Dive Bomber Down

ALSO BY BRYAN J. DICKERSON
AND FROM McFARLAND

*The Liberators of Pilsen: The U.S. 16th Armored
Division in World War II Czechoslovakia* (2018)

Dive Bomber Down
James A. Nist, Naval Aviator in the Pacific War

Bryan J. Dickerson

McFarland & Company, Inc., Publishers
Jefferson, North Carolina

ISBN (print) 978-1-4766-9246-3
ISBN (ebook) 978-1-4766-5045-6

LIBRARY OF CONGRESS AND BRITISH LIBRARY
CATALOGUING DATA ARE AVAILABLE

Library of Congress Control Number 2024001028

© 2024 Bryan J. Dickerson. All rights reserved

No part of this book may be reproduced or transmitted in any form or by any means, electronic or mechanical, including photocopying or recording, or by any information storage and retrieval system, without permission in writing from the publisher.

On the cover: Ensign James A. Nist in his dress whites (family photograph); USS *Bunker Hill* as seen from battleship USS *New Jersey* off of Japan in March 1945 (Naval History and Heritage Command [Photo 80-G-373737] / National Archives); F6F Hellcat (Naval History and Heritage Command [Photo 80-G-K-605] / National Archives)

Printed in the United States of America

McFarland & Company, Inc., Publishers
Box 611, Jefferson, North Carolina 28640
www.mcfarlandpub.com

To the late James A. Nist
and the Members of Navy Fighting Squadron 84

Table of Contents

U.S. Navy Officer Ranks in World War II	ix
Prologue: Off the Coast of Imperial Japan	1
Introduction	3
1. James A. Nist—His Life Before the U.S. Navy	5
2. Naval Aviation Cadet	15
3. Ensign James A. Nist, Naval Aviator	49
4. Navy Fighting Squadron 84	78
5. Deploying on USS *Bunker Hill*	114
6. Tokyo and Iwo Jima	127
7. With the Fast Carrier Task Force in March 1945	154
8. The Invasion of Okinawa	173
9. The War Goes On	178
10. Missing in Action	185
11. Honors and Tributes	196
12. Shorty Nist's Final Mission	200
Epilogue	204
Appendix: Nist Chronology	205
Chapter Notes	209
Bibliography	237
Index	245

Lord, guard and guide the men who fly
Through the great spaces in the sky,
Be with them always in the air,
In dark'ning storms or sunlight fair.
O, Hear us when we lift our prayer,
For those in peril in the air.

—The Navy Hymn (Eternal Father, Strong to Save)

U.S. Navy Officer Ranks in World War II

The following abbreviations are used for U.S. Navy officer ranks in this book.

FADM—Fleet Admiral
ADM—Admiral
VADM—Vice Admiral
RADM—Rear Admiral
COM—Commodore
CAPT—Captain
CDR—Commander
LCDR—Lieutenant Commander
LT—Lieutenant
LT(jg)—Lieutenant Junior Grade
ENS—Ensign

Prologue

Off the Coast of Imperial Japan

About 130 miles off the coast of Imperial Japan, F4U Corsairs and F6F Hellcats belonging to Carrier Air Group 84 were spotted on the deck of the aircraft carrier USS *Bunker Hill* (CV-17). Their engines were roaring and the propellers turning, their aircrews eagerly awaiting the signal to launch. This was *Bunker Hill*/Air Group 84's second fighter sweep of the day against Japanese airfields in and around Tokyo. Similar scenes were playing out aboard other carriers of the U.S. Navy's Fast Carrier Task Force (TF-58). The weather was terrible with overcast skies, intermittent rain and snow squalls and turbulent sea conditions. The day was 16 February 1945, and the U.S. Navy was making its first air strikes against the Japanese Home Islands.

In the cockpit of the F6F-5P Hellcat number 72614 was LT(jg) James A. Nist, USNR. Nist was a fighter pilot with Navy Fighting Squadron 84 (VF-84). Originally from Squankum, New Jersey, Nist had enlisted in the Navy as an aviation cadet after graduating from Rutgers University in 1942. After training for several months as a dive-bomber pilot, Nist had been transferred to newly formed VF-84 on 13 May 1944. VF-84 was equipped with the Vought F4U Corsair, the most powerful fighter aircraft in the U.S. Navy's arsenal. Nist had been training in Corsairs since joining VF-84. But today, Nist was seated in the cockpit of a Grumman F6F-5P Hellcat equipped with cameras for aerial photo reconnaissance. While his squadron mates would be strafing Japanese airfields and aircraft on the ground, Nist and another VF-84 pilot would be recording the results with camera-equipped Hellcats. Nist was about to undertake his first combat mission as a naval aviator against one of the most heavily defended targets in the Japanese Empire. Nist was in good company, as most of the other TF-58's aircrews were also making their combat debuts.

The launch signal was given. One by one, the heavily laden American warplanes started hurtling down *Bunker Hill*'s flight deck and up into the stormy skies off Japan. When it was his turn, LT(jg) Nist gunned the engine of his powerful warbird, released the brakes and roared down the flight deck. Just before the flight deck ended, Nist pulled back on his control stick and the laws of physics took over. Aided by the wind coming over the flight deck and *Bunker Hill*'s forward speed, his Hellcat achieved lift and climbed into the skies, heading for history.

Introduction

James Arthur "Shorty" Nist was an extraordinary young man who accomplished a great deal in just a few years. He graduated from high school at age 16, was the first in his family to earn a four-year college degree, earned a private pilot's license while pursuing his undergraduate studies, was commissioned as a naval officer, earned his naval aviator wings and flew with one of the most successful Navy fighter squadrons on one of the most decorated Navy warships in World War II.

James Arthur Nist was also my great-uncle, the youngest sibling of my grandmother Kathryn Nist Dickerson. Sadly, he lived his amazing life long before I was born. So, what I know of him comes from stories that my grandmother told me, his personal papers that she entrusted to me prior to her death and official Navy records from the National Archives. This book is the culmination of my efforts to learn more about the great-uncle who died long before I was born.

In preparing this biography of James A. Nist, I am indebted to several persons who assisted me in various ways. My late grandmother Kathryn Nist Dickerson entrusted me with her late younger brother's personal papers. These papers contain personal letters, Navy orders, official Navy correspondence, his aviator logbooks and photographs. Genealogical information on the Nist Family was provided by my late uncle Dr. Richard Conrad, husband of Joan (Kathryn's daughter and my father's sister). An expert in genealogical research, Uncle Richard spent several decades researching the various family lineages that comprise the Nist/Dickerson/Conrad extended family. The staff of the National Archives II in College Park, Maryland, assisted me with finding many of the official documents that I utilized for this biography. In addition, the website fold3.com worked with the National Archives to digitize a huge volume of Navy World War II records, and this effort has been very useful to me. I also thank the staff of the Tailhook Association for providing a copy of an excellent history of Air Group 84 by Barrett Tillman and Jan Jacobs, which they published in their association magazine back in 1990. This is the only secondary source that I know of specifically about Air Group 84. Lastly, I would like to thank LT Jeremy R. Lauber, USMS, and Stephanie Apperio of the Schuyler Otis Bland Memorial Library at the U.S. Merchant Marine Academy for providing a copy of Wilbert Popp's *The Survival of a World War II Navy Fighter Pilot*. Popp was my great-uncle's roommate aboard *Bunker Hill*.

1

James A. Nist—His Life Before the U.S. Navy

James Arthur Nist was born and raised on a farm in central New Jersey. He spent his formative years in the volatile period between the end of World War I and the beginning of World War II. This period saw economic prosperity, then the ruinous Great Depression and the rise of totalitarian regimes in Italy, Germany, Japan and the Soviet Union.

James Arthur Nist was born on 14 December 1921 to Martin Nist and the former Ethel Hayes in Lakewood, New Jersey. Ethel's ancestors had emigrated from England and France in the late 18th and early 19th centuries. She was born on 24 August 1890 in Howell, New Jersey, to Sarah Stokey and Jonathan Hayes. Sarah and Jonathan had two other children, Frederick S. and Chester.[1]

Martin's ancestors had emigrated from German states in the mid–19th century. Johann Martin and Magdelena Nist (Martin's grandparents) had emigrated with their son Jacob (Martin's father) from the Palatinate region to New Orleans in January 1861. During the Civil War, Johann Martin had served in the First Louisiana Infantry Regiment of the Union Army for a time. After the Civil War, the Nists came north and settled in Jersey City, New Jersey. Martin was born on 21 June 1890 in Jersey City, New Jersey, to Jacob Nist and Margaretha née Herbst. Margaretha and Jacob had seven children: Katherine, Magdelena, Margaretha, Wilhelmina, Jacob, Karl Heinrich and James's father, Martin. Only Margaretha, Wilhelmina and Martin lived past the age of six years old. Jacob Nist moved his family down to Monmouth County in 1895.[2]

Ethel Hayes and Martin Nist were married on 22 April 1910. They lived the early years of their marriage in an apartment on Squankum Road in Howell. They later purchased a farm across the street. Martin became a very successful farmer and a prominent local Democratic politician. Ethel and Martin had four children, all of whom survived childhood. The oldest, Martin Frederick, was born 19 June 1911 in his maternal grandparents' home. Next came Kathryn Louise (the author's grandmother), who was born 6 September 1913. She was also born in the Hayes home. Five years later, Margaret Elizabeth was born on 21 September 1918 in her family home. The youngest son, James Arthur, was born on 14 December 1921.[3]

After a couple of years of apartment living, Martin and Ethel purchased an 18-acre farm near the building that contained their apartment. The farm included a house, barn, chicken coops, shed and a privy (outhouse). Later in life, James's sister Kathryn would describe the Nist Family home:

The house had a small enclosed back porch, a kitchen with a metal sink and hand pump, a large pantry, a living room with an enclosed stairway and a sun porch with a hidden stairway in the floor leading to a dirt floored cellar. Upstairs there were two bedrooms and a large hall. The kitchen had a wood burning range and the living room had a pot-bellied stove for heat. There were registers over each stove to heat the bedrooms.[4]

Martin proved to be an adept farmer and businessman working cooperatively with his father. He soon added additional acres to his farm. Martin and Jacob's lands were separated by 13 acres of land owned by relatives Sam and Rose Burdge. Sometime after Kathryn's birth, Martin and Jacob began taking their produce to sell in Asbury Park. At first, they transported their produce using a horse-drawn wagon. Then they switched to a truck.[5]

James Arthur Nist: The Early Years

James Arthur Nist was born on 14 December 1921 in Paul Kimball Hospital in Lakewood. He was the youngest of the four children of Martin and Ethel Nist. Paul Kimball Hospital had opened only in 1913 and James was the first of his family born there. Older sister Margaret had been born in the family home, and his older siblings Martin and Kathryn had been born in the Hayes home in Howell Township.

Years later, Kathryn would describe her younger brother's birth. In her unpublished memoirs, she wrote, "On Dec. 14, 1921 my brother James Arthur was born in Paul Kimball Hospital. We expected my mother to be home for Christmas but the doctor said no. Two weeks was the customary time they kept new mothers in bed at that time. Santa Claus found us all staying with my grandmother Nist that year."[6]

By the time of James's birth, the Nist Family was well established in Howell Township. Jacob and his wife, Margaretha, were still living when James was born. James's aunts Wilhelmina and Margaretha (father Martin's older sisters) were also living in Howell Township. Neither had married and they would remain unmarried for the rest of their lives. The extended Nist family were members of All Saints Episcopal Church in nearby Lakewood, as was Ethel's mother, Sarah Stokey.

Space was already cramped in the Nist family home prior to James's birth. Martin and Ethel had one of the house's two bedrooms. Kathryn and Margaret shared the other bedroom. Eldest son Martin slept in a bed in the hallway. The hallway also contained his bureau. The elder Martin had plans drafted for a new home to be built on the opposite end of the farm.[7]

Sam Burdge's death scrapped Martin's plan to build a new home. His widow decided to sell their home and farm and move to Lakewood. Martin purchased the Burdge home and farm and moved his family into the much larger Burdge home. The land purchase also made all of the Nists' land holdings into one contiguous tract.[8]

The Burdge home that Martin and Ethel purchased for their family was a two-story structure that had four rooms and a kitchen on the ground floor, four bedrooms and a bathroom on the second floor, and a basement. The home was heated by the kitchen stove and a potbellied stove. To provide adequate heat for his family in winter, Martin and a neighbor installed a hot water heater, radiators in each room and a wood-burning stove in the basement.[9]

James Nist received his elementary school education at Farmingdale Grammar School, which was located in nearby Farmingdale Borough. There he attended kindergarten and grades first through eighth. On 14 June 1934, James graduated from Farmingdale Grammar School at the age of 12 years old. The commencement ceremony included a musical play titled *Reward of Friendship*. James played the part of Ted, the son. There were 12 members of the Class of 1934. James also served as the class treasurer.[10]

The Nist family were congregants of All Saints Episcopal Church in Lakewood. James received his catechetical instruction in the Christian faith at All Saints Church. On the ninth day of May 1938, he received the Sacrament of Confirmation.[11]

Like his older siblings before him, James Nist attended Lakewood High School as a tuition student in nearby Lakewood as Howell Township did not have a high school yet. Having been born in December, James was one of the youngest in his academic class. He began his first year in September 1934. That academic year, he took English I, Algebra I, History, Latin I, Manual Training and Physical Education, earning B grades in every class except for a C in Manual Training. In his second year, he took English II, Biology, Plane Geometry, Latin II, Manual Training and Physical Education and earned B grades in every class except for a C in English II. In his third year at Lakewood High School, Nist earned B grades in English III, Chemistry, Algebra II, French I and Physical Education and an A grade in Printing.[12]

James Nist began his fourth and final year at Lakewood High School in September 1937. He earned B grades in English IV, American History, French II and Physics and an A grade in Physical Education. During that year, he worked on the staff of the *Pine Needle*—Lakewood High School's yearbook. He was described in the yearbook as "[s]mall, well-built, the class baby by popular acclaim, James maintains himself above average scholastically and popular socially. To the girls he seems just **too** [emphasis in original] too cute for words."[13]

The commencement ceremony for the Lakewood High School Class of 1938 was actually held at the Clifton

James Arthur Nist's high school graduation photograph (Dickerson Family photograph).

Avenue Grade School at 8:00 p.m. on Friday, 17 June 1938. There were 152 members of the Class of 1938. The invocation was offered by the Rev. Frank Adler. Mildred Silverman offered the salutatory address and Edward Marks offered the valedictory address. The commencement speaker was Dr. Samuel Steinmetz. Then came the presentation of diplomas and finally the benediction. At the time of his graduation, James was 16 and a half years old.[14]

In early August 1938, James Nist was contacted by Monmouth County Superintendent of Public Instruction Thomas B. Harper via letter. In his letter, Superintendent Harper informed Nist that he had recommended him for a State Scholarship under the Act of 1864 for Monmouth County. Not long after, Nist was awarded the scholarship, which would be of significant assistance in his attending college and earning a four-year degree.[15]

Martin and Ethel Nist at their 50th wedding anniversary (Dickerson Family photograph).

Rutgers University

James Nist's academic abilities earned him a State Scholarship to attend Rutgers University in New Brunswick, New Jersey. He was only 16½ years old when he matriculated at Rutgers College of Rutgers University in September 1938 as part of the Class of 1942. At Rutgers, he majored in biology, with a focus on pre-medicine. Despite his young age, Nist did well academically at Rutgers. At the time, the university used a grade scale of 1 to 6, with 1 being "Distinction" and 6 being "Failure."[16]

During his freshman year (1938–1939), Nist took two terms each of English Composition, General Chemistry, General Botany and German Language, and a semester each of Algebra and Trigonometry. He also completed two terms of mandatory Military Science as part of the university's Army Reserve Officer Training Corps (ROTC) program. He earned grades of 2—"High Quality"—in all of his classes. James's grades earned him a place on the College of Arts and Sciences Honor School.[17]

In his sophomore year (1939–1940), James Nist's classes at Rutgers grew more challenging. He had two terms of General Zoology, Physics, Analytics, German Language, Mathematics and Military Science. During the first term (fall semester), he earned 3—"Fair" grades—in General Zoology, Analytics, Mathematics and German, and 2—"High Quality" grades—in Physics and Military Science. His grades declined in the second term (spring semester), earning 3 ("Fairs") in Zoology and Physics, a 4 ("Poor") in Military Science, a 6 ("Failure") in math and 2 ("High Quality") in German and Analytics.[18]

James Nist improved academically during his junior year at Rutgers. In his first term of the 1940–1941 academic year, he earned grades of "3—Fair" in Organic Chemistry and General Psychology, and grades of "2—High Quality" in General Bacteriology, General Physiology and Animal Parasites. In the second term, he began the second section of General Psychology but withdrew. He earned grades of "3—Fair" in Organic Chemistry and Pathological Bacteriology, and grades of "2—High Quality" in the second section of General Physiology and Mathematics. He also earned his first grade of "1—Distinction" in Controlled Private Flying. James Nist's venture into flight will be discussed in a following section.[19]

During his junior year, James was a member of the university's Biology Club. The 1941 edition of Rutgers's yearbook, *The Scarlett Letter*, contained this description of the Biology Club: "The club strives to provide a means for the expression of individual biological interest in the form of organized activity." Club activities included student discussions, field trips and club dinners with guest speakers. Dr. Samuel L. Leonard served as faculty adviser. Including James, there were 25 members of the Biology Club.[20]

Academic year 1941–1942 was James A. Nist's fourth and final year of studies at Rutgers University. In Elementary Bio-chemistry, he earned grades of "3—Fair" for the first term and "2—High Quality" for the second term. In public speaking, he earned grades of "2—High Quality" for the first term and "3—Fair" for the second term. In both American Government and American Literature, he earned grades of "2—High Quality" for both terms of study. For two terms of Physical Education, he earned grades of "Satisfactory." He completed the second section of General Psychology during the second term, earning a grade of "2—High Quality." He also earned grades of "1—Distinction" for two classes taken in the first term that were part of his pilot training, namely Aircraft Navigation and Powerplants.[21]

James Nist was also active in several extracurricular activities. In addition to competing as a collegiate wrestler, James was a member of the Scarlett Barb Council and vice president of the Winants Club. The Scarlett Barb Council was a student governing body that coordinated the neutral groups and independent undergraduates at Rutgers University. James was not a member of a social fraternity. The Winants Club was composed of independent students, i.e., those not in Greek fraternities and sororities, who lived in Winants Hall. Winants Hall was a student residential dormitory built in New Brunswick in 1890. In the 1942 edition of *The Scarlett Letter*, the Winants Club was described as such: "The organization promotes friendship and provides social and educational activities for its members."[22]

One of Jimmy's close friends at Rutgers was Alfred Messer. They were roommates for two years and both were engaged in the same course of studies. Messer would later become a psychiatrist. "Among other things, he [Jimmy] took great delight in throwing me all over a wrestling mat, although I am somewhat heavier than he," Messer wrote to Jimmy's parents in 1946.[23]

Rutgers University Wrestling[24]

In addition to his academic pursuits, James Nist embarked upon an athletic career as a wrestler. At the end of his freshman year, he was awarded class numerals by the Department of Physical Education for his proficiency in wrestling. The Rutgers wrestling team was coached by Fred Shepard.[25]

The following year, 1939–1940, the Rutgers wrestling team had its best season in its history thus far. The team amassed seven victories and two losses. They defeated Haverford College, Columbia University, Muhlenberg College, Johns Hopkins University, Lafayette College, the University of Maryland and New York University. They lost to Princeton University and the U.S. Military Academy. During the February 1940 match against USMA, James Nist wrestled at the 121-pound class in substitution for the injured Dick Mansfield; he was pinned by the West Point cadet that he wrestled. Rutgers also won the Middle Atlantic States Collegiate Wrestling Championship and Nist earned a third-place medal for his weight class. He also earned a Rutgers athletic letter for wrestling.[26]

The 1940–1941 wrestling season appeared promising for James Nist. Writing in Rutgers's daily newspaper, *The Targum*, Dick Nelson observed, "The little flyweight from Squankum began improving rapidly toward the end of last year and by the time the Middle Atlantics rolled around had absorbed enough knowledge and experience to grab a third place medal for himself."[27]

Unfortunately, the 1940–1941 season was a difficult one for Rutgers wrestling. In eight dual meets that season, the team defeated Columbia University, Muhlenberg College and Ursinus College, lost to Princeton University, Lehigh University and Lafayette College and tied the University of Maryland and Montclair College for a record of three wins, three losses and two ties.[28]

James Nist had mixed results during the season. "Little Jimmy Nist scored a startling victory over George Sickles in the 121-pound curtain raiser," declared *The Sunday Times* of New Brunswick after the Montclair match. Nist also earned wins against the University of Maryland and Ursinus College but lost to Princeton and Columbia wrestlers. During the Princeton match, Nist pulled several shoulder muscles, forcing him to sit out the Muhlenberg match. His shoulder was sufficiently healed to wrestle against Maryland and earn a victory.[29]

On 7–8 March 1941, the Rutgers wrestlers competed in the Middle Atlantic Collegiate Wrestling Association's Sixth Annual Championship Meet, held at Lafayette College in Easton, Pennsylvania. Teams from six colleges—Haverford, Lafayette, Rutgers, Muhlenberg, Ursinus and Gettysburg—competed. Haverford won the tournament. James Nist had a first-round bye, then lost to a Haverford wrestler in the second round to finish third in his weight class.[30]

During the 1941–42 wrestling season, the team's coach, Fred Shepard, was called to active duty for World War II. Wilfred Cann took over coaching duties. The wrestling team amassed a record of six wins, two losses and one tie. They defeated Montclair College, Muhlenberg College, Colgate College by a shutout, Lafayette College, Gettysburg College and Ursinus College. They lost to Columbia University and Lehigh University and tied Princeton University. James earned his third athletic letter for wrestling.[31]

On 6–7 March 1942, the Rutgers wrestlers competed in the Middle Atlantic Collegiate Wrestling Association's Seventh Annual Championship Meet, held at Gettysburg College in Gettysburg, Pennsylvania. A total of six collegiate wrestling teams competed. In addition to Rutgers and host Gettysburg College, Haverford, Lafayette, Muhlenberg and Ursinus also competed. The Rutgers wrestlers left New Brunswick for Harrisburg, Pennsylvania, on a Pennsylvania Railroad passenger train on the morning of 6 March. Then they took a bus to Gettysburg and stayed at the Hotel Gettysburg, which was located on Lincoln Square in the heart of the historic town. The wrestlers competed Friday night and Saturday before returning home to New Brunswick via Harrisburg. James Nist had a first-round bye, then lost to a Haverford wrestler in the second round to finish third in his weight class.[32]

Flight Training

In 1938, the Civil Aeronautics Act created the Civil Aeronautics Authority (CAA) and the Civilian Pilot Training Program (CPTP). Students at Rutgers were able to participate in the CPTP for college credit. Under the direction of Professor Ubert C. Holland, the assistant dean of the School of Engineering, the program began with ground school classes taught in two sections. The primary section consisted of classes in meteorology, civil air regulations, navigation and aircraft management, which were held twice a week from 7:00 p.m. to 10:30 p.m. in the Engineering Building. The secondary section consisted of classes in aerodynamics, power plants, celestial navigation, radio work, aircraft structures, instruments and parachutes. These classes met three times a week from 7:00 p.m. to 10:30 p.m. After completing ground school, the CPTP students took part in flight training, which covered the fundamentals of flying and a short cross-country flight. The students flew both with an instructor and solo.[33]

James Nist enrolled in the Civilian Pilot Training Program during his junior year at Rutgers. He completed the classroom training successfully. His flight training commenced on 14 March 1941 at Hadley Field in New Brunswick. The training was conducted by Ungar Aircraft Distributors. His instructor was Carl M. Rasmussen. There would be four stages to Nist's flight training. Stage A would consist entirely of flights conducted with the instructor. Stages B, C and D would consist of flights with the instructor and solo flights.[34]

James Nist began his flight training with preliminary ground instruction on 14 March 1941. The one-hour-long instruction consisted of airplane familiarization and an explanation of the controls, instruments, throttle, brakes, fuel system, fire extinguishers, first aid kits, safety equipment and local traffic rules. That afternoon, he undertook his first instructional flight. Instructor Carl Rasmussen demonstrated taxiing on the ground, performed the aircraft's takeoff and demonstrated climbs, turns, level flight, descents and landings. After landing, Rasmussen had Nist taxi the aircraft back to the hangar. Total flight time was 40 minutes.[35]

Beginning at 4:20 p.m. that same afternoon, Nist and Rasmussen performed the former's second instructional flight. This time, Nist taxied to the takeoff point and Rasmussen got the plane in the air. Once airborne, Nist practiced level and straight flight. At the end of the 35-minute flight, Rasmussen took over the controls and landed the plane. Nist then taxied to the hangar.[36]

James Nist progressed steadily through Stage A. He went two or three times a week, often performing two flights per day. With each instructional section, he was taught and practiced progressively more advanced flight maneuvers such as takeoffs, landings, recovering from stalls, S-turns and flying around pylons. On 9 April 1941, less than a month after starting flight training, Nist completed the required eight hours of dual flight instruction and progressed to Stage B. He began Stage B by performing his first-ever solo flight. He taxied out, took off, circled the airfield to make a 180-degree approach and landed the aircraft. He repeated this sequence two more times.[37]

Now in Stage B, Nist and Rasmussen settled into a training routine. Each session began with a 15-to-20-minute dual check flight with Rasmussen. Then Nist would land the aircraft, Rasmussen would disembark and Nist would perform 30 to 45 minutes of solo flight practice.

On 18 April 1941, Nist practiced solo flight for 35 minutes, then went aloft with Rasmussen for a dual check flight that lasted 45 minutes. During this time, Nist passed the test for all of the maneuvers that he had thus far learned.[38]

Stage C began for James Nist the following day. He flew with Rasmussen for a 30-minute dual check flight and then flew solo for another 30 minutes. In Stage C, the flights became longer with more complicated maneuvers such as spiral approaches and spins. By now, Nist was flying solo up to an hour at a time. He completed Stage C on 15 May 1941.[39]

The most important part of Stage D was a solo cross-country flight. To prepare for this, instructor Rasmussen accompanied Nist on a dual cross-country instructional flight with a heavy emphasis on navigational procedures. The instructional flight followed a triangular route with two checkpoints for each leg of the route. Leg One departed from Hadley Airport at 1:48 p.m. on 20 May 1941 and headed southwest to Mercer Airport near Trenton, New Jersey. Rasmussen landed the aircraft as Nist would have to do on his own solo flight, and then immediately took off for Red Bank Airport to the east. He landed the aircraft at that airport briefly and then returned to the air for the third and final leg of the flight. Rasmussen and Nist returned to Hadley Airport at 3:28 p.m. Total flight time was one hour, 40 minutes.[40]

Thus familiar with the procedures, James Nist took to the skies an hour and a half later to perform his solo cross-country flight. He departed from Hadley Airport at 5:05 p.m. on a compass heading of 238 degrees and at an altitude of 1,800 feet. He successfully located his two intermediate checkpoints and arrived at Mercer Airport at 5:37 p.m. He landed and had his logbook signed by airport attendant B. Dale Edgerton. Then, Nist returned to the skies and headed southeast on a compass heading of 105 degrees. Again, he located his two intermediate checkpoints and landed his aircraft at Red Bank Airport at 6:23 p.m. Airport attendant Louis H. Miller signed his logbook and he took off to complete the third and final leg of his cross-country flight. He located his final checkpoints and then landed at Hadley Airport at 6:58 p.m., having successfully completed his solo cross-country flight in one hour, 50 minutes of flight time.[41]

After successfully completing the solo cross-country flight, Nist had to pass a private flight test with his instructor. During the next four flight sessions, he reviewed what he had learned and practiced for the test. On 7 June 1941, Nist took his private flight test. For the next 65 minutes, instructor Rasmussen evaluated Nist on his judgment and his skills in performing taxiing, takeoffs, climbs and turns, glides and turns, approaches, landings, forced landings and other essential flight skills. When the test was over, Rasmussen wrote in Nist's log, "Passed private flight test." The Civil Aeronautics Administration issued him Certificate No. S214709 in recognition of him successfully completing their pilot training program. To accomplish this, he had completed 21½ hours of flight training with the instructor and 14 hours, 35 minutes of solo flying for 36 hours, 5 minutes total flight time.[42]

Graduation

James Nist had done well during his four years at Rutgers University as a student and an athlete on the wrestling team. Having earned enough credits, Nist graduated with the Class of 1942 in May of that year.

In recognition of the academic achievements of its graduates, Rutgers University held two major events: a baccalaureate service and a graduation ceremony. The 176th anniversary baccalaureate service was held at 11:00 a.m. on Sunday, 3 May 1942, at Kirkpatrick Chapel in New Brunswick. The service began with a processional hymn, "A Mighty Fortress Is Our God." Dr. William H.S. Demarest offered the invocation. Rutgers president Robert C. Clothier offered a scripture lesson, and the baccalaureate address was given by Dr. Rufus Jones.[43]

James Nist in his Rutgers University Class of 1942 graduation photograph (Dickerson Family photograph).

The 176th commencement ceremony for Rutgers University was held on 10 May 1942. The ceremony opened with the hymn "Onward Christian Soldiers" and the "Star-Spangled Banner." Dr. John Howard Raven offered the invocation. Rutgers University president Robert Clarkson Clothier gave the commencement address, which was titled "The Critical Hour." Then followed another hymn, "The Battle Hymn of the Republic." Next, there was the recognition of the graduates in military science. Nearly all of these graduates had only recently been commissioned into the U.S. Army or the U.S. Army Air Corps. Following this was the conferring of degrees by school or college. James Nist was one of 29 students to receive a bachelor of science degree. Afterward, honorary degrees were conferred and the benediction was offered by Dr. Samuel Arthur Devan. When James Arthur Nist graduated from Rutgers University, he was the first member of his family to earn a four-year college degree.[44]

Having earned a bachelor of science degree in biology with an emphasis on pre-medical studies, James Nist probably would have continued on to medical school in his pursuit of a career as a doctor. This had been his intention when he began studies at Rutgers University in 1938. But the world of 1942 was a very different place from what it was in 1938. The nations of the world and the United States were engaged in a horrific global war.

World War II very soon would dominate the remainder of James A. Nist's earthly life.

2

Naval Aviation Cadet

Throughout the 1930s, totalitarian regimes in Italy, Japan, Germany and the Soviet Union aggressively conquered various other nations and peoples of the world. The Second World War broke out in September 1939 when Nazi Germany and the Soviet Union jointly invaded and conquered Poland. Initially, the United States remained out of the widening global conflict. After Germany swiftly conquered France and most of western Europe in the spring of 1940, Congress approved a massive expansion of the U.S. Navy. Later that year, the National Guard and the Reserves were mobilized and the nation's first peacetime draft was instituted.

Imperial Japan attacked naval and military facilities and forces on Oahu, Hawaii, on 7 December 1941, and suddenly America was in the Second World War. Over the next six months, Japan captured the Philippines, Indonesia, Singapore, Guam and Wake Island, and threatened Australia. As James Nist was completing his studies at Rutgers University, the U.S. Navy turned back a Japanese invasion force in the Battle of the Coral Sea. A month later, the U.S. Navy decisively defeated the Imperial Japanese Navy at the Battle of Midway, sinking four Japanese aircraft carriers while losing the aircraft carrier USS *Yorktown* (CV-5).

In February 1942, Nist registered for Selective Service with Local Board Number 1 for Ocean County in Lakewood's Municipal Building. He listed his occupation as "Student" at Rutgers University. At the time of his registration, Nist was 5'5" tall and weighed 120 pounds. He was described as having brown eyes and brown hair.[1]

Jimmy Nist graduated from Rutgers in June 1942. Like many other members of his graduating class, Jimmy did not wait to be drafted. He wanted to do his part to defend his country sooner rather than later. On 2 September 1942, James A. Nist submitted his "Preliminary Application for Flight Training in the U.S. Naval Reserve and Marine Corps Reserve." The application was a standard Navy form that captured basic personal information such as home address and contact information, date and place of birth, education, ethnicity, religion and marital status. On the form, Nist indicated that he had received a bachelor of science degree from Rutgers University, earning a total of 137 credits in the process. He listed his height at 5'5" and weight at 125 pounds. He had no physical deformities, did not wear glasses, had good teeth, was not color-blind and had perfect hearing. He indicated that he did not have any flight training in the U.S. Army, Navy or Marine Corps, but he did have 15 hours of primary and 22 hours of secondary training with the Civilian Pilot Training Course. In answer to the question, "Have you had any Military or Naval Training?" Nist answered "Yes" and stated, "At Rutgers University, I had two years of basic R.O.T.C. training." When asked if he had taken any Civilian Pilot Training Courses, Nist answered, "I have completed both the primary and secondary C.P.T.P courses. The ground school courses were taken at Rutgers University and the flight training occurred at Ungar Aircraft, Inc., Dunellen, N.J." His application was accepted and James A. Nist enlisted in the U.S. Naval Reserve as an aviation cadet on 7 October 1942.[2]

James A. Nist reported for active duty as an aviation cadet in training on 6 January 1943. After in-processing in New York City, Nist and 200 other cadets traveled by train to Chapel Hill, North Carolina. In a letter home to his parents, Nist wrote, "The trip down was awful." The train did not have any sleeper cars and the heating system in his car was broken. As such, he was unable to get any sleep on the trip down. The train arrived in Durham, North Carolina, at 0620 on Thursday, 7 January 1943.[3]

The University of North Carolina at Chapel Hill was one of numerous colleges and universities that the Navy utilized for pre-flight aviation cadet training. The Navy Pre-Flight School at UNC Chapel Hill was commanded by Commander John P. Graf, USN (Ret.), with Lieutenant Commander James P. Raugh, USNR, as executive officer. Nist's group was merged with 75 cadets who had arrived from Baltimore the day before to form the school's 17th Battalion. Aviation Cadet James Nist was assigned to Room 214 in Grimes Hall. His first day consisted of in-processing and uniform issue. The rules of the school were explained to the cadets. They included being restricted to the UNC Chapel Hill campus except for authorized off-campus liberty on Saturday and Sunday afternoons, having to salute all officers, room inspections three or four times per day, and not being allowed to drive or ride in cars. Nist and the other cadets were issued eight pairs of pants, six shirts, six sets of underwear, six pairs of socks, one pair of dress shoes, one pair of work shoes, three covers (hats in civilian parlance), two sets of dress white uniforms and one dress blue top coat. They were measured for their dress blue uniforms. Weekday lights out was from 2200 to 0530. On weekends, they could sleep in until 0700. Weekend liberty secured at 2330.[4]

Aviation Cadet James Nist shared Room 214 with three roommates: Ed DeGaspar, Jim Smiley and Richard Rudolph "Satch" Sachsel. Nist knew Sachsel from Rutgers University, where they had both competed on the wrestling team. Sachsel was born on 16 March 1922 in New York City and later moved with his family to Garwood, New Jersey. Sachsel had earned a varsity letter in basketball at Dayton Regional High School in Springfield. Entering Rutgers in September 1940 as part of the Class of 1944, Sachsel switched to wrestling and dominated on the mat. He was an American Athletic Union and Middle States wrestling champion. During his final season at Rutgers, he lost only two matches. He left Rutgers before graduating in order to enlist in the Navy as an aviation cadet. He officially entered the Navy on 31 December 1942 and was immediately sent to UNC Chapel Hill.[5]

In his first letter home to his parents dated 7 January 1943, Aviation Cadet Nist described the UNC campus and Navy Pre-Flight School. "The place [UNC] is huge but there are still a few civilians around, especially babes," he wrote. He described the weather as warmer than home but "far from spring." He commented favorably on the abundance of food served to the cadets, which was necessary because the daily physical fitness program consisted of several hours of exercises, conditioning and team and individual sports.[6]

The Navy had a well-established pilot training program that dated back to the early days of aviation prior to World War I. In 1935, Congress enacted the Aviation Cadet Act, which established the grade of aviation cadet and a pilot training program for college graduates ages 18 to 28. Created in response to the rise of fascism in Europe, this program created a pool of trained reserve naval aviators to be called upon in the event of war or national emergency. This program underwent several subsequent modifications as the world plunged into its Second World War.[7]

Just as James Nist was entering naval service in January 1943, the Navy's pilot training program underwent a major change. In that month, the Navy opened flight preparatory schools at 20 civilian colleges and universities, including the University of Pennsylvania, Colgate University, Wesleyan University and the University of North Carolina at Chapel Hill. The Navy flight preparatory schools provided aviation cadets with three months of intense academic studies and physical conditioning. After completing the flight preparatory schools, aviation cadets proceeded to elementary flight and ground school. Aviation cadets who successfully completed flight training were then commissioned as ensigns. Flight training continued with the new pilots being trained on specialized aircraft such as scout bombers, fighters, torpedo bombers and large multi-engine aircraft. For those destined for carrier service, there was training aboard two Great Lakes steamers that had been converted into training carriers—USS *Wolverine* and USS *Sable*.[8]

Aviation Cadet Nist's second day at Navy Pre-Flight School was just as busy as his first. He received a number of inoculations. He passed a physical exam that included pull-ups, push-ups, an obstacle course and a five-minute timed pack test. For this last test, cadets put on a pack weighing a third of their body weight and had to step up on an 18-inch-high bench with both feet, step back down to the floor and repeat. Cadets who failed the physical exam were placed in a "weak squad" and they lost their Saturday liberty.[9]

The Navy Pre-Flight School placed a huge emphasis on physical fitness conditioning and competitive sports such as football, boxing and swimming. Each cadet was assigned to an intramural squadron for competitions. There were 10 intramural squadrons; Cadet Nist was assigned to the Vindicator Squadron. The Vindicator Squadron was the dominant intramural squadron, at one point having won the weekly intramural squadron competition for 11 weeks in a row. There were weekly hikes with packs on Saturday mornings. Initially the hike was six miles in distance and was lengthened with each successive hike. Success in sports was rewarded with an extra hour of liberty on Saturday afternoons. In his first full week at Navy Pre-Flight School, Nist and his Vindicator Squadron teammates were victorious over the other intramural squadrons and so earned that coveted extra hour of liberty. "I am going to spend my extra hour in bed," Nist wrote home to his parents.[10]

As Aviation Cadet Nist progressed in Navy Pre-Flight School, his letters home shared more and more details about his experiences there. He was regularly attending Sunday church services. "Everything down here is rush, rush," he wrote on 10 January 1943. "You have to eat as fast as you can, report for duty on the double or even on the triple, which is wide open." In another letter written around 17 January, he wrote, "Saturdays and Sundays are the only time we have to even breathe without hurrying." With all of the physical activity, food was in abundance to fuel the cadets. Writing home on 23 January, Nist informed his parents, "You can eat all you can possibly hold at each meal and an hour later you're as hungry as ever."[11]

In a letter written on Saturday, 16 January 1943, Nist informed his parents that "Wednesday damn near killed me." His day began at 0530, followed by battalion formation at 0550 and breakfast at 0600. The cadets returned to the dormitories at 0630 and cleaned their rooms for the next half hour. At 0710, they began a hike with packs that lasted until 0925. The hike was followed by classes from 0930 to 1145. At 1155, there was another battalion formation, followed by lunch at 1210. After lunch, the cadets were permitted to rest for 10 minutes between 1245 and 1255. Then there was another battalion formation at 1300. The remainder of the afternoon was spent in sports. The cadets participated in boxing from 1310 to 1415, tackle football from 1415 to 1530 and wrestling from 1545 to 1730. After sports, the cadets returned to their rooms and changed into the uniform of the day. Formation was at 1750, then dinner at 1800 and back to the rooms at 1845. Evening formation was at 1910, followed by classes until 2045. They returned to their rooms after classes and lights out was at 2130.[12]

Academics were just as important as physical training. Classes were held on aircraft and ship recognition, Morse code, flag semaphore code, blinker light code, rifle marksmanship and hand-to-hand combat. "I am in the smartest platoon of the battalion," Nist proudly wrote home. In the third week of January, 17th Battalion took their first quizzes. Nist scored a 3.88 out of 4.0 on his first math quiz. The following week, Nist scored a 4.0 on a gunnery quiz, 4.0 on math and 3.7 on plane recognition. In the radio Morse Code quiz, Nist took down seven words per minute, missing only three out of 80 words transmitted. Each word consisted of five letters and numbers. A score of eight words per minute without errors was necessary to complete the course. "Satch and I are both working like heck to get out of here in 10 weeks," he informed his parents in his 23 January 1943 letter. "Getting out of here early means getting upstairs [i.e., flying] two weeks early."[13]

Wrestling was a major component of the Pre-Flight School physical training and Nist's experience on the Rutgers University wrestling team served him well. In one match, the 125-pound Nist wrestled at the 138-pound level and pinned his opponent in 56 seconds. That performance earned Nist and the Vindicator Squadron an extra hour of Saturday liberty. Nist's success in intramural wrestling led him to be selected for the Navy Pre-Flight School's intermural wrestling team. Richard Sachsel, Nist's roommate and Rutgers wrestling teammate, was also selected for the team. The team was coached by LT Charles Speidel, assisted by LT(jg) F.D. Gardner, LT(jg) C.A. Schellenberger and Ensign G.E. Raab. On 23 January 1943, Nist and Sachsel wrestled on the Navy Pre-Flight School team for the first time. Their opponents were from Appalachian State University. Nist wrestled at the 121-pound class; Sachsel wrestled at the 145-pound class. Oddly enough, the Nist Papers do

The Navy Pre-Flight School at University of North Carolina—Chapel Hill wrestling team. Aviation Cadet Nist is seated on the left of team coach LT Charles Speidel (Dickerson Family photograph).

not contain the results of this competition. The Navy Pre-Flight School team competed against schools such as North Carolina State, Duke University and Virginia Polytechnic Institute. Cadet Nist did quite well in these competitions, even winning five matches in a row. In the North Carolina State match, Nist pinned his opponent twice. Sachsel and the other Navy wrestlers were doing well too. "A guy has to be really good to beat a cadet," Nist informed his parents in late January. "After two weeks in this place, we are in super-shape."[14]

Being a member of the Navy Pre-Flight School wrestling team had certain benefits that were not enjoyed by other cadets. When wrestling matches were held on Saturdays, team members were excused from the morning hikes. Several matches were held at the opposing team's home university, giving team members the opportunity to do some traveling. After the Duke match, the Navy wrestlers were granted liberty in Durham.[15]

Toward the end of January, the 17th Battalion was spending a lot of time preparing for the swim tests. During the last week of January, Nist passed the "B" swim test. To pass this test, the cadets had to successfully swim three-quarters of a mile without using the backstroke, swim the length of the pool while carrying another cadet, swim three laps using the backstroke, sidestroke and forward crawl, and swim 75 feet underwater at a depth of four feet. The latter was intended to simulate swimming below burning oil on the surface of the water and to escape from being shot. On Friday of that week, the cadets learned how to use their pants as flotation devices. They also practiced "Abandon Ship!" drills. For these drills, the cadets climbed a cargo net that hung from the rafters 20 feet above the water. Then they would jump into the water from that height and swim underwater to escape from

Top: The Navy Pre-Flight School wrestling team. Aviation Cadet Nist is third from the left (Dickerson Family photograph). *Bottom:* Group photograph of Seventeenth Battalion, Navy Pre-Flight School at University of North Carolina—Chapel Hill. Aviation Cadet Nist is at the right end of the back row (Dickerson Family photograph).

the sinking ship. After passing the "B" swim test, the cadets had to pass the "A" swim test, in which they had to swim one mile.[16]

Military and naval training can sometimes turn deadly. The 17th Battalion lost one of its own on the afternoon of Wednesday, 3 March 1943. The incident happened in the Bowman Gray Pool while the cadets were doing their routine swim exercises. That night, James Nist penned a letter home to his parents to inform them of what had happened. He wrote:

> We lost one of our room-mates—the hard way. Dick Sachsel died this afternoon in the swimming pool. We all saw it happen and we've heard it announced a dozen times. That's all the regiment is talking about, but we still can't quite believe it. We were swimming six laps to get warmed up. He was right alongside of me at the beginning but he got ahead of me. Then whatever happened did happen. Somebody dove in and got him out. He was only in the water about ten seconds.[17]

Aviation Cadet James Kieran Foley was on the side of the pool when Sachsel went into distress. Seeing his shipmate in trouble, Foley dived in to try to save him. Foley brought Sachsel to the surface and the side of the pool where he was pulled from the water. Artificial respiration was attempted but Sachsel died despite all efforts to revive him. Later, Navy Pre-Flight School commanding officer CDR John P. Graff issued Foley a Letter of Commendation for his actions. "You are hereby commended for your presence of mind and the skill and speed with which you went about your rescue work," wrote Graff. "The fact that Cadet Sachsel failed to revive doesn't minimize the fine part you played."[18]

Since James Nist was Richard Sachsel's roommate at Navy Pre-Flight School and a former Rutgers classmate of his, Nist was detailed to escort his shipmate's body home to his family and participate in the funeral. Sachsel's friends from Rutgers University served as pallbearers. Nist knew all of them personally. The U.S. Coast Guard's Rahway Barracks provided a ceremonial firing squad and bugler for the committal ceremony. "I [led] the procession and didn't have any job except to look good," Nist wrote to his parents afterward. "Everything went according to schedule." Following the funeral, Nist boarded a train in Cranford on the afternoon of Monday, 8 March, for the trip back to Chapel Hill. He arrived back there at 1130 on Tuesday morning and resumed his training.[19]

Over the next week or so, Nist completed a 15-mile hike with his battalion; finished ship recognition, physics and blinker code; and participated in an inter-squadron track meet. He continued to help the Vindicator Squadron keep up its dominance of intramural sports at Navy Pre-Flight School.[20]

On Friday, 19 March 1943, Aviation Cadet Nist wrote home to his parents. "This news is so hot it won't keep until tomorrow," he began. That night at supper formation, an announcement was made that 10 17th Battalion cadets would be graduating early with the 16th Battalion. Nist was one of those 10 fortunate 17th Battalion cadets. "Yeah, I finally made it," he wrote. The following day, he found out that he was heading for Naval Air Station Glenview, Illinois.[21]

Four days later, Cadet Nist wrote home again to his parents. Over the weekend, he had gone on liberty to Greensboro, home of the Women's College of the University of North Carolina. "There were 2300 females and about fifteen cadets," he wrote.

"We had our pick of the lot." Then on Monday, 22 March, Nist completed the academic portion of his Pre-Flight School, passing his final exams in physics, aerology, semaphore, blinker and radio. On 24 March 1943, Nist, the other nine selected 17th Battalion cadets and 16th Battalion departed from Navy Pre-Flight School Chapel Hill to begin flight training at bases across the country.[22]

Flight Training in Illinois

Naval Air Station Glenview was located in the suburbs of Chicago, Illinois, near Lake Michigan. The air station began its life as Curtiss-Reynolds Airport, a civilian airfield run by the Curtiss Flying Service, in October 1929. After leasing space for several years, the Navy purchased the property and renamed it Naval Reserve Air Base (NRAB) Chicago. Now known as NAS Glenview, the naval air station had been expanded significantly to handle the major influx of aviation cadets and pilots undergoing flight training.[23]

After arriving at NAS Glenview, Aviation Cadet James A. Nist was assigned to Class 3-B and berthed in Barracks 22 at the air station. Unlike his previous duty station, NAS Glenview was a naval installation. Several weeks after arriving there, Nist described the naval air station in a letter home to his parents. He wrote:

> There is enough concrete in the runways, mats and aprons to build 210 miles of dual highways. We have two circular landing mats each almost a half mile in diameter. That really takes concrete. And an apron in front of the hangars about a hundred and fifty yards wide and over a mile long.[24]

In successive letters to his parents, Cadet Nist described his newest duty station. "I thought Chapel Hill was tough, but this place is worse," he wrote on 30 March 1943. Nist and the other cadets were working long hours on the flight line and attending classes in ground school. The cadets were actually working on the flight line gassing up the aircraft that were used for flight training. The training was continuous, even on the weekends. "We didn't get much time off in Chapel Hill, but we don't get any here [emphasis in original]," he wrote to his parents on Saturday, 3 April 1943. "We're flying all day tomorrow, just as we did last Sunday. Sunday is just like any other day here. As long as we're flying though, who cares?"[25]

Aviation cadets at NAS Glenview were flying the Naval Aircraft Factory N3N-3, an aluminum biplane that was also known as the "Yellow Peril" after its distinctive yellow paint scheme. The Navy had been using the Yellow Peril as a primary trainer since June 1935. It was 25' 6" in length with a wingspan of 34' and a height of 10' 10". It had a maximum speed of 126 miles per hour, a service ceiling of 15,200 feet and a rate of climb of 900 feet per minute.[26]

The Class 3-B aviation cadets immediately began flight training. Aviation Cadet Nist took his first U.S. Navy flight as a passenger in an N3N on 28 March 1943. For an hour and a half, he rode while an instructor pilot performed acrobatics. This was repeated on 29 March and 31 March. In three days of flying as a passenger, Nist logged 4.5 hours of flight time.[27]

Since most of these cadets were destined for service aboard aircraft carriers,

The Navy N3N-3 Trainer, popularly known as the Yellow Peril (Naval History and Heritage Command [Photo 80-G-K-13392] / National Archives).

the flight training focused heavily on landing aboard carriers. "They start right out on precision approaches and tail low landings (so the landing hook will catch if you were on a carrier)," he wrote on 30 March 1943. Referring to the aircraft at NAS Glenview, Nist added, "They have the cream of the Navy out here as far as ships go. The dream ship came in yesterday. Three Corsair F4U-1s." He also noted that there was a B-17 Flying Fortress at the air station. Developed by Chance Vought Aircraft Company, the F4U Corsair was just entering service. A heavily armed, fast and maneuverable fighter, the Corsair would soon garner a fearsome reputation in the Pacific War.[28]

Besides flight operations, Nist commented on the weather. "It's always blowing a gale," he wrote on 30 March. "Don't know how they expect us to learn anything when the planes just about jump off the ground of their own accord." Two days later, Nist again complained about the weather. "This weather out here is positively the worst I've ever seen," he wrote to his parents. "It's usually clear but the wind blows so hard, we can't fly. Or rather we shouldn't."[29]

The newly arrived aviation cadets quickly learned how dangerous flying could be. On Monday, 29 March, a flight student fell out of a trainer aircraft while his instructor was demonstrating a slow roll. Fortunately, the student deployed his parachute and landed safely behind a farmer's house. When naval personnel arrived to retrieve him, the student still had his parachute ripcord in his hand. Per tradition, the student owed a quart of whiskey to the riggers who had packed his parachute.[30]

Cadet Nist's first several flights at NAS Glenview were accompanied by an instructor who either demonstrated maneuvers and/or had Nist perform maneuvers under instruction. He flew twice on 1 April and two more times on 2 April for a total of five hours of flying time, all as a passenger.

On Thursday, 1 April, Nist had his first opportunity to pass a "check flight" so as to qualify to fly solo. Due to the persistent high winds, he did not receive an "up check." In a letter to his parents, Nist described his harrowing experience:

> Everything was okay and good until I had to land. I don't know the wind is blowing so hard and neither does my check instructor till I head into the wind for the landing. Instead of gliding down, I have to pull it down with almost full throttle. It was a perfect three-point landing, the tail wheel, the starboard wheel and the starboard wing tip. But the damage was slight and he [the instructor] let me go. He said he probably would have done the same thing himself.

Nist's difficulties continued on the ground. The high winds made taxiing on the ground extremely difficult, so Nist and two of the aircraft mechanics had to lie on the wings of the plane to hold it down while the instructor taxied the plane to the flight line. Several other pilots also scraped wings due to the high winds.[31]

On 2 April, Aviation Cadet Nist soloed and completed A Stage. He went up at the controls of N3N Number 2726 and flew 1.5 hours of acrobatics. "Well yesterday, I got the best of my Yellow Peril N3N-3 and showed it a few things," he proudly wrote to his parents on 3 April 1943. "As a result, I am now out of A Stage. I soloed the damn thing yesterday. I was the first one in our wing." The following day, three more from Nist's class soloed.[32]

It was around this time that James Nist received some news about his sister Kathryn Nist Dickerson from his other sister, Margaret, a.k.a. "Wootz." "Also heard I'm going to be an uncle again," he wrote his parents, referring to Kathryn's fourth pregnancy. Kathryn already had a son, Walter, Jr. (a.k.a. "Dickie"), and two daughters—Patricia and Joan.[33]

Three weeks after arriving at NAS Glenview, Nist was reunited with Ed DeGaspar and his former shipmates from Navy Pre-Flight School 17th Battalion. DeGaspar et al. became Class 4-A. As the most recent arrivals at NAS Glenview, they assumed responsibility for cleaning the Ready Room, gassing airplanes and all other drudge work. "3-B is thru the dirty work," Nist wrote home jubilantly.[34]

The weather at NAS Glenview could turn ugly with alarming speed. On Saturday, 3 April, Nist went up for a solo flight amid clear skies. After 90 minutes, weather conditions rapidly deteriorated. Visibility dropped to one mile and the cloud ceiling dropped to 800 feet. Nist was practicing at another airfield farther inland and had trouble finding NAS Glenview. All further flight operations were canceled due to the weather.[35]

The atrocious weather was not the only hazard at NAS Glenview. With all those aviation cadets aloft performing their flight training, the air space around NAS Glenview could become heavily congested in a hurry. Nist commented on this in a letter to his parents on 11 April 1943:

> When the hop is due back, there are two hundred airplanes trying to land at once. If you don't keep your eyes open, some dodo will chew your tail or wings off. And in airplane traffic, you can't put on the brakes and stop and you have three directions to watch instead of only two. The favorite pastime out here is landing on top of someone else. They ought to put a window in the floor [of the airplane] so you can see down.[36]

While at NAS Glenview, Aviation Cadet Nist's free time was extremely limited. On Sunday, 11 April, he attended Protestant worship services and received "Navy communion with grape-juice." On one Friday, wind conditions were too dangerous to fly, so the aviation cadets were given liberty until 2200. "I didn't go anywhere," he informed his parents. "The only place worth going is Chicago and I didn't feel like going all the way there for a couple of hours." Instead, he used the time to study. The attrition rate was about a third of those enrolled. "If they can't fly, out they go," he wrote.[37]

Aviation Cadet Nist continued to make steady progress in his flight and classroom training throughout April. In Stage B, cadets were required to land straight through the center of a 50-foot circle painted on the runway as preparation for landing on aircraft carriers. "I'm showing them the little guys can fly as well or better than the big ones," he wrote home on 12 April 1943. Academically, Aviation Cadet Nist was doing exceptionally well with grades in his classes, ranging from 3.7 to 4.0. "The top 20% of the class have their choice of duty and I want myself a brand-new Corsair to fly around at 425 miles per hour," he wrote. The flight instruction schedule was physically demanding. "There's nothing like three hours of flying to beat you up. Especially when we go way upstairs," he wrote. "Its cold as heck and with open ships and no extra oxygen, it really leaves you with a going over."[38]

Flight operations continued to be plagued by frequent rain, sleet, snow and high winds. Cadet Nist described one challenging flight in a letter to his parents dated 16 April 1943:

> You should see the blizzard we had out here the other day. And we flew through it all. I was flying my Yellow Peril blind without instruments. Visibility zero, ceiling zero. We had to stay up. We couldn't see to land for a while. Finally, it quit snowing and we came back at almost twice tree top altitude. What a time.[39]

Other pilot trainees were not so fortunate. In one 10-day period in April, four pilots from NAS Glenview died and another went missing for over a week due to weather-related flight mishaps. Two more pilots were killed due to weather mishaps on 17 April. Due to the atrocious weather and fatal mishaps, flight operations had to be scaled back for safety reasons.[40]

Sunday, 18 April 1943, was a most memorable occasion for the Aviation Cadets at NAS Glenview. That day, the air station hosted a Tea Dance with female college students from Northwestern University. Music was provided by Navy musicians. Nist enjoyed the female company and raved about the music. "They've got a bluejacket orchestra here which has got about half of the big-name bands beat seven ways from Sunday," he wrote to his parents.[41]

The next day, Aviation Cadet Nist had his first "down check." Nist's aircraft had a recurring problem of the throttle sticking. He began the check flight flying solo. The aircraft was performing normally until it came time to land and pick up his evaluator, Ensign Glista. "The throttle wouldn't close under 1200 R.P.M. and that's just enough to hold the damn ship in the air," he wrote later. "So I miss six circle landings in a row." Nist then remembered that an instructor pilot had unstuck a stuck throttle the week before by making the fuel-air mixture lean. So Nist made the fuel-air mixture so lean that the engine barely kept the aircraft aloft. The throttle became unstuck and Nist was able to land. Glista then questioned him about his difficulties in landing. Nist explained about the stuck throttle, but Glista did not believe him. He then took Glista aloft for his check flight. At the conclusion of the flight, Glista gave Nist his first-ever "down check."[42]

Having received his first "down check," Aviation Cadet Nist became highly anxious about his future in naval aviation. The B Stage was notorious for washing out cadet pilots and Nist was expecting to wash out any day now. Adding to his concerns, several of Nist's shipmates had also flown their first B check flights and received "down checks." Nist was also mad at Ensign Glista for not believing him about the stuck throttle.[43]

Fortunately, Nist's anxieties soon passed. On 22 and 23 April, he flew twice and got "up checks" on both flights. "The two last check pilots said I gave them both good rides," he proudly reported.[44]

In discussing the week's events, the cadets quickly saw a pattern. "So we figure they give us the first down regardless of how we fly," he wrote home to Martin and Ethel. "That puts the pressure on good and proper (as if it ain't always hard on). Any guy who can't fly with the chips down gets washed out." Nist understood the logic behind the first "down check" but he was still rattled by the experience.[45]

On 24 April, Cadet Nist began stunt flying with the N3N-3. Acrobatic maneuvers were flown at a high enough altitude so that the trainee could use a parachute if he ran into serious trouble. "So the first solo I decide to have it out once and for all with my pet Yellow Peril," Nist wrote to his parents on 26 April. "I must have been hot that day 'cause she behaved all right. I snapped rolled her for an hour and a half straight.... It's a good thing she behaved or I would have taken them off [the aircraft's wings]."[46]

On Saturday, 25 April 1943, Aviation Cadet Nist and two shipmates went to Chicago by train on liberty. They arrived in Chicago at around 2030 (8:30 p.m.) and went to the Hotel Sherman, which was regarded as the headquarters for cadets on liberty in Chicago. The hotel was located on Clark and Randolph Streets across from City Hall. It was built after the Great Fire of 1871 and renovated extensively around the turn of the century. Boasting some 1,600 guest rooms and a world-class restaurant, Hotel Sherman was purported to be the largest hotel west of New York City. In the 1920s, it was frequented by some of Chicago's most notorious gangsters, including Al Capone. The hotel had a well-established reputation for its jazz performances and was one of Chicago's premier night spots. Those who performed there included famed jazz singer, dancer and band leader Cab Calloway.[47]

For service members, the city of Chicago was very accommodating. There were reduced prices for railroad tickets for service members. There was no cover for service members at the Hotel Sherman's Dome Room. Servicemen's Centers offered free tickets to sporting events, movies and other entertainment. Many other businesses and venues offered free or discounted prices for service members.[48]

Upon arrival at the Hotel Sherman, Nist and his two wingmen began searching for female companionship. "The town [Chicago] is pretty good and the girls are even nicer," he wrote home. They soon met up with a group of five girls. Since the cadets-to-female ratio was three to five, the three aviation cadets each paired up with a girl, then added three more cadets to round out their group. Nist and his group spent the evening enjoying the entertainment at the famed Dome Room. "Cab Calloway was there and the place was about ready to bust at the seams," he wrote home. After an enjoyable evening, the six cadets escorted their dates home but, in doing so, missed the last train back to the naval air station.[49]

Having missed the last train of the night, Nist and company were forced to wait until the next morning to catch a train back to NAS Glenview. They arrived back there at 0730. Nist caught a couple of hours of sleep, then went back up in the Yellow Peril. While aloft, he performed snap rolls, Immelmans, loops, split S's, falling leafs and pylon 8s.[50]

Around this time, Nist received a letter from his sister "Wootz." In that letter, Wootz enclosed a news clipping about the "Navy's Beloved Yellow Perils," which incurred the anger of her brother. "They might be beloved in Corpus Christi," he wrote to his parents, "but I'll be damned if they are around Glenview, Illinois."[51]

On the morning of 28 April 1943, Aviation Cadet Nist had a particularly harrowing training flight. The winds were so strong that flight operations were suspended. After circling the airfield twice, he saw that the recall flag had been hoisted, indicating that all aircraft were to land. The winds were blowing faster than the N3N-3's landing speed. Nist failed on his first two attempts to land. Worse yet, his aircraft was burning up fuel and becoming lighter by the minute. At one point, Nist thought he might have to bail out. On his third attempt at landing, he cut the engine. "She lands once, takes off again, lands again, takes off and lands," he described in a letter to his parents. "The third time the wind slackened a little and with the aid of a couple guys on the wings I get her in." He fully expected to get disciplined for his less-than-ideal landing but that fortunately never happened.[52]

The high winds were just as bad the following day. For the first time, Nist flew above the clouds and broke out into sunshine. Despite the high winds, Nist managed to land without experiencing a mishap, but others were not so fortunate. High winds caused over a quarter of the planes to have mishaps on landing. Fortunately, most were minor. Three cadet pilots went up on the nose of their aircraft and 25 others dragged wing tips. Another cadet was forced to land in a farmer's plowed field and wrecked his airplane. "Someday they'll learn better that to send us up in such weather," he wrote.[53]

April 1943 was a busy month for Aviation Cadet Nist. During that month, he went on 42 flights, of which 26 were solo. He logged 37.5 hours of flight time as a pilot and 22 hours as a passenger for a total of 59.5 hours of flight time that April. Nist's hatred of the Yellow Peril was also softening. "Now that I'm doing acrobatics, my pet seems to be behaving a little better," he wrote to his parents. "Sometimes I almost weaken enough to call it a good airplane, but that would be a little too much."[54]

As May 1943 opened, Cadet Nist was learning to do inverted spins. "It's a regular spin only you're upside down and instead of being held in, you are thrown out against the safety belt," he informed his parents. "They about cut you in half." Inverted spins were very difficult to perform and two Yellow Perils were lost in late April while attempting the maneuver.[55]

Aviation Cadet Nist wanted to fly the F4U Corsair, the Navy's newest and fastest fighter plane. "One of my dream bubbles burst the other day," a dejected Nist informed his parents. "The famed Vought-Sikorsky F4U-1 Corsair has been removed from carrier service. So they're turning it over to the Marines for land-based use." The Navy determined that the Corsair was unsuitable for carrier operations and so would operate from land bases. That summer and fall, fighter squadrons like the Navy's VF-17 (CDR Tom Blackburn) and the Marine Corps' VMF-214 (Major Gregory "Pappy" Boyington) would employ the Corsairs with devastating results against the Japanese in the South Pacific.[56]

Despite his disappointment, Nist did have some hope for flying the Grumman F6F Hellcat in the future. "They're even better than the Corsair but not nearly as good looking," he wrote home. "So I guess I ain't going to fly a Corsair, unless I don't qualify for carrier duty. I'd better, that's all."[57]

Cadet Nist continued to have issues with Ensign Glista, the instructor who had given him his only "down check" thus far. With Glista at the controls, the two had gone up on a dual flight. Glista performed a low-altitude half-roll, which Nist did not find amusing. "Ensign Glista might be okay, but he scared me more than I've been scared in one long time," he wrote to his parents. With that experience and the repeated mishaps occurring, it's no wonder then that Nist decided to quote the Navy Hymn in his latest letter:

> Lord, guard and guide the men who fly
> Through the great spaces of the sky.
> Be with them traversing the air
> In darkening storm and sunlight fair.
> Oh, hear us when we lift our prayer
> For those in peril in the air.[58]

On liberty, James Nist had met a young woman who took an interest in him. Dottie Schultz was a five-foot-three-inch-tall brunette. "She ain't so bad looking, and she dances like a fiend," he casually informed Martin and Ethel. In four days, she had written him four letters.[59]

On the night of Wednesday, 6 May, Cadet Nist began training for night flying. He flew as a passenger for an hour of night flying orientation. The following night, he flew solo at night for 1.5 hours. In a letter to his parents, he described the experience of simulated night carrier landings at NAS Glenview and included a hand-drawn sketch. "There are no lights to light the runway," he wrote. "The carrier deck is outlined by eight lights like this, and the lights are little flares like in the truck…. So we start landing about 25 feet up and slowly stall it down trying to keep it level and straight without anything to go by. Some fun, but it sure gave the nerves a workover."[60]

On the night of Friday, 8 May 1943, Nist was tested on simulated night carrier landings. After an hour of dual flight, Nist took the aircraft up solo. Fog and rain added to the difficulties of the simulated night carrier landings. Due to the poor visibility, Nist nearly struck the crash truck during takeoff. Nevertheless, Nist got an "up check" for this crucial test and passed stimulated night carrier landings.[61]

Nist was progressing well through his training. He was second in his class to a former Navy enlisted sailor who had served as a gunner on a scout plane. Nist had passed A, B and C Stages and was poised to test to pass D Stage. Most of his shipmates were still in B or C Stage. "The first guy in our outfit to washout left yesterday, but there are about five more ready to go," he informed his parents. "They're on their last leg." Another aircraft was lost to an inverted spin; fortunately both trainee and instructor successfully bailed out.[62]

Sunday, 9 May 1943, was Mother's Day and Jimmy Nist was sure to mail his mother a greeting card. That day, Nist got an "up check" for D Stage. To ensure that he was well rested for this critical flight, he had skipped the Saturday night trip into Chicago. Nist's check pilot was a tough one like his nemesis Ensign Glista. The check pilot reamed out Nist for not performing strange field procedures to his satisfaction, then made him fly S-turns into circles. He failed to execute the first attempt but then was successful on the next five. "So he comes back all smiles, says they were good, and off we go," Nist wrote home the next day. The check pilot had Nist perform several forced landings. After the last forced landing, the check pilot switched seats with Nist. Normally during dual flights, the instructor sat up front and the trainee sat in the back of the two-seat Yellow Peril. With Nist piloting from the front seat, the two went aloft again. "So we go up and fool around for a half hour with me flying from up front (quite a difference)," he wrote. Nist got his coveted "up check." He also ended the flight on better relations with his check pilot, who "really turned out to be a swell guy."[63]

A couple of days later, there was another serious incident at NAS Glenview. It involved one of the six cadets who came early with Nist from North Carolina. During a night takeoff, his plane ran into the crash truck. His plane's propellor chewed through the truck's cab, killing both sailors who were inside. The cadet escaped with minor injuries and was sent to sick bay for treatment, unaware that the two sailors had been killed. Nist expected that this fatal event would terminate the cadet's flying career.[64]

During the week of 9–15 May 1943, Aviation Cadet Nist completed his flight training. He was the second cadet in his class to "check out"; the first cadet was the former Navy enlisted sailor. In seven weeks at NAS Glenview, Nist had logged 102 flight hours. Added to the 77 flight hours that he had logged during his training with the Civilian Pilot Training Program, Nist now had 179 hours of flying experience. Nist still had to complete ground school but would continue to log flying time to maintain his skills.[65]

Formation flying was one of the final tasks that Nist had to successfully perform in order to complete his flight training. He thoroughly enjoyed this type of flying and stated as much in his 14 May 1943 letter to his parents. On this particular day, Nist went aloft three separate times and logged 4.5 hours of formation flying. In his letter, he wrote:

> You can't take it easy like you can flying alone. You've got to stay on the ball all the time.... When you're in formation, you keep your eyes on the leader every second. You can't even take a look at your instruments. So he has to go in the right places, fly at the right speed, etc.

Nist quickly proved adept at formation flying and spent most of this period of instruction flying as the flight leader.[66]

That weekend, Cadets Nist and DeGaspar had liberty from 1700 on Saturday until 2200 Sunday. On Saturday night, Nist, DeGaspar and another shipmate took the train into Chicago. At Hotel Sherman, the three aviation cadets met three female students from the University of Indiana. "From there on, things were swell," Nist wrote to his parents, offering no further details.[67]

With his flight training completed, Nist was eager to clear out of NAS Glenview. After finishing ground school, he would get nine days of leave and then report to NAS Corpus Christi, Texas. "Will I be glad to get to Corpus Christi," he wrote his parents on 16 May 1943. "They [his instructors] say everything is swell down there and the weather is beautiful."[68]

Aviation Cadet Nist sent his final letter home from NAS Glenview to his parents on Saturday, 22 May 1943. In this letter, he wrote about completing ship and aircraft recognition. On his final exam for this topic, he correctly identified 40 of 40 aircraft and 37 of 40 ships. He was also studying air navigation over water, learning how to find ships at sea, take off from carriers on scouting missions and return to the carrier without running out of fuel, how to use radio bearings to determine position when lost and how to search by changing course every 15 minutes and not get lost.[69]

On 26 May 1943, Cadet Nist took his final flight at NAS Glenview. He went up for 1.5 hours of flying to maintain his skills. Soon after, he left Glenview and went home on leave. He was granted a total of nine days leave, including two travel days.[70]

Flight Training in Texas

Aviation Cadet James Nist was sent to Naval Air Station Corpus Christi for further flight training. Encompassing some 20,000 acres on the Texas Gulf Coast, NAS Corpus Christi was the largest naval air station in the world. It was located about 12 miles east of the city of Corpus Christi, adjacent to Corpus Christi Bay and Oso Bay. Prior to construction, the site was covered with mesquite brush and scrub oak trees. Construction began on 30 June 1940 and the facility was commissioned on 12 March 1941. The new NAS Corpus Christi included seaplane hangars and ramps, runways, taxiways, barracks, hangars and support buildings. Flight training began on 5 May 1941. The station's first commanding officer, CAPT Alva D. Bernhard, declared the station to be "the University of the Air." The station trained pilots, navigators, aerologists, aerial gunners and radio operators. During World War II, 35,000 pilots trained there, including future president George H.W. Bush, who earned his naval aviator wings there in June 1943.[71]

After the United States entered World War II, NAS Corpus Christi was rapidly expanded to accommodate the immense need for trained pilots. Over the next two years, eight auxiliary airfields and 25 outlying practice landing fields were constructed. Aviation training was divided among the main airfield and its auxiliary airfields. The main station was used for aircraft maintenance and seaplane and observation training. Basic and intermediate flight training was conducted at Naval Auxiliary Air Station (NAAS) Cabaniss Field and NAAS Cuddihy. NAAS Cabaniss Field was located on the Oso Creek 12 miles west of NAS Corpus Christi and about

10 miles south-southeast from the city of Corpus Christi. NAAS Cuddihy was about 15 miles west of NAS Corpus Christi and about 10 miles west of Corpus Christi. Primary flight training and bombing training were conducted at NAAS Rodd Field, located seven miles southwest of NAS Corpus Christi. Advanced fighter training was done at NAAS Kingsville Field, located near Kingsville. Training for torpedo bombers was done at NAAS Waldron Field, which was located about seven miles south of NAS Corpus Christi. Pilots learned instrument flying at NAAS Chase Field in Beeville, 74 miles to the north of main station. Six of the auxiliary stations were named for naval aviators who had perished in the line of duty.[72]

The commandant of Naval Air Station Corpus Christi was Rear Admiral Charles P. Mason. Originally from Harrisburg, Pennsylvania, Mason was a 1912 graduate of the U.S. Naval Academy. He became a naval aviator in 1917 and served in the European Theater in World War I. Following the Battle of Midway, CAPT Mason assumed command of the aircraft carrier USS *Hornet* (CV-8), which operated in the southwest Pacific. She was sunk during the Battle of Santa Cruz on 26 October 1942. Mason earned a Navy Cross for heroism and leadership during the battle. Promoted to rear admiral, Mason continued serving in the southwest Pacific until he contracted malaria. He returned Stateside for treatment and to assume command of NAS Corpus Christi.[73]

Cadet Nist reported to NAS Corpus Christi during the second week of June 1943 and was assigned to Class 6B of the Cadet Regiment. In one of his first letters sent home from here, Nist wrote about conditions at NAS Corpus Christi:

> Texas isn't too bad when you get a little used to it, but it's still a long ways from being good. The heat is still as bad as ever, maybe a little worse. We try to sleep nights, but it's so hot we're just as tired when we get up as when we went to bed. Beginning to get a little tan but I've got a long way to catch the boys who have been down here for a few weeks. They're about thirteen shades darker than I used to get last summer.[74]

Before flight training, Nist and his fellow cadets had to undergo a high-altitude test. The cadets were put in a chamber that simulated conditions at various altitudes. They were then given a series of tests at different altitudes to evaluate their ability to perform. "We took it at sea-level, again after being at 18,000 feet for thirteen minutes without oxygen, and again at 28,000 feet breathing pure oxygen," he wrote in his 11 June letter home. At sea level, Nist scored 200 out of a possible 243 points. At 18,000 feet without oxygen, Nist scored 181 out of 243 points. While breathing pure oxygen at 28,000 feet, Nist scored 191 out of a possible 243 points. In doing so, Nist earned the second-highest scores of his class. "The oxygen made quite a difference," he wrote home. "A few more minutes without it and a lot of the boys would have passed out. We all felt dizzy enough to teach us it ain't good to fly without oxygen." He also described the effects of diminished oxygen at higher altitudes. "The guys acted just like drunks," he wrote. "They were silly, couldn't move very gracefully. One guy started tearing things up and they had to take him out."[75]

During the high-altitude test, the cadets' vital signs were monitored and recorded. Nist's resting pulse at sea level was 72 beats per minute. Without oxygen at 18,000 feet, his resting pulse was 84 beats per minute. At 28,000 feet with oxygen, his resting pulse was 76 beats per minute and his blood pressure was 100 over 58. Nist's performance on the high-altitude test was impressive considering that he had spent nearly his whole life in coastal New Jersey close to sea level. After the high-altitude test, the cadets were given a complete physical exam. Nist passed his exam with a Schneider Rating of +14. "If they stick me in a damn P-boat after that performance, there'll be a war on right in Texas," he wrote, referring to the Navy's PBY Catalina amphibious patrol aircraft. "That rates an F6F or an SB2D any day."[76]

On Sunday, 13 June, Nist and his shipmates were transferred over to Cabaniss Field for three weeks of basic flight training. Afterward, they would return to NAS Corpus Christi for double ground school, then be moved to another auxiliary field for instrument flying and, after that, be moved to a third auxiliary field for advanced squadron.[77]

Training at Cabaniss Field was intense. The training day was packed with ground school, study time and 4.5 hours of flying, much of which was in formation. "This place tops anything I've seen before," he wrote to his parents on 16 June 1943. "They roll us out at 0515 and we just don't have time for anything the whole damn day. Or night—not even sleep…. It's a good thing we're only here for three weeks." Chow was at 0530, 1315 and 2000, and not to Nist's liking. "If anybody asks you why they don't get any mail, just tell them that I'm in Shangri-La on restriction," he advised his parents.[78]

Nist and the other cadets were flying a more powerful aircraft, the SNV-1 Vultee Valiant. The Valiant boasted a 450-horsepower engine, landing flaps, retractable wheels, a cockpit cover, propeller pitch control, landing lights and a cruising speed of 178 knots. The Valiant was nicknamed the "Vibrator" because its propeller produced a distinctive vibration.[79]

On 14 June 1943, Nist went up in a Valiant for the first time. Nist rode as a passenger while an instructor pilot, LT Tunner, demonstrated the aircraft's flying characteristics for 1.4 hours. Over the next three days, Nist performed four flights accompanied by an instructor. Two days later, he soloed for the first time in a Valiant. He flew two solo flights performing acrobatics and a third flight to practice formation flying. From here on out, Nist would alternate between dual and solo flights.[80]

Aviation Cadet Nist quickly became fond of the more powerful Valiant. "Such an airplane," he informed his parents. "Sweetest thing on wings so far. And twice as hot as anything so far." Comparing the Valiant with the Yellow Perils that he had previously flown, he wrote, "Quite a jump from something that lands at 43 knots to a job that lands at 80 knots, with flaps down." He went on to offer a detailed description of the Valiant and its attributes:

> Besides the flaps and controllable pitch prop to learn, we've got an oil heater, fuel tank selector valve (three gas tanks on her), a whole lot of new instruments including all those we need to fly blind, electric starters, and radios [emphasis in original].
>
> That's the best part. We can talk to anybody we want, but we have to be careful what we say because everybody can hear you. We get instructions from the tower by radio. The helmets have earphones. And the planes have a crash-harness in place of safety belt. It fits over your shoulders so you can't fall into the instrument panel. Oh yeah, we've got cock-pit covers and don't have to wear goggles anymore. And trim tabs so you can trim the ship to fly perfectly level and straight.[81]

The SNV-1 Vultee Valiant, popularly known as the "Vibrator" due to the distinctive vibration caused by its propeller, was used by both the U.S. Army Air Forces and the U.S. Navy. The USAAF version is pictured here (U.S. Air Force).

As Aviation Cadet Nist continued to develop as an aviator, he became concerned about being assigned as an instructor pilot. One of his instructors had previously been a fighter pilot but had not deployed. "That's what I'm afraid of," Nist wrote home in one of his letters. "Will be murder if they make an instructor out of this cay-det."[82]

In his 19 June 1943 letter to his parents, Nist described one particularly noteworthy training flight that he had had a couple of days prior. He wrote:

> We were in formation the other day. An instructor leads us and two of us fly on his wing. He broke us up and told us to follow him. So we chased his tail for about 10 minutes. He was trying to lose us by dodging around the clouds at 180 miles per hour. He finally did by slowing way up, cranking down his flaps so he could turn real sharp and then beating it away while we were still trying to turn. Most fun I ever had.[83]

In that same letter, Nist gave his parents a preview of the next part of his training at Cabaniss: gunnery. Training for aerial gunnery actually began on the ground. First, the cadets would learn to shoot skeet and trap using shotguns. This would develop their skills in firing at moving targets. Next, the cadets would fire at model airplanes using machine guns that fired BBs (small .177-caliber metal balls). Friendly airplanes were interspersed with enemy airplanes. Hitting a friendly airplane would result in losing all of one's score. Lastly, the cadets would use machine-gun sights like those used in naval aircraft.[84]

The ground school component of the training at Cabaniss focused heavily on aerial navigation. Nist quickly demonstrated an aptitude for navigation. Nist was still worried about being assigned as an instructor pilot after completing his flight training, but he was starting to become concerned that the Navy might want to use his exceptional navigational skills as a pilot in a scout-observation aircraft such as a PBY Catalina or SBD Dauntless.[85]

Each training flight was being graded. Four "down" checks would get a cadet washed out of the program. The grueling flight training and ground school was taking a toll on the aviation cadets, and cadets were starting to quit. "I can understand quitting at Pre-Flight, but after going all the way through that and then primary and with the Wings almost in sight, I think they're crazy," he wrote to his parents on 25 June 1943. "The day they make this [emphasis in original] cay-det say 'Uncle' will be one helluva day." Other cadets had become complacent and were failing to meet the Navy's standards, so more cadets were being washed out of the program.[86]

Cadet Nist was doing exceptionally well in his ground school classes, especially aerial navigation. "I feel very proud of myself today," he informed his parents on 25 June. "I became the fourth caydet [sic] in the history of Cabaniss Field to finish the first course in navigation with a straight 'four-oh.'" Nist earned 4.0s grades on five quizzes and the final exam. Next Nist would be working on the second course of instruction for navigation. "Nobody has ever finished the second course with a 4.0 average so I got something to shoot for," he wrote.[87]

The cadets at Cabaniss Field were logging many hours flying at night. "The night flying was swell down here," Nist wrote on 25 June. "Not like the rat-race at Glenview. We had the whole runway to land on and it was outlined with flares. Also, the Vultees have landing lights which helped no end. And the land is dark down here. In Chicago, there were so many lights we couldn't tell planes from houses or stars. Really was great stuff."[88]

As the end of the month neared, more cadets were getting washed out of the program. On Monday, 28 June, four of the cadets were washed out, including a cadet who had been in Nist's platoon at NAS Glenview. That particular cadet had gotten four "down checks." "Seems too many guys have been getting killed for no good reason except their own mistakes," Nist wrote.[89]

In the last week of June, Nist and his fellow cadets began shooting trap and skeet with 12-gauge shotguns in preparation for aerial gunnery. Both trap and skeet involve shooting shotguns at moving targets (clay pigeons). Both shooting disciplines involve leading the target sufficiently so that the target flies into the shotgun pellets fired ahead of it by the shooter. The idea is to fire where the target is going to be, not where it already is. The same basic principle applied to aerial gunnery, which is why aerial gunners and fighter pilots trained in skeet and trap.[90]

For the month of June, Nist logged 8.1 hours of dual flight time and 20.7 hours of solo flight time. This included an hour of flying solo at night just before the month ended.[91]

In a major departure from his usual topics, Cadet Nist wrote about watermelons in his 2 July 1943 letter to his parents. Apparently, he had developed a craving for watermelons that could not be satisfied at NAS Corpus Christi. "Can't afford them on cadets' pay," he informed his parents. "The little ones sell for a dollar and the big ones as high as three." In his next letter, however, Nist had found a solution to his watermelon predicament. Apparently, he found somewhere on base where he could get some watermelon for a nickel.[92]

An important part of the training at Cabaniss Field involved using a Link Trainer. The Link Trainer was invented by Edwin Link, a private pilot who worked at his father's piano and organ company. In the late 1920s, Link developed a machine to simulate flying conditions using a scaled-down fuselage and cockpit mounted on a movable control base. The Link Trainer consisted of an aircraft cockpit with instruments and flight controls and an instructor station that recorded aircraft movements. A hood enclosed the cockpit to eliminate outside references so that the trainee was forced to "fly" solely using instruments. Use of the Link Trainer helped shorten the time required to train a pilot and enabled trainees to learn and develop their flying skills in an environment where mistakes were not fatal.[93]

While at Cabaniss Field, Aviation Cadet Nist successfully completed training in the Link Trainer. The training was conducted by a member of the Navy's WAVES (Women Accepted for Volunteer Emergency Service) program. "When I climbed out of the thing she says 'I'll fly with you anytime. Your radio procedure was perfect and you sure can handle that Link,'" he informed his parents. "The thing that got me the good grade was that I figured out a way to make the Link fly straight and level without even touching the controls. Thus, I concentrated on flying the beam and hit it perfect."[94]

Saturday, 3 July, witnessed a near mishap that could have ended disastrously. An Army Air Force plane was attempting to land at Cabaniss Field but its landing gear would not come down. The pilot radioed the tower and informed them of his situation. The tower cleared the runway and positioned a crash truck in anticipation of the Army pilot attempting a wheels-up belly landing. Fortunately, one of the Navy instructors rushed up into the tower. He advised the Army pilot to gain altitude and perform a snap-roll to hopefully unjam the landing gear. The Army pilot did so and the landing gear lowered properly. He then landed safely.[95]

On the Fourth of July, Ed DeGasper and several other of Nist's Chapel Hill shipmates arrived at NAS Corpus Christi. Unfortunately for Nist, his former roommate was immediately reassigned to Cuddihy Field.[96]

Two days later, Cadet Nist returned to NAS Corpus Christi's main facility, a.k.a. Main Station. For the first few days, Nist was in ground school learning celestial navigation, ship and aircraft recognition, gunnery and radar. The radar class was taught in a high-security facility. "Its so secret, there's a guard at each door and around the building with rifles to see that nobody gets in who shouldn't," he informed his parents. Nist had wanted to move on to NAS Corpus Christi's outlying station at Beeville for instrument flying so he could fly the SNJ Texan training airplane, but he remained at the Main Station for the month of July.[97]

Around this time, Cadet Nist got a letter from his nephew Walter Dickerson, Jr. "Dickie," as he was nicknamed, the oldest child of his sister Kathryn and her husband, Walter Dickerson. Referring to his nephew's letter, Nist wrote, "It was short but he didn't do so bad."[98]

On Friday, 9 July 1943, Nist and the other cadets submitted their final preferences for advanced flight training and their sentiments for each choice. Nist listed his preferences as:

1. Fighters—very pleased if I got them
2. Scout bombers—pleased if I got them
3. Torpedo bombers—pleased if I got them
4. Land based twin and multi-engine bombers—satisfied
5. Scout observation catapults—disappointed
6. Patrol bombers—Very disappointed

According to Nist, 70 percent of the cadets got their first preference and over 90 percent got their first or second preference. With so many of his fellow cadets requesting fighters, Nist recognized that he might not get his first choice. He would be okay with getting scout (dive) bombers or torpedo bombers instead.[99]

That same day, Nist and 249 of his fellow cadets were treated to a lecture by a lieutenant junior grade that he derisively referred to as "some ninety-day wonder." "He is as wise and smart as they come. Typical Corpus Christi attitude and he starts giving us the same old stuff," Nist wrote in a letter to his parents. Apparently, neither Nist nor any of his shipmates were in the mood for the lieutenant (jg)'s attitude and they let him know so. As Nist described:

> So two hundred and fifty of us are on report with ramp duty to walk off. Hope he feels better but so do we. An hour of ramp duty was a cheap price for showing one of those high-and-mighties what we think of them. We're all going to walk it off together tomorrow morning. But willingly and smiling.[100]

Saturday, 10 July 1943, was notable for another reason besides the lecture. "It actually rained today," Nist informed his parents. "First time I've seen it in Texas."[101]

Cadet Nist was very much looking forward to graduation, even though it appeared to be anticlimactic from his description of it. In his 10 July 1943 letter, he described a graduation that he had recently attended:

> Graduation down here isn't the occasion you'd expect. There are very few guests, mostly girl friends of the boys from Texas and Louisiana, etc. The admiral says a few words and the commissions are passed out. The wings are already on. It's all over in half an hour.[102]

Nist did well in instrument flight training. For the first two weeks, he trained exclusively in the Link Trainer. Then on Saturday, 17 July, Cadet Nist took his first flight using instruments. He went aloft in an SNV-1 number 12709 with instructor Second LT Collins, USMC, for 1.4 hours. For the rest of the month, Nist flew with an instructor nearly every day and sometimes twice a day to perfect flying on instruments. He logged 21.7 hours of flight time in July, only 3.1 hours of which was solo. Thus far, he had logged 148.5 hours of flight time as a naval aviation cadet. Other cadets were not doing as well as Nist. "They've been quitting in droves," he informed his parents on 17 July 1943.[103]

On Monday, 26 July 1943, an aircraft with an instructor and cadet aboard crashed on takeoff at NAS Corpus Christi. The instructor was at the controls. "I never saw such a wreck in all my life," Nist wrote home. "It was one tangled up mess of wheels, motors, wires and twisted aluminum."[104]

On 27 July 1943, Cadet Nist went aloft in SNV-1 number 12707 for an instrument and acrobatics training flight with Second LT Collins. This flight was not one of his better ones. "I couldn't make that airplane do anything," he wrote to his parents later that day. "I was doing steep turns and lost 600 feet in two turns. I lost half a minute on a leg of a pattern we fly and gained half a minute on the next leg.... I can do the stuff, but I couldn't today." Fortunately, his instructor was generous and still gave him an "up check" for the flight.[105]

Later that day, Cadet Nist did some shotgun shooting. In less than half an hour, he fired off two boxes of shotgun shells. On the skeet range, where two targets were launched in opposite directions, Nist hit 21 of 25 clay pigeons. On the trap range with only single targets, however, Nist hit only 12 of 25.[106]

With NAS Corpus Christi being located on the Gulf Coast, hurricanes were serious events. At the end of July, one menaced Corpus Christi. "There's a hurricane supposed to be on its way," Cadet Nist wrote home on 27 July. "It was supposed to arrive at 5 o'clock. It's nine now and still no sign of it. Guess it missed us. But they've got everything battened down and I guess we're ready for it."[107]

While Corpus Christi escaped damage, other parts of the Texas Gulf Coast were not so fortunate. The storm formed in the Gulf of Mexico off the Mississippi River delta, gained strength rapidly and headed west toward the Texas Gulf Coast. Due to wartime censorship, news about the hurricane's existence was suppressed. Its "unexpected" arrival led to the storm being dubbed "the Surprise Hurricane." The hurricane came ashore on the Bolivar Peninsula of Galveston Bay on the afternoon of 27 July. With maximum sustained winds of 104 mph, the hurricane was the most severe storm to strike the Galveston area since 1915. It caused $16.5 million in damages to Texas and killed 19 persons. On 27 July, the first two aerial flights ever to penetrate the eye of a hurricane occurred. First, Lieutenant Colonel Joseph B. Duckworth, an instrument flight instructor at USAAF Bryan Army Air Field, and navigator Lieutenant Ralph O'Hair flew an AT-6 Texan trainer into the hurricane's eye. During his second flight, LtCol Duckworth was accompanied by the base's meteorologist, Lieutenant William Jones-Burdick, who recorded meteorological observations.[108]

Several days later, Cadet Nist wrote to his parents about the hurricane and its aftermath. "We missed it, all but a thunderstorm," he wrote. "But it tore hell out of Galveston. They recorded a wind velocity at the weather station of 132 miles per hour. That's some wind. It also rained over 17 inches in twelve hours and that is something. Water up to the second stories in almost level country."[109]

Aviation Cadet Nist completed his instrument flight training at NAS Corpus Christi main station on Saturday, 31 July 1943. "For a day, I thought my address was going to be Ex-Av.Cad. Nist, Great Lakes Training School, Chicago, Illinois," he wrote to his parents afterward. On Friday, Nist had gone up with Second LT Collins and received a "down check" ... only the second one of his naval career. "I deserved that one," he later wrote.[110]

On Saturday, Nist got his chance at redemption. Nist was to fly to Rockport Field using instruments only. Since Nist's instructor, Ensign Knickerehn, was in the front seat of the plane, he did the takeoffs and landings. The flight got off with an ominous start. "I am sitting back there 'fat, dumb and happy' as they say," he later wrote to his parents. "I hear a swish. When I look down, I see all my radio charts and map of the area has blown out." Fortunately, Nist found a diagram of the Rockport Radio Range. Using the Vultee's intercom radio, Nist informed his instructor of what happened. The instructor dictated the bearings of the radio beams for the Corpus Christi Range. With this scant information, Nist then drew up a radio navigation diagram. "That's all I had to go by," he wrote. He then explained what happened next:

> So I proceed to find myself, make an instrument approach that was a beauty and 'break through the overcast at 500 feet.' We report to the instructor when we think (or know) we are over the field at 500 feet. So he says to open the hood and sure enough, there is Rockport Field dead underneath.[111]

Having passed the test, Nist and Knickerehn returned to NAS Corpus Christi without further incident. After landing, his instructor let him put his mark on the flight board indicating that he had completed instrument flight training. Nist drew a huge up arrow through his name. "As of that moment, I was through instrument squadron," he proudly reported.[112]

Nist had become so proficient at instrument flying that he was asked repeatedly to become an instructor. One of his instructors even offered to put in a good recommendation for him. Finally, Nist politely and firmly turned down the offer. "So I told him it was all I could stand just flying instruments one [emphasis in original] hop a day, let alone four or five," he wrote home to his parents. "I said I wanted to go to sea on one of the new carriers, so he says, 'So do I but they won't let me.'"[113]

Sunday, 1 August 1943, was an exceptional day for Jimmy Nist. "What a day! What a day! What a day!" he wrote to his parents. "Started out at 0800 this morning after absorbing nine solid hours of beautiful sleep. Went to chow and had the best breakfast since I hit Texas." He didn't have to play sports because it was Sunday. From 1000 to 1100 he attended a lecture, then loafed around the barracks until noon chow. Nist described noon chow as "like a country club" because of the quality of the food and an 11-piece Navy dance band that played the latest popular music.[114]

After noon chow, Nist and his shipmates had an orientation for the North American SNJ-4 (AT-6) "Texan" trainer aircraft, or the "J" for short. The Texan was used by the U.S. Navy and the U.S. Army Air Forces. The Texan had a wingspan of 42', a length of 28'11 7/8" and a height of 11'8½". With its 550 horsepower Pratt & Whitney radial engine and two-bladed propeller, the Texan could reach 21,500 feet in altitude and a maximum speed of 205 knots ground speed at 5,000 feet of altitude. With 25 instruments and 66 controls, levers and switches, the "J's" cockpit was much more complicated than anything Nist had heretofore flown in.[115]

After an hour's instruction on the aircraft, Nist and his shipmates were each taken up with an instructor to get a feel for the aircraft. Everyone passed their first check ride in the SNJ-4. Then it was their turn to solo. "One guy refused to take it up alone without more instruction," Nist reported. "But the rest of us calmly (?) climbed back into the things and soloed them." Nist then offered a detailed description of his first flights in the SNJ-4:

> They fly swell. Just a little tricky landing and taking off 'til we get used to them. Boy—they are the dream deluxe. They slow roll just as easy as another plane flies level. Of course, after we

The SNJ Texan was used by both the U.S. Navy and U.S. Army Air Forces as a trainer aircraft (Naval History and Heritage Command [Photo 80-G-K-13381]/National Archives).

got them upstairs we had to try them out. Went higher and faster that ever before. Was almost to 9,000 feet and had the thing to 180 knots which is somewhere in the neighborhood 210 miles an hour (that was level flight). These things really move when you shovel "all the coal in."[116]

Over the last several weeks, Jimmy Nist had sprinkled cryptic references to a young woman named June in his letters to his parents. Apparently, Jimmy was in contact with her and a long-distance relationship was developing. In late July, he had sent a photo of her to his parents. On 2 August, he wrote to his parents, "This kay-det thinks she's pretty nice. Wait 'til you see the live model."[117]

Jimmy Nist did not provide many biographical details on the mysterious Miss June. Her full name was June G. Smith. She lived in a two-story home in New Brunswick, New Jersey, several blocks away from the campus of Rutgers University's Douglass College.[118]

The high-stress tempo of training at NAS Corpus Christi was taking its toll on the aviation cadets both physically and mentally. Finally, the flight surgeon intervened. As Nist informed his parents, "He's a captain so he ain't afraid to speak up. He went right to the admiral and spoke his peace." That admiral was Rear Admiral C.P. Mason, the commandant of the Naval Air Training Center at NAS Corpus Christi. RADM Mason heeded his flight surgeon's professional opinion. Flying and sports on Sundays were ended and Sunday reveille was set at 0700. Physical drill was lessened and more time was allotted each day for relaxation.[119]

On Monday, 2 August, Nist and 12 of his shipmates were transferred to Naval Auxiliary Air Station Kingsville, Texas. Within six hours of arriving, Nist and seven other cadets had been appointed to leadership positions within the 10th Cadet Battalion. They also found out that their training at NAS Corpus Christi was going to last six or seven more weeks, not the four weeks like they originally believed.[120]

NAAS Kingsville was located three miles east of Kingsville, Texas, and about 45 miles southwest of NAS Corpus Christi. NAAS Kingsville had been constructed in 1942 to support aviation training at NAS Corpus Christi. Originally intended as a wartime expedient, NAS Kingsville continues to serve naval aviation to this day.[121]

Kingsville was also home to the King Ranch. At 825,000 acres, the King Ranch was one of the largest ranches in the world and larger than the state of Rhode Island. "I'm waiting to get a look at it from up-stairs," Nist wrote to his parents. "Probably wouldn't even be able to fly around it without running out of gas."[122]

After only a day aboard NAAS Kingsville, Cadet Nist already had some strong opinions about his new duty station. He wrote to his parents:

> Kingsville is really in the sticks. I thought we were bad off at Cabaniss but we're sixty miles further out in the underbrush. Away from the Gulf and twice as hot here. But things in general are a lot nicer. We've got nicer barracks, better chow, they aren't quite so eager here, we get one day a week off and we have about an hour and a half of real honest-to-goodness time off (when we're not on watch). The big trouble with this outfit is that we're so darn far from civilization.[123]

Despite the living conditions, Cadet Nist was very much enjoying the flying at NAAS Kingsville. While here, Nist and his shipmates performed high-altitude flights using oxygen; scouting flights over the Gulf of Mexico; formation flying involving six, 12 and 18 aircraft; ground strafing; and dogfights using camera-guns to record the results. Nist expected to log a hundred flight hours while here. The training was conducted by experienced pilots of Navy Fighter Training Squadron 14 (VF-14).[124]

On Saturday, 7 August, Nist returned to the cockpit of an N3N-3 "Yellow Peril." "We had to go up and show them [the instructors] we could go into and come out of an inverted spin today," he wrote to his parents afterward. "Took me just one spin and about thirty seconds. But I can say I was flying again anyway."[125]

That same day, a ground mishap seriously damaged two of the SNJ trainer aircraft. Afterward, Nist wrote:

> Two less airplanes today. This time it was an instructor and not a kidoodle who pulled the dumb one. He guns the thing and plows head on into another plane. His prop chewed completely through the other guy's wing so that the wing tip just dropped off. His wing smashed the whole tail off. And his own plane got tore up with a smashed wing, landing gear and prop all busted up. Nobody even scratched—but scared.[126]

After just eight hours of flight time, Nist was confident in his ability to fly the SNJ. On 11 August, he wrote to his parents:

> Well, I think I have mastered the "J" by now. Ready for bigger and tougher game. Sort of had us a little leary in the beginning but we're doing okay now. We went out and shot precision landings yesterday for two hours and started acrobatics today. We have a sequence of maneuvers we run through without stopping. Loop, right slow roll, right chandelle, right Immelmann, loop, left slow roll, left chandelle [a 180 degree turn while climbing—BD], left Immelmann and two turn precision spin. The plane is upside down more than its right side up.[127]

Besides the flying, the 10th Battalion cadets were still taking ground school classes. On 11 August, Nist tested to check out of code class. The test consisted of taking 12 words per minute for six minutes for a total of 72 words (360 letters) with no mistakes. Each word consisted of a five-letter group generated at random so the test taker could not guess.

Nist missed three words out of 72. He did pass the semaphore, blinker code and hand-tapping code tests.[128]

On Saturday, 14 August, Cadet Nist went up again in a Yellow Peril and successfully checked out of inverted spins. "You know about Perils and inverted spins," he wrote to his parents. "No trouble at all yesterday. She fell into it beautiful and came out just as nice."[129]

On Wednesday, 18 August, Cadet Nist and his shipmates had a check flight on division tactics. A division consisted of nine planes. The check flight consisted of repeatedly changing formations. The formations included "Vee," "Vee of Vees," "Echelon of Echelons," "Echelon of Vees," and "A-B-C formation" and "Column." If one pilot got a "down check" for unsatisfactory flying, then the whole division got a "down check." For three hours, the nine pilots practiced transitioning from formation to formation. Then they completed a 1½-hour check flight. Cadet Nist led the division for 30 minutes of that check flight.[130]

Cadet Nist and the others of his company were also learning fighter tactics. "During section tactics the other day we had a fight with our instructor," Nist wrote to his parents. "My J wouldn't go quite as fast as his, and of course he knows a little more about fighting than we do. Consequently, we got beat. But it sure was fun."[131]

Toward the end of the third week of August, the Navy made a startling offer to the aviation cadets at NAS Kingsville. Originally, Nist and the other cadets were told that they could go back to civilian life if they washed out of flight training. Now, the Navy changed the rules and gave the cadets two options. They could quit now and go back to civilian life, or they could stay in but if they stayed in and washed out, then they would go to the fleet as a seaman second class. Apparently, a lot of cadets had been washing out of flight training. In his 22 August 1943 letter to his parents, Cadet Nist related his reactions and those of his shipmates.

> For a lot of the boys it was the last straw. Believe it or not, almost half of the boys just quit, with a month or less to go. One boy had less than a week. All together [sic], there was between 400–500 that quit. I figured that I'd got this far, I'd take a chance on three weeks more. If I get the boot now, I'll be a seaman second-class, with bell-bottomed trousers. They've got us shaking in our boots.[132]

Also around this time, Nist and the other remaining cadets started aerial gunnery. An aircraft pulled a large fabric sleeve as a target for the other pilots to shoot at. To qualify, the pilot had to get four hits on the sleeve out of 80 shots fired from his aircraft's machine guns. In one practice session, Nist hit the sleeve three times out of 50 shots. On another flight, Nist piloted the aircraft towing the sleeve.[133]

Aerial gunnery was performed out over the Gulf of Mexico. While this improved the safety of the training, it presented other challenges. "If your motor conks out, you get a bath, with maybe a parachute ride thrown in for good measure," Nist wrote. He then described how one cadet had to bail out over the Gulf and spent half a day adrift before being picked up by a rescue boat. Otherwise, Nist enjoyed flying out over the Gulf as he described to his parents:

The other day was the first time we were ever out of sight of land. Every gunnery hop we fly out for half an hour and then turn around and come back. Half an hour at about 157 [mph] is seventy-five miles. Quite a swim back to shore. We've got Mae-Wests and the instructor has a life raft in his ship to drop to anybody if they go down. I wish my engine would quit sometimes. That would be fun, but it would be the end of one SNJ-4. And they cost around $50,000 so I guess it wouldn't be such a good idea.[134]

Near the end of August 1943, Aviation Cadet Nist's future as a naval aviator went into serious jeopardy. On one of his gunnery flights, Nist flew in a five-plane flight with each pilot taking turns at the target sleeve. When the results were tallied afterward, there were only 15 holes in the sleeve. With each pilot firing 80 rounds of ammunition, that meant the five pilots fired a total of 400 rounds and hit the target sleeve only 15 times. One of Nist's shipmates scored nine hits, another scored four hits and a third pilot scored just two hits. Nist and the fifth pilot did not score any hits on the target sleeve. Because of their dismal performance, Nist and the other four pilots went before the squadron review board to determine if they would be terminated from flight training. "Well, seeing as we had good records beforehand in the Navy, and that we were all in the same flight (indicating maybe our instructor wasn't too sharp in gunnery), they gave us three more chances to qualify—or else," Nist informed his parents.[135]

Aviation Cadet Nist and the other pilots of his flight got their chance at redemption on the morning of Tuesday, 24 August. A new instructor was brought in and he gave a two-minute explanation on how to qualify successfully. Then as Nist wrote in his letter:

> I made up my mind to get enough to qualify. Came so damn close to that old sleeve, I could count the threads. Figured I might as well get washed out for hitting the sleeve and wrapping up a "J" in the drink than for not getting hits. So I need 5% of my bullets to qualify. Shot 104 cartridges and low and behold when we got down and looked the sleeve over, there were twenty-four green holes in it. Well, the guy looks at me and says "that's pretty good. Guess you just didn't have the right word before..." Anytime I can put 25% of my bullets in a Mitsubishi '01 Zero, I'll be very happy.[136]

Since he had qualified, Nist's instructor gave him the option of skipping the remaining two qualification flights. Nist chose to go up again and get in some extra aerial gunnery practice. Unfortunately, an ordinance mate hadn't loaded Nist's guns correctly and so they jammed. Nevertheless, his score from the first flight was more than adequate to qualify. "My regular instructor damn near dropped dead when he found out how many hits I got," Nist wrote. "That Joe only got fourteen out of eighty yesterday."[137]

On Monday, 23 August, two cadets flying a combat training exercise collided in midair. One aircraft sustained only damage to a wing tip. The other aircraft, however, suffered heavy damage to its tail. Its rudder was inoperable and its elevators only barely operable. The cadet pilot refused to bail out and tried to get the aircraft back to NAAS Kingsville. By cutting the throttle, he was able to descend. To gain altitude, he increased throttle. To make gentle turns, he dipped a wing and let drag turn the aircraft in the direction he wanted to go. In this way, the cadet was able to land successfully. "Never saw anything like it," Nist wrote. "If that happened to me, you'd have seen 24 feet of nylon against the Texas sky. I'll stick by the 'chute."[138]

Now in advanced gunnery, Nist and his shipmates had to hit the target sleeve with 10 percent of their bullets in order to qualify. On Friday, 27 August, they went up on a training flight with their new instructor. To his parents, he later wrote:

> We got back from the hop and he really gave us hell. He says "If any of you got any hits, they were just luck. Couldn't you see how I was making the approaches? You'll never get any hits the way you guys fly." So we go out to the target sleeve and look it over. His Nibs has exactly two hits in the sleeve. He never said a word, just turned around and walked away.[139]

The deadline for quitting the Navy to avoid washing out was fast approaching, and so more aviation cadets had quit, including two of his former roommates at main station. "Guys have been quitting and getting commissions in the Army Air Corps," he wrote to Martin and Ethel on 28 August. "And some guys go further than the guys who quit, get washed out and end up as Seaman 2/C. Don't seem quite fair to me. When that instructor gave us hell yesterday, all of Flight 72 almost went to San Antonio to see the Army. Still have three days to quit. It sure looks tempting."[140]

Apparently, the topic of quitting had come up in conversation with his girlfriend back in New Brunswick, New Jersey. "She was mad I even thought of it," he wrote to his parents. "Says she'd rather see me a 'swab-jockey' than to see me quit. Guess that settles the question. But I sure will be 'coming in on a wing and a prayer' from now on!"[141]

Cadet Nist continued to be concerned that he would be assigned to instructor duty after earning his wings. Instructor options included NAAS Cabaniss, San Diego, California; Hollywood, Florida; Miami, Florida; or Cherry Point, North Carolina. If he had to choose, Cherry Point was his preference. "That's within 600 air miles of Jersey isn't it?" he wrote to his parents. "Any time I got two days off, I could borrow a J and come home. After we get our commissions we can go on cross-country hops up to 600 miles any time we've got off and there's a plane available. I guess there's quite a list waiting on a J tho.'"[142]

On 28 August 1943, Aviation Cadet Nist received orders from BUPERS (Navy Bureau of Personnel) that detailed the next phase of his naval career. The president of the United States had appointed him as an ensign in the Naval Reserve with his rank to date from 1 September 1943. After taking the oath and accepting his new rank, Nist would be officially commissioned as an ensign. Then he was to report to the commandant, Naval Air Training Center, Corpus Christi, Texas, for flight duty. The exact date for the commissioning was dependent upon when he completed his training. Of course, if he washed out, then there would be no officer commissioning for Jimmy.[143]

The following Sunday, a sudden change of weather disrupted Cadet Nist's morning aerial gunnery training flight. He was piloting an SNJ that was towing a gunnery sleeve out over the Gulf of Mexico. "One minute we could see five miles and the next we couldn't see five hundred feet," he wrote to his parents later that day. He turned his SNJ around and headed back to base. For a while he tried to locate the rest of his flight. Eventually, he met up with his instructor and the two of them flew back together. "For about ten minutes I was out there alone over the drink, flying on instruments," he wrote. "Sure feel better now that I know they can actually be relied on. I ended up exactly where I started from. Hit the beach right where I had left it when I headed out to sea." When Nist and his instructor got back to base, they discovered that the rest of the flight was already there. The target sleeve that Nist was towing slowed his aircraft considerably, thus enabling the other pilots to return ahead of him. The weather cleared later on and Nist went up two more times that day. Altogether that day, Nist spent 4.4 hours aloft on three separate training flights.[144]

Throughout August, Nist had also been concerned about flying at night, which he had not done yet in Texas. On the night of Tuesday, 31 August, he got his first crack at night flying. The following day, he wrote to his parents:

> The night flying that was supposed to be so wicked turned out to be quite a lot of fun. Was just as easy as daytime, except formation. That was a little hard when all you could see of the plane you were flying on was the wing and tail light and the exhaust stack flame. But it sure was nice. Cool, and at night the air is smooth as silk.[145]

August had been a very busy month. Nist had logged 59.8 hours of flight time, both solo and with an instructor. On 31 August alone, he had flown five training hops for 5.7 hours of flight time. Nearly all of this flight time was logged in an SNJ.[146]

All throughout flight training, Cadet Nist had been desirous of becoming a fighter pilot and flying the F4U Corsair or F6F Hellcat. His 4 September 1943 letter to his parents showed a dramatic change in Nist's hopes for the future. He wrote:

> Finally found the place for me in the Naval Air Corps. My shooting ain't so hot and my fighter tactics could stand improvement, but boy, can this boy put the bombs on the target in dive-bombing. Dropped ten bombs last time we had dive-bombing and got five direct hits and four near-misses. Have ten more today and all I need is one more hit or two near misses to qualify. There isn't much wind today so I'm looking forward to putting about seven or eight on the target today. And its really a lot more fun than fighting. There isn't so much glory in it, but they're the boys who do the damage. Too bad it wasn't one of Tojo's battlewagons I was dropping bombs on instead of just a circle on the ground. If I get to Operational, I'm going to ask for dive-bombers. Everybody gets the same training in advanced now and get put into their squadrons at Operational according to what the fleet needs. Still can end up a fighter, dive-bomber, or a "pickle lugger" as they call the torpedo bomber boys. An F6F wouldn't be bad, yet, but this dive-bombing is really great stuff. And if the new SB2D comes out pretty soon, that's for me, but definitely.

Nist finished his dive-bomber qualification by scoring six hits and four near misses out of 10 bombs dropped.[147]

On 8 September, Nist and the others went aloft to practice combat air patrols. One section of planes acted as bombers and two other sections acted as fighters. The bombers were supposed to attack the "target," which was defended by the two sections of fighters. The fighters had to make attack runs on the bombers. If the fighters were able to make four attack runs on the bombers before the bombers reached the target, then the bombers were considered to be shot down. If the fighters failed to make four attack runs before the bombers reached the target, then the target was considered to be destroyed. Nist led one of the fighter sections. "It was awful cloudy but I spotted them [the bombers] way off, so down went the first section," Nist wrote later on. "Succeeded in making twelve runs before the instructor called us off."[148]

Having done so well as fighters, the instructor had Nist's section act as the bombers on the next turn. They nearly made it to the target before they were spotted. Before the fighters were able to make an attack run, Nist's bombers flew into a cloud bank. They were flying in echelon formation about 30 feet apart but quickly loosened up the formation to avoid hitting each other. "It's the first time I ever had to fly on instruments to save my neck," Nist later wrote. "Was this boy doing some sweating." When they emerged from the clouds five anxious minutes later, there was about a half mile between them.[149]

The flight ahead of Nist's earned their wings and commissions and departed NAS Corpus Christi for their next assignments on Saturday, 11 September. Most of these newly commissioned pilots were heading for operational training. Twenty-three of them were assigned to instructor school and eventually would become instructors flying the Yellow Perils and Stearmans.[150]

Training flights in September were becoming steadily longer and more complex. "The hops we used to have were an hour or an hour and a half," Nist informed his parents. "We used to be able to fly three or four a day. But we can only get one of these long ones in." Nist was eager to leave Texas. "But I've seen ever part of—every part of what I'm deep in the heart of," he wrote. "Got too much of Texas!" The weather was making it difficult to complete the remaining training flights.[151]

On the morning of 12 September, Cadet Nist performed his toughest training flight yet. The flight was a three-hour navigation flight out over the Gulf of Mexico. They flew two triangles and covered about 400 miles by Nist's estimation. "Our navigation must have been okay because we got back," he wrote that night. "The wind changed a little and we missed our point by about five miles but after flying four hundred, that was almost as good as an Army navigator could do with a broken octant."[152]

In his 12 September letter to his parents, Jimmy mentioned that he had gotten a letter from his sister Kate, who was pregnant with her fourth child. "She says I'll have a nephew or niece by the time I get home," he wrote. "He or she will probably be walking around by the time I get to see him, unless I get an instructor job. No leave if you go to Operational."[153]

Weather, again, proved to be problematic. While on one of their extra gunnery training flights, the weather turned bad and visibility dropped to near zero. "The instructor led us back and we were flying so close to him it wasn't even funny," Nist wrote home later that day. He continued:

> The worse the weather, the closer you have to get. The worst thing that can happen is to get separated and have five or six guys flying on instruments in the same cloud bank. I've been in tight formations before but this one was like a Scotchman.[154]

James Nist was hoping to graduate on Saturday, 18 September, but the extra training flights and the repeated problems with the weather made that highly unlikely. Then, a tropical disturbance began forming in the Gulf of Mexico some 270 miles southeast of Matamoros, Mexico. The storm intensified and became a Category One hurricane on 15 September. As this occurred in the era before hurricanes were given names, the storm became known as Hurricane Six.[155]

Early on the morning of Thursday, 16 September, Nist and the other cadets were woken up and informed that a hurricane was heading for the air station. They immediately went to hurricane stations. Then about 0900, the cadets of the Flight 72 and the other senior flights were ordered to report to the flight line to fly aircraft out of NAAS Kingsville. At 1000, they left NAAS Kingsville to escape the coming hurricane. Nist was at the controls of SNJ number 51630. Though offshore, the hurricane was already affecting flight conditions.[156]

About two hours later, Nist and the other Navy pilots arrived at San Marcos Army Air Force Field in San Marcos, Texas. San Marcos AAF Field was about halfway between San Antonio and Austin and almost due north from NAAS Kingsville. "When we landed at San Marcos we scared them to death with our Navy landings," Nist reported. "They have real narrow runways and land one plane at a time. We did wingover landings two abreast and took off in three plane formation in a vee. Had the whole base watching us."[157]

After refueling, Nist and his group took off, continuing their journey north. Their destination was Perrin Army Air Force Base, just north of Sherman, Texas, and about 70 miles northeast of Dallas. Flight conditions were still poor until they got about 75 miles from Perrin. Around 1600, the Navy pilots arrived at Perrin AAF Base. Altogether they had flown about 500 miles and logged three hours of flight time to escape the hurricane.[158]

While landing at Perrin, the Navy pilots repeated the feat of landing in twos that had startled the AAF personnel at San Marcos. "These Army boys land straight and level for about three or four miles," Nist wrote to his parents. The Navy pilots, however, had been training for carrier landings, which had much shorter and much steeper approaches. "Got right over where we wanted to land and cut the throttle," he wrote. "These SNJ's glide like a streamlined brick and it scared hell out of the Army to see us dropping so fast."[159]

Perrin AAF Base quickly became packed with airplanes escaping Hurricane Six. "All the instructors are up here and about a hundred and fifty cadets," Nist wrote to his parents. "There are over 700 Navy planes here, plus the Army ships that belong here. Never saw so many airplanes in my life."[160]

Now that the planes from NAS Corpus Christi and its satellite fields were safely inland, there was nothing really for Nist and the others to do except wait out the storm. "We're living a life of Riley up here," he wrote to his parents. "Don't have to get up or go to bed 'til we want to. All we have to do is stand-by." If the weather got too bad, then they would have to fly their aircraft further inland. But for now, Nist and the others were enjoying the recreation facilities and the company of WAACS (Women's Army Auxiliary Corps).[161]

Hurricane Six reached its peak strength on the night of 16–17 September, becoming a Category Two hurricane. While the hurricane was some 80 miles off the coast, Freeport, Texas, recorded winds of 62 miles per hour. Then a high-pressure system over the northern Plains States caused Hurricane Six to do a counter-clockwise loop off the Texas coast. The next day, the hurricane resumed its northerly track but began losing strength rapidly. When it came ashore in southwestern Louisiana, Hurricane Six was no longer a hurricane or even a tropical storm. Nevertheless, the storm's heavy rainfalls caused widespread flooding in low-lying areas.[162]

The displaced Navy flyers left Perrin AAF Base on Sunday, 19 September 1943, after Hurricane Six had proceeded far enough north to permit their return home.

Nist again was flying SNJ number 51630. "When we left Perrin, we really put on a show for them," Nist later wrote. As Perrin was a basic flight training field, the Army aviation cadets had never flown in formations before. When the Navy pilots left Perrin, they took off in three-plane formations with the two trailing aircrafts' wing tips nearly touching the section leader's tail. Nist's squadron was the last to leave Perrin, so they got to watch the Army's reactions to the Navy takeoffs. Nist wrote:

> There was an Army colonel and a lieutenant colonel looking at each other and shaking their heads as much as to say, "I'm seeing things. It can't be done." We were watching all this and as each squadron took off, the one's left would swear they could fly a tighter formation. By the time it was our turn, we were flying so close we were almost chewing each other's wings off with the props. I don't think Perrin Field will recover for some time. And all the time we were standing there with a very bored expression like this was an every day occurrence and laughing ourselves sick inside.[163]

When it was Nist's squadron's turn, they too took off in very tight three-aircraft formations. Once airborne, they immediately did a steep bank turn with the inside aircraft's wing tip barely 20 feet off the ground. But after they left Perrin Field, it was all business.[164]

Flying conditions were worse on the return flight than on the flight up to Perrin. Nist described this in a letter to his parents the following day, writing:

> We ran into a cold front and got caught "over the top" and had to let down thru 1500 feet of clouds. Didn't know how low they came to the ground either. Had about four hundred foot ceiling and about a mile of visibility when we broke out and we were right over Dallas. We could count the shingles in the roofs and the bricks in the street. Headed south and the ceiling lowered to about a hundred feet. We flew about a half hour fifty feet over the ground. The instructor was leading us and the visibility was so poor we couldn't find the airport we were looking for. Finally found it and landed okay. Was this boy glad to put SNJ#81 on terra firma—but gently?

Nist and the others stayed on the ground for about five hours. After the weather cleared, they took to the skies again and resumed their journey back to NAAS Kingsville. Despite the difficult flying conditions, Nist considered it to be a good experience.[165]

Nist and his colleagues returned to NAAS Kingsville Sunday night after having flown another three hours and 500 miles. Hurricane damage at NAS Kingsville was minimal. Moving those 700 aircraft prevented them from getting damaged or destroyed by the hurricane. With SNJs running $50,000 each (about $796,000 in 2019 dollars), Nist estimated that those 700 aircraft were worth $35 million. Only two aircraft were lost due to mishaps. One was flown by an instructor and one by a cadet with a mechanic aboard.[166]

In his final week at flight training at NAS Kingsville, Nist performed two training flights in the SNJs. On Monday, 20 September, he went aloft for 1.7 hours, and the following day, he flew for 2.3 hours. That brought his total flight time for September 1943 to 45.6 hours and his overall total flight time with the Navy to 253.9 hours.[167]

The day of Aviation Cadet James A. Nist's commissioning finally came on Saturday, 25 September 1943. Accordingly his enlisted service was terminated in order for him to accept an officer commission as an ensign. He was appointed by RADM

Charles P. Mason, the commandant of the Naval Air Training Center at NAS Corpus Christi, as a naval aviator (heavier-than-Air) on 25 September 1943. Also that day, he accepted his commission, executed the oath of office and reported for temporary active duty involving flying on 25 September 1943. The oath of office read in part:

> I, James Arthur Nist, having been appointed an Ensign, U.S. Naval Reserve, do hereby accept such appointment and do solemnly swear (or affirm) that I will support and defend the Constitution of the United States against all enemies, foreign and domestic; that I will bear true faith and allegiance to the same; that I take this obligation freely, without mental reservation or purpose of evasion; and that I will well and faithfully discharge the duties of the office on which I am about to enter: So help me God.

The oath of office was sworn and executed before LtCol R.C. Mangrum, USMC.[168]

After earning his designation as a naval aviator and being commissioned as an ensign, James Nist did not remain much longer at NAS Corpus Christi. He received orders assigning him to operational training at Naval Air Station Miami, Florida. He would not be getting leave in between assignments. As he was going to operational training, he was to proceed directly to NAS Miami. At 2300 that very night, Nist boarded a train for his next duty assignment. His orders directed him to report for temporary duty involving flying under instruction. He was afforded six days of travel time to get to NAS Miami.[169]

3

Ensign James A. Nist, Naval Aviator

Having been commissioned as an ensign in the U.S. Navy Reserve and having earned his much-coveted gold naval aviator wings, James Nist embarked upon the next phase of his journey—operational flight training. This next phase of his career would see him learn the skills of dive-bombing, carrier takeoffs and carrier landings and be assigned to an operational scout-bomber squadron preparing for war.

Journey East to Florida

Ensign Nist's rail journey took him from Corpus Christi to New Orleans, Louisiana. The Nist family had a historical connection with the city of New Orleans. James's great-grandfather Johann Martin Nist and great-grandmother Magdalena Nist had first arrived in New Orleans in the early days of the American Civil War. After the war, they moved their family north to New Jersey.

Nist disembarked at a train station in New Orleans to change trains. With some free time before his next train, he went out sightseeing and met a young lady with blonde hair. So he decided to stay an extra day in New Orleans. Then Nist boarded another eastbound train and he traveled to NAS Miami in Opa-locka, Florida, arriving there on Friday, 1 October 1943.[1]

Several other squadron mates from NAAS Kingsville had made the trip with Ensign Nist. Since they did not have to report until 2 October, Nist and his friends used the intervening time to explore the nearby city of Miami. One of the first things that Nist noticed was his change in status. "The gold bars sure make a difference," he wrote to his parents. "Everybody treats us about a thousand times better than when we were kidoodles."[2]

While exploring, Nist and his friends met two other naval aviators who had been training at NAS Miami for some time. These two aviators informed them about their new duty station. Flight training was conducted six days a week, with one day off. The pilots were granted liberty every night until 2200 (10:00 p.m.). The pilots attended ground school for half the day and flew the other half. Most of the flight training was conducted using the SNJs but the pilots would also get to qualify in Brewster F2A Buffalo fighters, Grumman F4F Wildcat fighters and Curtis Helldiver scout/dive-bombers. The primary focus of training at NAS Miami was learning to land aboard carriers. The pilots would perform three or four training flights to the Bahamas flying Helldivers. After five or six weeks of training, they would return to NAS Glenview to qualify in carrier landings aboard two training aircraft carriers, USS *Wolverine* and USS *Sable*, which the Navy operated on Lake Michigan. At around Thanksgiving or Christmas, they would be granted leave to visit home.[3]

NAS Miami

Naval Air Station Miami began naval service in 1918 when the Navy set up a blimp hangar in Opa-locka. A Naval Air Reserve training base was established in the early 1930s. When war threatened, the Navy made major upgrades to the installation and commissioned the facility as NAS Miami in August 1940. Less than two years later, the Navy purchased Miami Municipal Field and Master Field and incorporated

Ensign James A. Nist, USNR (Dickerson Family photograph).

them into NAS Miami. The base conducted intermediate flight training and also became home to Headquarters 7th Naval District, Marine Corps Air Station Miami, a Coast Guard Station, a naval aerial gunnery school and a small craft training center.[4]

Ensign James A. Nist reported to NAS Miami at 1900 on 2 October 1943 and checked into the bachelor officer quarters. For the next several days, Nist went through the check-in process. He was assigned to Training Division, Flight F-115.[5]

As part of the check-in process, the newly reported pilots underwent a high-altitude test in an air pressure chamber on Tuesday, 5 October. "We bundled up in heavy flight gear and went to 35000 feet for an hour," Nist wrote the next day. "The temperature was 20 degrees below zero, so that flight gear came in handy." After some time had passed, the instructor in charge of the altitude chamber asked for volunteers to remove their masks and try writing. The volunteers could put their masks back on at any time. This was to demonstrate what would happen if a pilot lost oxygen at that altitude. One of the volunteers went 48 seconds without oxygen, before trying to put his mask back on. The lack of oxygen inhibited his motor skills to the point where he needed assistance to get his mask back on.[6]

Ensign Nist also volunteered to experience life in a low-oxygen environment. In his 6 October letter to his parents, he described what happened:

> So I start writing. Everything seemed okay to me, but in 63 seconds I was out. It just sneaks up on you. The flight surgeon was kidding me and wanted to know why I didn't put the mask back on. I said I didn't know because I didn't remember anything. He told me to look at the writing and it was just a lot of scratching. He said I had tried to put the mask back on three times but was too far gone. At 35,000 feet we're breathing pure oxygen and a couple of breaths fires you right up. It was fun and we sure learned what we were supposed to. Especially me.[7]

Ensign Nist quickly became quite happy with his new duty station. "This base is swell as far as living goes," he wrote to his parents. As an officer, Nist ate in the officers' mess, lived in the bachelor officer quarters (BOQ), socialized at the officers' club, had liberty every night until 2200 (10:00 p.m.) and got every sixth day off. "We're treated as full-fledged officers, despite the fact we're still learning," he wrote. As an ensign, Nist was earning $150 per month plus $75 per month in flight pay, which was considerably more than he had earned as a cadet. That was important because he was in debt after having purchased his officer uniforms back at NAS Corpus Christi. The weather here was a huge improvement over arid south Texas.[8]

The leave situation was very frustrating to Ensign Nist. Since he was expecting to get leave after finishing at NAS Corpus Christi, his girlfriend, June, took her vacation from work in September. The Navy, however, had other plans for Nist, and that did not include leave after NAS Corpus Christi.[9]

NAS Jacksonville in northeastern Florida was stocked with F4F Wildcats and F4U Corsairs. "There's some talk of getting them here," Nist wrote to his parents. He was eager to fly the Corsair in particular. "It's supposed to be the hottest thing the Allies have got except the Spitfire Mark X," he wrote. "She'll outrun (by 30 knots), outmaneuver, out-climb and has twice the fire power of the latest version of the Zero. And even better than the Hellcat. The Navy boys are supposed to be cleaning up the Japs at about 12 or 15 to 1."[10]

Ensign Nist went up for the first time at NAS Miami on Thursday, 7 October 1943. He rode as a passenger in an SNJ flown by Ensign J.A. McChesney for an hour-long orientation flight. The next day, Nist flew two training flights in an SNJ for a total of 2.9 hours of flight time. He flew two training flights again on Saturday, 9 October, for a total flight time of 3.1 hours.[11]

After completing his two Saturday training flights, he found some time to write home and describe his first week at NAS Miami. "Situation far from normal—everything is just swell down here," he wrote. "We've been flying three days now and it's really great. We do things here they never dreamed of in Kingsville." Flight F-115 was learning fighter tactics using four-plane divisions. He described a training maneuver called "snake-dances." Nist wrote, "It's just follow-the-leader but the way they play it and what they do is really something to see. There were seven of us doing slow-rolls today at the same time in a line."[12]

James's sister Kathryn finally had her baby, a boy that she named James Ronald after her youngest brother. James did not get word of his new nephew's birth until several days later. "Say Hello to my new nephew for me," he instructed his parents. "He'll be big by the time I get to see him (I don't hope.)" James was puzzled by the origin of his new nephew's middle name. No one in either the Nist or Dickerson families had that name. Kathryn and Walt had chosen James to be the godfather of his namesake. "I'm honored, of course, but he's liable to grow up to be a wild Navyator."[13]

After a week of training, Ensign Nist had completed advanced combat training and was still raving about NAS Miami. On Thursday, 14 October, he wrote to his parents:

> It's a pretty swell place. The flying is really fun. They always said we'd learn more about flying when we started flying without an instructor. They sure were right. And ground school is much better here. We don't do as much here as we did when we were cadets and we're getting three times as much pay.[14]

Judging from Nist's letters from NAS Miami, communication with his sweetheart, June, up in New Brunswick, New Jersey, seemed to be improving since he moved from Texas to Florida. June had mailed him a package but she wouldn't tell him what was in it. He was really eager to get leave and come home to visit. He preferred Christmas but expected to be home before that. Thanksgiving was also preferable, especially since June's birthday was 28 November.[15]

June and Jim's parents had also had some time to talk by phone. "Tried to find out if you and June traded any secrets but she wouldn't tell me," he wrote to his parents. "Wouldn't tell me anything except that she thought you both were swell. I knew that all along. I think she's pretty swell too. The four of us will have to get together when I get home."[16]

On 18 October, Ensign Nist and the others of his flight got word that they were being transferred. They were told to pack up and be ready to depart the following day. "Everybody is all pepped up about leaving," he wrote to his parents. "This is one swell place and we probably will be going to one not quite as nice, but we'll be upstairs in a Wildcat and that's what we want.... The Wildcats aren't the fastest thing in the world, but it's a service type ship and they used it in the fleet until they got the new Hellcat." Nist was expecting to be transferred to NAS Jacksonville in northeastern Florida or NAS Sanford north of Orlando, Florida.[17]

As it turned out, Nist was not heading for the cockpit of a Grumman F4F Wildcat. Nor was he headed for NAS Jacksonville or NAS Sanford.

NAS Daytona Beach

Ensign Nist remained at NAS Miami for 20 days, then was transferred to NAS Daytona Beach for flight instruction in scout/dive-bombers. He left Miami at 1000 on 22 October and arrived in Daytona Beach at 2000 the following day. There he joined Scout-Bomber Squadron 59 (VSB-59). Soon after reporting to VSB-59, Nist was assigned as the squadron navigation officer as a collateral duty.[18]

Naval Air Station Daytona Beach was formerly the Daytona Beach Municipal Airport. It was built in 1930, and Florida senator Claude Pepper and local leaders had convinced the Navy to acquire the airport for use in training Navy pilots. NAS Daytona Beach was commissioned in December 1942 and later added four outlying airfields.[19]

The commanding officer of NAS Daytona Beach was CAPT Willis E. Cleaves, USN. A 1924 graduate of the U.S. Naval Academy, Cleaves earned his naval aviator wings in 1926. When war broke out, Cleaves was in command of Patrol Squadron 74 (VP-74) on the island of Bermuda. In August 1942, CDR Cleaves was placed in command of the seaplane tender USS *Casco* (AVP-12). While operating in the Aleutian Islands, *Casco* was torpedoed by the Japanese submarine *RO-61*. Despite being wounded, Cleaves saved his ship from sinking by beaching her. She was later repaired and refloated, and Cleaves was awarded the Silver Star. Following operations to retake Japanese-held Attu Island, Cleaves assumed command of NAS Daytona Beach.[20]

Ensign Nist wanted to fly fighters but the Navy decided to train him to fly dive-bombers. He would begin by learning the Douglas SBD Dauntless dive-bomber. The Douglas SBD Dauntless was the standard scout/dive-bomber aircraft of the U.S. Navy for most of the war. At Battle of Midway, Navy Dauntlesses sank four Japanese aircraft carriers, marking a pivotal turning point in the war in the Pacific. The Dauntless was powered by a Wright R1820–66 Cyclone nine-cylinder radial air-cooled engine that gave the aircraft a maximum speed of 253 miles per hour at 14,000 feet, a cruising speed of 185 miles per hour and a service ceiling of 25,200 feet. The maximum range of the dive-bomber version was 456 miles. The scout bomber had a maximum range of 773 miles. The Dauntless could carry 2,250 pounds of bombs and was armed with four machine guns. The aircraft was crewed by a pilot and an enlisted sailor who operated the radio and the rear-facing machine guns. When dive-bombing, the radio operator/gunner called out the altitudes so that the pilot could concentrate on hitting the target. Both the Navy and the Marine Corps used the Dauntless. The Army Air Force version was called the A-24. While at NAS Daytona Beach, Nist would fly four of the five Dauntless models currently in service.[21]

On 26 October, Nist took his first flight at NAS Daytona Beach. "Had a solo hop in a J to get familiar with the area around here so we wouldn't get lost when we took a Dauntless up," he reported to his parents. "The country around here looks swell from the air." He expected to spend two months here at NAS Daytona Beach flying SBDs and log 120 hours of flight time.[22]

Ensign Nist and the other new pilots of VSB-59 spent their first few days at NAS Daytona Beach learning about the SBD Dauntless but not actually flying in them yet. In his 27 October 1943 letter to his parents, Nist described the differences between the SNJs they had been flying and the SBDs that they would be flying soon:

> There are quite a few new things to learn about. We've got a three bladed electric propellor to work now. We jump from a 650 hp. engine to 1200 hp. The propellor is geared and the supercharger has two speeds. Then there are diving brakes to work, plus better radio equipment, about six bomb racks and selector switches to operation, and something new—radar. So it takes a few days of studying to learn how to fly the darn things. It might seem funny learning to fly by reading a book, but that's just what we're doing. We're better off going through dive-bomber operational. It will give us that much more experience in heavier planes.[23]

Another major difference between the SNJs and the SBDs was that the SBD was a two-person aircraft: pilot and radio operator (radioman)/rear gunner. Nist had

The SBD-5 Dauntless dive-bomber, pictured here flying above the aircraft carrier USS *Enterprise* (CV-6) during operations in the Pacific in 1944 (Naval History and Heritage Command [Photo 80-G-251065]/National Archives).

numerous hours in two-seater aircraft, but that second person most times had been an instructor, not a crewmember. The SBD required two people working as a team to operate and fight the aircraft successfully. The new SBD pilots would fly 7.5 hours in the SBD before they would start flying with the rear seater. "I've met him though," Nist reported. "It looks okay." *Him* was a Navy enlisted sailor named Stallknecht. In the rear seat of the cockpit, there was an auxiliary stick, rudder pedals and controls for the throttle and elevators but no controls for the landing gear or the flaps. In an emergency, the radio operator/rear gunner could fly the aircraft but could not lower the flaps or landing gear to land the aircraft. The pilots were responsible for teaching their enlisted aircrewmen about the aircraft, including the rudiments of flying so that he could fly the aircraft. On 30 October, Nist flew in the back seat of a Dauntless. "That boy can have his job," he wrote to his parents. "I'll stick to the front cockpit."[24]

Nist was eagerly hoping to get home for the holidays. In his 29 October letter to his parents, he told his parents, "I'd give a month's pay to get back to Jersey for a few days at Christmas. I've never missed one home yet but it looks like I will this year. I'd like to see my nieces and nephews, especially my new one." When he finally did get leave, he would have 15 days of it. He planned on splitting his time home between Squankum and New Brunswick.[25]

VSB-59 also had a penalty system for errors and infractions committed by the

Pilots and enlisted aircrewmen of Navy Scout-Bomber Squadron Fifty-Nine at NAS Daytona in fall 1943. Noteworthy members include Ensign J.A. McChesney (at the end of second row), Aviation Radioman Third Class Stallknecht (in the back row second from left) and Ensign James A. Nist (standing in third row third from left) (Dickerson Family photograph).

pilots. The penalty fines ranged from 25 cents to $5. Breaking taxiing rules cost 25 cents. Pilots were charged $5 for landing wheels up, dropping bombs without arming them first so that they failed to detonate on impact and pulling out of a dive under 300 feet. The fines went into a pool that was then used periodically to offer cash prizes for the best bombing or gunnery score.[26]

On Tuesday, 2 November 1943, Ensign Nist finally got to solo-pilot an operational Navy warbird: the Douglas Dauntless scout-bomber. For an hour and a half, Nist and the other new joins flew Dauntlesses on an orientation flight. That afternoon, Nist wrote to his parents:

> The SBD ain't so bad. It handles okay, cruises about 192 knots but she won't climb for love or money. Most I could get out of mine was a thousand feet a minute and you can climb that fast in an N3N-3 (remember that one? That's a Yellow Peril.) It takes about 45 minutes to climb to 20,000 feet with any kind of bomb load.... If I hadn't heard the tires screech when I hit, I don't even believe I'd have known I was on the ground.

With VSB-59, Nist continued to train in instrument flying. "An SBD's second home is in a cloud," he explained to his parents. "That's why they teach us so much instrument flying. When things get tough, the dive-bombers have to run and hide and leave the fun up to the fighter boys."[27]

Nist's first experience with the Dauntless was tempered by an encounter with the Grumman F6F Hellcat. He described the encounter to his parents afterward:

Then, just as I was beginning to think we had a pretty nice airplane, along comes six F6Fs and ruined things. At first, I didn't mind dive-bombers, but every time I see one of them Hellcats, I like the idea less. The Hellcats today were just idling and they went past a J like he was going backwards. The hot rocks that were flying them took them off in about 50 feet, then stuck their nose up in the air like a debutante and went upstairs.[28]

Ensign Nist continued to log more flight time in the Dauntless and learn more about the plane. On Thursday, 4 November, he wrote about the plane to his parents:

They're designed for high speed so that they handle nice in a dive. We were up playing around today and that diving is really fun. Twice today I pushed over at twelve thousand and pulled out at about three thousand. With the diving flaps open they'll only go about 220 knots straight down. So when you pull out there isn't even a suggestion of a blackout. It's a fair airplane. The ones we have here are pretty beat up.[29]

The next day cloudy weather conditions enabled Nist to write again to his parents. "I dove one yesterday from 11000 feet to 3000 feet without using the diving brakes and all I could get out of the thing was between 350–360, straight down," he wrote. "And to think that a Hellcat will go faster than that level. Yipe! And it took almost two miles straight down to get the 350 m.p.h."[30]

In his first few flights at the controls of an SBD, Ensign Nist quickly discovered that dive-bombing put significantly more physical stress on both aircraft and aircrew than the flying he had previously done. Several months later, Nist described the physics of dive-bombing in response to a question posed to him by his parents. He wrote:

A "G" is the force of gravity or rather is a force equal to the force of gravity. When you are standing on the ground or sitting in an airplane flying straight and level, you've got one G on you, but when you are in a turn or pulling out of a dive, you've got centrifugal force behind it helping it along. When I say an SBD is stressed for 19 "G"s I mean that an SBD weighs 8,000 lbs normally, but the extra "G"s due to centrifugal force put a load on the wings equal to the weight times the number of "G"s. And the wings on an SBD stay on up to 152,000 lbs or 75 tons so you can see why Ensign Nist lost the struggle with P-10. When you're under G strain, you tire out real quick. Pulling out of a dive, you get about 5 "G"s so at the bottom of each dive, Ensign Nist with his 130 lbs soaking wet weighs up around six hundred and fifty pounds. If you want to see something funny, just try lifting your arm at the bottom of a dive.[31]

Something mysterious was going on between Jimmy's parents and his sweetheart, Miss June Smith. Apparently, his parents had written asking for his ring size "pronto." After asking several questions to find out what was really going on, he relented and told them that his ring size was 8.[32]

On Wednesday, 10 November, Ensign Nist experienced mechanical problems with his SBD dive-bomber. The diving flaps on his Dauntless would not function, so he "downed" it and turned it over to the aircraft maintainers for repairs. "I'll do most anything, but that is one thing I refuse to do—dive bomb without diving flaps," he wrote later that day. "If we ever got caught within 5000 feet of the ground without dive flaps we'd be slaughtered, one way or another, probably by the plane, otherwise by our squadron skipper."[33]

In the second week of November, Nist began dropping practice bombs. Their aiming point was a circle 10 feet in diameter. To qualify, the pilots had to drop 20 individual bombs and average within 100 feet of the target. The results of his first attempt were poor. However, on his second flight, he dropped four bombs for an average of 130 feet from the target.[34]

In his 14 November 1943 letter to his parents, Nist mentioned having received a letter from his sister Kate. According to his sister, Jimmy's nephew Ronnie "is growing like a weed." He also mentioned that some unnamed members of the family did not like the name "Ronald" for his nephew. Jimmy sprang to the defense of his nephew's name. "I think it's a darned good one," he wrote. "Ronald Reagan is no sissy, is he?" He also quoted his sister, who was requesting a photo of him in uniform so "Ronnie can see what his uncle looked like." To which, Jimmy added, "He'll see me in my uniform. There's still enough fighting left for that!"[35]

On 16 November, Ensign Nist began flying with his radio operator/rear gunner aboard. Unlike Nist, Seaman Second Class Stallknecht was an enlisted sailor straight out of recruit training (boot camp) with hardly any flying experience. On his first flight with Nist, the gunner started being affected by airsickness. Nist wrote, "He wasn't looking so sharp, so like a Good Samaritan, I pulled out of a dive a little easier than usual and went too low." In doing so, Nist went below 1,000 feet and was fined a dollar for going below the altitude for safe pullouts. "Theoretically, if we were using big bombs, if we went below that we'd be hit by our own bomb fragments," he explained. That day, Nist and Stallknecht went up for two training flights for a total of 3.1 hours of flight time.[36]

As November steadily progressed, it became more apparent that Jimmy was not getting leave to return home before the end of the year. Around 20 November, he found out that he and his squadron mates were heading west to Chicago for carrier qualifications on 27 December 1943. Hopefully after carrier qualifications, he would get leave to visit home.[37]

Saturday, 20 November, was a costly day in the air for Ensign Nist. He was fined six dollars for infractions. That day, he went up for dive-bombing practice with the rest of his squadron. His gunner was Seaman Second Class Stallknecht. Nist described the fateful flight to his parents in a letter written later day:

> An SBD has four gas tanks: a left auxiliary, left main (90 gals.), a right main (90 gals.) and a right auxiliary. Ordinarily, the auxiliaries hold 60 gal. a piece, but here we don't need them so they only put 15 gal. a piece in them and we never use them. There's a selector valve so we can choose which tank we want to use. We never, never NEVER [emphasis in original] take off on an auxiliary tank, even if they're full [emphasis in original] because they've only got one drain pipe while the main tanks each have four drain pipes. I got the valve in the wrong position, on left auxiliary. Warming the ship up and taxiing out is using up that measly 15 gals. fast, but I take-off fat dumb and happy on left aux. I get six hundred feet of altitude and the damn thing runs out of gas. Well, the first thing you do when an engine quits is switch to a new gas tank so in the space of one second and with only two hands, I keep flying the plane, switch gas tanks, turn on the fuel booster pump, richen the mixture, increase prop pitch and open the throttle on the Rambling Wreck. She loses a couple of hundred precious feet of altitude and then starts again. I still don't know I was flying on left aux. and think I was on left main and the line was stopped up. We're on a dive-bombing hop so I figure to go out and make a couple dives on the right main tank and come home alone. I call the skipper up and tell him and he says okay. So I make two dives (particulars later on) and start home. Here's where the fun comes in. There are two radio systems in an SBD, one is called ICS

(inter-cockpit system) so the pilot and gunner can talk without broadcasting over the air (it's like a telephone) and the other to broadcast with. There's a switch to use to choose which one to use. When I called the skipper, he says to check the gas selector valve and make sure it was okay. I do, and still [emphasis in original] don't catch on I was flying on an aux. tank. When I start back, I'm halfway home when I suddenly see the light and discover my stupid (putting it mildly) mistake. I switch to the left main (the one which was supposed to be clogged) and she runs beautiful. So with 90 gals. left, I head back to the dive-bombing target. Here comes the best part. I pick up the microphone, thinking I'm on inter-cockpit and give out with a beautiful string of anything but the King's English and tell my gunner what had happened. So I go back to the target, make two more dives, and come back with the squadron. The skipper and all the guys are smiling and I can't figure it out. I thought it was a secret between my gunner and I. Seems I'd broadcast my lovely string of @*?!#@'s [emphasis in original] over the air and everybody is in on the fact that I took off on an auxiliary tank. The skipper gets out the fine book and the boys gave me a going over. I was charged with a Dilbert act (the take-off), unnecessary radio transmission, swearing on the air and to top it off I get charged a buck for pulling out of one of the dives too low. I got off easy in several ways. The Dilbert act was supposed to cost $5 alone (a serious one). But the big item was the fact that the Rambling Wreck is still in one piece and Ensign Nist and Aircrewman Stallknecht are walking around. Another couple of minutes of warming up and she'd have run out of gas at about 50 feet altitude and piled SBD, pilot and gunner into a beautiful swamp. So I figure six bucks is getting away pretty darned easy.... I think the best thing was what Stallknecht said when he came down. He says, "Sir, when that engine quit, I unbuckled my safety-belt and was ready to bail out. I was waiting for you to tell me to jump."[38]

Ensign Nist was able to correct his fuel tank mistake, complete the training exercise and land safely. Two other aircrews that same day were not so fortunate. Two SBDs had a midair collision while performing gunnery practice. The pilot and gunner of one of the SBDs bailed out. The pilot of the other stricken SBD was able to ditch his plane in the ocean. Afterward, that pilot swore that his gunner had gotten out of the plane and onto its wing, had retrieved the life raft from its compartment and was yelling for the pilot to "Get out!" before the plane had stopped on the water.[39]

Ensign Nist's next letter home to his parents was written on Monday, 22 November. The topics included Thanksgiving, the training schedule, the latest "Dilbert" act and new Navy warships. VSB-59 had Thanksgiving off because the holiday fell on their normal day off. So VSB-59 would be enjoying turkey dinner and relaxation. All of the other squadrons at NAS Daytona Beach were flying on Thanksgiving. Nist also wrote about USS *Bataan* (CVL-29), an *Independence*-class light aircraft carrier that had just been commissioned, and the new *Iowa*-class battleship USS *New Jersey* (BB-62). "If old Tojo ever saw the figures on her, he'd have apoplexy," Nist informed his parents. "She totes nine sixteen-inch rifles but the speed is the thing. Absolutely terrific."[40]

At present, VSB-59 was conducting aerial gunnery. The SBD Dauntless was armed with two .50-caliber machine guns in the nose. The rear seat gunner operated twin .30-caliber machines from his position. On Tuesday, 23 November, VSB-59 would be dropping 500-pound bombs for the first time. Thus far, they had been dropping small practice bombs. "That ought to be good, but how the Rambling Wreck is ever gonna get off the ground with a 500 lb. bomb in her rack is more than I can figure," he wrote. "Hope she's in a good mood."[41]

The latest VSB-59 "Dilbert" act occurred on the afternoon of 22 November following a gunnery training flight offshore. Visibility was so poor that they could not determine where they were when they made landfall. The wind was blowing out of the north, so Nist and 10 of the pilots reasoned that they had drifted south. Accordingly, they turned north and, sure enough, returned to NAS Daytona Beach without any trouble. The 12th pilot, however, for reasons unknown turned south. He ended up 70 miles south of his home base at NAS Banana River, where he landed nearly out of gas. He refueled, took off and returned to NAS Daytona Beach. In the meantime, three other aircraft were sent out to find the "missing" pilot. He would have his fate decided the following day.[42]

Thursday, 25 November, was Thanksgiving Day. Ensign Nist was still in NAS Daytona Beach, about a thousand miles from home. Instead of sharing the holiday with his family and his sweetheart, Ms. June Smith, Ensign Nist shared Thanksgiving dinner at a dining facility at NAS Daytona Beach with his roommate, another Navy pilot, that pilot's wife, who was a lieutenant (junior grade) and a Navy nurse, and her mother. In his letter home, Nist wrote:

> We've had the day off, we had a good dinner but it didn't seem like Thanksgiving Day to me. There were a few things missing. You could have done that turkey a lot more justice than the stewards did, and then I wasn't eating with the same people I usually do and one other person I haven't yet. I guess I should be thankful I was in VSB-59 and wasn't flying today. Still, it would have been lots nicer in Jersey.[43]

The pilots of VSB-59 continued to rack up the fines for mistakes. To date, the squadron had $71 in the pool. On one hop alone, VSB-59 pilots were fined a total of $25. Those who were fined included the squadron executive officer, who was a lieutenant (O-3) and a Naval Academy graduate. "What a squadron party we're going to have!" he wrote home.[44]

After having the day off for Thanksgiving, VSB-59 was back in the air dropping practice bombs. Their Saturday, 27 November, dive-bombing practice happened to coincide with the annual Army-Navy game between the cadets of the U.S. Military Academy and the midshipmen of the U.S. Naval Academy. Navy defeated Army 13–0. With Nist's permission, radio gunner Stallknecht changed the coils in the SBD's radio receiver and the two got to listen to the Army-Navy game while flying their training mission. Apparently other VSB-59 aircrew had done the same because, according to Nist, dive-bombing scores were not very good. Nist himself got an average of 140 feet. Clouds and wind over the target also affected bombing results.[45]

Ensign Nist's leadership and flight skills were being recognized. On that same day, Nist was promoted to be section leader of VSB-59's Second Section, which pleased Nist very much. The preceding section leader's performance had left much to be desired.[46]

Friday, 3 December 1943, was a day of mixed results for the pilots and sailors of VSB-59. Their first training flight of the day lasted 1.9 hours. The flight was particularly jarring for the newly promoted Stallknecht. When it was their turn to bomb the target, Nist put the Dauntless into a vertical dive. He wrote about it in a letter to his parents the next day:

We hit two thousand feet still going straight down and he [Stallknecht] yells "Pull out" at the top of his lungs. I wanted to get a good hit so I waited a couple of hundred more feet and then pulled out hard. When we got back, he said, "I decided if you were going to kill us both, that you'd die with broken ear drums."[47]

That night, the VSB-59 aircrew started night flying. With Stallknecht in the rear seat, Nist flew for two hours in the dark. "We were all scared to death and it turned out to be the easiest night flying we've ever done," Nist wrote home. "Just like in the day time only more fun. All we do in the daytime is fly formation all the time. Last night we flew alone."[48]

Also around this time, Nist and Stallknecht went out on a sub-hunting training mission. For this training, a boat towed a target that was shaped like the conning tower of a submarine. The goal was to bomb it from as low an altitude as possible. Nist found the training to be "fun." "My gunner says next time we do sub bombing, he's going to take a fish line and troll for tarpon," Nist wrote to his parents.[49]

The SBD Dauntlesses used by VSB-59 had seen a lot of usage out in the fleet and in training units Stateside. As a result, there were frequent maintenance issues with the aircraft, as Ensign Nist testified in his 4 December 1943 letter. Of the Dauntlesses, he wrote:

> They're fun and new ones would be okay, but you get tired of flying planes where there's at least one thing wrong with it all the time. If the radio works, the hydraulic system won't, and if they both work, either the bomb racks and guns jam or the engine hasn't any power. These planes have all been to the fleet and have been around here for over a year, flying six or eight hours a day.[50]

There were lighter moments in Nist and Stallknecht's training. "He's a good kid but I have to laugh at him sometimes," Nist wrote to his parents. Stallknecht liked to sing a popular tune of the time, "Pistol Packin' Mama," over the SBD's inter-phone while they were flying. The song had been recorded by Bing Crosby and the Andrews Sisters earlier that fall. One of these lighter moments occurred at Stallknecht's expense. "He was getting out of the rear-cockpit after a hop the other day when his rip-cord handle [for his parachute] caught on a knob," Nist wrote. "The next thing he knew, there was 24 feet of beautiful white silk hanging over the side of the ship and laying on the ground."[51]

Ensign Nist was unable to get home for Miss June Smith's birthday. For her birthday, he sent her a miniature officers insignia pin with a miniature ensign rank insignia attached to it by a small chain. Previously he had sent her the Navy wings he had earned back at NAS Corpus Christi. "They say there's ten women wearing Navy wings for every Navy flier," Nist later explained to his parents. "That's an old custom to send them to the little girl who's waiting back home."[52]

During the second week of December, VSB-59 performed six consecutive nights of night flying.

On 7 December, they practiced dive-bombing at night. On 9 December, Nist and Stallknecht flew a two-hour sub-hunting mission during the day and then a 2½-hour cross-country training flight at night. Leaving NAS Daytona Beach, they flew south to Vero Beach, then north to Melbourne, then northwest to Orlando and finally northeast to return to NAS Daytona Beach. On 10 December, Nist flew his final night training mission to practice glide-bombing.

To perform glide-bombing, the aircraft approaches the target at a shallow angle without using dive brakes. After releasing his bomb, the pilot does not have to pull up sharply to avoid slamming into the ground. "If they didn't teach me anything else here, I've learned to like night-flying," Nist wrote to his parents. "With a beautiful full moon, its more fun than flying in the daytime."[53]

Next the VSB-59 pilots moved on to field carrier landings, which Ensign Nist described in his 10 December letter to his parents. The outline of an aircraft carrier was painted on the runway. This gave the pilots the rudiments of landing on the carrier without having to worry about missing the deck and landing in the water or hitting the superstructure (island) of the carrier. "You fly around the field at 100 feet altitude and make your approach at about 5 knots above stalling speed," he wrote. "Then when you want to land, you just cut the throttle and land her on a dime, right now! [emphasis in original]"[54]

On 13 December, Ensign Nist received orders from the Chief of Naval Air Operational Training Command (NAOTC) at NAS Jacksonville. When he had completed flight training with that command, he was to detach from VSB-59 and proceed to Commander, Fleet Air, West Coast at NAS San Diego for assignment involving flying. The exact date for his transfer to the West Coast would occur after he had completed all of his required training with NAOTC.[55]

On the night of Thursday, 16 December, VSB-59 had their squadron Christmas party. The party was held in the ballroom of the Riviera Hotel in Daytona Beach. The party had been funded by the fines levied on VSB-59 fliers for various infractions occurring over the preceding weeks.[56]

By now, Ensign Nist knew that he would be heading for NAS Glenview, Illinois, on or about 27 December 1943, for carrier qualifications on one of the Navy's converted aircraft carriers that operated on Lake Michigan. After completing carrier qualifications, Nist would receive an operational assignment. He would get 23 days to report to his next assignment, during which time he would go home on leave. Afterward, he would report to NAS San Diego. There he expected to be assigned to a fighter squadron.[57]

During his time in Florida, Jimmy Nist had developed a friendship with another fellow SBD pilot, Ensign J.A. McChesney. McChesney was engaged to a young woman from San Francisco, California, named Alice Richards. In late December, Nist and McChesney learned that they would be parting ways with Nist headed for California and McChesney headed for Seattle, Washington. McChesney told Nist to look up his fiancée, Alice, if he got assigned to duty in the San Francisco area.[58]

Over the last several months, VSB-59 had earned an excellent safety record with no casualties to either aircrew or aircraft. That record was broken when one of the pilots suffered an engine failure on a training flight. The pilot made a wheels-up forced landing on the beach. The SBD's propeller was bent and the landing flaps were ruined. Most important, neither the pilot nor his radio gunner was injured.[59]

On Wednesday, 22 December 1943, Ensign Nist completed his flight training with VSB-59 and successfully qualified in field carrier landings. It had been a very busy month. In December alone, Nist had logged 144 flight hours. In his final two days of field carrier landings, Nist did 23 straight field carrier landings with an "OK" score.[60]

Having qualified with carrier landings onshore, Nist was ready to qualify aboard an actual ship underway. "Those carrier approaches and landings are the big difference between Army and Navy fliers," Nist explained to his parents. To qualify, Nist would need to perform eight carrier landings aboard ship successfully.[61]

On 27 December 1943, Ensign Nist received orders detaching him from NAS Daytona Beach and assigning him to the Carrier Qualification Training Unit at NAS Glenview, Illinois. He left Daytona by rail at 1700 on 27 December 1943.[62]

Return to NAS Glenview, Illinois

Ensign Nist arrived in NAS Glenview, Illinois, and reported for duty at 1630 on 28 December 1943. He joined the Carrier Qualification Training Unit, which was commanded by Commander James O. Vosseller, USN. Nist was back at NAS Glenview, where he had undertaken his first flight training with the Navy some nine months before.[63]

Carrier qualifications were conducted aboard USS *Wolverine* (IX-64) and USS *Sable* (IX-81). Both ships had begun their lives as coal-fired sidewheel steamers that operated on the Great Lakes. The Navy acquired them in 1942 and converted them to aircraft carriers by adding a flight deck. On the inland waters of Lake Michigan, thousands of Navy carrier pilots were qualified in carrier landings and take-offs without being menaced by German and Japanese submarines. *Wolverine* was constructed as the steamer *Seeandbee* by the American Shipbuilding Company of Wyandotte, Michigan, for the Cleveland and Buffalo Transit Company. She had a displacement of 7,200 tons, a length of 500', a beam of 58' 1" and a draft of 15'6".[64]

Nist was hoping to get his carrier qualification done and be on his way home in just a few days. Unfortunately, that was not to be as the weather was characteristically uncooperative. "They're talking about securing the carriers for the winter and letting us go home," Nist wrote to his parents on 2 January 1944. "Then we'd have to check out at San Diego when we got there. Suits me." Apparently, there was a shortage of SBDs at NAS Glenview, so Nist would probably be doing his carrier qualifications in an SNJ. Unable to fly because of the weather, the pilots had very little to do. "All we do is lay around and sleep and eat all day and go into Chicago at night," he wrote to his parents.[65]

Ensign Nist celebrated the new year in Chicago with a new young lady that he met after arriving at NAS Glenview. "We really had a swell time on New Year's Eve," he later wrote. "You never saw such bedlam in your life as the Loop was. Worse than Times Square in New York." The Loop was Chicago's central business district.[66]

On Monday, 3 January 1944, Ensign Nist finally got his chance to qualify for carrier landings. As he expected, Nist's qualification flights were done in an SNJ. He went up twice on 3 January and successfully performed eight carrier landings aboard USS *Wolverine*. The next day, *Wolverine*'s flight officer, LT R.W. Fleming, USNR, made the following entry in Nist's flight log:

> 4 JAN 1944
> Qualified this date aboard
> The USS WOLVERINE in Carrier
> Landings in SNJ airplane.

Altogether, Nist logged 3.6 hours of flight time during his carrier qualifications. This brought his total Navy flight time to just over 400 hours.[67]

That same day, Ensign Nist received orders detaching him from the Carrier Qualification Training Unit and ordering him to report to the Commander Fleet Air West Coast at Naval Air Station San Diego, California, later that month. He detached at 0930 and left Chicago by train heading for home.[68]

Jimmy Nist had not been home since the previous June. No records exist that detail what he did at home on leave, but one can surmise from his letters around this time what he did. Jimmy availed himself of his mother's home cooking. The extended Nist family got together to welcome home Jimmy and to celebrate a belated Christmas. Jimmy got to meet his namesake and newest nephew, James R. Dickerson. He renewed his budding romance with Miss June Smith and introduced her to his parents. Apparently, Jimmy also proposed marriage to June while home on leave because he started referring to her as his "fiancée" in his February 1944 letters. In his 15 February 1944 letter to his parents, Nist described the engagement ring that he gave to June as a "twelve cylinder chunk of ice."[69]

Then it was over. Leave ended and Ensign Nist had to head west for the next phase of his naval career. He boarded a train and left for California via Chicago.

From Chicago, Nist went west aboard the Atchison, Topeka and Santa Fe Railroad's "The Chief." The train departed Chicago and headed for Albuquerque, New Mexico. Along the way, however, a major train crash delayed "The Chief's" progress for 18 hours while the accident was cleared. Writing from New Mexico, Nist described what he saw:

> It was the damnedest mess I ever saw. One freight ran into the back of another one. It must have been going like hell, because it smashed about twenty cars to kindling wood and match sticks. The one locomotive was all bashed in and the rails broke like they were twigs.[70]

After arriving in Albuquerque, Nist was able to make up the lost time caused by the train crash. He took a train that left a day earlier than the one he had originally been scheduled for. The only available spot was in a sleeping car. Nist shared a room with an Army first lieutenant who was with the horse cavalry. Like Nist, the Army lieutenant was returning from leave.[71]

Killing Time in San Diego

Naval Air Station San Diego was located on the north end of Coronado Peninsula at the entrance of San Diego Bay. To the west of the peninsula was the Pacific Ocean. To the east was San Diego Bay and farther east was the city of San Diego. The area was also known as North Island. North Island first became associated with aviation when aviation pioneer Glenn Curtiss started using the area in 1911. Both the U.S. Army and the U.S. Navy utilized North Island for aviation beginning in

1913. Four years later, Congress purchased the land and both the Army and Navy established airfields there. Naval Air Station San Diego was commissioned in 1917. In 1924, the Navy homeported its first aircraft carrier, USS *Langley* (CV-1), at NAS San Diego. On 9 May 1927, aviation pioneer Charles A. Lindbergh took off from the Army's Rockwell Field in the *Spirit of St. Louis* heading east to undertake his historic first trans-Atlantic flight from New York to Paris. Twenty years later, the Army ceased operations at North Island and the whole area became the Navy's. In 1943, NAS San Diego was a major center of naval aviation and a key component of the Navy's operations in the Pacific theater. In 1955, NAS San Diego would be renamed NAS North Island.[72]

On 26 January 1944, Ensign Nist reported to the office of Commander of Fleet Air, West Coast, at NAS San Diego. Fleet Air, West Coast was commanded by Rear Admiral William K. Harrill. The following day, he received orders sending him to Carrier Aircraft Service Unit Five (CASU-5), which was also in San Diego, for flying duty involving scout-dive-bombers. He reported to CASU-5 the same day. Nist had been expecting to be assigned to fly F6F Hellcats, so these orders were a major disappointment for him.[73]

Carrier Aircraft Service Unit Five was commissioned at NAS San Diego on 21 July 1942. The function of a CASU was to provide aviation ground support for Navy aviation squadrons either in the process of organizing or refitting after a combat deployment. CASUs performed basing facilities, aircraft maintenance and administrative support. CASU-5 consisted of administration, personnel, ordnance, engineering and operations, supply, medical and communications divisions. Within a year, CASU-5 grew substantially and ultimately was responsible for detachments at MCAS El Centro, Naval Air Auxiliary Station (NAAS) Brown Field at Otay Mesa, NAAS Ream Field at Imperial Beach, NAAS Holtville and NAAS San Clemente Island. From its commissioning until February 1944, CASU-5 supported 33 air groups and squadrons.[74]

Ensign Nist was now in a pool of pilots awaiting further assignment. Until that happened, they would be sitting around NAS San Diego killing time. "The life isn't too bad, but if we don't get something to do pretty soon, we'll go crazy," he informed his parents on 31 January 1944. "They were in such a hurry to get us out here and now they haven't got any place or planes for us, not even an old SBD." He was able to go into San Diego on liberty. With each passing day, more pilots joined CASU-5, including some of Nist's shipmates from VSB-59.[75]

A week went by and the frustration was mounting in Ensign Nist. "Nobody around here has the slightest idea as to what is going on," he wrote to his parents on 5 February. "To date, the only thing I've logged any time in is my bunk and the only shoving off is three times daily to the chow hall," he continued. "If things don't change soon, I'm going to start going out on submarine patrol as a gunner on a PBY. At least, that's a way to get flight pay." On 5 February, a large group of pilots left for the New Hebrides Islands in the South Pacific ... but Nist was not one of them.[76]

Adding to his frustrations, Nist learned that his carrier qualifications back aboard *Wolverine* were not sufficient. "They sure did us up fine in Chicago—making us check out in SNJ's," he wrote to his parents on 6 February. "They promised us up there it wouldn't make any difference. But out here, it does. We have to check out on a carrier all over again, this time in an SBD." He had no idea when he would get a chance to qualify with the SBD.[77]

Ensign Nist's stay in San Diego finally came to an end in the second week of February 1944. On 9 February 1944, he received orders to return to Commander Fleet Air, West Coast that same day. The next day, Commander Fleet Air, West Coast issued him orders to report to the Commander, Fleet Air, Alameda, at NAS Alameda, California, for assignment to Carrier Aircraft Service Unit Six (CASU-6). CASU-6 was in the process of fitting out Bombing Squadron 303 (VB-303). At NAS Alameda, Ensign Nist would be joining VB-303 for flying duty. The Disbursing Office at NAS San Diego issued Nist a first-class train ticket from San Diego to Oakland aboard the Atchison, Topeka and Santa Fe Railroad.[78]

Naval Air Station Alameda, California

From San Diego, Ensign Nist traveled by train north to Oakland, California. Along the way, the train passed through the San Joaquin Valley. For the Jersey farm boy Nist, seeing the vast agricultural areas was a fascinating experience, even if it was from the train. To his parents, he wrote, "They were planting spuds and you should see the fields. Saw one farm with 7000 acres of just peaches and apricots. Biggest farm like it in the world." He arrived at NAS Alameda and reported to Commander, Fleet Air, Alameda on 11 February 1944 at 2000 local time. The following day, he received orders to report to CASU-6 for assignment to Bombing Squadron (VB) 303. Nist reported as ordered later that day.[79]

Naval Air Station Alameda was located on the eastern side of San Francisco Bay on the island of Alameda and adjacent to the city of Oakland. NAS Alameda began its existence in 1927 when the city of Alameda filled in some wetlands to construct an airport. The U.S. Army Air Corps and Pan American World Airways both used the west end of Alameda Island, with the Army Air Corps calling their area Benton Field. On 1 June 1936, the city of Alameda ceded Alameda Municipal Airport to the federal government for use as a naval air station and the Army Air Corps transferred Benton Field to the Navy as well. Construction to expand the naval air station began in February 1938. Some 15 million cubic feet of dredge material from San Francisco Bay was used to expand the land areas of the naval air station. Barracks, operational buildings and support facilities were constructed in phases. Further improvements were made in 1940, including building two seaplane hangars and seaplane ramps, and a concrete pier to accommodate aircraft carriers. Naval Air Station Alameda was placed in commission on 1 November 1940. Several outlying fields were constructed in 1942. When Ensign Nist reported in 1944, NAS Alameda had five runways varying in length from 3,500 to 6,000 feet and running in four directions.[80]

Carrier Aircraft Service Unit Six (CASU-6) was commissioned at NAS Alameda on 19 September 1942. CASU-6 consisted of administration, personnel, ordnance, engineering and operations, supply, medical and communications divisions and sections for recognition training, athletics and the first lieutenant. From its commissioning until December 1944, CASU-6 supported 41 air groups and squadrons.[81]

CASU-6 was organizing and equipping Bombing Squadron 303. VB-303 would be a land-based dive-bomber squadron employing the latest version of the dependable SBD Dauntless. "That gyps us out of the life aboard ship," he lamented in a letter to his parents. "We'll be crawling around in the mud on some island when we go, but we won't have to worry about home getting torpedoed and sunk while we were in the wild blue yonder." While not ideal, Nist did prefer flying the Dauntless to the Curtiss-Wright Helldiver, which was developing a negative reputation among naval aviators. Two other former VSB-59 pilots were assigned to VB-303. "So all in all, things are fair to middling," he concluded.[82]

Despite his new assignment, Ensign Nist's frustrations with the Navy continued unabated. "Situation normal, all fouled up," he wrote on 15 February to his parents. "Our airplanes haven't arrived yet. We get brand new ones, when they get here. Our squadron can't be commissioned until they do. I hope they hurry up." Instead of flying, Nist and the other VB-303 pilots were spending their days in ground school and performing athletics.[83]

Meanwhile, the war was raging across the globe. Allied forces were fighting in Italy, the Marshall Islands and New Guinea, and Soviet forces were fighting in Poland. This caused Ensign Nist to lament about not being actively involved in the war. He wrote to his parents:

> People will start calling us draft-dodgers. <u>Me?</u> [emphasis in original] Why I was in the battle of Daytona Beach the time the German Navy got within four thousand miles of the Florida coast. And the battle of Corpus Christi! Over half the cadets in that battle got washed out! Then the time a squadron of Japanese beetles invaded California. I got the Purple Heart for getting sunburned one day. Let me tell you, that California sun was something to put up with. But we got most of the Japanese beetles and the rest got killed by the first frost.[84]

With no airplanes to fly, VB-303 training consisted of ground school and athletics. On 16 February, Ensign Nist scored a 4.0 on a navigation test. The following day, Nist passed a swim qualification. Henceforth he only needed to take a "maintenance" test once a month. That test entailed a quarter-mile swim in 10 minutes. To maintain their swimming skills, the squadron's aircrew were required to swim at least once a week. Though swimming was performed in a heated outdoor pool, the air temperature was in the 40-degree range. "You climb out of the pool and run like hell for the locker room to keep from freezing," he explained to his parents.[85]

Being located on San Francisco Bay meant that personnel assigned to the naval air station were able to visit San Francisco periodically. Ensign Nist made his first venture into San Francisco a few days after arriving at NAS Alameda. One of the first places that he visited was Nob Hill. "The Officers Club is in a hotel on Nob Hill," he explained to his parents in his 19 February 1944 letter. "It's a swell place. What I wouldn't have given to have had you-know-who with me. I never knew I could miss anybody so much."[86]

Being located on the opposite coast from his fiancée was not easy. June and Jimmy mostly communicated by mail but on occasion they were able to talk on the phone. June worked for the telephone company, which helped somewhat with phone communications. "I was talking with Smitty for about fifteen minutes the other night," he informed his parents on 21 February. "She called from work. Oh, brother, was that ever a welcome sound."[87]

Around the last week of February, the pilots destined for VB-303 finally got some aircraft. "We've got our six airplanes flying every day all day, but divided up between twenty-eight pilots, that ain't much for one guy," Nist wrote to his sister Margaret, a.k.a. Wootz. "We're supposed to get some more someday but Lord knows when."[88]

Ensign Nist got his first look at the Navy's *Essex*-class aircraft carrier around this time too. USS *Lexington* (CV-16) pulled into Alameda on or about 24 February 1944. Though in service for barely a year, *Lexington* had already amassed an admirable war record. He wrote to his parents singing her praises:

> One of the "Queens of the Fleet" was in this morning. The new Lex, named after the old one that the Japs sunk. Newer, bigger, faster and better. What a wagon. Would I like to park my SBD on that and call in home for a while. Its got a flight deck almost 900 feet long. Couldn't very well miss that after the Wolverine. But it don't do any good to wish. She's on her way now.[89]

When Nist was at NAS Glenview getting his carrier qualification, the chief flight officer had him and his group qualify using SNJs, saying that it would not make any difference in their future assignments. As Nist was finding out in California, qualifying in an SNJ *did* make a huge difference. Nist's frustration ... and anger ... intensified after running into another pilot who had recently returned from the war. The pilots who were with Nist in San Diego that had qualified for carrier landings using Dauntless dive-bombers, Hellcat fighters and Avenger torpedo bombers all were immediately transferred to Naval Station Pearl Harbor and assigned to fleet aircraft carriers as replacement pilots. Nist's acquaintance had been assigned to a fighter squadron aboard a fleet carrier, and participated in the Navy's huge air strikes that devastated the Japanese naval base at Truk Island. He had earned an Air Medal and his squadron had destroyed 27 Japanese aircraft in the air and on the ground without suffering a single loss. Now this pilot was going home for 30 days of leave. "I don't mind the leave," Nist wrote home. "They could have forgotten about that. But if I'd have checked out in a D [Dauntless] instead of a J, yours truly would probably have paid a visit to Truk Island."[90]

Compounding Nist's misery was the appalling weather. Six days straight of rain and poor visibility had virtually grounded the few planes that VB-303 actually had. In his 4 March 1944 letter to his parents, Nist complained about the heavy rains:

> Oh, I forgot to tell you. I broke my leg and both arms yesterday, to say nothing of being all bruised up. Here's how it happened. I was swimming in the pool and it was raining pretty hard. I kept sinking to the bottom and I couldn't get any air. So I had to keep swimming upwards. I thought the water was awful deep for such a little pool when it suddenly dawned on my that I wasn't in the pool anymore but swimming around in a big rain cloud. (It really rains out here.) I says to myself "My God, I'd better get out of here before it stops raining." Well, you know how it is, speak of the Devil and here he is. It stops raining quick as a flash. Well, you know what happens when you spin in from 500 feet. I think I'm pretty lucky. I probably owe my life to the fact that it had rained so hard, the water was 450 feet deep and I only fell fifty feet and landed in the water. I almost drowned as I couldn't swim with two

busted arms and a busted leg but an SBD came floating by and I hung on to that 'til the water went down. And that son, is how I got my bronze star on the Purple Heart I got for getting sunburned.[91]

On Sunday 5 March, Ensign Nist went into San Francisco on liberty. While he was there, he saw the movie *The Song of Bernadette*. The ticket cost $1.10. Based on the Franz Werfel novel of the same name, *The Song of Bernadette* tells the story of the French peasant girl who was visited by the Virgin Mary in the town of Lourdes in 1858. These apparitions and the miraculous healings associated with the Lourdes spring have made Lourdes one of the most important Catholic pilgrimage sites in the world. The movie was nominated for 12 Academy Awards and won four. Jennifer Jones won the Oscar for Best Actress and Arthur C. Miller won the Oscar for Best Cinematography (Black and White). "Easy to see why Jennifer got her Oscar," Nist wrote to his parents.[92]

In the first full week of March, VB-303 was still not in commission but it had acquired a few more aircraft. Another dive-bomber squadron had shipped out for the war zone. Squadrons heading off to war were issued new aircraft. So this squadron gave eight of their old SBDs to VB-303.[93]

Ensign Nist had not piloted an aircraft since carrier landing qualifications at NAS Glenview back in early January. Finally on 8 March 1944, Ensign Nist took to the skies again. On that day, he went aloft in an SNJ to perform an instrument check flight. Later that day, he gleefully described his first flight in two months to his parents:

> Started the instrument course and finished it all in the same hop. That wasn't bad at all. I have flown better instruments, but considering that I hadn't flown in two months and the plane was a refugee from a scrap heap, I was really in there pitching. Started out doing an instrument take-off, went out to the area, did wing-overs, crash descent, power spirals, antiaircraft evasive tactics, unusual positions and flew all the way back, the return journey being only with the aid of four instruments altimeters, airspeed indicator, ball bank indicator and compass. So now I'm all through except that I have to check out of the damned Link.[94]

On 8 March 1944, Nist passed his instrument navigation check flight and completed his third pressure chamber test. The latter was to evaluate a new type of oxygen mask that was coming into use. Nist and several other pilots went into the pressure chamber and were subjected to conditions that simulated 30,000 feet of altitude, though without the extreme cold. "One of the guys demonstrated breathing at 30,000 feet without oxygen like I did at Miami and promptly but surely went out," Nist informed his parents. Each pilot performed a different test. Nist's test involved a simulated "bailing out" at 30,000 feet. "A couple of breaths of oxygen, then bail out quick and wait 50–60 seconds before pulling the ripcord. After that it's okay because by then you're down to where you can breathe okay, at about 12–14,000 feet."[95]

On Monday, 13 March 1944, Ensign Nist finally went up at the controls of a Dauntless for the first time since leaving NAS Daytona Beach at the end of December 1943. This was the first time he had piloted the SBD-5 model. On this day, he took aircraft number 28450 up for a 1.3-hour test flight. The Dauntlesses that VB-303 had inherited had been overhauled so Nist and several others took the aircraft aloft to test them out. Writing later that day, Nist described his day's flying for his parents:

We climbed them to 10,000 feet to check the supercharger in high gear, dove them once to make sure the flaps worked okay and brought them back. Did a few wingovers, but I didn't feel up to any slow-rolls, seeing as I hadn't flown in two and a half months. The landing was the thing, though. I was afraid I was going to make a real sloppy one, but what a surprise. She touched the ground like a feather, rolled as straight as an arrow. Up came the landing flaps and it was all over with. It was the first time I had ever flown an SBD-5. I flew 1's and 2's and 3's and 4's at Daytona Beach, but no 5's. They didn't have any. These have got 1200 horsepower, much better radios and a lot of other improvements.

There was a significant downside to the flying, however. Due to a shortage of 100-octane aviation gas, Nist and the other VB-303 pilots had to use 91 octane in their Dauntlesses. Unfortunately, the planes' Wright-Cyclone engines did not run well on the lower-octane fuel, so performance suffered.[96]

Meanwhile, Miss June Smith was busy working with the telephone company back in New Jersey. She was working nights and acting as the second-in-command of the switchboards while the chief operator was out sick. She did find some time to get the inside of her engagement ring engraved with "Smitty-Shorty."[97]

Bombing Squadron 303

On 15 March 1944, VB-303 was commissioned and Nist officially became a member of the new squadron. At the time of commissioning, VB-303 had six SBD-5 Dauntless dive-bombers officially assigned to it. A sister squadron, VB-302, had been commissioned two weeks prior by CASU-6. "We're flying regular now with our six airplanes," he wrote to his parents. "Six divided up among twenty-eight pilots gives us about an hour a day at most." The weather also improving.[98]

The commanding officer of the new Bombing 303 was LCDR John Reginald McCarthy. He was born on 1 March 1918 in Saint Paul, Minnesota. He was commissioned as an ensign in the prewar Navy and earned his naval aviator wings. On 7 December 1941, he was serving with Scouting Six (VS-6) aboard the aircraft carrier USS *Enterprise* (CV-6) when the Japanese attacked Pearl Harbor. *Enterprise* was returning to Pearl Harbor at the time and, as was standard procedure, had launched a number of her aircraft on ahead to land prior to the ship's arrival. As misfortune would have it, McCarthy and the other *Enterprise* pilots were attacked by Japanese fighters when they arrived over Pearl Harbor. McCarthy and several others were shot down. Bailing out, he sustained a broken leg when he landed in a tree.[99]

Ensign McCarthy recovered from his injuries and resumed flight operations with Scouting Six. He participated in the June 1942 Battle of Midway and helped sink the carrier *Kaga*. After dropping his bomb on *Kaga*, McCarthy and his radio operator/gunner ARM 2/c Earl Howell joined up with five other Dauntlesses led by LT Charles S. Ware. The six Scouting Six Dauntlesses were attacked by Japanese Zero fighters. Through skillful maneuvering and aerial gunnery, the six Dauntlesses survived the attacks. Howell shot down two Zeros and assisted with a third. Now they had to return to the *Enterprise.* When McCarthy realized that they were flying on the wrong heading, he communicated this to LT Ware but to no avail. So McCarthy and Howell struck out alone. Ware and the other five Dauntlesses were never heard from again. McCarthy and Howell found the aircraft carrier *Yorktown* and ditched in the water near the destroyer *Hamman*. For his heroism during the Battle of Midway, McCarthy was awarded the Navy Cross.[100]

The new Bombing 303 included two pilots who would become among Ensign Nist's closest friends in the Navy: Ensigns R. Elmer "Dusty" Miller and Gene Scruggs Powell. Dusty Miller, Jr., was born on 29 March 1922 in Oklahoma City, Oklahoma, and raised there. After high school, he went to work for the General Motors Acceptance Corporation in that city. On 30 June 1942, he registered with Selective Service. Sometime afterward, he entered the Navy as an aviation cadet, earned his naval aviator wings and was commissioned as an ensign. He was 5′ 8″ tall and weighed 134 pounds at the time of his draft registration. He had blue eyes and blond hair.[101]

Gene Scruggs Powell was born on 11 September 1920 in Cherokee County in northwestern South Carolina. He registered for Selective Service on 16 February 1942. At the time, he was living in Gaffney, South Carolina, and working for the Sleep Easy Mattress and Upholstering Company. He stood 5′11½″ tall and weighed 150 pounds at that time. He had blond hair and blue eyes. Like Nist and Miller, Powell entered the Navy as an aviation cadet and earned his wings and officer commission through that process.[102]

Toward the end of the week, VB-303 received 13 more SBD-5 Dauntless dive-bombers, bringing their total aircraft complement up to 19. These aircraft were not in good shape. "The SBD's out here are so beat up that by the time the 91 octane gets to work on them, they aren't worth a damn," he wrote to his parents.[103]

Though they had more aircraft available, notorious San Francisco Bay weather

Pilots and enlisted members of Bombing Squadron 303 in the spring of 1944. Noteworthy members include Squadron Commander LCDR John McCarthy (seated in center), Ensign James A. Nist (second row fifth from left), Ensign Gene Powell (on Nist's left) and Ensign Elmer Miller (on Powell's left) (Dickerson Family photograph).

was making flight operations difficult. "For the past two days it is so bad we've only flown once in a while when it lifts for a few minutes," he wrote to his parents. On 18 March, Nist went up in an SNJ with another pilot to practice instrument flying. "We take turns going up with each other and I was under the hood today," he wrote to his parents. "I'm getting pretty sharp on these instrument take-offs."[104]

Now with a full complement of aircraft, Bombing 303 was able to practice its attack formations. The lieutenants and lieutenant junior grades led the dive-bomber sections with the ensigns flying on the wing positions. Ensign Nist was assigned to fly on the squadron commander's port wing. During an attack to port, Nist would dive second after the commander. During an attack to starboard, he would dive third. "The boys in the other divisions are gonna be out of luck because we'll have everything sunk or blown to hell by the time they get to dive," he wrote to his parents.[105]

Monday, 20 March, was a very busy day for Ensign Nist. He flew three training flights for a total of 5.2 hours. The first flight was in an SNJ to perform 1½ hours of instrument flying. During the other two flights, Nist trained in dive-bombing tactics at high altitude using oxygen. The following day, he described the training in a letter to his parents:

> We practiced high speed break-ups in which we follow each other in the dive at an interval of four seconds. That makes a whole division of six planes in a dive all at the same time. We weren't too sharp at it yesterday, seeing as it was the first time, but we'll have it down pat before long and then it will really be a sight to see. We could do much better with some good airplanes.[106]

Nist and the other pilots of VB-303 continued to endure the shortcomings of their SBD-5s and the lower-quality aviation fuel. He wrote to his parents, "Most of the ones we have now are in pretty sad shape, despite the fact that they were just overhauled." Then with some optimism, he informed them that the squadron would get the new SBD-6 model Dauntlesses in the near future. This latest version of the dauntless Dauntless boasted an extra 250 horsepower and lighter weight, which improved its performance.[107]

That night, the sailors and marines at NAS Alameda were treated to a live concert by Bob Crosby and the Bob-Cats. Crosby was a jazz singer and band leader and the younger brother of legendary performer Bing Crosby. After the U.S. entered World War II, Bob Crosby had joined the Marine Corps and been commissioned as an officer. He and his band toured, performing morale concerts for service members. In his 21 March letter to his parents, Nist wrote about attending the concert:

> You didn't happen to hear the Old Gold radio show with Bob Crosby last night (Sunday) did you? He broadcast from Alameda NAS and of course everybody went over to hear him. He was pretty good, but the best part didn't go over the air. The Bobcats played about fifteen minutes before broadcast time and they were really hot.[108]

The culmination of Ensign Nist's memorable day came after the concert around 2030. Nist was relaxing in his room at the BOQ when a sailor knocked on his door and informed him that he had a long-distance phone call. In his 21 March letter, he described what happened next:

Well, I was pretty sure who that would be and I set a new record between building 84 and main B.O.Q. Some twelve minutes after arriving there, I departed again, a very much happier lad. So today I am singing praises to Alexander Graham Bell for inventing the telephone. So far I've talked to her from Texas, Florida, and California. Someday I might even call from New Zealand or maybe I'll try one from Tokyo.[109]

On the morning of Sunday, 26 March, two of the VB-303 Dauntlesses experienced mechanical problems and were forced to land at one of NAS Alameda's outlying airfields. Ensign Nist and another pilot were tasked to fly mechanics out to the outlying airfield so that they could fix the aircraft. The mechanics were able to fix one of the broken planes but could not fix the other one. So Nist, his fellow pilot and the mechanics flew back to NAS Alameda, arriving there at 1900. Then, Nist packed up his gear and belongings because the squadron was moving the next morning to another airfield.[110]

On Monday, 27 March, VB-303 moved about 48 air miles north-northwest to Naval Auxiliary Landing Field Santa Rosa. Located just north of the city of Santa Rosa, NALF Santa Rosa had been constructed in 1943 and had two 7,000-foot runways in an X shape. "The base up here is swell, but definitely on the rugged side," Nist informed his parents. "Everything wood, the hangars are open lean-to's."[111]

The following day, Nist flew back to NAS Alameda to pick up some items, then took another pilot back to the outlying field he had previously flown to on Sunday. The aircraft that had landed there with mechanical problems was now fixed, so Nist's passenger flew it to rejoin the squadron at NALF Santa Rosa.[112]

Bombing 303 was led by an experienced and veteran dive-bomber pilot. The lieutenants and lieutenant junior grades were former SNJ instructors and Vought OS2U Kingfisher observation floatplane pilots. The ensigns had all completed three months of training in Dauntlesses to include dive-bombing and carrier operations. Due to rank, the lieutenants and lieutenant junior grades occupied all of the flight leadership positions, leading the divisions and sections. The ensigns flew the wing positions. Having inexperienced but higher-ranking pilots leading more experienced but lower-ranking pilots created some serious tensions within the newly formed Bombing 303. Ensign Nist wrote about this in his 30 March 1944 letter to his parents:

> Things reached the boiling point today when we started dive-bombing. In all my days in the Navy, I have never seen anything so fouled up. They [the LTs and LT(jg)s] had no idea what the score was. And of course, they were far above taking a suggestion or two from a lowly ensign, even if the suggestion was thought up by Admirals and Captains in Florida and was merely being passed on in good faith. So things continue to be SNAFU or TARFU and will [emphasis in original] continue that way until they decide to let somebody explain a few of the simpler details of how one goes about hitting a target or brings a squadron back to a flat-top. I was so disgusted at one time I talked myself into turning my wings in. It ain't safe in the same sky with guys who just won't listen. But I'll wait a couple more days before doing anything drastic. I talked myself out of it by the time I landed.[113]

As March gave way to April, the flight leadership situation in VB-303 seemed to have improved. Apparently the squadron commander recognized that the former SNJ pilots/LT(jgs) were not as skilled as the ensigns in flying dive-bomber formations. So the best ensigns were now taking turns in the lead positions and the LT(jgs) were flying the wing positions. In his 2 April 1944 letter, Ensign Nist explained how this came about:

> This happened after a carrier break-up led by one of the "J-boys" which ended up in a general melee. The next hop, the ensigns took over, the j.g.'s started flying wing positions and everything went as smooth as silk. The "J-boys" don't like the idea of flying wing on an ensign but we sure did improve matters. Now we know what to expect anyway.[114]

Despite the "rugged" conditions, Ensign Nist was enjoying the new environs. In his 2 April 1944 letter, he described flying in this part of California:

> We were out on some navigation hops this week over eastern California and I saw some of the prettiest and most rugged country I ever saw. No houses for fifty or sixty miles but it sure is pretty. Mountains 6–8,000 feet high covered with fir and redwood trees and snow. One minute you're over a peak clearing the ground by a mere 500 feet and the next you're over some gorge four or five thousand feet deep. We saw Shasta Dam and a whole lot of lumber camps with flumes for the logs and copper, silver, and gold mines. It's really pretty but such country to fly over. If the old Wright Cyclone gets tired, you take to the silk elevator.[115]

Ensign Nist had been frequently flying a Dauntless that was named "Peter Ten" after its radio call sign. Around this time, Peter Ten came to a sudden and violent end. Another pilot had just taken off when Peter Ten's engine failed at 200 feet of altitude. The Dauntless was a poor glider so with his aircraft falling fast, the pilot tried to make it to a nearby road to land the stricken aircraft. About 10 feet off the ground, the aircraft's port wing clipped a telephone and Peter Ten crashed hard. The pilot escaped with a minor head injury but Peter Ten was a total loss. "We ought to do that with the other seventeen and maybe we'd get some better ones," Nist observed.[116]

Thursday, 6 April 1944, was a very busy flying day for VB-303. On that day, Ensign Nist went up three times and logged a total of seven hours of flight time. In a letter written the next day, Nist described one of the training missions:

> We were up dive-bombing yesterday by divisions pulling high speed break-ups at 11,000 feet. There were five of us diving, following each other at three second intervals. Out of the five guys, the first four of us were so close to the bulls-eye they were called direct hit (its only seven or eight feet in diameter) and the fifth guy only missed by about fifty feet. It was the prettiest piece of bombing I have ever seen or hope to see. The skipper dove first. I was flying wing on him and went second so the only bombs I saw hit was the skippers. I sure would have liked to have been last guy and seen them all hit.[117]

Nist also reported that the ensigns and LT(jgs) were getting along somewhat better now. Apparently, the LT(jg)s attitudes toward the ensigns changed for the better after they witnessed the ensigns' superior bombing and carrier landing skills. While the LT(jg)s were scattering their bombs all over the place, the ensigns were consistently putting their bombs on target. While the LT(jg)s were making long, gradual approaches and landings, the ensigns were making good carrier approaches and landings. The LT(jg)s had resumed flying the lead positions but relations between the two groups were better.[118]

The pilots of VB-303 were putting in long hours and not just in the air. In his 13 April 1944 letter to his parents, Nist narrated a typical day for him. The pilots were flying four to six hours per day. They had been flying upward of nine hours per day but that proved to be too much. On the ground, the pilots were helping prepare their aircraft for training flights. They attended ground school classes and participated in athletics. They participated in post-flight critiques of their performance on training missions. As VB-303's navigation officer, Nist was responsible for maintaining the squadron's navigational equipment and the squadron log. On a rotational basis, Nist served as squadron duty officer and squadron security officer. The security watch officer supervised the sentries that were posted around the airfield and was provided with a jeep to use for inspecting the posts.[119]

On 16 April 1944, VB-303 experienced a ground mishap. A pilot taxied into the end of Ensign Nist's roommate's SBD. The resulting collision caused significant damage to both aircraft, requiring the replacement of the wings and the tail assembly of the aircraft that was struck, as well as the propeller and engine of the aircraft that taxied into Ensign Nist's roommate.[120]

Jimmy Nist was a naval aviator perfecting the art of dive-bombing but he had been raised on a farm and so farming was still very much a part of him. With spring progressing, Nist's letters frequently mentioned the start of the growing season back in New Jersey. He took a keen interest in the farming taking place around him. "The farms out here are all busy now," he wrote to his parents on 23 April 1944. "I saw acres and acres of red stuff growing on the way to Frisco Friday. They didn't look like too much like beets, but I guess they were sugar beets." He also mentioned seeing numerous orchards of various kinds of fruit trees.[121]

On the afternoon of Monday, 24 April, VB-303 took some time off from its intense training schedule for a little recreation and relaxation. The squadron held a picnic off base at a park in a redwood forest near a mountain stream. The menu included fried chicken, potato salad, potato chips, pickles, olives, bread, butter and three kegs of beer. When the food ran out, a collection was taken up to buy more. The food detail returned with ample supplies of food, including 60 hamburgers. Squadron personnel went swimming in the stream and attempted (often unsuccessfully) to navigate a canoe on it. There was a bonfire that consumed six cords of wood.[122]

Along with VB-303, there were two other Navy dive-bombing squadrons at Santa Rosa training for war: VB-301 and VB-302. The Bombing 303 pilots were feeling pretty skilled in the art of dive-bombing so on 25 April they challenged sister squadron Bombing 302 to a dive-bombing contest. The contest was to be held the following day. Each squadron would be represented by 12 pilots. The bet was $5 per pilot for a grand total of $120 at stake. To make it fair, both squadrons would use the same SBDs. The target for the contest was an outline of a cruiser. The squadron with the most hits would win. Ensign Nist was chosen to be one of the 12 pilots representing Bombing 303.[123]

On the morning of the dive-bombing contest, the competitors from VB-303 went up for some bombing practice. The results were discouraging. However, VB-302 backed out of the contest at the last minute, which was probably fortunate for them. VB-303 went up that afternoon and really plastered the target. "We made three dives and I got three hits," Nist later wrote. "Out of the 36 dives, I don't think there were more than a half dozen misses."[124]

Then, the pilots and sailors of Bombing 303 found out that the Navy was going to decommission its land-based dive-bombing squadrons, including VB-301, VB-302 and VB-303. On 1 May, Nist wrote to his parents:

> The squadron is going to be decommissioned Thursday. What happens to us then nobody knows. Scuttlebutt is as thick as ticks on a sheepdog. Some say we're going into SB2Cs, some say F6Fs with diving flaps (Hellbombers), some say F6Fs without flaps (fighters and that's for me) some say TBFs (torpedo bombers). The most logical one seems to be that half of us go to divebombers in SB2Cs and the other half in TBFs as torpedo pilots. From what I have seen and heard about both the SB2C and TBF, if they ask me what I want, I'm going to be an ex-divebomber [emphasis in original] and try my luck and skill at torpedo-bombing.[125]

Even though the future was uncertain, VB-303 continued with its training. On one training mission, the squadron practiced dropping 1,000-pound bombs, averaging 16 feet from the target. Nist put his bomb 10 feet from the target.[126]

On Monday, 1 May 1944, Ensign Nist passed a significant milestone in his flight training. On that day, he completed his 600th flight hour with the U.S. Navy. He had begun flying N3N "Yellow Perils" at NAS Glenview, then moved on to SNV-1 Vultee Valiants and SNJ "Texans" at NAS Corpus Christi. After being commissioned as an ensign and earning his wings as a naval aviator, Nist had begun training as a dive-bomber flying the SBD Dauntless.[127]

Undoubtedly, Tuesday, 2 May 1944, was one of the best days in Ensign Nist's naval career thus far. On that day, the list of pilot reassignments was posted. An ecstatic Nist wrote to his parents that day, "I've taken a lot of raw deals before from the Navy but what they just did to me sort of makes up for all of them." Of the 26 pilots still with VB-303, 10 were being transferred to Bombing Squadron 84 (VB-84), nine were being transferred to torpedo bomber squadrons and seven were being reassigned to Fighting Squadron 84 (VF-84). The 10 pilots being transferred to VB-84 included the commanding officer of VB-303, LCDR John R. McCarthy. The seven pilots heading for VF-84 were Ensigns Applegate, Elmer Miller, Phillip C. Helms, Gene Powell, McBride, Sheaffer and James A. Nist. "It is supposed to be the official word, but it is so good I will not believe it until I see my orders with my own eyes," he wrote to his parents. "And then I'll probably spend the next week pinching myself to see that I'm not asleep and dreaming."[128]

As of 2 May, officially there was no word as to what aircraft VF-84 would be flying. The squadron was still in the process of organizing. VF-84 might be equipped with Grumman F6F Hellcats or the FM-2 Wildcat. The latter was a version of the F4F Wildcat built under license by Eastern Aircraft Company from Grumman. Expectations were, however, that VF-84 would be flying the Vought F4U Corsair, the Navy's most powerful fighter-bomber. Nist described the Corsair as "that beautiful streamlined hunk of aerodynamic beauty with the inverted gull-wing."[129]

Not everyone was as happy as Ensign Nist was with his new assignment. That included Nist's radioman/gunner. The VB-303 pilots who were either staying with dive-bombers or moving over to torpedo bombers were able to retain their radioman/gunners but those destined for fighters had no need for a radioman/gunner. At least 10 enlisted sailors of VB-303 were being transferred to VB-84. Oddly enough,

Nist never identified who his radioman/gunner was in any of his letters. In his 2 May 1944 letter, he referred to him as "a pretty good kid." The young sailor was very saddened to be parting ways with his pilot.[130]

On Thursday, 4 May 1944, Ensign Nist and the other VB-303 members flew from NALF Santa Rosa back to NAS Alameda. For the next few days, they waited for their orders to come through. On Sunday, 7 May, he wrote to his parents describing his activities around this time. "We haven't done a darn thing since Thursday," he wrote. "We've been in San Francisco all the time except when we were asleep and that's not very often."[131]

Ensign Nist's tenure with VB-303 officially ended on 4 May 1944. Per orders issued this day, Ensign Nist was detached from VB-303. He was transferred back to CASU-6 pending further assignment by the Commander Fleet Air, West Coast. Nist, however, was not notified of this until several days after the fact.[132]

While waiting for his days in NAS Alameda to end, Ensign Nist found time to make a new female friend. A friend from VSB-59, Ensign J.A. McChesney, was engaged to a girl named Alice who lived in San Francisco. Back in December 1943 when McChesney learned he was heading to Seattle and Nist was going to NAS Alameda, McChesney gave Alice's phone number to Nist and encouraged him to look her up if he was in the area. Jimmy got to NAS Alameda in early February but did not call Alice for two and a half months. In the meantime, McChesney and Alice had broken off their engagement. Finally, on Friday, 5 May, Jimmy called up Alice and they went out to see the movie *School for Brides* starring Roscoe Karns and Glenda Farrell. "It was pretty darn good," Jimmy later opined. Later that night, they went to a social club called the Zebra Room. Three months later, Jimmy would inform his parents, "somewhere along the course of the evening, I came to the conclusion that the girl I was out with was just a little on the special side." The following night, Jimmy and Alice went out again.[133]

Alice Marie Richards was 5'2½" tall in heels, about 115 pounds and had brown hair. She was 21 years old and had attended junior college. At present, she was working for Bank of America in San Francisco. She was Catholic and had five brothers and sisters. Her youngest brother was

Miss Alice Richards (Dickerson Family photograph).

only a month old. She lived with her family on 28th Avenue in the Sunset District on the west side of San Francisco and was a communicant of Saint Anne's Catholic Church.[134]

On Sunday, 7 May, Jimmy and Alice again went out together. First they went to Omar Khayyam's restaurant in downtown San Francisco. The restaurant was established by Armenian émigré George Mardikian and it served Armenian and Middle Eastern–style food. "The salad was raw spinach with some kind of dressing and it was about the best salad you ever ate," Nist described to his parents later. "The coffee though was this sweet syrupy stuff and I'll stick to Yankee coffee." Afterward, Alice took Jimmy to see Chinatown. "We went to Chinatown then as she said nobody could be in San Francisco and miss Chinatown," he wrote. "It's some place. Just like China. There's no English to be seen anywhere."[135]

Alice made quite an impression upon Jimmy. At some point, Jimmy started fondly calling her "Butch." After these three dates, Jimmy was seriously regretting having not called her sooner. "In spite of Smith-Nist, Butch was just one of those things too nice to forget about so we wrote to each other pretty often plus a couple of phone calls," he reported to his parents three months later.[136]

On Monday, 8 May 1944, Ensign Nist and the several other former dive-bomber pilots of the now decommissioned Bombing 303 departed Naval Air Station Alameda and headed south to San Diego, California, to join up with their new squadron, Navy Fighting Squadron 84.[137]

4

Navy Fighting Squadron 84

Jimmy Nist had wanted to fly carrier-based fighter planes since before he had joined the Navy. The Navy trained and assigned its pilots primarily based upon the needs of the service and not so much upon the preferences of said pilots. Initially, the Navy chose to train Jimmy Nist as a dive-bomber pilot, which he enjoyed but was not what he really wanted. From October 1943 until early May 1944, Nist trained as a dive-bomber pilot—first in Florida and then in California. But then the Navy decided it did not need so many dive-bomber pilots and squadrons. Much to Jimmy Nist's good fortune, the Navy reassigned him to one of its carrier-based fighter squadrons. Jimmy Nist would serve out the remainder of his naval career as a member of Navy Fighting Squadron 84.

South to San Diego

Ensign James Nist and the other six former members of Bombing 303 left NAS Alameda by train bound for San Diego. They were given five days to report to their new command, so Nist and the others decided to stop off in Los Angeles along the way for some sightseeing. They spent two days in LA, then continued on to San Diego.[1]

On Friday, 12 May 1944, Ensign Nist and the six others reported to Commander Fleet Air West Coast at NAS San Diego. The following day, 13 May 1944, Nist reported to his new squadron, Fighting Squadron 84 (VF-84). He met the squadron commanding officer, LCDR Roger Hedrick, and the executive officer, LT Raymond E. Hill. Nist described both officers as "pretty good guys." In a letter the next day, Nist informed his parents, "He [Hedrick] assured me that I would like a Corsair and said I'd 'probably' find it a 'little' faster than an SBD."[2]

VF-84 was formed at NAS San Diego on 1 May 1944 on the same day as parent Air Group 84. Following the activation ceremony for Air Group 84, the group's three subordinate squadrons relocated to their respective ready rooms for their own squadron activations. As the senior officer present, LT Raymond E. Hill assumed command as the acting squadron commander for VF-84. At the time of its activation, the squadron consisted of only nine officers and no enlisted sailors. LCDR Roger Hedrick assumed command of the squadron on 5 May 1944. By month's end, there would be 49 officers and 16 enlisted sailors aboard.[3]

VF-84's commanding officer, LCDR Roger Hedrick, was a distinguished naval aviator. He had been born in Pasadena, California, on 2 September 1914. He attended Los Angeles City College. He and his wife, Barbara, had a daughter and a son. Prior to assuming command of VF-84, Hedrick had served as executive officer of the famed Navy Fighting Squadron 17 (VF-17). VF-17 had been one of the first Navy squadrons equipped with the F4U Corsairs and originally had been assigned to the aircraft carrier USS *Bunker Hill* (CV-17). The Navy instead had sent it to the South Pacific theater to operate from land bases. Under the command of the legendary LCDR Tommy Blackburn, VF-17 pilots had decimated the Japanese in the skies over the Solomon Islands, shooting down 152 Japanese aircraft. Eleven VF-17 pilots became aces. Hedrick had shot down three Japanese aircraft and had three probables during aerial combat in the South Pacific. His former CO, Tom Blackburn, described him as "by far the best fighter pilot with whom I ever served."[4]

In addition to LCDR Hedrick, VF-84 had several other former VF-17 pilots. They included LT(jg) Doris C. Freeman, LT(jg) Wilbert P. Popp, LT(jg) William P. Meek, LT(jg) James C. Dixon, LT(jg) J.O. "Fatso" Ellsworth, LT(jg) John Malcolm Smith, LT(jg) H.L. Mathews, LT(jg) J.E. Diteman and VF-84's executive officer, LT Raymond E. Hill. Flying with VF-17, Smith had shot down three Japanese fighters, for which he had been awarded the Distinguished Flying Cross. Freeman and Popp had each shot down two Japanese fighters and Dixon, Meek and Ellsworth downed a Japanese fighter each. Several of these veteran former VF-17 pilots were surprisingly young. LT(jg) Smith and LT(jg) Popp were 22 years old, and LT(jg) Dixon was 21. Chief Aviation Machinist Mate George Mauhar was an enlisted alumnus from VF-17.[5]

LT(jg) Wilbert P. "Beads" Popp was born on 15 November 1921 in Fresno, California, and later moved to Portland, Oregon. He studied at Multnomah College in Portland before joining the Navy as a naval aviation cadet on 7 May 1942. He was 6' tall but barely made the Navy flight program's minimum weight requirement. After completing flight training, he was assigned to VF-17 in October 1943 and fought with the squadron during its aerial battles in the South Pacific. He shot down two Japanese fighters during his time with VF-17. While serving in the South Pacific, he earned his nickname "Beads" due to the beads of sweat that appeared on his forehead on his first combat missions.[6]

LT(jg) Doris Clyde "Chico" Freeman was 24 years old and from Los Angeles, California. He was a graduate of Ventura Junior College, in Ventura, California. While serving with VF-17 in the South Pacific, Freeman shot down two Japanese aircraft and probably four others. LCDR Hedrick assigned him to serve as the VF-84 personnel officer.[7]

Ensign Nist was clearly ecstatic to be part of VF-84 with its legendary pedigree. On 16 May 1944, he wrote to his parents describing his new squadron:

> Boy, do I ever have to get on the ball to live up to this squadron's reputation. Ever hear of Blackburn's Bearded Pirates, otherwise known as the Jolly Roger Squadron? It's the most famous squadron in the Navy. They knocked down Japs at better than 12 to 1. Well, they're back in the States now and seventeen of its old members are in VF-84. I guess we'll have good teachers. Those boys really ought to be able to give us the word. And everybody in the squadron is swell. None of these j.g. instructors from Corpus who think they invented the airplane. We'll be flying wing on these experienced guys I guess. But that suits me.[8]

Officers of Navy Fighting Squadron Eighty-Four in the fall of 1944. Noteworthy members include Squadron Commander LCDR Roger Hedrick (front row center), Executive Officer LT Raymond Hill (to Hedrick's left), Ensign Elmer Miller (second row second from left), Ensign Leroy Wallet (second row sixth from left), LT(jg) Ike Kepford (second row ninth from left), Ensign Curtis Jefferson (back row left end), LT(jg) John Sargent (back row fifth from right), Ensign Jimmy Nist (back row second from right) and Ensign Gene Powell (back row right end) (Dickerson Family Photograph).

VF-84 was staffed with veteran pilots from other squadrons as well. LT Ellis J. Littlejohn had previously served with Bombing 98 (VB-98) in the South Pacific. LT(jg) John T. Gildea piloted an SBD Dauntless dive-bomber with Bombing Five (VB-5) aboard USS *Yorktown* (CV-10). LT(jg) William L. "Flip" Gerner had previously served with Bombing 17 aboard *Bunker Hill*. LT(jg) John J. Sargent, Jr., had gone to sea aboard *Bunker Hill* in 1943–44 as part of Fighting Squadron 18 (VF-18). While piloting F6F Hellcats, Sargent had shot down five Japanese aircraft and probably downed three others. This accomplishment earned him the Distinguished Flying Cross.[9]

LT(jg) Wilton H. "Hoot" Hutt was born on 15 December 1922 in Norwood, Colorado—a small town high up in the Rocky

VF-84 Squadron Commander LCDR Roger Hedrick (Naval History and Heritage Command [Photo 80-G-220754]/National Archives).

Mountains. After the Pearl Harbor attack, he enlisted in the Navy. While at Naval Station Great Lakes, he was selected for officer flight training, even though he did not have any college education. After completing flight training, he served with Fighting Six (VF-6) aboard USS *Independence* (CVL-22) and USS *Cowpens* (CVL-25), and then Fighting Three (VF-3) aboard USS *Intrepid* (CV-11).[10]

Two of the new VF-84 pilots, LT Philip C. Helms and LT Earle C. Gillen, were survivors from the ill-fated escort carrier USS *Liscome Bay* (CVE-56). LT Gillen formerly served with Torpedo Squadron Three and LT Helms had flown scout-observation aircraft from the cruiser USS *Chester* (CA-27) before joining Composite Squadron 39 aboard *Liscome Bay*. While supporting the invasion of Makin Island in the Gilbert Islands group on 24 November 1943, *Liscome Bay* was sunk by a torpedo fired from the Japanese submarine *I-175*. Six hundred and forty-four of her crew were lost; LT Helms and LT Gillen were among the only 272 survivors.[11]

Air Group 84

Fighting Squadron 84 was one of three squadrons assigned to Air Group 84 then forming at Naval Air Station San Diego. The other squadrons were Bombing 84 (VB-84) and Torpedo 84 (VT-84). VB-84 was equipped with 36 of the new Curtiss SB2C-3 Helldivers dive-bombers and VT-84 was equipped with 18 of the Grumman TBF-1 Avengers and General Motors TBM-1 Avengers bombers. Air Group 84 officially was commissioned at Hangar 525 at NAS San Diego on 1 May 1944 with LCDR John P. Conn in temporary command. Following the ceremony, VF-84, VB-84 and VT-84 relocated to their respective Ready Rooms and performed their squadron activation ceremonies.[12]

Conn was in command only until LCDR Roger Hedrick reported to serve as acting commanding officer. Conn then assumed command of Bombing Squadron 84. Hedrick performed this role until the permanent commanding officer, CDR George M. Ottinger, USN, assumed command on 29 May 1944.[13]

CDR George Malone "Bunky" Ottinger was born on 10 May 1910 and was raised in Memphis, Tennessee. He was accepted into the U.S. Naval Academy. As a midshipman, Ottinger participated in wrestling, cross-country and track. The Naval Academy's yearbook, *The Lucky Bag*, described him as "There is nothing indefinite about Bunky. He makes up his mind to do a thing and does it. Always ready to do a good turn, a truer friend never lived." He graduated as part of the Class of 1932 and was commissioned in the Navy as an ensign. He earned his naval aviator wings on 1 October 1935, becoming naval aviator #4152. Subsequently he served as the landing signal officer of USS *Ranger* (CV-4) and as the executive officer of an escort aircraft carrier (CVE). He was married to the former Mary Suitor.[14]

Down in San Diego, other VB-303 alumni had been assigned to Bombing Squadron 84. Now they were flying SBC Helldivers. The former VB-303 pilots now assigned to VF-84 and VB-84 were both staying in the same bachelor officer quarters. Former squadron mates now became friendly rivals. "The argument goes on and on and on about who's got the better airplane," Nist informed his parents. The arguments quickly escalated into good-natured pranks. "It's more fun than the best circus you ever saw."[15]

The Corsair

In transferring to VF-84, Ensign Nist and his colleagues from VB-303 would have to learn not only a new aircraft but a new type of aircraft as well. VF-84 flew the Navy and Marine Corps' premier fighter-bomber: the Corsair.

The F4U Corsair was developed and manufactured by Vought Aircraft Company. To meet the high demands for the aircraft, the Corsair was later built by Goodyear Aircraft Corporation and Brewster Aircraft Company as well. First flown in 1940, the Corsair was built around a powerful Pratt & Whitney R-2800 engine. To accommodate this very large engine, the Corsair had a long nose that placed the cockpit significantly farther aft than other single-engine aircraft. In order to accommodate the Corsair's large propeller, the wings were designed with an inverted gull shape and tall landing gear that retracted into the gull wings. The combination of the powerful engine, large propeller and unique design made the Corsair an exceptionally fast naval fighter capable of surpassing 400 mph with ease. Having the cockpit so far aft on the fuselage made for poor visibility on landing approaches and while taxiing on the ground. The Corsair could attain speeds of 446 miles per hour, a service ceiling of 41,500 feet and a range of over 1,000 miles.

The Corsair was supposed to be a carrier plane but during its trials, senior naval aviation leaders had concerns about its ability to operate from carriers. So, the Corsair was restricted to shore facilities. As such, land-based Marine Corps and Navy squadrons in the South Pacific theater were the first ones to take the Corsair into combat.

Marine Fighter Squadron VMF-214 was one of the first squadrons to employ the Corsair in combat. The squadron was led by the legendary Major Gregory S. "Pappy" Boyington, who ultimately would become the Marine Corps' leading fighter ace. Originally, VMF-214, a.k.a. "the Black Sheep," flew Grumman F4F Wildcats, but in May 1943, they swapped them for Corsairs. "The Corsair was a sweet-flying baby if I ever flew one," wrote "Pappy" Boyington in his memoirs. Boyington had previously flown Wildcats and P-40 Tomahawks against Japanese Zeros and scored victories despite the shortcomings of these aircraft. He continued:

> No longer would we have to fight the Nips' fight, for we could make our own rules. Here was a ship that could climb with a Zero, only with a more shallow angle of climb, and one that had considerably more speed.[16]

Another proponent of the Corsair was Navy CDR Tom Blackburn, commanding officer of Navy Fighter Squadron VF-17. In 1943, VF-17 was assigned to the aircraft carrier *Bunker Hill*. "The airplane was huge, far bigger than any fighter I had ever seen," Blackburn wrote his memoirs. "Most of it seemed to be engine." He also noted that the fighter had poor ground visibility due to its long nose, which stretched 12 feet in front of the cockpit windshield. Blackburn became a strong proponent of the

Corsair. When Commander, Naval Air Forces Atlantic (COMAIRLANT) attempted to replace VF-17s with Grumman F6F Hellcats, Blackburn and *Bunker Hill*'s commanding officer, CAPT John J. Ballentine, vigorously opposed the decision. Ultimately, VF-17 kept its Corsairs but was replaced aboard *Bunker Hill* by a Hellcat fighter squadron. VF-17 was sent to the South Pacific to operate from land bases. There the squadron achieved one of the Navy's highest aerial victories records.[17]

VF-84 was equipped with Corsairs manufactured by Goodyear known as the FG-1A. Ensign Jimmy Nist got his first opportunity to fly the Corsair on Thursday, 18 May 1944. For his first time in the cockpit of a Corsair, he took aircraft number 13843 aloft for an orientation flight that lasted 1.5 hours. Then he went up a second time at the controls of aircraft number 13819 for 1.4 hours. Later that day, he described the experience for his parents in a letter:

> I spent three of the most enjoyable hours of my life today falling in love with 2250 horses and a gull wing. Boy, there just ain't words built that can describe that airplane. It was the biggest thrill of my life when I set that baby down gently at around 85 knots, brought her back and climbed out. The first time up in a new plane, you're always just a little bit scared of what's going to happen. So I took it easy the first time and just got used to her. The second hop I took her up and knocked myself out. She got the works from loops, Immelmann's, slow rolls, split-S's to just plain straight level flying. She's just like a good race-horse or a red-head. She's perfection personified and a honey, but she's a little temperamental at times. But there never was a plane built to match her. The biggest trouble I had was trying to slow the thing up. All you've gotta do is suggest that you're going to put the nose down and you're doing 250 knots at cruising throttle.[18]

Three days later, Jimmy Nist was still raving about the Corsair. In his next letter to his parents, he offered another description of his time flying the Corsair:

> I fell in love with it the first time I flew it, but every time I take it up I like it more. I really wrung it out the other day over some small town east of here. I'd like to do that over Squankum. Started out with a split "S," then three rolls in a row followed by two Immelmann's, two slow rolls and another split "S" without stopping. It does stunts just about as nice as the Waco I used to fly in New Brunswick. The thing will out climb anything in the Navy as well as out-run them, including the Hellcat. Besides that, there's a new version coming out that we'll get before we leave the states (Sept 1 or later).[19]

Training for War in San Diego

Much like his previous commands, swimming was a major part of VF-84's fitness program. "If you never believed in evolution, you will when I get home," Nist wrote to his parents on 24 May 1944. "I've spent so much time in the pool that I've grown fins. There are also some slits starting to grow in my neck that can't be anything but gills."[20]

Only a few days into its operational existence, VF-84 suffered its first fatal mishap. On 9 May 1944, a midair collision occurred between Ensign Paul D. Bucher and LT(jg) Wilbert Popp in the skies above Escondido. LT(jg) Popp was leading a four-plane division against another four-plane division in practice aerial dogfights. Bucher was Popp's wingman but instead of flying on his wing, Bucher was following

Flight of five F4U Corsairs from VF-17. LT(jg) Kepford is flying Corsair closest to camera (Naval History and Heritage Command [Photo 80-G-217817]/National Archives).

Popp. While maneuvering, Bucher lost Popp in the sun and struck Popp's Corsair aft of the cockpit. "My plane exploded," Popp later wrote. He continued:

> However, in that split section between the collision and the disintegration of my plane, I was able to open my hatch. Fortunately, for me, my plane at that time was inverted and gravity threw me loose from the plane. On the instant of the collision I thought I had bought the farm.[21]

At the time of the collision, Popp and Bucher were at about 6,000 feet and flying in excess of 300 knots. When Popp fell out of his cockpit, his leather flying helmet and sunglasses were ripped from his head. The sudden blast of air caused the unprotected blood vessels in his eyes to rupture. Popp landed in a field and sprained his right ankle. A farmer picked up Popp and drove him to a medical clinic in Escondido. Along the way, they passed aircraft wreckage. An hour later, a Navy ambulance arrived and drove him to the medical clinic at Marine Corps' Camp Pendleton in Oceanside. From there, he was transported to the dispensary at NAS San Diego, where he spent a week recovering from ruptured blood vessels in his eyes, second-degree burns on the right side of his face and a sprained right ankle.[22]

Popp survived the harrowing ordeal. Unfortunately, ENS Bucher did not. The wrecked aircraft that Popp had seen on the way to the medical clinic in Escondido was Bucher's. As they passed the wreckage, the farmer informed Popp that the pilot was still in the plane. Apparently, he had checked the crash site before coming to Popp's aid. A brief inquiry was undertaken by Navy officials, during which the other six pilots who witnessed the mishap corroborated Popp's recollections of the tragic event.[23]

There was a tradition in the Navy that someone who successfully used a parachute in an emergency situation would reward the parachute rigger who packed it with either a box of cigars or bottle of whiskey. After being discharged from the dispensary, Popp met with parachute rigging shop's leading chief petty officer and the seaman second class who had packed Popp's parachute. Popp's parachute was the first one packed by the young seaman. Per the seaman's preference, Popp subsequently presented him with a box of cigars in grateful appreciation.[24]

The following October, Popp was officially inducted into Switlik Parachute Company's "Caterpillar Club" in recognition of his successful use of a parachute manufactured by them. In a letter dated 11 October 1944, Stanley Switlik presented Popp with a Caterpillar Club Membership Certificate and insignia.[25]

The high-performance Corsair was everything that Jimmy Nist had hoped for. After getting a taste of the Corsair and its capabilities, he was eager to get as much flight time as he could, but it was not enough for him. For the month of May, Nist flew 21 training flights for a total of 25.2 hours of flight time. Of this, 17 flights (20.6 hours) were flown in the Corsair with the remainder in SNJs.[26]

Apparently, Ensign Nist had been neglecting his spiritual training; 28 May was a Sunday, so Nist attended an Episcopal Communion Service at the base chapel. "It's the first time I've been to church in a long time," he informed his parents. "It will probably do me some good."[27]

The month of May was very busy for VF-84, despite the difficulties with the weather. Squadron pilots flew 1,384 flight hours that month. They also expended 3,688 rounds of .50-caliber machine gun ammunition. Unfortunately, the squadron lost one pilot and three aircraft in mishaps.[28]

On 2 June 1944, Ensign Nist broke two personal flight records. Nist went on a high-altitude training flight at the controls of FG-1A Corsair number 13979 and reached an altitude of 37,000 feet. That was about 15,000 feet higher than he had ever flown. None of the aircraft that he had flown previously was capable of reaching such a height. "Believe it or not, but at that height there was still clouds above us," he wrote to his parents later that day. "And then we were making our own clouds—some of the nicest vapor trails you ever saw." Nist also set a new personal speed record. Nist and his group did a dive from 37,000 feet and exceeded 450 knots, the first time that Nist had exceeded 400 knots.[29]

Ensign Nist had been with VF-84 for not quite a month but his enthusiasm was unabated. On 2 June, Nist wrote to his parents.

> What an outfit this is going to be! We've really got the talent! ... Most of the experienced pilots were in this 'Skull and Crossbones' squadron that is the talk of the Navy. The skipper says we have the making of the hottest bunch of fighters that ever hit the blue for Uncle Sam. About half the fellows have been out before and know the ropes. It all depends on us new boys to make it a hot outfit and we're doing our damnedest. I was mad 'cause I didn't go to sea in January but this was sure worth waiting for. I still can't get over how sweet the U [Corsair] is. Every day it seems nicer.[30]

Probably what prompted this glowing description of VF-84 was the squadron's newest pilot. "Who should join our ranks today but Lt.(j.g.) Ira 'Ike' Kepford, leading Navy flier with a score of sixteen," wrote Nist. Ira Cassius "Ike" Kepford was born 29 May 1919 in Harvey, Illinois, and later moved to Muskegon, Michigan. He played football at Muskegon High School and was captain of the undefeated team that won the state championship in 1937. After graduating from high school, Kepford enrolled in Northwestern University to study dentistry. He also played halfback and on defense for Northwestern's football team. In 1941, Kepford enrolled in the Civil Aeronautics Administration pilot program but was dismissed by the administrators before completing it. Expecting to be drafted into military service at some point, he enlisted in the Navy Reserve during halftime of Northwestern's final game of the 1941 season. The Navy recognized Kepford's potential and appointed him as an aviation cadet in April 1942. He earned his wings in November of that year. Ensign Kepford's first operational assignment was with LCDR Tommy Blackburn's VF-17 in the South Pacific theater. While flying combat air patrol on 11 November 1943 for three U.S. aircraft carriers attacking Rabaul, Kepford shot down four Japanese aircraft and damaged a fifth one. This action earned him one of his two Navy Crosses. During aerial combat in the South Pacific, Kepford achieved 16 aerial victories, making him the Navy's leading ace at the time.[31]

At NAS Corpus Christi, Ensign Nist was introduced to fighter tactics as part of his flight training, but then was trained in dive-bombing. Now that he was with a fighter squadron, he had to learn and master fighter tactics. In his 6 June 1944 letter to his parents, Nist described some of the fighter tactics that he was learning. Two aircraft made up a section with a section leader and a wingman. Two sections made up a division. He wrote:

> You see, in a fighter squadron, there are leaders and wing-men. The leaders do the fighting and the wingmen protect the leader and do all the dirty work. Naturally, the best job is a division leader (he leads four planes). That is strictly up to the experienced boys. Considering that there are 46 guys in the squadron, 19 of whom have seen action and practically all the rest are operationally trained in fighters, I used to think I'd be lucky to fly wing on the first team. (36 guys play the first team—the other 10 warm the bench). Well, tomorrow I get my crack at leading a section. I've been doing pretty sharp flying wing and I'm keeping my fingers crossed. If this boy can get section lead, he'll be a pretty happy character. Always knew I wasn't cut out to be a dive-bomber.[32]

In his 10 June 1944 letter to his parents, Ensign Nist offered some observations about his current squadron, VF-84, and his previous squadron, VB-303. "There's a big difference between VF-84 and VB-303 and it's the kind of difference that makes for a good outfit," he wrote. "We've got some guys who know what they're talking about now instead of a bunch of j.g.'s that were instructors at Corpus Christi. Here, everybody helps everybody else instead of trying to be a big shot." According to Nist, even the ensigns were free to criticize and comment on how the other pilots were flying, including the lieutenant commanders.[33]

In this same letter, Nist described what it was like to fly at high altitudes. "How cold is it seven miles up?" he wrote.

LT(jg) Ike Kepford (Naval History and Heritage Command [Photo 80-G-220348]/National Archives).

"Somewhere in the vicinity of 35 or 40 below zero. But it's nice and warm in a Corsair, even in shirt sleeves." With a closed canopy and a cockpit heater, the pilots were flying in coveralls to keep from overheating.[34]

By now, VF-84 had started aerial gunnery training using camera guns instead of live ammunition. These cameras were linked to the machine gun triggers so when the guns fired, the camera would record the results. To practice aerial gunnery, a pilot would tow a 30-foot-long banner as the target that the other aircraft would "shoot at." The tow cable stretched some 900 feet as a safety precaution for the tow aircraft. Another aircraft flew as escort to keep other aircraft from flying into the tow cable. When the training was finished, the pilot of the tow aircraft would release the tow cable so that he could safely land.[35]

The squadron pilots took turns flying the tow plane. On one of these training missions, Nist had a problem with the tow cable. "When I went to release the target and drop it so I could land, the damned release broke and I had to land with 900 feet of tow line and a thirty foot target on the end," Nist wrote to his parents. "But I got down without dragging the tow through anybody's back yard."[36]

Flying the Corsair was much more physically demanding than flying the SBD Dauntless. "She really treats you rough on gunnery runs," Nist wrote. "You dive down a couple of thousand feet and then pull out at about 325 knots and you feel like somebody is running a steam roller over you.... Pull-outs in an SBD were nothing but they are in these jobs."[37]

When his Corsair came due for its 60-hour check, Ensign Nist performed some of the maintenance work. "Of course, I don't know much about airplane engines but I helped change spark-plugs and fooled around a little," he informed his parents. "It runs a lot better with the new spark-plugs." The Corsair's Pratt & Whitney R-2800 Double Wasp engine had 36 spark plugs, so changing them was rather involved.[38]

On 13 June 1944, Air Group 84 participated in an amphibious assault training exercise on an uninhabited island about 50 miles off the coast of San Diego. Part of VF-84 would provide fighter escort for VB-84's Helldivers and VT-84's Avengers while the other part would conduct strafing runs preparatory for the amphibious landing. Ensign Nist would be one of the VF-84 Corsairs doing strafing runs. Another air group would perform the role of Japanese fighter defense. Targets had been erected ashore so the fighter would be using live ammunition and the bombers would be dropping real bombs.[39]

The amphibious training exercise proved to be a disappointment for the Air Group 84 aviators. Apparently, it was not even worth mentioning in the War Diaries for Air Group 84 and its three subordinate squadrons. "The fighters did okay but the dive-bombers were SNAFU," Ensign Nist informed his parents. "Didn't get a chance to do much shooting. Had 2400 rounds of .50 caliber ammunition aboard and brought about 2350 rounds back." One of the VF-84 Corsairs ran out of fuel returning from the training exercise. Both pilot and aircraft ended up in the Pacific Ocean. The pilot was rescued; the Corsair was not.[40]

The next day, Ensign Nist flew a total of 5.5 hours. "An hour in a Corsair is just as much work as two or three hours in an SBD," he wrote to his parents. "What makes it tough is that you're always tensing to keep from blacking out.... At three hundred and fifty knots, a sharp turn or a slight pull up is like breaking the light bulb in a haunted house at midnight."[41]

Fighting Squadron 84 was now using live ammunition for aerial gunnery training. The Corsair was armed with six .50-caliber machine guns, three in each wing, but they were only using two machine guns in training—one in each wing. "The first time up I didn't even touch the [target] sleeve as it takes a while to get used to converging fire," Nist wrote on 18 June 1944. "The second hop I came back with the top score of the day (not bad for an SBD pilot). There are usually six guys in a hop. Today I tied for second place."[42]

By month's end, VF-84 had reached its authorized strength of 51 officers and 16 enlisted sailors. The squadron also had its full complement of 36 FG-1 Corsairs. Squadron pilots had logged 2,649.5 flight hours, an increase of 1,265.5 hours over the previous month. They had also shot 112,144 rounds of .50-caliber machine gun ammunition and dropped 1,777 miniature practice bombs.[43]

Ensign Nist got considerably more flight time in June than the preceding month. In June, he logged 53.9 hours of flight time, nearly all of which was in FG-1 Corsairs. That brought his total flight time while in the Navy up to 608.3 hours.[44]

Romantic Troubles

Military service, especially during a time of war, places tremendous stresses upon relationships. This includes prolonged periods of physical separation, fears and worries about the service member's safety, and uncertainties about the future, to name just a few. Many a relationship has succumbed to the stresses of military service.

Not surprisingly, Ensign James Nist's wartime service had presented some difficulties with his engagement to Miss June Smith. During their engagement, Jimmy had been in Florida and California while June had been in New Jersey. They last had seen each other in January 1944 when Jimmy had come home on leave. Then on Monday, 12 June 1944, Jimmy Nist got the official notification that he had been expecting. On that day, he received a letter from June confirming that she had decided to call off their engagement. That same day, he also received a very sympathetic letter from June's mother. Mrs. Smith held Jimmy in high regard and was saddened by the wedding being called off.[45]

Jimmy Nist handled the news of the ending of his engagement with June well, all things considered. In his 12 June 1944 letter to his parents, he wrote:

> I can't exactly say I'm happy about the whole affair, but it was a little easier to take seeing as we hadn't seen each other in about five months. I suppose the usual thing to do is to get mad, but that's one of those things that have to be two-way—they don't work otherwise. The break is what you might call irreparable and it's all over. However, in spite of what happened, she's still one swell girl and she'll always be tops with me.... It's a pretty hard thing to explain in a letter and perhaps it all turned out for the best anyway. Time will tell. Please don't hold anything against Smitty—I don't—she's playing it square like she should.[46]

With the engagement officially terminated, there was the matter of the engagement ring. Jimmy addressed this situation in his 12 June 1944 letter to his parents. "You'll be getting the ring back in a few days I guess," he wrote. "I'll have her send it to you. I won't want it out here. I've already got my F4U to take care of me and she doesn't want a ring." Jimmy's parents finally got the engagement ring and the set of Jimmy's naval aviator wings from June in August.[47]

Jimmy would later come to find out the primary reason she called off the engagement. June had met and fallen in love with another pilot, a lieutenant in the Civil Air Patrol. June and the Army flyboy were married after a very short engagement. Even with that startling news, Jimmy was still not angry with her. Her ending their engagement enabled him to develop a romance with his new friend, Alice Richards.[48]

Moving On

A few weeks back, Jimmy Nist had met the ex-fiancée of Ensign J.A. McChesney in San Francisco and spent some time with her. She must have made quite an impression on him because not only had he kept in contact with her, but he had also named his Corsair "Little Miss Butch" in her honor. In his 14 June 1944 letter to his parents, he described Alice Richards as "a pretty nice girl." Apparently, he had made quite an impression on her, too, because Alice was coming down to San Diego for part of her vacation.[49]

By the end of the month, Jimmy Nist was clearly moving on after the end of his engagement. On 25 June, he wrote to his parents about Alice Richards's upcoming visit:

> Well, in a couple of weeks, Little Miss Butch will be down. Guess she's going to stay a week, so I'd better lay up a good supply of sleep. I'd rather be up in San Francisco, though. There's nothing to do down here at all, unless that squadron party hits the right day.

What Jimmy was referring to was a squadron party that was being planned.[50]

July 1944 Begins

When July 1944 began, the leadership of VF-84 was in the midst of reorganizing its tactical arrangements. "The squadron has just been reorganized on the basis of performance," wrote Ensign Nist to his parents. "Our division (four planes) was so good we didn't need reorganizing."[51]

The nation celebrated the 168th anniversary of its independence on 4 July 1944. Ensign Nist went to a fireworks display that night. "It was supposed to be the best display in the country. Guess it was, too," he wrote to his parents. That same night, Ensign Nist started night flying. The moon was nearly full and the sky was clear. "Night flying is beautiful until it comes time to land," Nist informed his parents.[52]

The next day, VF-84 pilots began using all six of the Corsair's .50-caliber machine guns. Ensign Nist flew five hours of gunnery training. During his morning hop, Nist shot the target tow rope—the first time he'd done that since NAS Corpus Christi. "Of course, hitting a quarter inch tow row is just luck, but that's the middle of the sleeve and that's where we're aiming," Nist wrote to his parents. Another pilot shot the tow rope on Nist's afternoon hop.[53]

North to Mira Loma

In early July 1944, Air Group Nine was stationed at NAS Pasco near Seattle, Washington, and was entering the final stage of their preparations for deployment back to the Pacific theater. The air group had previously served aboard *Essex* for combat operations in 1943–44. As part of their preparations, the air group relocated to NAS San Diego.

The relocation of Air Group Nine had a major but temporary impact upon Air Group 84. To make room for AG-9 at NAS San Diego, AG-84 was temporarily relocated to Mira Loma Army Air Field in Oxnard, California—about 60 miles north of Los Angeles. The Navy was in the process of acquiring the airfield from the Army Air Force. AG-84 found out about the move on Friday, 7 July, and moved there on the morning of Monday, 10 July. Due to the short notice of the move and its limited duration, VF-84 could take only a limited amount of its squadron and personal gear.

The living accommodations at Mira Loma were sufficient but the aircraft maintenance facilities were not. "We're stuck at a little air strip—one runway—with hardly any facilities to see how good we are at making out alone," Nist observed in a letter to his parents. Years later, LT(jg) Popp wrote in his memoirs, "Bunk room, community showers, lousy beds and the lack of privacy i.e., snorers galore, made life less than pleasant." The VF-84 pilots also found Oxnard devoid of liberty opportunities. "There is nothing at all to do up in this neck of the woods," he complained in his 17 July 1944 letter to his parents. "Such a town I never saw in all my life."[54]

The arrival of AG-84 at Oxnard was quite startling for the 8,500 or so residents of the small town. Previously, the USAAF had been using Stearman biplanes with 250-horsepower engines at the airfield. Now, AG-84 brought in some of the Navy's premier warbirds with high-performance engines. VF-84's pilots enjoyed flying their high-performance Corsairs at very low altitudes over the town. Such were the VF-84's antics that the head of the local hospital complained about them to squadron commander LCDR Hedrick, who put an immediate stop to them.[55]

This sudden and unexpected move to Mira Loma caused major complications for Ensign Nist's social life. "Well the moving fouled things up in general," Nist wrote to his parents after arriving at Mira Loma. "Things are not only SNAFU, but TARFU (Things are really fouled up) and FUBAR (Fouled up beyond all recognition)." First, the move forced the postponement of the much-anticipated squadron party. Worse, the move occurred right after Alice Richards's arrival in San Diego. Alice had come down from San Francisco with a friend whose fiancé was a patient at the naval hospital in San Diego. "Alice arrived Saturday afternoon and we were all set for a week of fun and here I be 200 miles from Diego," he lamented to his parents.[56]

Jimmy Nist tried to make the best of a bad situation. Fortunately, he had liberty from Saturday afternoon until 0900 Monday morning. "The time sure went quick though," he wrote to Martin and Ethel. "We had a swell time while it lasted. It just didn't last long enough." He tried to find a place for Alice and her friend to stay near Mira Loma AAF so that they could come visit him on their way back to San Francisco but was unsuccessful. So Alice and her friend decided to stay in San Diego and try to meet up with Jimmy in Los Angeles on the following Saturday afternoon.[57]

Jimmy met up with Alice in Los Angeles on Saturday, 15 July. He got liberty early Saturday afternoon and they went out that night. They began the evening with dinner at the famous Brown Derby restaurant in Hollywood. Jimmy was less than impressed with the place, saying it "wasn't too sharp except the price." Afterward they went over to The Tropics cocktail lounge and restaurant. The night had to end early because nightspots had to close at midnight.[58]

Then on Sunday morning, Jimmy did something that was surprising for an Episcopalian Protestant Christian. He went with Alice to a Roman Catholic church for Catholic Mass. This was his first time attending Mass. "She said I did pretty good—only made a few mistakes that were to be expected," he reported to his parents. They spent the rest of the day together and he saw her off at the train station at 1830 for her return trip to San Francisco.[59]

Back to NAS San Diego

VF-84's temporary exile to Mira Loma ended on Wednesday, 19 July 1944. That morning, the squadron flew back home to NAS San Diego. After returning, Nist wrote to his parents, "I must say I was sure glad to see this place again." On the way out of Mira Loma, LT "Ike" Kepford broke up his flight and led them in buzzing Oxnard. Then they did a simulated strafing run on Mira Loma's control tower at an altitude of only 50 feet. Since the tower was only 40 feet high, Kepford's Corsairs cleared it by only 10 feet or so.[60]

The VF-84 pilots had been authorized to have names painted on their aircraft. Jimmy Nist was the first to do so. He had been calling his Corsair "Little Miss Butch," in honor of Alice. He made it official by having the name painted on the side of his Corsair. Soon other names started appearing on the sides of the squadron's Corsairs, including "Emmy Jane," "Baby" and "Bronx Express."[61]

On 27 July 1944, Jimmy Nist wrote to his older sister Margaret, a.k.a. "Wootz," and updated her on his blossoming relationship with Miss Richards. He wrote:

> She is really a swell girl. Told Mom and Dad as much and will probably hear something about it but I don't care. She's a lot too nice to forget about—nicer by far than somebody else I used to think wasn't bad. Too bad she's in California or I'd show you just what a nice one I'd found.[62]

Jimmy's engagement with Miss June Smith had been steadily in decline for quite some time before June made it official in June. Miss Alice Richards entered into the picture around the time Jimmy was coming to that realization. By mid–July, Jimmy's romantic orientation was solidly toward Alice and June was rapidly fading into the past. "Smitty don't know what a favor she did me," he informed his parents, referring to her calling off the engagement. Martin and Ethel had some concerns about his getting romantically involved so soon after his engagement ended but he brushed them off.[63]

Around the last week of July, VF-84 got some ominous news. Under authority of the Chief of Naval Operations, ADM Ernest J. King, VF-84 would be exchanging its Corsairs for F6F Hellcats sometime in August. Manufactured by Grumman Aircraft, the Hellcat was the second fighter of its famed "Cat" series. It was the first American fighter that could outperform the vaunted Japanese A6M Zero fighter. Like the Corsair, it was armed with six .50-caliber machine guns mounted in the wings. With a maximum speed of 391 miles per hour, the Hellcat was slower than the Corsair but better suited for carrier operations. "Haven't got anything against the F6F not having flown it, but it will really have to be a good plane to even come close to 'Little Miss Butch I,'" Nist wrote to his parents. Then to his sister "Wootz," he wrote, "Have never flown one [Hellcat] but the guys who have flown them both think the Corsair is much nicer."[64]

Tragedy struck VF-84 on Sunday, 23 July 1944, while it performed attack tactics training over the Pacific Ocean. About 10 miles offshore and at an altitude of 10,000 feet, the Corsairs piloted by LT(jg) William P. Meek and Ensign Archie L. Beene collided. Both aircraft plummeted into the ocean and both pilots were killed. "They were both pretty good boys, too," Ensign Nist lamented. Accordingly, the squadron party scheduled for that night was canceled. Three days later, memorial services were held for the two pilots.[65]

During the month of July, VF-84 pilots logged 2,117.25 hours of flight time, expended 90,261 rounds of .50-caliber machine gun ammunition and dropped 960 miniature practice bombs.

The squadron temporarily relocated to Mira Loma AAF for 10 days and, while there, conducted field carrier landings. They had started training to employ the Corsair as dive-bombers. "It's a pretty good dive-bomber, too," wrote the former dive-bomber pilot Ensign Nist. Ensign Nist logged 33.1 hours of flight time in the month of July 1944—nearly all of which was flown in FG-1 Corsairs.[66]

August 1944: Changes in the Southern California Winds

August 1944 was a month of major changes for Fighting 84. The squadron switched from Corsairs to Hellcats. This transition caused some administrative and operational difficulties as the pilots had to adjust to the new aircraft types. This set back the squadron's training. To make up for it, the pilots worked longer hours to be ready for deployment. VF-84 also underwent an organizational change from a 36-aircraft squadron to a 54-aircraft squadron.[67]

VF-84's switch from the FG-1 Corsair to the Grumman F6F Hellcat began during the second week of August 1944. Both Air Group 84 and Fighting 84 leadership opposed this switch to the Hellcats. "This command has urgently pleaded that this be reconsidered and the F4U be retained, fairly believing it to be superior to the F6F," wrote CDR George Ottinger in the air group War Diary for July 1944. "This was a very great disappointment to the pilots as all were unanimous in their opinion that the F4U was the finest military fighter plane in operation today," recorded the Squadron History. "The fellows have been griping about getting them ever since we definitely found out that we were going to get them," Ensign Nist informed his parents in a 12 August 1944 letter.[68]

Ensign Nist flew an F6F-3 Hellcat for the first time on 11 August 1944. "Had one of them up last night for the first time and they weren't bad at all," he wrote to his parents. "They are slower than the Corsair but definitely not as hot or tricky." A week later, Nist wrote again about the Hellcat: "It's a pretty nice airplane. But it just doesn't stack up to a Corsair for stunting, climbing or just plain going like hell in a straight line."[69]

Early on the morning of 18 August, Air Group 84 conducted a simulated air attack on an aircraft carrier. VF-84 Hellcats escorted VT-84 Avengers and VB-84 Helldivers against the carrier, which was defended by its own Hellcats. With both the attackers and the defenders flying Hellcats, there was a great deal of confusion in the air. "We were weaving with their planes instead of our own and making runs on our own instead of them," Nist wrote afterward. "They were having trouble too, but their main target was the bombers."[70]

Around the middle of August, VF-84 celebrated the wedding of LT(jg) R. Elmer "Dusty" Miller, Jr., and his fiancé, Lois Evelyn. A short wedding ceremony was held

F6F Hellcat (Naval History and Heritage Command [Photo 80-G-K-605]/National Archives).

for "Dusty" and Lois at the naval air station chapel. Nist assisted with the wedding. This was followed by a steak dinner at the officers' club and a celebratory bottle of champagne. "The whole squadron was at the O-Club so the champagne was spread pretty thin," wrote Nist to his parents afterward. The newly married pilot was one of "Shorty" Nist's roommates and closest friends in Fighting 84.[71]

On 22 August, VF-84 changed from a 36-aircraft fighter squadron to a 54-aircraft fighter-bomber squadron. To do so, an 18-aircraft fighter-bomber unit and 27 pilots were added. Due to a shortage of Hellcats, this unit had FM-2 Wildcats. Originally, the fighter-bomber unit would conduct bombing. However, it was soon decided to train all VF-84 pilots in fighter and bomber tactics so that every pilot could perform in both roles.[72]

In his 23 August 1944 letter to his parents, Ensign Nist described conditions in the cockpit when they were flying their training missions here in Southern California. "You don't know the meaning of the word [hot] until you've flown in it," wrote Nist. At 37,000 feet, the outside temperature was -40 degrees Fahrenheit. Yet, the engines of the Corsairs and Hellcats generated enough heat to keep the pilots warm, even in shirtsleeves. However, what was a blessing at 37,000 feet was a curse at 3,000 feet when the temperature was 85 to 90 degrees. "We have to be completely covered, even to gloves as fire protection and the sweat just trickles all the time," Nist wrote.[73]

Another of Ensign Nist's roommates was the squadron gunnery officer. The roommate was dating a Navy nurse named Ensign Isabel Stout from Belvidere, New Jersey. She had never been in an airplane before. Since her boyfriend was not a pilot, Ensign Nist took her up in an SNJ on Sunday, 27 August 1944. "She wouldn't let me try any fancy stuff," Nist later wrote to his parents. "Tried two wing-overs and she told me to stop because 'she was afraid she'd fall out.'"[74]

Due to the changes in both organization and aircraft types, VF-84 looked very different at the end of August than it did at the beginning of the month. At month's end, VF-84 consisted of 75 officers and 28 enlisted sailors. As a result of these changes, VF-84 had nine F6F-5 Hellcats, 15 F6F-3 Hellcats, 18 FM-2 Wildcats and 15 FG-1 Corsairs at month's end.[75]

Despite the organizational and aircraft changes, VF-84 still was able to complete a great deal of flight training. During August, squadron pilots flew 3,076.5 hours, including 86.5 hours at night. They also expended 194,406 rounds of .50-caliber machine gun ammunition and 184 miniature bombs. For his part, Ensign Nist logged a total of 56.6 flight hours—31.3 hours in FG-1 Corsairs, 2.7 hours in SNJs, 4.2 hours in F6F-3 Hellcats and 18.4 hours in F6F-5 Hellcats.[76]

Back to Corsairs

Just as Ensign Nist and the other Fighting 84 pilots were getting used to the Hellcats, the chief of naval operations switched VF-84 back to Corsairs on 31 August 1944. The following day, Ensign Nist shared the good news with his parents:

> I was flying when the news arrived. The Commander walked in the ready room and told the boys who weren't flying. Silence for about ten seconds and then all hell broke loose. They met us on the line when we got back. Gene (my roommate) was on my wing and told me before I even had a chance to cut my engine.[77]

The effect on squadron morale was tremendous. Nist wrote to his parents:

> The old swagger is back, the chip rides our shoulder once again and the outfit is twice as cocky as it ever was. They just couldn't keep a fighting outfit down. We were a pretty sorry bunch when we lost them and weren't half the squadron with Hellcats. Our morale was all gone. But if you never saw a sharp bunch of boys, you'd like our outfit now. Man, they're so crazy now there's no holding them.

That night VF-84 held a huge celebration at the Hotel Del Coronado to celebrate getting their Corsairs back. "Nobody liked the F6Fs and didn't care who knew it," Nist wrote.[78]

VF-84 continued its preparations and training for war throughout the fall, growing in personnel and aircraft strength and developing into a lethal aerial fighting force. The squadron exchanged its Hellcats for Corsairs. The squadron also received three F6F-3P photographic aerial reconnaissance versions of the Hellcat fighter and three Chance-Vought F4U-1C Corsairs. The latter were armed with four 20 mm cannons instead of six .50-caliber machine guns.[79]

In September 1944, Fighting 84 picked up several pilots from Bombing 84. These included LT Willis G. Laney, a recipient of the Distinguished Flying Cross. He and LT Caleb Kendall had previously served with Bombing Six (VB-6) aboard the aircraft carriers USS *Enterprise* (CV-6) and USS *Intrepid* (CV-11). LT(jg) William L. Gerner and LT(jg) Ralph K. Coconougher had served with Bombing 17 (VB-17) during USS *Bunker Hill*'s (CV-17) 1943–44 operations in the Pacific.[80]

Ensigns "Dusty" Miller, Jimmy Nist and Gene Powell and an unidentified lieutenant with dates at VF-84 squadron party in August 1944 (Dickerson Family Photograph).

The latter part of September was rough on VF-84 aircraft. Several days of difficult crosswinds caused a number of mishaps. Two pilots flipped their Corsairs and demolished them. Another pilot caused significant but repairable damage to his aircraft. Three pilots damaged wings or flaps by dragging them on the ground. Fortunately, there were only two minor injuries. Nist missed most of this by being up in San Francisco on leave.[81]

In the month of September, VF-84 added to its personnel strength and reached a complement of 83 officers and 29 enlisted sailors. The squadron also had acquired a unique mixture of aircraft. At month's end, VF-84 had 18 Chance-Vought F4U-1D Corsairs, two Chance-Vought F4U-1 Corsairs, three Chance-Vought F4U-1C Corsairs, 16 Goodyear FG-1 Corsairs, four Goodyear FG-1A Corsairs and two Grumman F6F-3P photo Hellcats. Squadron pilots logged 2,200.2 hours of flight time, including 22 hours of night flying. They fired 103,934 rounds of .50-caliber machine gun ammunition and 5,840 rounds of 20 mm cannon ammunition. During September, Ensign Nist logged 25.6 hours of flight time, of which 7.8 hours were flown in F6F Hellcats, 15.2 hours were flown in FG-1 Corsairs and 2.6 hours were flown in F4U Corsairs. In doing so, Nist ran his total Navy flight time to 723.6 hours.[82]

Wedding Banns

In late September, Jimmy took a few days leave and went up to see Alice in San Francisco. Hitching a ride on a bomber, he made it up there in two and a half hours. When Alice was working, Jimmy met her for lunch and wandered around the city.

While he was there, Jimmy proposed marriage to Miss Alice Richards and she accepted. He did not recycle the engagement ring that he had given to Miss June Smith. Jimmy presented Alice with a ring made of palladium. On each side of the ring there was a small diamond baguette.

"Naturally I met all the Richards family and they're all swell," he wrote to his parents. "Her grand-dad is an old ex-chief in the Navy and he's quite a guy." On Sunday afternoon, Alice's parents held an open house at their home to celebrate the engagement. Someone had made up matchbooks for the occasion that declared "Alice Jimmy It's A Match." The engagement was not a surprise for Jimmy's parents back in New Jersey. In fact, they were expecting him to tell them that he had gotten married.[83]

The Richards family lived on 28th Avenue in San Francisco in the Sunset District of the city. Her mom, Alice Susan Richards, was born on 23 May 1902. Her father, Bertram Aloysius Richards, was born on 4 June 1895. Her father was a veteran of World War I. At the time, he was working as an assistant chief clerk for the Southern Pacific Railroad in San Francisco. Bertram and Alice Richards had four daughters (Alice, Patricia, Mary and Susan) and three sons (Charles, Joseph and George). The Catholic faith was very important in the Richards family. They were parishioners of Saint Anne's Church on Judah Street, where Bertram had been a parishioner since 1904. Alice's aunt Mary (her father's sister) was a religious sister of the Sisters of the Holy Family. Alice's uncle Vincent (her father's brother) was a priest.[84]

The engagement of Alice and Jimmy presented several issues that needed to be resolved. First, Jimmy and Alice had decided not to get married right away. With Jimmy preparing for a combat deployment in the near future, they decided to hold off getting married until either the Japanese surrendered or Jimmy returned from his deployment. Second was the issue of employment and residence. Jimmy was hoping to continue in the Navy after the war's conclusion. However, he recognized that a lot of others had the same idea and the Navy couldn't keep everyone in service after the war. "She's got a pretty good job and she might as well keep it," Jimmy informed his parents. From his 29 September 1944 letter, it appeared that Jimmy was planning on relocating to the San Francisco area if the Navy discharged him.[85]

Alice and Jimmy also resolved another major issue confronting their planned marital union. Alice was a Roman Catholic and Jimmy was an Episcopalian. Jimmy had discussed this issue with his parents at some point previously. "Always did think Catholics had something Protestants didn't anyway," he wrote to Martin and Ethel in his 29 September letter. "So sometime in the future, probably before I go out, I'm turning Catholic."[86]

Squadron Training in October 1944

Around the beginning of October, the VF-84 leadership did some reorganizing of the squadron. Ensign Nist was temporarily promoted to section leader. This occurred because his previous division leader and section leader each got promoted to be flight leaders leading eight aircraft.[87]

On Wednesday, 11 October 1944, Ensign Nist went up in a Dauntless dive-bomber for the first time since joining VF-84. "It sure felt funny to be crawling along at 130 knots," he wrote to his parents. "What a difference between that and taking off in a Corsair."[88]

A presidential election was being held in 1944. President Franklin Delano Roosevelt was running for an unprecedented fourth term. Many Democratic Party officials were concerned about the president's declining health and were opposed to his current vice president, Henry Wallace, due to his strong leftward leanings. Senator Harry S. Truman of Missouri was chosen at the party convention to run with Roosevelt as his vice presidential candidate. The Republicans chose two governors as their candidates: Thomas E. Dewey from New York for president and John W. Bricker from Ohio for vice president.

The Nist Family was traditional Democratic and Martin Nist was active in local politics. Jimmy Nist, however, was very outspoken in his dislike for Roosevelt. Jimmy did not like Thomas Dewey much either but decided he was better than FDR. "Dewey made a big mistake in blaming him for not preparing for war though," Nist wrote back in late September. "I hate to think what would have happened if some joker like Landon or Hoover had been in there." Jimmy voted via absentee ballot on 10 October 1944. For president, he voted for Dewey/Bricker, though he was realistic about the New York governor's chances for election. "Guess Dewey needs all the votes he can get in Jersey," Jimmy wrote to his parents afterward. "He sure won't take California. Too many shipyards and airplane factories." During the general election in New Jersey, an election was being held to fill the unexpired term of Senator W. Warren Barbour, who died in office. Republican H. Alexander Smith was running against Democrat Elmer H. Wene. Jimmy voted for Smith for U.S. Senate. For local offices, he voted for George Matthews for Howell Township Committee and Joseph Dilatush for tax collector."[89]

In October 1944, VF-84 rotated three groups of pilots through Naval Auxiliary Air Station Twenty-Nine Palms out in the Mojave Desert for rocket training. "Living accommodations were very comfortable and pleasant and, except for the distance to the nearest liberty towns, little was left to be desired," recorded the Squadron History. "From the standpoint of training, Fighting Squadron EIGHTY-FOUR broke all existing rocket records at Twenty-Nine Palms." Rocket training had to be discontinued on 7 November when heavy rains flooded out the airfield.[90]

Ensign Nist was part of the first group rotated out to Twenty-Nine Palms. They arrived there on or about Sunday, 15 October 1944. "We were the guinea pigs and the whole arrangement turned out pretty good," he wrote to his parents on 21 October. "We're having fun roughing it out here." After returning to NAS San Diego on 24 October, Jimmy wrote to his parents, "We had a pretty good time in Twenty-Nine

Palms. They sure kept us busy out at the desert, though. Three and four flights a day." He flew 18 training flights for a total flight time of 12.3 hours with each flight lasting less than an hour.[91]

Just as the month of October ended, VF-84 lost another pilot. On 30 October, ENS Robert M. South crashed near San Clemente Island.[92]

October 1944 was a very busy month for Fighting Squadron 84 and for Ensign Nist in particular. He logged 50.7 hours of flight time. This brought his total Navy flight time to 774.3 hours.[93]

November 1944: Alice Visits Jimmy and Jimmy Visits Takanis Bay

Alice Richards, the future Mrs. James A. Nist, came down to visit her fiancé in San Diego on the night of 3 November 1944. The timing was perfect because Jimmy and Alice were able to spend over a week together right before he went out to sea for carrier qualifications. They went dancing and played miniature golf. About the former, Alice later wrote to Jimmy's mother, "My goodness, I just about have to drag Jimmy on the dance floor but once he's there he is swell." They visited with her younger brother who was training with the Marines in San Diego. On Monday, 6 November, Jimmy and Alice went south of the border and visited Mexico. "There wasn't much too it, but at least I can say I've been there," he wrote to his parents on 12 November. "Seemed crazy to spend six plus months eighteen miles from Mexico and not go." In her 21 November 1944 letter to her future mother-in-law, Alice wrote that she and Jimmy had "loads of fun" in Mexico.[94]

On Saturday night, 11 November, Air Group 84 held a huge party in which members of all three squadrons participated. "I met the skipper and the Executive Officer along with the other fellows in the squadron," Alice wrote to Jimmy's mother on 21 November 1944. "We had a grand time and the fellows are swell."[95]

Then their time together had to come to an end. On Sunday, 12 November, Alice took Jimmy to Catholic Mass. "I certainly had a wonderful time there and sure hated to come home," she wrote to Ethel Nist on 21 November. "The time went all too quickly for us." Then she boarded the 1030 bus for her journey home to San Francisco. Jimmy was looking forward to his postdeployment leave so he could bring Alice back east to meet everyone.[96]

A week after returning to San Francisco, Alice sent a letter to Jimmy's mother describing their recent time together and their engagement. "I have a very lovely ring and am very proud of it," she wrote to Ethel. "It has a solitaire and two baguettes on the side." She also wrote about their engagement party. "When Jimmy was here last time [in San Francisco] we had a party and announced our engagement," she wrote. "Everyone thought Jimmy was just tops and I certainly agreed with them. We have such fun together doing just little things and we're really happy together." She also told Ethel of her wanting to meet Jimmy's family. "I'm sure looking forward to the day when I can meet you and hope it won't be too long a wait," she wrote.[97]

Just five days after ENS Robert South's crash on San Clemente Island, VF-84 lost another pilot to a flying mishap. On 4 November, ENS Oscar W. Hickey, USNR, was killed during a night familiarization flight off NAS North Island.[98]

The 1944 General Election occurred on Tuesday, 7 November. Not surprisingly, Roosevelt defeated Dewey with 432 electoral votes to 99 electoral votes. In the popular vote, Roosevelt won with 25,612,916 votes (53.39 percent) to Dewey's 22,017,929 votes (45.89 percent). Dewey won only 12 states with Roosevelt winning every other state, including New York and New Jersey. In New Jersey, Roosevelt received 987,874 votes (50.31 percent) and Dewey received 961,335 votes (48.95 percent). Among military voters like Ensign Nist who were voting via absentee ballot, Roosevelt outpolled Dewey 95,581 votes to 64,748 votes. In Monmouth County, Dewey defeated Roosevelt, earning 49,349 votes to 34,720 votes. In the special election for U.S. Senate, Republican H. Alexander Smith defeated Democrat Elmer H. Wene 940,051 votes (50.44%) to 910,0096 votes (48.84%). This was a gain for the Republican Party as the Senate seat was previously held by a Democrat.[99]

As one would expect, Jimmy Nist had something to say about the election results. Though Dewey lost, Nist did take some consolation in Smith defeating Wene for U.S. Senate. After the election, Jimmy wrote to Martin and Ethel:

> Well, for a while I thought New Jersey was going to be one of the few states to get the straight word, but I see in the end, they went the way of all flesh. Was bragging to everybody that Jersey would never go for Roosevelt and they let me down…. Dewey could have won if he'd cared to come out against the Old Guard G.O.P. on foreign policy instead of sitting on the fence with a lot of double-talk. He wouldn't commit himself on anything.[100]

That same month, VF-84 was issued the night fighter version of the F6F Hellcat. F6F-3E was the standard Hellcat equipped with AN/APS-4 radar equipment. Radar equipment was carried in a pod that was mounted on the outer leading edge of the starboard wing. Ensign Nist got a chance to fly the night-fighting Hellcat for nearly an hour on the night of 9 November. "It's pretty good stuff, but here's one boy who'll stick to flying in the daytime and trust his eyes rather than a bunch of instruments," he wrote to his parents a couple of weeks later.[101]

VF-84 added another member to its roster in November. The squadron adopted a pedigreed cocker spaniel puppy. At present, he was 8" long and coal black in color. Accordingly, they named him "Blackout." The puppy was issued an identification tag, a serial number (000–00–0 ½), an official health record and the rank of ensign (junior grade).[102]

In mid–November, Air Group 84 squadrons embarked on the escort carrier USS *Takanis Bay* (CVE-89) for carrier qualifications. *Takanis Bay* was constructed by the Kaiser Shipbuilding Company in Vancouver, Washington, and placed in commission on 15 April 1944. She had a length of 512' 3", a beam of 65' 2", a draft of 22' 6" and displaced 9,570 tons. She could operate 28 aircraft. She spent the war training carrier pilots out of San Diego. From 14–20 November 1944, Torpedo Squadron 84 and Bombing Squadron 84 conducted their qualifications aboard *Takanis Bay*. From 20 to 25 November, a group of VF-84 pilots conducted carrier qualifications aboard *Takanis Bay* and successfully completed 187 landings.[103]

While VB-84 and VT-84 were doing their carrier qualifications aboard ship, VF-84 was still practicing ashore. On 18 November, VF-84 went out to one of NAS

San Diego's outlying fields to practice landing on a mock-up of an aircraft carrier. A wooden platform had been constructed about the size of a carrier flight deck. A cable was strung across the deck for the aircraft's tail hook to catch just like the arrestor cables aboard ship. "We made four landings a piece," Nist wrote to his parents. "It was fun after the first one. Sure is different than landing an SNJ aboard the Wolverine in Lake Michigan."[104]

Before embarking aboard *Takanis Bay* for carrier qualifications, VF-84 and VB-84 performed a public air show over San Diego as part of the kickoff for the Sixth War Loan Drive. Forty VF-84 fighters and 18 VB-84 dive-bombers participated. First VF-84 fighters flew a large V of divisions. Next, 20 fighters performed a weave maneuver over the rest of the fighters and dive-bombers. After that, all of the fighters flew over in a column of Vs. Then, the squadron broke into four-plane divisions and buzzed the city. In a letter written later that day, Ensign Nist described this aspect of the air show to his parents:

> Some boys claim they were low enough to read the menu in the El Cortez Hotel. Ike [Kepford] claims he got a girl's name and address, and other stories. I won't lie like that, but I was looking up [emphasis in original] to see the top of the Post Office when we went by.

The air show ended with LCDR Roger Hedrick leading a 16-plane tail chase over the city that did not include Nist. "Some fun we had!" Nist reported.[105]

Ensign Nist had previously qualified for carrier operations aboard *Wolverine*, a Great Lakes sidewheel steamer that had been converted to a training aircraft carrier. While *Takanis Bay* was nearly the same size as *Wolverine*, Nist would be flying a high-performance fighter plane instead of a low-speed SNJ trainer plane.

Weather conditions conspired against VF-84 in their carrier qualifications. For the first couple of days, there was insufficient wind for carrier operations. When flight operations commenced, Ensign Nist was able to make four landings without a single wave-off. A "wave-off" occurred when the carrier's landing signal officer determined that an incoming pilot was not going to safely land aboard the carrier and directed him to abort the landing and go around to make another attempt. Fighting Squadron 84 accomplished 200 successful landings with only one minor mishap. Fighting Squadron 12 was qualifying aboard a full-size aircraft carrier, USS *Ranger* (CV-4), at the same time. In contrast, they had four major mishaps with their F6F Hellcats. One Hellcat nosed over after landing and three slammed into the crash barrier.[106]

VF-84's attempts at carrier qualifications had major significance beyond the squadron's readiness for deployment. "We were being watched," Nist reported to his parents afterward. "A few of the big boys still think Corsairs are not for carriers and are watching us for a chance to give us Hellcats again. But we showed them."[107]

On their third day at sea, a major storm hit. At first the storm hindered air operations, but then air operations had to be canceled on Friday, 24 November. "Rolls of 25 degrees were noted and winds of 38 knots velocity (true winds) were recorded," stated *Takanis Bay*'s War Diary. As a result of the heavy seas, the deck and after bulkhead in the number two clipping room on the port side forward buckled. One sailor was injured.[108]

Thanksgiving Day was 23 November and VF-84 celebrated the holiday aboard *Takanis Bay* with the ship's company. The event was memorable but not for good reasons. First, the ship's officers ate before VF-84's officers, and because of that, there was no turkey left when the latter reported for chow. So they had to settle for baked ham. Second, storm conditions made eating very difficult. As Ensign Nist would later describe to his parents, "we had to hang on with one hand and eat with the other. The soup was all over the table and you couldn't put your coffee down or that would have gone too."[109]

The storm intensified throughout the day and night. Ensign Nist described conditions aboard ship in his 26 November 1944 letter to his parents. "We had quite a night that night with chairs, ash-stands and everything sliding all over the cabin," he wrote. "It broke all the dishes (not all, but a lot anyway) in the galley." Unfortunately, Ensign (junior grade) Blackout seemed to get the worst of the storm. He was sleeping with one of the pilots in a top bunk. When the ship rolled, he fell out and onto the steel deck, suffering some bleeding to his mouth.[110]

Due to the terrible sea conditions, *Takanis Bay* returned to NAS San Diego. Some of VF-84's pilots were able to fly off the escort carrier on 25 November. Ensign Nist and the remainder of the squadron's personnel disembarked the next morning when she tied to the pier at NAS San Diego.[111]

Upon his return to NAS San Diego, Jimmy Nist experienced Christmas a month early. Several Christmas packages from his family back east were waiting for him when he got back. It was unofficial squadron policy that edible gifts from home were to be shared among the rest of the squadron. "The fruit cake didn't last long in the ready room," Nist informed his parents. "I've been eating up everybody else's Christmas."[112]

Fighting 84 did not remain on shore for long. The very next day, all three Air Group 84 squadrons went aboard the carrier USS *Ranger* (CV-4) for carrier qualifications and air group operations. Commissioned on 4 June 1934, *Ranger* was America's first aircraft carrier built from the keel up as an aircraft carrier and not a conversion from another ship type. In the first year of America's involvement in World War II, *Ranger* operated in the Atlantic Ocean and supported the Allied invasion of North Africa in November 1942. Transferring to the Pacific in 1944, *Ranger* trained carrier pilots off the West Coast of California. *Ranger* had a length of 769,' a beam of 81' 8", a draft of 19' and a displacement of 14,500 tons.[113]

Ensign Nist performed seven successful landings aboard *Ranger*: one on 28 November, five on 29 November and one on 2 December. That gave him a total of 19 carrier landings aboard *Wolverine*, *Takanis Bay* and *Ranger*. "After landing the Corsair aboard, I'm more convinced than ever that it's the sweetest hunk of airplane ever designed," Nist wrote to his parents on 3 December. For the month of November, Nist had flown 24.9 hours, all but 2.8 hours of which were flown in either F4Us or FG-1s. He also flew in an F6F-3E Hellcat and an SNJ. This gave him a total Navy flight time of just under 800 flight hours.[114]

While aboard, VF-84 broke three of *Ranger*'s records. On 28 November, the flight led by LT(jg) Ira Cassius "Ike" Kepford performed 56 landings in one hour, setting a new record for most landings aboard *Ranger* in a single hour. The next day, the squadron set a new record for most landings (312) in a single day. Lastly, the

USS *Ranger* (CV-4) underway in 1942 in Hampton Roads, Virginia (Naval History and Heritage Command [Photo 80-G-10786]/National Archives).

squadron set a new record for the most landings without a carrier landing accident: 698. Altogether, VF-84 pilots performed 710 landings aboard *Ranger*. They remained aboard until 3 December 1944.[115]

As Ensign Nist reported to his parents via letter written the day he returned to NAS San Diego, VF-84 time aboard *Ranger* was very successful:

Fighting 84 continues to amaze everybody with its record aboard ship. We had a few minor accidents which were to be expected, otherwise everything is swell. We have evidently proven that we can fly Corsairs off a carrier, because in the very near future we are getting our planes that we're going to take out with us—forty-eight spanking new F4U's. Squadrons usually pick up their new planes at Pearl Harbor, which leads us to believe we're going to get our ship here in California rather than out at Pearl.[116]

In his next letter written on 5 December 1944, Ensign James Nist covered a variety of topics. First, he compared flying from a land based versus off a carrier:

Well, we're flying on dry land once again and it's a little bit different landing on acres and acres of macadam and rolling to a stop than landing on a pitching carrier deck some 80 feet wide and stopping like you'd just run through a few feet of reinforced concrete. A change, but not altogether so welcome. Flying off a flat-top isn't so tough, but it's sure a little more exciting. That's why I joined the Navy for, a Corsair and a carrier.[117]

James Nist had been in the Navy for nearly two years. In his 5 December letter, he reflected on his aviation cadet days back at the University of North Carolina—Chapel Hill. Of his four roommates at Chapel Hill, he was the only one actually flying. Richard Sachsel had died during training at Chapel Hill. Jim Smiley washed out of primary flight training. Ed DeGasper had washed out of flight training at NAS Corpus Christi.[118]

On 5 December, Ensign Nist performed two high-altitude training flights using oxygen. After taking them up high, Nist and the others did high-speed dives. Nist estimated that they exceeded 450 knots. "Those babies will really travel when you want them to," he wrote. "But at twenty thousand feet you don't even notice you're moving except for the noise."[119]

Also making 5 December noteworthy was another important milestone in "Shorty" Nist's naval career. On that day, he found out that he had been promoted to lieutenant (junior grade) effective 1 December 1944. Rather than outright tell his parents and Alice, Jimmy simply started adding the new rank to his return address on the letters he sent them. By 15 December, none of them noticed, so he had to tell them. "Thought I'd see how long it took you to notice the change in return address without telling you," he chided his parents.[120]

Around this time, Vice Admiral Marc A. Mitscher was in San Diego on leave. Mitscher was one of the leading naval aviators in the U.S. Navy. Marc Andrew Mitscher was born on 26 January 1887 in Hillsboro, Wisconsin. He grew up and was educated in Washington, D.C. Appointed to the U.S. Naval Academy, he graduated with the Class of 1910. After spending a few years with the surface fleet, he switched to aviation and earned his naval aviator wings on 2 June 1916. He was naval aviator number 33. In 1919, he was awarded the Navy Cross for serving as a flight crew member aboard a NC-1 seaplane when it flew with two other seaplanes from Newfoundland to the Azores. He then served in a succession of shore and sea billets all within naval aviation. In June 1929, he became executive officer of America's first aircraft carrier, USS *Langley* (CV-1). From June 1934 to June 1935, he served as executive officer of USS *Saratoga* (CV-3). Barely two months prior to the Pearl Harbor attack, Mitscher assumed command of the new carrier USS *Hornet* (CV-8). CAPT Mitscher commanded *Hornet* during the April 1942 Doolittle Raid against Japan and the June

4. Navy Fighting Squadron 84

1942 Battle of Midway. Promoted to rear admiral, Mitscher served as commanding officer of Patrol Wing Two; Commander Fleet Air, Noumea; Commander Air Solomon Islands; and Commander, Carrier Division Three in succession. In March 1944, he assumed command of First Carrier Task Force and Task Force 58, leading them during the Marianas Islands invasions and the June 1944 Battle of the Philippine Sea. During the later stages of the Pacific War, the U.S. Navy alternated command of its fighting forces between leadership teams led by Admiral Raymond Spruance and Admiral William F. Halsey. Thus while Admiral Spruance was in command, the Navy's striking assets were designated as Fifth Fleet with Mitscher in command of the Fast Carrier Task Force/Task Force 58. These same assets were designated Third Fleet and Fast Carrier Task Force/Task Force 38 when Admiral Halsey was in command.[121]

Not surprisingly, Ensign Nist was very familiar with VADM Marc Mitscher. In his 5 December 1944 letter to Martin and Ethel Nist, he wrote:

> We've got one friend who'll stick up for our Corsairs anyway and he seems to carry quite a bit of weight—none other than Vice Adm. Marc A. Mitscher. He was in San Diego on leave and he wants something faster than an F6F next time he goes out. Of course, VF-84 would give its eye teeth and two months flight pay to get on his carrier. Which, by the way, could quite possibly be.[122]

At some point in November or December, LT(jg) Nist and the other VF-84 participated in a navigation training event that involved the pilots viewing a movie that depicted a cross-country flight. In one of his February 1945, he described the training:

> While I was in San Diego, we had a new-fangled navigation set-up where we did the navigation and the terrain we flew over passed by on a movie screen. Well, they said we were starting from Lakehurst but I didn't pay much attention as I was busy getting my plotting board squared away. I looked up in time to see the Metedeconk River by Point Pleasant go by. Then we swung in to Lakewood and the lakes and everything were plain as anything. Then we headed for Freehold and then the real shock. As plain as day, there was Nist Farms on one side of the screen. It was taken too high to see any buildings but the railroad and road showed up and the strip of swamp between home and the farm were real clear. Almost passed out. The boys got quite a kick out of it, to say nothing about me.[123]

Major Changes in Air Group 84

Around the middle of December, Air Group 84 underwent another major reorganization. Torpedo Squadron 84 and Bombing Squadron 84 were reduced in size to 15 aircraft each. Fighting Squadron 84 was reorganized from a 54-aircraft squadron down to a 36-aircraft squadron with 48 pilots. "They threw out 8 LT's, 2 (j.g.'s) and twenty ensigns (mostly the new fellows in the squadron as of a couple months ago)," LT(jg) Nist wrote angrily to his parents on 10 December 1944. "Am very pleased and proud to be one of the boys still with the squadron, since the skipper naturally got rid of the boys he didn't think too sharp," he added.[124]

The major downsizing of VF-84 caused some major reorganization of its leadership as well. "Howsomever, with the squadron half the size and still having all the experienced boys with us, I'm no longer a section leader," Nist lamented. "Just about everybody got knocked down a rung. The whole outfit is much better now and when you improve an already hot outfit, you've really got something." With fewer pilots in the squadron, even the experienced ones were being dropped down in their leadership positions. The reorganization affected Nist's division of four aircraft. One of the flight leaders was a lieutenant with combat experience. Under the reorganization, he was made Nist's division leader. This caused the existing division leader—a lieutenant (j.g.) with combat experience—to be dropped down to section leader. Both Nist and the fourth pilot in the division had formerly been section leaders. Neither pilot had combat experience yet. "Put that together and you really have a sharp division," Nist proudly proclaimed. "And the whole squadron is just about like that. I don't think the Japs are going to like us a bit."[125]

While VF-84, VB-84 and VT-84 all experienced reductions in their aircraft and pilot strengths, Air Group 84 actually grew in size. The increasing lethality of Japanese kamikaze attacks upon Navy vessels prompted U.S. naval leaders to increase the numbers of fighter aircraft assigned to aircraft carriers. This included assigning U.S. Marine Corps fighter squadrons to carrier air groups. Accordingly, Marine Fighter Squadrons VMF-221 and VMF-451 were assigned to Air Group 84 in mid-December 1944. Organized on 11 July 1941 at San Diego, VMF-221 had participated in the Battle of Midway Island in June 1942 and fought in the South Pacific from land bases for most of 1943. Major Edwin S. Roberts, Jr., assumed command of the squadron on 12 October 1944. VMF-451 was commissioned on 15 February 1944 in Mojave, California, under the command of Major Henry A. Ellis, Jr., and trained there throughout 1944. Like VF-84, the two Marine squadrons were equipped with F4U Corsairs. Between the two Marine squadrons, there were nine combat veterans. They included Majors Archie G. Donahue and H.H. "Trigger" Long of VMF-451 and CAPT James E. Swett of VMF-221, who were all veterans of the Solomons Campaign. While flying an F4F Wildcat on his very first combat mission on 7 April 1943, Swett earned the Medal of Honor for shooting down seven Japanese Val dive-bombers in 15 minutes. Swett's own Wildcat was heavily damaged by Japanese fire and he was forced to ditch the plane.[126]

Both Marine squadrons came to AG-84 without carrier experience so getting the Marine pilots carrier qualified was a high priority. They began with field carrier landings at Ream Field five miles south of San Diego. Unfortunately, Second Lieutenant Richard Shasserre of VMF-221 was killed in a landing mishap. Following field carrier landings, the Marine pilots performed carrier landings aboard *Ranger*. "The Marine units were qualified in carrier work during the latter part of the month," reported CDR George Ottinger. "They are enthusiastic at the prospects ahead."[127]

Fighting 84 had another round of downsizing right before Christmas. Six more pilots were detached to make room for six pilots who had specially trained for aerial photographic missions. These photo pilots would join VF-84 in the future. "It had been rumored for several days but the axe fell yesterday. Well, yours truly escaped again for some reason," LT(jg) Nist wrote to his parents on 22 December. During December, VF-84 had been cut practically in half.[128]

The addition of the aerial photographic capability for VF-84 opened another unexpected opportunity for LT(jg) Nist. He was selected as one of four VF-84 pilots to attend photo school and be trained to fly aerial photographic aircraft. They would be using the F6F-3P Hellcat, which was the basic Grumman Hellcat fighter equipped with cameras for aerial photographic intelligence gathering. "Just a little something extra it doesn't hurt to know," he wrote on 22 December 1944.[129]

Nist and the other VF-84 pilots were actually taking the course twice so that they would really be proficient in aerial photography. "It's a lot of fun except that we have to fly Hellcats," he wrote to his parents on 28 December. "In between photo hops, we're doing a little practice to learn how to exterminate suicide bombers.

Aerial photograph of San Diego showing Lindbergh Field (now San Diego International Airport) and vicinity. At the time, Lindbergh Field was being run by the U.S. Army Air Forces. LT(jg) Nist took this photograph while learning to be a photograph reconnaissance pilot (Dickerson Family photograph).

Guess they're raising hell with the fleet out there now. But I don't think they'll raise much hell with '84's' flattop—not with seventy-two fighter-bombers looking after her." Nist and his squadron mates finished photo school on Sunday, 31 December 1944.[130]

During the month of December, VF-84 pilots logged 3,049.4 hours, including 236.5 hours at night. They also expended 81,200 rounds of .50-caliber ammunition. At month's end, the squadron had 48 officers and 29 enlisted sailors. At month's end, the squadron had 19 F4U-1D Corsairs, nine F4U-1 Corsairs, one Brewster F3A-1 Corsair, seven FG-1 Corsairs, one F6F-3P Hellcat and one F6F-5E Hellcat.[131]

LT(jg) Nist had a very busy month of December. He logged 53.3 flight hours, nearly all flown in the F4U and FG1 Corsairs. He even got an hour in the Brewster F3A version of the Corsair on 17 December. He flew one training mission in an SNJ-3 for nearly an hour. Toward the end of the month, he flew F6F-3P Hellcats as part of the photo reconnaissance school and logged 2.2 hours in them. At month's end, Nist had flown a total of 850.3 hours in his naval aviation career.[132]

As 1944 concluded, Navy Fighting Squadron 84 had developed into a well-trained, highly proficient combat force led by combat experienced officers. The squadron leadership and staff structure looked as thus, with previous combat commands indicated:

Commanding Officer	LCDR Roger R. Hedrick	VF-17
Executive Officer	LCDR Raymond E. Hill	VF-17
Engineering Officer	LT Earle C. Gillen	VC-39
Flight Officer	LT Philip C. Helms	VC-39
Gunnery Officer	LT Willis G. Laney	VB-6
Navigation Officer	LT C.T. Larsen	VB-21
Material Officer	LT(jg) John T. Gildea	VB-5
Communications Officer	LT Ellis J. Littlejohn	VB-98
Personnel Officer	LT(jg) Doris C. Freeman	VF-17
Radio Officer	LT(jg) Wilton Hutt	VF-3
Safety & Parachute Officer	LT(jg) G.E. Roberts	
Building & Grounds Officer	LT(jg) R.J. Vaughn	
Welfare Officer	LT(jg) Ralph K. Coconougher	VB-17
Oxygen Officer	LT(jg) John J. Sargent, Jr.	VF-18
Athletic Officer	ENS G.S. Powell	

The Squadron also had four non-flying officers attached. They were:

LT J.L. Lewis	Aviation Equipment Officer and Assistant Flight Officer
LT M.B. Seigler	Photographic Officer and Assistant Gunnery Officer
ENS Sydlowski	Assistant Engineering Officer
ENS J.J. Frazer	Air Combat Intelligence Officer and Historical Officer[133]

Christmas and New Year's

Jimmy got three days off for Christmas and so he made plans to fly up to San Francisco to spend it with Alice and her family. LCDR Hedrick authorized him to fly up there using a Corsair. The only possible problem was the weather. Jimmy's plan was a "no-go" if the weather did not cooperate.[134]

Unfortunately for Jimmy and Alice, the weather did not cooperate. Accompanied by another aircraft, Jimmy took off from NAS San Diego in early afternoon of Saturday. They made it as far as Los Angeles before heavy rain forced them to turn back. The rains continued on Sunday, and on Christmas Day. "So I spent a very disappointed two days in San Diego. We did have two very good Christmas dinners with everything except the right atmosphere," he wrote to his parents on 28 December. Christmas dinners were served at noon and again at night, and Jimmy indulged in both. Though Christmas did not turn out as planned, Jimmy and Alice had a backup plan. She would come down to San Diego for New Year's.[135]

Jimmy and Alice's plan for New Year's did work out. Alice flew down from San Francisco on Saturday 30 December. It was her first time in an airplane and she enjoyed it. The trip took a total of seven hours because she had to get off in Burbank and wait there for a couple of hours for another flight. Apparently, her seat on the airplane was needed for a priority passenger. Nevertheless, she made it down to San Diego. The return flight went much smoother. She left San Diego around 1830 on New Year's Day and got home in four hours. "Sure was swell to see her again," Jimmy wrote to his parents afterward. "She is sure one swell girl."[136]

A week after returning home to San Francisco, Alice Richards penned a letter to her future mother-in-law and father-in-law. Referring to her weekend with Jimmy over New Year's, she wrote, "I don't believe there is any other words to use in describing it except to say it was certainly perfect." Alice and Jimmy went out on New Year's Eve with his roommate LT(jg) Dusty Miller and his wife. They also saw Alice's brother at the Hotel Del Coronado. On New Year's Day, Jimmy took Alice around the naval air station and showed her his squadron ready room, the hangars and the bachelor officer quarters.[137]

The New Year Begins

Air Group 84 went back aboard *Ranger* in early January 1945 for carrier qualifications. On 2 January, AG-84 accomplished 47 night landings but also sustained one minor crash into the ship's island, a major crash into the crash barrier and a major crash into a catwalk. Fortunately, there were no injuries in any of these crashes. That night, VF-84 qualified 24 of its pilots in night landings without any mishaps. The next day, AG-84 and VMF-451 performed 173 day landings without mishaps. In the "oh dark early" hours of 5 January, VT-84 performed 24 night landings without any mishaps. After the sun rose, VMF-221 completed 229 day landings with only one major catwalk crash. Fortunately, there were no injuries. AG-84 finished its training aboard *Ranger* on 6 January and returned to NAS San Diego.[138]

The Fighting 84 pilots headed off for *Ranger* on the morning of 2 January 1945, but LT(jg) Nist and the other photo pilots were not with them at first. "We stayed behind for some field carrier landings in F6F's and we're going out in the morning," Nist informed his parents. "We have to qualify all over again in them in the daytime and in both the F6F and the F4U at night so the next day or so should be pretty busy." In addition to doing the field carrier landings, Nist and the other photo pilots got some experience in carrier catapult launches using their Hellcats. "It's not very much, except it's quite a jolt at first and you take off in nothing flat," he wrote.[139]

After completing their field carrier landings, "Shorty" Nist and the other photo pilots flew out to *Ranger*. Nist earned his carrier landing qualifications, successfully landing his F6F Hellcat aboard *Ranger* five times. That made for a total of 24 carrier landings in three different aircraft types.[140]

In early January 1945, VF-84 received new F4U-1D Corsairs; these would be the aircraft that the squadron would take to war. The Corsairs were checked out, equipped and prepared for the upcoming combat deployment. Also around this time, Fighting 84 and the rest of Air Group 84 learned the key details of their upcoming deployment. They would be joining up with the fleet aircraft carrier USS *Bunker Hill* (CV-17) at NAS Alameda, California. In addition, *Bunker Hill* would be serving as the Flagship for VADM Marc A. Mitscher, commander of Fifth U.S. Fleet's Task Force 58 (the Fast Carrier Task Force).[141]

In his 5 January 1945 letter to his parents, LT(jg) Nist shared some of this news about their deployment. He told them that they would be leaving from Alameda but withheld the name of their ship and their deployment for operational security reasons. He did tell them that their ship was going to be Vice Admiral Mitscher's flagship—a fact that he was justifiably proud of.

"We're getting 26 planes for 42 pilots and yours truly has one all to himself," he wrote. He had decided to name the plane "Misbehavin' Butch" in honor of his fiancée.[142]

On 4 and 5 January, LT(jg) Nist had a chance to evaluate the performance of the F4U Corsair versus the F6F Hellcat. He flew an F4U Corsair on 4 January and then flew an F6F Hellcat against a Corsair the following day. He recorded the experiences in his letter to his parents:

> Had a chance to race a Hellcat against a Corsair today [5 January]. I was in the Hellcat and tried to get an advantage by jumping the gun. I got the advantage all right but I didn't hold it long. Dusty Miller (he's the guy I helped get married) was in the F4U and he went by me going a good thirty knots faster. Had a Corsair to almost six hundred [knots] yesterday at 25,000 feet and that is really moving. Not level of course, that was with her nose headed straight down.[143]

Fighting 84's deployment to the Pacific theater was rapidly approaching. The squadron would be meeting up with their aircraft carrier in the San Francisco area and leaving from there. This was fortunate for Jimmy and Alice because they might get to see each other one more time before deployment. The reality of his upcoming deployment was weighing heavily upon Miss Alice Richards. She shared her feelings about this with Martin and Ethel Nist in her 8 January 1945 letter to them. On one hand, she was very proud of Jimmy for his recent promotion and his completion of photo school. "Jim certainly looked swell with his new half-stripe," she wrote. "Golly certainly am proud of him."[144]

On the other hand, Jimmy would be leaving for war in the very near future. "Sure will hate to see him leave, but I guess I don't have to tell you about that as you know how it is," she wrote to her future in-laws. "[Jimmy] Says the sooner he goes the sooner he'll be back, so I try to look at it that way."[145]

As more details about their upcoming deployment were revealed, Nist experienced one disappointment regarding his aircraft. He was planning on naming his Corsair after his fiancée but he came to find out that that would not be possible. As a photo pilot, he would be flying one of the squadron's two F6F Hellcat photo planes that would be shared with the squadron's other three photo pilots. "The photo deal is mostly taking pictures of battle damage, and when I fly the photo plane, I'll miss out on the actual strike," he explained in a 17 January 1945 letter to his parents. "Should fly with the squadron most of the time though, in a Corsair [emphasis in original]."[146]

When Nist was flying a Corsair, he would not be flying *his own* Corsair either. "Having a plane of your own doesn't mean a thing aboard ship because we fly in a certain order and have to take off in that order," he informed his parents. "A carrier is too crowded to move the planes around much, so we fly whichever one we happen to be assigned after they're arranged."[147]

In his 17 January 1945 letter to Martin and Ethel, Jimmy was able to reveal the name of his ship:

> Well, we're going aboard the Bunker Hill which will be Mitscher's flag ship (quite a feather in our cap). It will probably be head of another big task-force, since Mitscher usually has a fleet of his own. Where we're going is anybody's guess, but knowing Mitscher, it will probably be someplace to knock hell out of things.[148]

When they deployed for combat, VF-84 would be equipped with a new innovation designed to prevent G-LOC or gravity-induced loss of consciousness. The effects of the earth's gravity increase dramatically with acceleration. With greater acceleration come greater forces impacting the body. These forces are known as "g" forces. The human circulatory system is heavily impacted by "g" forces. When an aircraft accelerates rapidly or changes direction abruptly, the blood in the body flows away from the brain. Too much blood flowing away from the brain will cause a "G-LOC." The likely result of the pilot losing consciousness during flight would be the aircraft crashing or getting shot down if engaged in aerial combat and the death of the pilot.

In his 17 January 1945 letter, LT(jg) Nist described the new flight suits that were being issued to VF-84 pilots to counter the effects of "g" forces during flight. He wrote:

> From now on, no Corsair will get the best of Lt(jg) Shorty Nist. Our new flying suits arrived yesterday that are designed to keep us from blacking out. They double our resistance to "g's" and are really supposed to be great things. There's an air pump that pumps air into the legs and front of the stomach part when "g's" are pulled—the more "g's," the more air. That keeps the blood from settling in the lower half of your body and keeps it up in your head where it belongs. That should be pretty good. That means we can turn much sharper without blacking out. If we can get a Jap on our tail, turn real sharp and black him out close to the water, into the drink he'll go.[149]

Three years ago, James A. Nist had first entered the United States Navy as an aviation cadet. Now he was on the verge of his first combat deployment as a fighter pilot. This certainly gave him pause for reflection. In his 17 January letter, he wrote:

> Yeah, I finally did make it up to being a Corsair pilot. It was a long struggle and Chapel Hill was part of it, but I think instrument training at [NAS] Corpus [Christi] was the worst. I

finally got what I wanted. I think about three-quarters of the guys who enlisted did so in hopes of some day climbing into a Corsair on a carrier. It really feels good to be one of the few and to be part of a really crack outfit like "84."[150]

Jimmy Nist spent his last night in San Diego on 17 January 1945. Earlier that day, he shipped much of his personal belongings home to his parents. Other items, most notably two dress uniforms, would remain at Alice's home in San Francisco. The following morning, Fighting Squadron 84 began moving north to NAS Alameda. The movement was conducted by plane, train and automobile and completed on 19 January 1945.[151]

Shorty Nist flew his final flight prior to deployment on 18 January when he flew an F6F-3P Hellcat from San Diego to NAS Alameda. The flight took 3.5 hours to complete. This flight gave him 22.2 hours of flight time for the month of January 1945 and a grand total of 850.3 of flight time for his naval aviation career.[152]

Back to NAS Alameda and Goodbye

VF-84 and Air Group 84 arrived at NAS Alameda between 18 and 19 January 1945. It was expected that they would be boarding ship and heading out immediately. However, USS *Bunker Hill* was still up at Navy Yard Puget Sound in Bremerton, Washington. So, while they waited for their ship to come in, Air Group 84 members were berthed at NAS Alameda and granted liberal amounts of off-base liberty.

Jimmy was expecting to be able to spend a day or two with Alice before shipping out. Instead, they got six days. Unfortunately, Alice had a cold so that limited their activities. Nevertheless, they did spend one night with Jimmy's squadron mates and attended a party another night. "We had a wonderful six days while he was here and he stayed at the house and the children all had loads of fun with him," Alice wrote to her future in-laws afterward.[153]

Jimmy was very much in love with Alice and his friends in Fighting 84 had become fond of her as well. In his 27 January 1945 letter to his parents, Jimmy wrote:

> If you like Alice as much as the boys in the squadron, everything will be swell. They all thought she was very nice and I had to keep my eye on several of them. Several of them said I was crazy not to marry her right away, but when I get back is soon enough. Has to be.[154]

In her January 25, 1945, letter to her future in-laws, Alice related their son's state of mind before he shipped out. "Jim was rather excited and a little anxious to get started too," she wrote. "After two years training I guess it feels pretty good to really be going although all he talked about was getting home to New Jersey when he got back. He's counting on spending the summer home so maybe it won't be too long." Alice also noted that Jimmy seemed a little disappointed at being assigned to fly Hellcats as well as the Corsairs.[155]

While he was in the Bay Area, there was a lot of uncertainty as to when exactly *Bunker Hill* was heading out. "I didn't know exactly when I was leaving so when I went over to the station each time, I'd say Goodbye to everybody," Nist wrote to his parents. "After a couple of times, her mother got quite a kick out of it."[156]

Not surprisingly, leaving was difficult for both Jimmy and Alice. "Alice was pretty good about it—cried quite a bit one night—but the last night she was okay," he wrote to Martin and Ethel. "So now we're just looking forward to our next date some several months hence."[157]

5

Deploying on USS *Bunker Hill*

LT(jg) James A. Nist, Navy Fighting Squadron 84 and Air Group 84 reported aboard the *Essex*-class aircraft carrier USS *Bunker Hill* (CV-17) on 24 January 1945 while she was berthed at Naval Air Station Alameda, California. They had been waiting for their ship to come in for six days.

USS Bunker Hill *(CV-17)*

U.S. carrier aviation had come a long way since Eugene Ely had flown a rickety early airplane off an improvised flight deck on the forward section of the light cruiser USS *Birmingham* (CL-2) on 10 November 1910. America's first three aircraft carriers (*Langley, Lexington* and *Saratoga*) all were converted from other ships. Beginning with USS *Ranger*, American fleet carriers were designed and constructed as aircraft carriers from the keel up. The *Essex*-class aircraft carriers were designed and constructed based upon the operational experiences of the Navy's preceding eight aircraft carriers. USS *Essex* (CV-9) was 70 feet longer and displaced nearly 10,000 more tons than the preceding *Yorktown*-class. The *Essex*-class carriers were larger, better armed, carried a larger aircraft complement and were better designed than their predecessors. They were the most advanced and lethal warships in the world at that time.

As well designed and technologically advanced as the *Essex*-class carriers were, they did contain several significant flaws that would later come back to haunt the Navy, especially when the Japanese resorted to kamikaze suicide aircraft attacks on U.S. warships. One of their most significant vulnerabilities was their unarmored flight decks. Their flight decks had only a few inches of steel and wood.

USS *Bunker Hill* (CV-17) was the 17th American aircraft carrier and the ninth of the *Essex*-class fleet aircraft carriers. She was laid down at Bethlehem Steel Corporation's Quincy, Massachusetts, shipyard on 15 September 1941 and launched on 7 December 1942, exactly one year after the infamous Japanese attack on Pearl Harbor. Mrs. Donald Boynton was her sponsor. Over the next several months, *Bunker Hill* was completed and fitted out. On 24 May 1943, she was officially placed in commission. Captain J.J. Ballentine was her first commanding officer.[1]

Like her *Essex*-class sisters, *Bunker Hill* was a marvel of technology and American industrial prowess. She was 872' long at the flight deck and 820' at the waterline. Her beam at the waterline was 93', which enabled her to fit through the Panama

USS *Bunker Hill* underway in October 1945. This photograph has been signed by Commodore Arleigh Burke (Naval History and Heritage Command [Photo NH 42373]).

Canal. Her maximum beam at the flight deck was 147'. The flight deck was only one-fifth of an inch of steel covered by 4" of teak wood. To save weight, ship designers had decided against an armored flight deck with greater protection against bombs. *Bunker Hill*'s draft was typically around 29' when loaded. Her height from waterline to the top of her mast was 190' and her height from keel to the top of her mast was 229'. She was designed to displace 27,100 tons. As the war progressed, additional equipment, personnel and weaponry were added, which in turn added to her displacement. During combat operations, she could displace over 41,000 when fully loaded.[2]

On the starboard side of the flight deck was located the island, *Bunker Hill*'s command and control center. Located in the island were the navigation bridge for steering and running the ship; the pilot house; the flag bridge and flag plot, which were used by flag officers and their staffs when embarked; communications equipment; radar; and primary flight control. The uptakes (or smokestacks) for the ship's boilers also were located in the island. At its base, the island was 60' wide.[3]

Immediately below the flight deck and island was the gallery deck. These spaces were literally suspended below the flight deck and above the hangar deck. The squadron ready rooms and spaces for communications and code encryption/de-encryption were located here. Located right below the unarmored flight deck, the gallery deck was one of the most vulnerable areas of the ship, but the pilots and aircrews needed spaces readily accessible to the flight deck.[4]

The hangar deck was located below the flight deck and the gallery deck. The hangar deck ran the length of the ship and had ceilings 25′ high. Here, the air group's aircraft were serviced and stored protected from the elements. The floor of the hangar deck was protected by thicker steel than its ceiling. Three elevators brought aircraft up to/down from the flight deck. The hangar deck could be subdivided by fire curtains to isolate fires that occurred and keep them from spreading.[5]

When designing warships, naval architects engage in a balancing act between weight and armor protection. Making a warship too heavy with armor protection will adversely affect the warship's performance and speed. Installing too little armor protection to gain additional speed makes the warship more vulnerable to battle damage. As a compromise between armor protection and weight, warship designers often opt for reserving the best armor protection for the most essential areas of the ship, namely the engineering spaces and magazines. *Bunker Hill* and her *Essex*-class sisters were constructed with a 500-foot-long armored box in which were located the engine and boiler rooms, fuel storage, munitions magazines, and other vital functions. To conserve weight, the ship's spaces above, forward, and aft of this armored box were constructed of lesser-strength armor.[6]

Bunker Hill's propulsion was provided by four boiler rooms and four engine rooms. The boiler rooms produced the steam that drove the engines. Working together, they generated 150,000 horsepower and provided the power that turned *Bunker Hill*'s four large propellers. *Bunker Hill*'s auxiliary power plant with its two 750-kilowatt electrical generators generated electrical power for the ship.[7]

Bunker Hill's primary offensive and defensive weapons system was her embarked aircraft. For defensive purposes, *Bunker Hill* also carried an extensive array of anti-aircraft weaponry. She had 52 20 mm Oerlikon light automatic anti-aircraft weapons, 68 40 mm Bofors medium anti-aircraft guns and 12 five-inch/.38-caliber dual-purpose guns mounted in twin-gun turrets. The Oerlikons and the Bofors were mounted in sponsons that ran alongside and below the length of the flight deck. The five-inch gun turrets were located forward and aft of the island. "Designed to fulfill the needs of battleships as well as destroyers, the 5-inch/38-caliber dual-purpose gun became one of World War II's best regarded and most versatile naval weapons," wrote naval historian Norman Friedman.[8]

Bunker Hill had already amassed an impressive war record when LT(jg) Nist, VF-84 and Air Group 84 reported aboard in January 1945. In her very first combat operations, *Bunker Hill* and her Air Group 17 participated in naval air strikes on the major Imperial Japanese Navy base at Rabaul. *Bunker Hill* supported the invasion of Tarawa in November 1943. In late January and early February, she supported amphibious operations in the Marshall Islands. From late February 1944 to early May 1994, she conducted air strikes on Truk Island, the Marianas Islands and the Caroline Islands. In June, *Bunker Hill* supported the amphibious assaults upon the Marianas Islands. When the Japanese fleet sortied to contest the Saipan Invasion, *Bunker Hill*'s aircraft participated in the wholesale destruction of Japanese airpower in the Battle of the Philippine Sea, which was dubbed the "Marianas Turkey Shoot" for the huge number of Japanese aircraft that were shot down. Her aircraft helped sink one carrier and destroyed many of the 476 Japanese aircraft lost in the battle. In the fall of 1944, she participated in aerial operations against the Western Caroline Islands, Okinawa, Luzon and Formosa. On 6 November 1944, *Bunker Hill* left the war zone for the Puget Sound Navy Yard at Bremerton, Washington. There she underwent repairs, refitting and upgrades.[9]

Organization of a Warship

An *Essex*-class fleet aircraft carrier such as *Bunker Hill* was an amazingly complex blend of technology and personnel. The most sophisticated weaponry and equipment of the day was impotent without the trained and proficient personnel to operate them. Accordingly, *Bunker Hill* personnel were organized for optimum performance and efficiency.

The organization of an aircraft carrier separated the ship's company from the aviation component. The ship's company operated and maintained the ship and all of its systems. The operation of the carrier's aircraft and the aircraft themselves were the responsibility of the embarked air group. In World War II, the air group typically remained with the carrier for only one or two combat deployments before being replaced by another air group. While *Bunker Hill* was in refit at Puget Sound Navy Yard, Air Group Eight disembarked and was later replaced by Air Group 84.[10]

Bunker Hill was commanded by CAPT Marshall R. Greer, USN. The ship's executive officer was Commander Howell J. Dyson. Two other officers were qualified to command *Bunker Hill*: CDR Shane King, who headed the Hull Department, and CDR Joseph Carmichael, who served as chief engineer and head of the Engineering Department. *Bunker Hill* had two assigned chaplains: Unitarian minister LT(jg) Abbott Peterson and Roman Catholic priest LT Robert E. Delaney.[11]

Like her *Essex*-class sister ships, *Bunker Hill*'s ship's company was organized into departments to accomplish the multitude of tasks required to operate the mighty ship. Each department was subdivided into divisions. The Air Department consisted of sailors and officers who operated the flight and hangar decks and supported the flight operations of the embarked air group. The Communications Department had the vital responsibility of providing for all of *Bunker Hill*'s incoming and outgoing communications and much of the ship's internal administration. The Engineering Department was responsible for *Bunker Hill*'s propulsion systems, boilers, main engines and certain auxiliary machinery. *Bunker Hill*'s defensive weaponry, magazines and fire control equipment were the responsibility of the Gunnery Department. This department included a Marine detachment of three officers and 75 enlisted Marines. The Hull Department was responsible for damage control, trash disposal, fire prevention, firefighting and construction and repair projects. The Medical Department consisted of doctors, dentists and pharmacists' mates who took care of the sailors and Marines' medical and dental needs and treated casualties. The Navigation Department was responsible for the ship's movements, including plotting the ship's courses, handling the ship while underway and in port and recording all information pertaining to the ship's movements. *Bunker Hill*'s band was also part of the Navigation Department. The Supply Department provided all of the supplies and consumables used by the ship and its air group. Its S-2 Division consisted of stewards and steward's mates who served meals in the wardrooms. In a Navy that was still racially segregated, the S-2 Division was the only unit of the ship where blacks were able to serve.[12]

USS Bunker Hill *in January 1945*

When January 1945 began, USS *Bunker Hill* was still undergoing refitting and repairs at the Puget Sound Navy Yard. In the middle of January, she loaded ammunition, supplies and stores and calibrated radio and radar equipment. On 19 January, *Bunker Hill* passed through the degaussing range. Degaussing was a process by which electrical currents were used to minimize the ship's magnetic fields and thus make the ship less vulnerable to magnetic sea mines. Following degaussing, *Bunker Hill* completed her repairs for the next two days and made ready to get underway.[13]

Bunker Hill was fully loaded and ready for war, except that she did not have an air group embarked. So, her next order of business was to steam south to San Francisco Bay and pick up Air Group 84 at NAS Alameda. On the evening of 20 January 1945, *Bunker Hill* tried to get underway, but dense fog forced her to anchor for the night. Overnight the weather improved so she weighed anchor at 1054 local time and got underway again. She steamed through Puget Sound and the Strait of Juan de Fuca and into the Pacific Ocean. Turning south, she steamed alone down the Washington and Oregon coast roughly along longitude 125 degrees west. Sometime before midnight on 22 January 1945, *Bunker Hill* passed through the Golden Gate and underneath the magnificent suspension bridge that spanned this historic entrance to San Francisco Bay. From here, it was a short run to NAS Alameda located on the eastern side of the bay. She anchored in the bay overnight and moored to Naval Air Station Dock #800-T in the morning. In total, she covered over 800 nautical miles.[14]

The morning of 24 January 1945 found *Bunker Hill* still at NAS Alameda. Changes were underway, however. At 0930, *Bunker Hill*'s commanding officer, CAPT M.R. Greer, turned over command of the mighty warship to CAPT George A. Seitz, USN. Originally from Rochester, New York, Seitz was a 1916 graduate of the U.S. Naval Academy and had also done graduate studies at the Massachusetts Institute of Technology.[15]

Two hours after the change of command ceremony, Air Group 84 reported aboard per order of Commander Fleet Air, Alameda, California. The air group as such was composed of Navy Fighting Squadron 84 (VF-84), Navy Torpedo Squadron 84 (VT-84), Navy Bombing Squadron 84 (VB-84), Marine Fighter Squadron 221 (VMF-221) and Marine Fighter Squadron 451 (VMF-451). The air group's aircraft and equipment were hauled aboard and stowed throughout the day.[16]

Upon reporting aboard *Bunker Hill*, Air Group 84's personnel were assigned berthing. Berthing was based upon rank. As a lieutenant (junior grade), Nist was assigned to a room with two other officers of his rank: Wilbert Popp and Leroy Wallet. "The rooms are pretty good, just a little crowded," Jimmy later wrote to his parents. The ensigns were less fortunate; they were all berthed in a large bunk room. The differences in berthing certainly made Jimmy more appreciative of his promotion the previous month. The air group's enlisted sailors rated less comfortable berthing spaces than the officers.[17]

In his memoirs, LT(jg) Popp described their berthing aboard *Bunker Hill*:

> We were assigned three officers to each stateroom. These were staterooms which normally only accommodated two officers, so the Navy had welded in a third bunk to the hull itself. The other two bunks were doubled bunked. My roommates were Anthony Nist [sic] and Leroy Wallet from Albany, Oregon. Since I was senior I chose the lower bunk. Wallet next chose the upper bunk, and Tony [sic] Nist, the junior of the group, got the bunk attached to the hull. Our stateroom was on the portside of the ship under the Focil (fo'c'sle) deck. Unfortunately, we were right behind Anchor room.[18]

In his letters home, "Shorty" Nist never identified the names of his roommates. "Beads" Popp's account in his 2004 memoirs was noteworthy for two significant errors in describing his roommate "Shorty" Nist. First, he got Nist's first name wrong, calling him "Anthony" instead of James. Second, Popp wrote that Nist was from San Francisco; Nist was actually from Squankum, New Jersey. Writing nearly 60 years afterward, Popp probably got the hometowns confused because Nist was engaged to a young woman who lived in San Francisco and spent a considerable amount of time there while VF-84 was at NAS Alameda awaiting their ship.

As officers, Nist, Popp and Wallet rated a steward's mate to attend to their stateroom. Their steward's mate was Steward's Mate First Class Norman Thomas Cola, whom they called "Coca-Cola." Originally from New Orleans, Louisiana, StM1c Cola made the pilots' beds and kept their stateroom supplied with towels and linens. Alcohol was prohibited by Navy regulations from being aboard ship. However, this was not widely enforced aboard aircraft carriers. Accordingly, Popp et al. had a small supply of whiskey that they kept in their stateroom safe. When "Coca-Cola" did a good job at keeping their stateroom shipshape, the pilots would periodically leave out a shot of whiskey for him as both a reward and an incentive. According to the ship's roster, Cola had reported aboard *Bunker Hill* on 25 May 1943.[19]

Haze Gray and Underway

That afternoon, *Bunker Hill* completed embarkation and cast off her lines. At 1608, she got underway. Again *Bunker Hill* passed beneath the Golden Gate Bridge and headed out into the Pacific Ocean bound for war on her own unaccompanied by any escort vessels. On the first night at sea, she ran into a storm. Shorty Nist had previously weathered a storm at sea aboard the escort carrier *Takanis Bay*. Being considerably larger, *Bunker Hill* handled the storm much better. Many others got seasick, but Nist was not one of them. "Our room is way forward, too, where you feel all the rolling and pitching," he later informed his parents.[20]

During that storm, Nist, Popp and Wallet soon found out the downside of being located near the ship's anchors. "During high seas as the ship's bow would dive into the sea, the force of the water would pull the anchors from the side of the hull and the sound of the anchor chain was loud and clangy," Popp wrote in his memoirs. "Then as the bow rose again the anchor would bang against the hull. That was not conducive to good sleep, but eventually we got used to it."[21]

Despite that first storm, LT(jg) Nist was quite happy with his new ship. "So far, everything has gone swell," he wrote to his parents. "The chow is very good, only hope it stays that way." For the moment, there was not much to do.[22]

Bunker Hill's first stop on the way back to war was Naval Station Pearl Harbor, Hawaii. The distance between San Francisco and Pearl Harbor was 2,096 nautical miles. *Bunker Hill* covered the distance in approximately 92 hours, averaging 22 knots. "One night en-route, the Captain ran it up to 28 knots," LT(jg) Popp later wrote. "The ship really shook." On 28 January 1945, *Bunker Hill* entered Pearl Harbor, steamed north past Hickam Airfield and Hospital Point and then into the North Channel. From there she eased to the west of Ford Island Naval Air Station and moored to Dock F-12 off Ford Island.[23]

Naval Station Pearl Harbor was not just a port of call on *Bunker Hill*'s voyage to war. This was where World War II officially began for the United States just three years before. America had begun World War II with a devastating defeat. Eight U.S. battleships and 15 other ships had been sunk or damaged, 188 aircraft had been destroyed and 2,335 service members and 68 civilians had been killed. The Japanese lost five midget submarines, 29 aircraft, 129 personnel killed and one taken prisoner. Most of *Bunker Hill*'s crew had not been in the U.S. Navy on 7 December 1941. They had been still in high school or working civilian jobs. Many, like LT(jg) James A. Nist, had been in college when Pearl Harbor had been attacked.

Even three years later, there were many visible reminders of the 7 December 1941 surprise Japanese attack. The heavily damaged battleship *Oklahoma* (BB-37) was awaiting scrapping. Though her superstructure and armaments had been removed in 1942, the battered hull of the battleship *Arizona* (BB-39) remained submerged at her mooring. The upturned hull of the former battleship *Utah* (BB-31/AG-16) remained near her original mooring. When *Bunker Hill* moored at Dock F-12 just north of Ford Island, she did so adjacent to the still visible hull of *Utah*.[24]

Bunker Hill's stay at Pearl Harbor was brief. Liberty was granted and many *Bunker Hill* sailors went ashore to explore Honolulu and Waikiki. "We didn't have much time to enjoy the beauties and relaxation of Hawaii," LT(jg) Popp later wrote. "We only had time for either downtown Honolulu or Waikiki and we foolishly stayed in Honolulu. Wasn't much to see."[25]

While *Bunker Hill* was in Pearl Harbor, seven pilots came aboard to serve as the ship's night fighter detachment. They would fly F6F-5N Hellcats in this role. At 0740 on the morning of 29 January 1945, *Bunker Hill* cast off her lines and got underway as part of Task Group 12.2 commanded by Rear Admiral Sprague. Task Group 12.2 consisted of the aircraft carriers *Saratoga* (CV-3), *Bunker Hill* (CV-17), *Bennington* (CV-20), *Randolph* (CV-15) and *Belleau Wood* (CVL-24), the cruiser *Alaska* (CB-1) and seven destroyers. As protection against Japanese submarines, the task group was zigzagging on a base course 270 degrees at a speed of 22 knots. Zigzagging, or frequently changing course, was designed to make it more difficult for enemy submarines to target ships. Task Group 12.2's destination was the U.S. fleet anchorage at Ulithi Atoll in the Caroline Islands some 4,200 nautical miles west/southwest of Pearl Harbor.[26]

Now steaming away from Pearl Harbor, the pilots and men of Fighting Squadron 84 found out what their next mission. "That night LCDR Hedrick called a squadron meeting in our ready room after the evening chow to tell us our first target was Tokyo," LT(jg) Popp later wrote. "It took me some time to finally go to sleep that night. All I could see was Zeros, Haps, Tojos, Tonys all shooting at me."[27]

Steaming west meant steaming toward the enemy. On 30 January 1945, Task Group 12.2 began maintaining combat air patrols and anti-submarine patrols to protect its ships and personnel. The aircraft for these patrols were provided by the task group's five aircraft carriers on a rotating basis. LT(jg) James Nist did not fly any of these missions on the voyage to Ulithi.[28]

On 6 February 1945, *Bunker Hill* and Task Group 12.2 steamed in the vicinity of Truk Island. Located in the Caroline Islands, Truk was a volcanic island with a superb natural harbor that the Imperial Japanese Navy used as a major support base for its operations. These were familiar waters for *Bunker Hill*. Almost exactly a year before, on 17–18 February 1944, *Bunker Hill* and Task Force 58 struck the Japanese bastion with devastating results. U.S. forces sank four destroyers, three light cruisers and 33 other ships and destroyed over 250 Japanese aircraft while losing 25 aircraft and 40 aircrew. A special task group centered on the battleships USS *Iowa* (BB-61) and USS *New Jersey* (BB-62) also sank several Japanese ships fleeing the carnage at Truk Lagoon.[29]

After the punishing Operation Hailstone raids, the Japanese never used Truk again for significant naval operations. Periodically hit with air strikes, Truk was neutralized and bypassed. Even so, Task Group 12.2 intensified its combat air and anti-submarine patrols, went to torpedo defense stations and manned half of all anti-aircraft guns.[30]

Having passed Truk without incident, Task Group 12.2 arrived at Ulithi Atoll the following day. At 1255, *Bunker Hill* anchored at Berth #24 inside the spacious atoll anchorage. Stretching out across the massive Ulithi Atoll was one of the largest assemblages of warships in history. "I went up to the Focil deck at dawn and tried to count," LT(jg) Popp later wrote. "I gave up way after 100."[31]

In February 1945, Ulithi Atoll was the most important forward base in use by the U.S. Navy. Ulithi Atoll is located in the western Caroline Islands in the Central Pacific Ocean. Guam and Peleliu are both 370 miles from Ulithi, albeit in opposite directions. Ulithi consists of several small islets and a long fringe of coral reefs surrounding one of the largest lagoons in the world. The lagoon stretches some 22 miles north to south and upward of 15 miles across. With an average depth of 80 to 100 feet, the lagoon provided U.S. forces with an ideal anchorage capable of accommodating several hundred warships at a time. Elements of the U.S. Army's 81st Infantry Division occupied Ulithi on 20 September 1944 without meeting any Japanese opposition. Within days, a Navy construction battalion began work to convert the atoll into an advanced support base. In a few short months, Navy Seabees had expanded the existing Japanese airfield on Falalop Island and constructed aviation support facilities. They also built a fleet recreation center on Mogmog Island, a hospital on Sorlen Island, a theater, a 500-seat chapel, warehouses, fuel storage and other facilities. Ulithi quickly became essential for prosecuting the war against Imperial Japan in the last year of the Pacific War.[32]

In his memoirs, LT(jg) Popp described their brief stay at Ulithi. He wrote:

> During our short stay in Ulithi there would be whale boats that came alongside and we would be able to get our land legs back to use. We were able to buy and drink beer when we got there. The beach was marked for Regular Officers and set-aside for Flag Officers, senior commander and above. There wasn't a hell of a lot to do but drink beer, bullshit with your buddies and urinate. The Navy provided sponsons for this purpose. The beach was called "Mog Mog" and I never understood how it got that name.[33]

U.S. Fifth Fleet

Back in the United States, Fighting Squadron 84 had learned that their carrier would be the flagship for Vice Admiral Marc Mitscher, commander of the Fast Carrier Task Force. Independent of *Bunker Hill*, Mitscher and his staff made their way across the Pacific with a stop in Pearl Harbor for meetings to discuss upcoming operations in the western Pacific. At 1339 on 7 February 1945, Mitscher and his staff came aboard *Bunker Hill* and she became the flagship for Mitscher's Fast Carrier Task Force.[34]

Mitscher's staff included Commodore Arleigh A. Burke. Born in Boulder, Colorado, on 19 October 1901, Burke graduated with the U.S. Naval Academy's Class of 1923. He served in a succession of assignments aboard battleships and destroyers and earned a master of science degree in chemical engineering from the University of Michigan. He commanded Destroyer Squadron 23 (DESRON 23) during combat operations in the South Pacific. In 20 engagements with the enemy, DESRON 23 sank a Japanese cruiser, nine destroyers and a submarine and shot down 30 aircraft. Burke also earned his nickname "31-Knot." In March 1944, Burke became chief of staff for Vice Admiral Marc Mitscher's Fast Carrier Task Force. This was an interesting assignment given that Burke had had no prior experience with naval aviation. Yet the team of aviation pioneer Mitscher and surface warfare expert Burke worked well together.[35]

Beginning in mid–1944, the Pacific Fleet's operating forces were organized into the Third and Fifth Fleets. Admiral William F. Halsey commanded Third Fleet while Admiral Raymond Spruance commanded Fifth Fleet with each admiral having his own large staff to plan and coordinate operations. The respective fleet commanders and staffs alternated commanding the warships of the Pacific Fleet. When Admiral Halsey and his staff were commanding the ships, they were known as Third Fleet. When Admiral Spruance and his staff commanded the ships, they were known as Fifth Fleet. While Halsey was out at sea with Third Fleet, Spruance with his Fifth Fleet staff were planning their next operations and vice versa. When Admiral Halsey was commanding Third Fleet, Vice Admiral John S. McCain commanded the Fast Carrier Task Force, also known as Task Force 38. When Admiral Spruance commanded Fifth Fleet, Vice Admiral Marc Mitscher commanded the Fast Carrier Task Force, also known as Task Force 58.

The most recent of these changes in command of Fifth Fleet and the Fast Carrier Task Force occurred at midnight on 26 January 1945. In the preceding several months, Halsey and Third Fleet had supported the liberation of the Philippine Islands, sortied through the South China Sea and conducted air strikes against French Indochina, the Chinese coast and Formosa. Now at Ulithi, command of the fleet passed from Halsey to Spruance, and Third Fleet once again became Fifth Fleet.[36]

While Third Fleet was pounding the Japanese in the western Pacific, Admiral Spruance, Vice Admiral Mitscher, COM Burke and their staffs had been planning the operations to commence in early 1945. The upcoming operations included air strikes on the Japanese Home Islands, supporting the invasion of Iwo Jima and supporting the invasion of Okinawa. The next several months were going to be very busy for the U.S. Navy in the western Pacific.

Now that Jimmy was aboard ship and heading to war, his mail was being censored for operational security reasons. "We censor our own mail or rather each other's without reading it, trusting each other not to divulge any military information," he admitted to his parents. Due to censorship, his several letters from the first weeks of his deployment were sparse on details. Essentially, all he was sharing was the squadron's daily exercise routine and talking about how tan he was getting from exercising on the flight deck. In one letter he talked about going to bed at 2100 each night, getting up for reveille very early and playing cards and records on the phonograph in the ready room to pass the time. "We have our record player in the ready room and it goes continuously with everything from boogie to Beethoven with emphasis on the former," he wrote to his parents on 13 February.[37]

Jimmy had left Alice behind in San Francisco only two weeks prior but he was missing her greatly. In his 7 February 1945 letter to his parents, Jimmy wrote:

> I sure wish you could have met her before I left. She surely is one swell girl. I know I said the same thing about June, but June was just an ordinary girl. I've never introduced Alice to a single person who hasn't later come around and raved about her, including such remarks as not knowing how a screwball like me ever rated such a girl. Sometimes I wonder about that myself, but that's the way it is.[38]

Back Underway

Bunker Hill's stay at Ulithi was brief. At 1009 on 10 February 1945, she weighed anchor and got underway as part of Task Group 58.3 with the commander of the Fast Carrier Task Force and his staff embarked. *Bunker Hill* and Air Group 84 were heading into harm's way. Though few at the moment knew, they were heading north to launch the first carrier air strikes on the Japanese Home Islands since *Hornet* launched Lt. Col. Jimmy Doolittle's B-25 bombers on their epic air raid in April 1942.[39]

Though he could not say in a letter, the Fast Carrier Task Force, *Bunker Hill* and "Shorty" Nist were rapidly approaching the Japanese Home Islands. To reassure his parents, he wrote on 13 February, "In a couple more days you'll know where we are by the newspapers, but once again I'll say there's not a thing in the world to worry about. Told you once before I didn't think the Japs were going to like Fighting 84 and their airplanes. That was quite an understatement on my part."[40]

Now underway, *Bunker Hill* was part of Task Group 58.3 of the Fast Carrier Task Force, U.S. Fifth Fleet. Overall command was exercised by Admiral Raymond Spruance. VADM Marc Mitscher commanded the Fast Carrier Task Force. Task Group 58.3 was commanded by Rear Admiral Frederick C. Sherman. A 1910 graduate of the U.S. Naval Academy, Sherman had commanded USS *Lexington* (CV-2) at the Battle of Coral Sea and had commanded carrier task forces during operations throughout the south and central Pacific and during the epic Battle of Leyte Gulf.[41]

Task Group 58.3 was a powerful assemblage of naval sea and air forces that dwarfed the Navy task force that had fought in the Battle of Coral Sea only three years prior. The task group's three aircraft carriers were USS *Essex* (CV-9), *Bunker Hill* and USS *Cowpens* (CVL-25), with *Essex* serving as Sherman's flagship. Commissioned on 31 December 1942, *Essex* entered combat service the following summer and served with distinction through numerous Pacific campaigns. In February 1945, her embarked Air Group Four consisted of two Marine fighter squadrons (VMF-124 and VMF-213) equipped with F4U Corsairs, Navy Fighting Squadron Four (VF-4) equipped with F6F Hellcats and Navy Torpedo Squadron Four (VT-4) equipped with TBM-3 Avengers. *Essex*'s air group boasted 36 F4U Corsairs, 48 F6F Hellcats, two F6F-5(P) photo Hellcats, four F6F-5(N) night fighter Hellcats and 15 TBM-3 Avenger bombers, for a total of 105 aircraft. *Cowpens* was an *Independence*-class light aircraft carrier. Commissioned on 28 May 1943, "Mighty Moo," as she was affectionately known, had participated in the Marshalls, Marianas, Philippines and South China Sea operations. She had a length of 622' 6", a beam of 71' 6", a draft of 26,' displaced 11,000 tons and could carry up to 35 aircraft. Her Light Carrier Air Group 46 was equipped with Hellcat fighters and Avenger bombers.[42]

The task group also included battleships USS *South Dakota* (BB-57) and USS *New Jersey* (BB-62), cruisers USS *Pasadena* (CL-65), USS *Astoria* (CL-90), USS *Wilkes-Barre* (CL-103) and USS *Indianapolis* (CA-35) and 13 destroyers. *Indianapolis* was the flagship for U.S. Fifth Fleet commander ADM Spruance. At that time, Spruance and *Indianapolis* were in the Marianas Islands while he conferred with the commander of the Joint Expeditionary Force, VADM Richmond Kelly Turner, about the upcoming Iwo Jima invasion.[43]

As large and powerful as it was, Task Group 58.3 was just one of five task groups that constituted VADM Mitscher's Task Force 58, also known as the Fast Carrier Task Force.

Task Group 58.1 included the three fleet carriers, one light carrier, two battleships, three light cruisers and 15 destroyers. Task Group 58.2 included two fleet carriers, one light carrier, two battleships, two heavy cruisers and 19 destroyers. Task Group 58.4 included two fleet carriers, two light carriers, two battleships, three light cruisers and 17 destroyers. A new innovation to the Fast Carrier Task Force was Task Group 58.5, which was a night aircraft task group. The task group's two carriers—USS *Enterprise* (CV-6) and USS *Saratoga* (CV-3)—were both equipped exclusively with night fighters and attack aircraft. In support, the task group also included two cruisers and 12 destroyers. Altogether, Task Force 58 boasted 11 fleet aircraft carriers, five light aircraft carriers, eight fast battleships, five heavy cruisers, 10 light cruisers and 77 destroyers. The task force embarked over 1,200 aircraft, including Helldiver bombers, Avenger bombers, Hellcat fighters and Corsair fighters, with fighters being the predominant aircraft type. This included eight Marine fighter squadrons (VMF), which were embarked aboard four of the task force's aircraft carriers. Altogether, the Marine component boasted 144 F4U Corsairs and 216 pilots or 16 percent of the task force's total fighter strength.[44]

Task Force 58 continued its northeastward passage on 11 February 1945 on a course that would take them to the east of the Marianas Islands. During the day, the task group conducted combat air patrols and anti-submarine patrols, as well as anti-aircraft gunnery practice. The carriers launched aircraft to conduct tactical exercises and simulated air strikes in conjunction with the Third Marine Division, which was on Tinian Island at the time. LT(jg) James Nist participated in one of these strike exercises, piloting an F4U Corsair for a four-hour training flight.[45]

Essentially, 12 February 1945 was a repeat of the previous day. Task Force 58 was now headed in a more northerly course. Anti-aircraft gunnery practice was performed in the morning with the task group's gunner firing at target sleeves pulled by aircraft from *Essex*. *Bunker Hill* provided Corsairs and Helldivers for combat air patrols and anti-submarine patrols. Again the carriers launched strike groups on training missions against Tinian. LT(jg) Nist piloted an F6F-5P Hellcat on a 3.3-hour training flight. That night, *Bunker Hill* and *Essex*'s night fighter Hellcats conducted training flights.[46]

The next three days were spent completing final preparations for the upcoming air strikes on the Japanese Home Islands. On 13 February, *Indianapolis*, with Admiral Spruance aboard, rendezvoused with Task Group 58.3, and Task Group 58.3 rendezvoused with the logistics vessels of Task Group 50.8. Underway refueling and replenishment was one of the most important capabilities of the U.S. fleet, enabling its ships to remain at sea for long periods of time at distances far removed from shore facilities. In the vast expanses of the Pacific Ocean, this capability was indispensable to the successful prosecution of the war against Japan. Three fleet oilers began underway refueling operations in early afternoon and continued until 1830. Refueling resumed the following morning and finished up at 1030. Replacement aircraft were transferred from Task Group 50.8's escort carriers to Task Group 58.3's carriers. Combat air patrols and anti-submarine patrols were aloft all day to protect the task force.[47]

Preserving operational security was essential for the success of the air strikes on the Japanese Home Islands and to protect the task force from Japanese aircraft and submarines. The task force's daily anti-submarine and combat air patrols continued in earnest. Marianas-based B-29 Superfortresses and B-24 Liberators and five U.S. Navy submarines scouted the projected route of Task Force 58. On 15 February, five U.S. destroyers were sent ahead of the task force to eliminate any Japanese craft that might detect the task force. Vectored in by a combat air patrol, the destroyer USS *Hailey* (DD-556) intercepted a small enemy vessel and sank her.[48]

Two years earlier, James Arthur Nist had entered the U.S. Navy as an aviation cadet with the intention of going to war as a carrier fighter pilot. Over the last two years, he had logged 880 flight hours in a variety of naval aircraft, including the SBD Dauntless dive-bomber, the F6F Hellcat fighter and the F4U Corsair fighter. He had served with training and operational squadrons in Illinois, Texas, Florida and California. Now he was about to put all of that training to the ultimate test, in arguably some of the most heavily defended enemy skies in the world.

6

Tokyo and Iwo Jima

Vice Admiral Marc Mitscher brought a very powerful striking force to the waters off the Japanese Home Islands. The centerpiece of this strike force was its carrier aircraft. Most of the pilots of these Navy warbirds had never seen combat before. Their first combat action would be against the very heart of the Japanese Empire.

Defenders of the Heart of the Japanese Empire

The Japanese Home Islands were among the most heavily defended areas of the world in early 1945. Japanese leaders had been utterly shocked and infuriated by the April 1942 Doolittle Raid in which USAAF B-25 bombers had flown off USS *Hornet* to bomb Tokyo and other Japanese cities. Nearly three years later, the war had come home to the Home Islands. Since November 1944, they had been under air attack from U.S. Army Air Forces B-29 Superfortresses, very heavy bombers operating from the Marianas Islands. U.S. forces were at long last liberating the Philippines from Imperial Japanese domination. Most Japanese leaders realized that it was only a matter of time before powerful U.S. naval forces began lashing at the Home Islands. Though preparations to defend the Home Islands against air and sea attack were underway, there still was much complacency in the Japanese high command.

Japanese aircraft factories were churning out warbirds despite the massive shortage of trained pilots to fly them. In January 1945, the Joint Target Group of the U.S. Army Air Forces estimated that the Japanese were producing 2,100 combat aircraft per month, of which 60 percent were fighters, 27 percent were bombers and the remaining 13 percent were reconnaissance aircraft. The Japanese had an estimated 2,470 fighters, 1,070 bombers and 990 other aircraft of all types serving in their front-line units as of 1 December 1944. Most of these planes were destined for use as kamikazes. The Japanese were also losing about 900 aircraft per month in combat and operational losses.[1]

The Japanese aircraft industry was concentrated around Tokyo, Nagoya and Kobe. The primary Japanese aircraft manufacturers were Mitsubishi, Aichi, Nakajima, Kawasaki and Kawanishi. Nakajima and Mitsubishi together produced about 80 percent of Japanese aircraft engines. Nakajima had one engine plant and two airframe plants in the vicinity of Tokyo. The heavily concentrated nature of the

Japanese aircraft industry made it highly vulnerable to air attack. This vulnerability apparently had not dawned upon Japanese leaders, even at this advanced stage of the war in the Pacific. "Those engine plants thus far covered by aerial photography are compactly built concentrations of large buildings," reported the Joint Target Group in January 1945. "They have been apparently designed and built primarily for production efficiency with no dispersal because of fear of bombing."[2]

To defend the Home Islands, the Japanese were using a multilayer defensive arrangement. Far out to sea, a ring of picket boats detected both air and surface forces approaching the Home Islands. The next layer of defense was fighter and bomber aircraft. Both the Imperial Japanese Army and Navy operated aircraft. Land-based Imperial Japanese Navy fighters and bombers would attack enemy ships and aircraft over the ocean while the Imperial Japanese Army Air Force would attack enemy aircraft over land. Japanese Navy fighters were responsible only for the airspace in the immediate vicinity of their airfields. The navy fighters were part of the Third Air Fleet. The army fighters were part of the 10th Air Division. According to staff officer Major Toga Horishi, the 10th Air Division had 200 fighters with which to defend Tokyo and its environs but was hampered by fuel shortages. There was no fighter direction or air defense center to coordinate the Japanese army and navy fighters but some liaison arrangements had been implemented. Lastly, the Japanese had extensive anti-aircraft installations positioned around their vital areas. Light Japanese anti-aircraft weaponry included 6.5 mm, 7.7 mm and 13.2 mm light machine guns, 20 mm cannon and 40 mm Bofors guns. These weapons protected the heavier anti-aircraft guns from strafing by enemy aircraft. Heavy anti-aircraft guns included 75 mm, 120 mm and 127 mm guns.[3]

Both the Japanese Army and Navy employed fighters for the defense of the Home Islands. Each fighter was deadly in the hands of a skillful operator but they were less well-armed and less survivable than their American opponents. Most Japanese fighters lacked armor protection and self-sealing fuel tanks. The army employed three fighters that were manufactured by Nakajima: Ki-43 "Hayabusa (Peregrine Falcon)," Ki-44 "Shoki (Demon)" and Ki-84 "Hayate (Gale)." The Allies assigned their own names to Japanese aircraft; thus, the Ki-43 "Hayabusa" was called the "Oscar" by the Allies. The Ki-43 (Oscar) could attain 333 miles per hour and had a range of 1,800 miles when fitted with drop tanks. Japanese fighters were typically armed with combinations of 12.7 mm and 7.7 mm machine guns and 20 mm cannon with at most four weapons per aircraft. The Ki-44 "Tojo" and Ki-84 "Frank" had weapons mounted in the wings and in the fuselage synchronized to fire through the propellor. Mitsubishi produced two fighters for the Imperial Japanese Navy: the J2M2 "Raiden (Thunderbolt)," or "Jack" as the Allies called it, and the A6M Type 00 "Reisen." Called "Zeke" by the Allies and popularly known as the "Zero," this carrier-based fighter came as a deadly surprise to Allied pilots in the early months of the war. The "Zeke" was highly maneuverable and fast, and had a high rate of climb, but lacked protective armor and was very vulnerable to machine gun fire. Over 10,000 Zeke fighters were built during the war in six models. By this stage of the war, American naval fighters were faster, more heavily armed and better protected than their Japanese counterparts.[4]

Name	Speed	Ceiling	Range	Armament
Ki-43 "Oscar"	333 mph	36,800 feet	1,800 miles with drop tanks	One 12.7 mm mg & one 7.7 mm mg or two 12.7 mm mg
Ki-84 "Frank"	427 mph	34,450 feet	1,339 miles	Two 20 mm guns & two 12.7 mm mg
Ki-44 "Tojo"	383 mph	36,745 feet	1,056 miles	Two 20 mm guns & two 7.7 mm mg
J2M2 "Jack"	365 mph	38,385 feet	1,179 miles	Two 20 mm guns & two 7.7 mm mg
A6M5 Type 00 "Zeke" Mk1	346 mph	38,520 feet	1,870 miles with drop tanks	Two 20 mm guns & two 7.7 mm mg
F6F-5 Hellcat	388 mph	37,300 feet	1,530 miles	Six .50-caliber mg
F4U-1 Corsair	446 mph	41,500 feet	1,005 miles	Six .50-caliber mg

Source: *Jane's Fighting Aircraft of World War II*

Plan of Attack

At 1900 on the evening of 15 February 1945, Task Force 58 began a high-speed run to the launch positions for the next morning's air strikes. VADM Marc Mitscher's intention was to deliver a surprise aerial attack on the Japanese Home Islands using a storm front to mask the approach of his carriers. Task Force 58 would approach to less than 100 miles from the Japanese coast and launch fighter sweeps to destroy Japanese aircraft on the ground and any that managed to get airborne. After the Japanese fighter defenses had been sufficiently degraded, then Mitscher would launch air strikes against key industrial targets, most especially the Japanese aircraft assembly and aircraft engine factories in and around Tokyo. The objectives were to destroy Japanese aircraft and aircraft manufacturing and to distract Japanese attention from the impending invasion of Iwo Jima, which was scheduled for 19 February 1945. Coupled with the U.S. Army Air Force's B-29 Superfortress air raids currently underway, the Navy air strikes would also deliver serious damage to Japanese morale by demonstrating the vulnerability of the heart of the Japanese Empire. Overnight, Mitscher's Task Group 58.5 night fighters would continue to harass the Japanese. After several years of waging war across the Pacific, the fight that Japan had initiated would be brought home to them in a powerful and undeniable way.[5]

Task Force 58 was bringing tremendous combat power to the very doorstep of Imperial Japan. Surprise was on their side. In the ready rooms and spaces of the task force's ships, nevertheless, there were no illusions about the enormity of their task. That night aboard *Bunker Hill,* Chaplains Abbott Peterson and Robert E. Delaney offered prayers via the ship's loudspeaker system.[6]

VADM Marc Mitscher was a veteran of carrier warfare since the first days of America's involvement in the Pacific War, but most of his pilots were not. Mitscher was cognizant of this fact. So, prior to these historic first naval air strikes on the heart of the Japanese Empire, VADM Mitscher had several classified memoranda issued to his commanders, pilots and aircrews to pass along his knowledge and experience of carrier warfare and to bolster their self-confidence in accomplishing their missions. The three most significant ones dealt with procedures for fighter sweeps in the Tokyo area, flak evasion and air combat methods for pilots.[7]

On 5 February 1945, VADM Mitscher's chief of staff, Commodore Arleigh A. Burke, put out a memorandum to all of the task force's aviators regarding tactics for evading enemy anti-aircraft fire. COM Burke stated that aircrews could expect two general categories of anti-aircraft weapons: heavy anti-aircraft guns (75 mm or greater size) and automatic weapons (40 mm or smaller in size). When in range of enemy anti-aircraft weapons, pilots were to vary their speed, course and altitude at irregular intervals to make targeting more difficult for the enemy's gunners. When seven miles from heavy anti-aircraft weapons, pilots were to change course by 30 degrees and/or altitude by 500 feet every 15 seconds until they were within range of automatic weapons. These methods should also be used when flying away from those weapons. Noting that automatic weapons fire was effective at a slant range of 2,500 yards, COM Burke wrote that pilots should use moderate evasive maneuvering but not to the detriment of their aircraft's speed.[8]

COM Burke had several general rules for flight crews to follow when dealing with flak. Pilots should strafe anti-aircraft gun crews, attack downwind and take advantage of the sun's position when possible. When making steep strafing attacks on well-defended targets, pilots should level off at 1,000 feet. Pilots must not follow each other through the same opening in cloud cover when they are flying over a defended area or fly just under cloud cover. This would make it easier for Japanese anti-aircraft gunners to determine their altitude and improve their chances of scoring hits on U.S. aircraft. Flak intelligence officers would provide course recommendations that took into consideration the location, number and type of anti-aircraft defenses.[9]

The following day, VADM Mitscher sent a top-secret memorandum for the commanders of his task groups with recommended procedures for the upcoming fighter sweeps against the Tokyo area. In stating the mission of these sweeps, Mitscher was direct and to the point: "Destruction of enemy aircraft wherever found in the air and on the ground." Mitscher expected "that enemy fighters will rise up in great numbers to defend the Tokyo area, its airfields, industry and harbor facilities."[10]

VADM Mitscher's recommendations covered all aspects of the fighter sweeps from takeoff to returning for landing. Mitscher wanted all task groups to launch their first three fighter sweeps at the same time so that the fighters would arrive over the target areas in sufficient strength. Each task group was to break their sweeps into three groups flying at three separate altitudes providing mutual cover. If enemy fighters were encountered over the ocean prior to making landfall, the fighter sweep leaders were to detach sufficient numbers of fighters to deal with the enemy and continue on to the targets with the remainder of the sweep group. Mitscher recommended arming the fighters of the first three sweeps with rockets, then adding bombs for succeeding sweeps. The fighters were to retain their drop fuel tanks for as long as possible in order to provide the most fuel possible for the fighters and to aid in identification to other friendly forces. Over the target, the low-level group would strafe first while the other two groups provided overhead cover against enemy fighters. Then the intermediate group would attack covered by the high group. The high group would wait until the next sweep arrived. The high group would brief the incoming sweep on the situation then proceed with their attack while covered by the follow-on sweep. Mitscher left target selection and priorities up to the individual task group commanders. The fighter sweep leaders were to designate rendezvous points offshore to gather their fighters together for the return to the carriers. Mitscher also recommended route and attack procedures for several weather scenarios likely to be encountered. Lastly, Mitscher wanted his fighter pilots prepared to fight enemy fighters near their task groups on the return to their carriers. To this end, each pilot was to retain 100 rounds of ammunition per machine gun if possible to deal with any enemy fighters threatening the task group. While Mitscher had excellent recommendations, he left the final decisions on tactics up to his individual task group commanders and their respective air group commanders.[11]

The third significant memorandum for the upcoming Tokyo air raids was addressed specifically to all Task Force 58 pilots. Titled "Air Combat Notes for Pilots," this memo was posted in all carrier ready rooms. The four-page memo covered aerial tactics for fighter and bomber pilots and for flight leaders at all levels. "The coming raid on TOKYO will produce the greatest air victory of the war for carrier aviation, but only if every air group commander, squadron commander, combat team leader, section leader and individual pilot abides by the fundamentals of air combat that have been taught to them since the war started," VADM Mitscher began. Predicting that the coming battle would primarily be fought by fighters, he wrote:

> The enemy will be forced to come up to protect the capitol of his empire. He will be aggressive and eager to display his ability to his people on the ground. In his eagerness and inexperience will he meet his downfall in great numbers but only if you keep your heads and apply your teamwork to the utmost.[12]

In paragraph three, VADM Mitscher focused on the torpedo and dive-bomber pilots. They would launch their strikes after the fighter sweeps had reduced enemy fighter strength. Friendly fighters would escort the bombers to and from the target and protect them from enemy fighters. Maintaining formation was essential for mutual protection and to assist the escorting fighters in protecting them. When attacking the target, each aircraft would dive from a slightly different angle than the preceding one to make it more difficult for the anti-aircraft gunners to hit them. After the target runs, the bombers were to quickly rendezvous at a designated point or on a designated course to assist the escorting fighters in protecting them for the return flight to the carrier. "Put your bomb on the target after carrying it all the way in there," Mitscher directed. "Usually an aggressive diving attack provides more safety than a high pull-out which only breaks the continuity of your dive and makes it difficult if not impossible to rejoin your division."[13]

Most Task Force 58 fighter pilots had never been in combat before. "This fact will not be too great a handicap if pilots will remember the fundamentals and keep calm," VADM Mitscher wrote. He stressed the necessity of teamwork and staying together. He cautioned them to be wary of decoys, to look all around for enemy aircraft before diving, and not be lured by decoys into anti-aircraft traps. Speed was also essential. Mitscher told his pilots to maintain 160 knots indicated air speed at a minimum and climb at high speed. Mitscher wanted his fighter pilots to be aggressive but also to work together. "Remember that your plane is superior to the Jap's in every way," he wrote. "He is probably more afraid of you than you are of him."[14]

As the first missions would be against Japanese airfields, Mitscher had instructions for strafing ground targets. He advised his pilots to pull out of their dives at 1,000 feet and to fire bursts of not more than six seconds. "Don't start strafing until you know you have a target and can hit it," Mitscher instructed. "Remember that a well place strafe will chew up an aircraft on the ground even if it doesn't burn." He warned his fighter pilots not to make repeated strafing runs on the same target without first retiring out of automatic weapons fire range.[15]

During the strike missions, the fighters' primary role was to protect the bombers from Japanese fighters. Mitscher directed his fighter pilots to maintain a tight weave over the bombers when the enemy was in sight. They were to stay with the bombers and not go chasing Japanese fighters. When an enemy fighter attacked the formation, the Navy fighter pilot was to aim at the enemy, open fire when the opportunity presented itself and quickly return to the weave over the bombers. When the bombers dived on their targets, fighters were to accompany them, and strafe enemy anti-aircraft guns.[16]

The mission was not over until the aircraft were back aboard the carriers. Mitscher emphasized that the fighter pilots should be vigilant on the return flight for any enemy fighters trailing them back to the carriers. Periodically, the fighters were to circle 360 degrees to check if they were being followed. He told them to descend to 3,000 feet or lower, which would force the Japanese to fly high and thus be easier for the picket destroyers and task group radar operators to spot. Mitscher also wanted his fighter pilots to keep 100 rounds per machine gun for use against any Japanese aircraft approaching the task groups.[17]

VADM Mitscher's concluding admonitions were directed at bomber and fighter pilots alike. He reiterated the need to stay together, to maintain at least 160 knots indicated air speed, to pull out of bombing and strafing dives at 1,000 feet and to join up with the nearest friendly plane if they became separated from their formation. "Let's bear down every minute between now and the big day which you alone can make the greatest day in history for naval aviation, AND THE SADDEST DAY FOR THE JAPS [emphasis in original]," VADM Mitscher wrote in conclusion.[18]

The First Day of Air Strikes

At dawn on 16 February, Task Force 58 was in position to launch its air strikes. The launch position was 125 miles southeast of Tokyo but only 60 miles from the coast of Honshu—the largest and most populated of Japan's Home Islands. So far, the task force had not been detected by the Japanese.

The weather enabled Task Force 58 to approach so close to the Japanese Home Islands undetected. VADM Mitscher had used the weather to his advantage. At launch time, the weather was completely overcast with a ceiling of 4,000 feet. Winds were out of the northeast at Force 6 to 7 (22 to 33 knots) with occasional rain and snow squalls. The atrocious weather had helped to conceal the task force from Japanese surveillance and lulled them into a false sense of security, but it also presented significant challenges for U.S. pilots and aircrew.[19]

The first air strikes of the morning were fighter sweeps to take out Japanese fighter defenses on the ground and in the air. The sudden appearance of American fighters over Japan took the Japanese completely by surprise. Only the first fighter sweep flown by Task Group 58.2 met serious Japanese opposition. Soon after crossing the Chiba Peninsula on the east side of Tokyo Bay, a group of 100 Japanese fighters attempted to intercept Task Group 58.2's fighters. Forty of the Japanese fighters were claimed by U.S. pilots. Otherwise, Japanese opposition was minimal or nonexistent. A fighter sweep by Task Group 58.3 in late morning earned them the distinction of being the first U.S. Navy fighters over Tokyo.[20]

In his postwar memoirs, Rear Admiral Frederick C. Sherman recorded his thoughts on the start of his Task Group 58.3's air strikes on Japan. "As our planes swept in from the sea over Tokyo and Yokohama, the ground was covered by a light fall of snow, and thick weather over the target area hampered the operations," he wrote. "It was a strange experience to all officers and men of the task force. After fighting so long in the tropics here we were off Tokyo at last, and we were amazed at the lack of determined air opposition. No Japanese aircraft came within 20 miles of our disposition and our planes roamed at will over the enemy's territory seeking their targets."[21]

Task Group 58.3's three aircraft carriers were very busy on the morning of 16 February. *Essex* provided combat air patrols and conducted four fighter sweeps against Tateyama, Hamamatsu and Tenryu Airfields near Tokyo. *Essex*'s fighters claimed 13 enemy aircraft in the air and another 16 on the ground. *Cowpens*'s fighters conducted three sweeps of Japanese airfields, destroying two aircraft on the ground and one in the air. *Bunker Hill* conducted four fighter sweeps.[22]

Bunker Hill launched her first fighter sweep of the day at 0710 in a combined mission with *Essex* and *Cowpens*'s air groups. Led by Major Roberts, 16 fighters from VMF-221 strafed aircraft and hangars at Tatayama Airfield and two small vessels off the coast, sinking one. CAPT William N. Snider and First LT Don McFarlane shot down a "Betty" bomber over Tatayama, thus scoring Air Group 84's first combat aerial victory. Three aircraft were destroyed on the ground by strafing and several hangars were set afire. The *Bunker Hill* flight landed back aboard ship at 0940.[23]

LT(jg) Wilbert Popp was part of one of Fighting 84's first fighter sweeps against Japan. Due to the heavy cloud cover, Popp and his associates had to climb up to 20,000 feet to find clear skies. The outside temperature was 60 degrees below zero. At one point, he saw Mt. Fuji, which at 12,589 feet was Japan's highest mountain. "It is a beautiful mountain, a perfect cone in snow white, similar to how our Mt. St. Helens looked prior to its eruption," he wrote in his memoirs. Later during this mission, Popp spotted a Japanese Tojo fighter and attempted an intercept with ENS Curtis Lee Jefferson as his wingman. With the Tojo in his sights, Popp fired his six machine guns but nothing happened. They had frozen at the high altitude. ENS Jefferson's guns had frozen too. "So my first trip of great expectations over Tokyo ended up as a colossal bust," he later wrote.[24]

Bunker Hill's second fighter sweep consisted of 12 Corsairs and two Hellcat photo planes. Again, *Bunker Hill*'s fighters were accompanied by those of *Essex* and *Cowpens*. Sweep #2 was led by Air Group 84 commander CDR Ottinger flying a

Corsair. This was VF-84's first combat mission of the Pacific War as a squadron. Sweep #2 took off at 0820.[25]

The F6F-5P Hellcat photo planes were flown by LT(jg) John J. Sargent and LT(jg) James A. Nist. Nist was flying aircraft number 72614. This was "Shorty" Nist's first combat mission as a naval aviator and he was flying into the heart of the Japanese Empire.[26]

Weather conditions prevented them from reaching their primary target area so CDR Ottinger diverted them to a secondary area closer to the coast. Finding an opening in the heavy clouds, the VF-84 Corsairs made one strafing run on Oi Airfield with no observed results. During his strafing dive, LT(jg) "Dusty" Miller's right aileron ripped off. He returned to the carrier accompanied by another Corsair. CDR Ottinger then led his fighters to Hamamatsu Airfield. Weather conditions were more favorable here. Fourteen single-engine Japanese aircraft and 179 twin-engine aircraft of various types were on the airfield. Ottinger and his Corsairs made two strafing runs on the airfield. Enemy anti-aircraft fire was medium in intensity but inaccurate. One Nakajima Ki-49 "Helen" medium bomber was destroyed on the ground. Four other "Helen" bombers and a Mitsubishi GM4 "Betty" twin-engine naval bomber was damaged. During the Corsair strafing runs, several Japanese aircraft attempted to take off. LT(jg) J.C. Dixon shot down one "Helen" medium bomber and Ensign J.O. Pini shot down a Mitsubishi Ki-24 "Topsy" twin-engine transport aircraft. CDR Ottinger and his wingman, LT(jg) Ralph K. Coconougher, damaged a "Helen" medium bomber that was taking off. Next, CDR Ottinger led the remaining Corsairs to strafe Tenryn Airfield.[27]

After strafing Tenryn Airfield. Ottinger and his Corsairs then rendezvoused about 10 miles south of the airfield over the water. LT(jg) J.E. Diteman's division was engaged by each a "Tojo," "Zeke" and "Hamp" fighter. Diteman damaged the "Tojo" fighter and the other three members of his division—LT(jg) Larson, LT(jg) Daniel and ENS C.S. Carter—all shot at and damaged the "Hamp" fighter. Then they rejoined the rest of Sweep #2 and headed back to *Bunker Hill*. LT(jg) Sargent and LT(jg) Nist made a total of six photo runs over the target areas. Sweep #2 returned aboard *Bunker Hill* at 1120. The mission took three hours to accomplish and covered some 300 miles total.[28]

Led by LCDR Roger Hedrick, fighter sweep #3 took off from *Bunker Hill* at 0930. They joined up with 11 Marine Corsairs from *Essex* and headed west to the island of Honshu. LtCol William Millington of VMF-124 from the *Essex* Air Group was in overall command. Finding the weather in their primary target area to be unsuitable for strafing, LtCol Millington led the *Bunker Hill/Essex* Corsair fighter flight south to attack Yaizu Airfield located on the western side of Suruga Wan (Bay). There the Marine and Navy Corsairs found two twin-engine bombers, 15 "Zeke" fighters, four "Val" dive-bombers and two single-engine trainers. Three strafing runs were conducted against minimal anti-aircraft fire from light machine guns. LCDR Roger Hedrick and LT Gardner each destroyed a "Zeke" on the ground. Marine Corsairs shot down four enemy aircraft in the air. The Corsairs destroyed at least one "Val" and six "Zekes" on the ground and damaged 10 others. Sweep #3 returned aboard at 1250.[29]

Bunker Hill launched sweep #4 at 1055. Sweep #4 consisted of VMF-451 Corsairs. The Marine fighters strafed a convoy of five ships and numerous small crafts and shot down a "Jake" fighter. On this mission, *Bunker Hill* and Air Group 84 experienced their first combat loss. Hit by anti-aircraft fire, First LT Forrest P. Brown, Jr., bailed out of his Corsair 16 miles from Sune Saki lighthouse. He was last seen in the water in a life jacket but a rescue submarine sent to retrieve him was unable to find him.[30]

Change of Plan

VADM Mitscher's original plan was to saturate Japanese airfields with fighters to destroy enemy fighters and facilities on the ground. Concerned about the worsening weather conditions, Mitscher decided at 1130 to move up the bombing raids. He ordered air strikes against the Nakajima Ota and Koizumi aircraft factories. Both installations had been previously attacked by B-29 Superfortresses.[31]

The Nakajima Corporation was Japan's oldest and largest aircraft manufacturer. The company had been founded on 6 December 1917 by Chikuhei Nakajima. As an engineer in the Japanese navy, Nakajima had studied aeronautics in the United States and even learned to fly at the Curtiss Aircraft Company's Dayton, Ohio, facility. After returning to Japan, Nakajima resigned his commission, secured financial backing and founded the Nakajima Aircraft Corporation. Nakajima constructed his first aircraft airframe assembly plant at Ota and in 1919 began producing planes for the Japanese army. A year later, Nakajima began producing airplanes for the Japanese navy as well. In 1924, Nakajima Corporation began producing aircraft engines as well. By early 1945, Nakajima was producing 47 percent of Japan's combat aircraft. This included the "Frank," "Tojo" and "Oscar" fighters and the

VADM Marc Mitscher (right) and his chief of staff, COM Arleigh Burke. discuss Task Force Fifty-Eight operations against the Japanese Home Islands in February 1945 while aboard USS *Bunker Hill* (Naval History and Heritage Command [Photo 80-G-303981]/National Archives).

"Helen" medium bomber. In addition, Nakajima was producing 32 percent of Japan's aircraft engines—a close second to Mitsubishi. By war's end, Nakajima had 121 manufacturing facilities in existence, of which 88 were operational.[32]

The Nakajima Corporation had concentrated its aircraft production in the vicinity of Tokyo. Airframe plants were located at Ota and Koizumi and an aircraft engine plant was located near Tokyo. Both airframe plants were massive complexes with about 2.5 million square feet of floor space in their various buildings. The Ota Airframe Plant was located some 55 miles or so from the coast near the city of Ota and about 40 miles northwest of Tokyo. Originally constructed in 1919, the plant became obsolete by 1934 so it was converted to a machine shop and a new, much larger airframe plant was constructed. The Ota complex occupied a rectangular area about 2,500' by 2,000', of which about 55 percent of this area had been developed. There were over 30 buildings of various sizes in the complex. Here the Nakajima Corporation assembled some 20 percent of Japan's combat aircraft, including the twin-engine "Helen" bomber and single-engine "Frank," "Tojo" and "Oscar" fighters. The Joint Target Group estimated that Nakajima Ota produced 100 "Frank" fighters, 50 "Tojo" fighters, 40 "Helen" twin-engine bombers and two Ki-83 twin-engine bombers in the month of December 1944. They also estimated that Nakajima Ota and the Tachikawa Aircraft Company together produced 270 "Oscar" fighters in that same month. Several days before the scheduled Navy air strikes, American B-29 Superfortresses had struck the Ota Plant, inflicting moderate damage on the facilities.[33]

In 1937, the Japanese government directed Nakajima Aircraft to expand its airframe and engine production capacity to fulfill the larger numbers of aircraft and engines being ordered for military use. In response, the Nakajima Corporation built a new airframe plant at Koizumi and a new engine plant at Musashi. Production of navy aircraft began in February 1941 and the plant was fully operational in March of 1944. The Koizumi Factory was located north of Tokyo in the town of the same name in the Gunma Prefecture and only a few miles south of Ota. The Koizumi complex consisted of nearly 60 buildings of various sizes. The Joint Target Group estimated that the Koizumi Factory produced 265 "Zeke" 52 fighters, 45 "Irving" twin-engine fighters, 75 "Frances" twin-engine bombers and 50 "Jill" single-engine bombers in December 1944. Altogether, the two Nakajima assembly plants and the engine plant produced some 51 percent of Japan's single- and twin-engine fighters, and 37 percent of all Japanese aircraft types.[34]

Task Group 58.3's primary effort for the afternoon of 16 February was a major air strike against the Nakajima Ota and Koizumi Aircraft Assembly Plants. Other U.S. aircraft had been unable to locate either plant due to the awful weather conditions. Strike A consisted of 13 Avengers, 11 Corsairs, six Hellcats and two photo Hellcats from *Essex*'s Air Group Four; four Hellcats and nine Avengers from *Cowpens*'s Light Air Group 46; and 18 Corsairs, 13 Helldivers and 14 Avengers from *Bunker Hill*'s Air Group 84. *Essex* and *Cowpens*'s air raiders would go after Nakajima Koizumi while *Bunker Hill*'s air raiders went after Nakajima Ota. Altogether, Task Group 58.3 would be sending 49 bombers and 39 fighters against the Nakajima targets. Overall command of the air strike was exercised by a strike leader from *Essex*.[35]

Heretofore, Air Group 84 had been launching only fighter sweeps. At 1440, the air group launched its first bombing raid on a Japanese target. The target was the Ota Airframe Plant. Strike A consisted of 14 Avengers from VT-84, 13 Helldivers from VB-84 and 18 rocket-armed Corsairs from VF-84. Overall command of Air Group 84's strike force was exercised by LCDR John P. Conn, Jr., commanding officer of VB-84. Amid wind and rain, the Air Group 84 raiders launched from *Bunker Hill*. Their approach to the Japanese coast was hindered by a 50-mile-per-hour headwind and a cloud ceiling that kept them below 8,000 feet.[36]

One of the Fighting 84 pilots participating in the Ota Plant airstrike was LT(jg) "Shorty" Nist. He was piloting Corsair Number 82204. This was his second combat mission of the day. In the morning, he had flown a photo Hellcat in support of a fighter sweep against several airfields.[37]

On the way to the target, *Essex*'s and *Cowpens*'s air groups encountered weather conditions so severe that the *Essex* strike leader decided to divert from the Nakajima Koizumi complex to Mawatari Airfield on the coast east of Tokyo. The airfield was strafed and rocketed. Twelve aircraft were destroyed on the ground. Several aircraft hangars and other buildings were set afire. One "Tojo" fighter was shot down too. The two air groups returned to their respective aircraft carriers without incident.[38]

SB2C Helldivers from Bombing Squadron Eighty-Four heading to bomb targets in the vicinity of Tokyo on 16 February 1945 (Naval History and Heritage Command [Photo NH 62573]/ National Archives).

Earlier in the day, strike groups from other carriers had found heavy cloud cover over the Ota Airframe Plant and been forced to divert to secondary targets. Weather conditions had improved considerably by the time Air Group 84's raiders arrived over Japanese land territory. "Sunlight cascaded down on the foothills leading to Honshu's interior," wrote Robert Olds in his *Helldiver Squadron* published later that year. "The planes were moving into perfectly clear weather." The formation climbed to 13,500 feet and headed inland with the foothills of Japan's mountainous interior ranging below them.[39]

Eleven operational Japanese airfields were located along the route to the target. By now, the Japanese defenders were alert and waiting for the American fliers. At least 15 to 20 Japanese fighters attempted to intercept the Air Group 84 warbirds. Japanese fighters followed them to the target and then back to the coast, seeking opportunities to strike at the American bombers. Along the way, one "Tony" and one "Tojo" fighter were shot down. A Tojo fighter surprised Second LT William M. Pemble of VMF-451 and shot him down.[40]

Arriving over the target, Air Group 84's warbirds found the skies suitable for bombing. With the Corsairs providing overwatch, the Helldivers and Avengers pummeled the target with 77 500-pound bombs and 12 250-pound bombs. "Twelve thousand pounds of general-purpose bombs from the bays of a dozen planes and an additional one thousand pounds from under the wings of four of them crashed down on the plant that had only been hit once before—by B-29s several days previously," stated Bombing 84's Aircraft Action Report for this mission. In addition to the Avengers and Helldivers, the Corsairs launched rocket attacks and strafed the factory facility. The carrier planes left the target with numerous buildings on fire and several appearing to be on the verge of collapsing.[41]

When it was his turn, "Shorty" Nist dove on the target and unleashed his rockets and machine gun fire. Then he rejoined the Air Group 84 formation and helped escort the bombers home to *Bunker Hill*. His flight time for the mission was 3.5 hours.[42]

This raid was the costliest of the day for Air Group 84. Three planes failed to return. In addition to Second LT Pemble's Corsair, two VT-84 Avengers were shot down with the loss of all six aircrew members. One Helldiver was so heavily damaged while landing aboard *Bunker Hill* that it was pushed over the side. *Bunker Hill* pilots claimed two "Tony" fighters and one "Tojo" fighter shot down.[43]

The Japanese were completely taken by surprise by Mitscher's air strikes on the Home Islands. Weather conditions helped to conceal American ships from Japanese surveillance efforts. Japanese fighter opposition was negligible. The few Japanese aircraft that dared to attack the task force were easily dispatched by combat air patrols far from the American ships. Japanese picket boats, however, actively sought the American ships. The destroyer USS *Haynsworth* (DD-700) sank three picket boats and rescued several survivors.[44]

In early evening, Task Force 58 retired eastward and spent the night undisturbed by Japanese aircraft as it prepared for another day of attacks on the Home Islands.[45]

Far to the south on Kyushu, the Commander-in-Chief of the IJN's Fifth Air

Fleet, Admiral Matome Ugaki, quickly became aware of the American air strikes. His aircraft had been searching the water east of Kyushu for the American ships but had failed to locate them because they were off the coast of Honshu. Late on 16 February, he wrote in his diary:

> In spite of repeated warnings that an enemy will come, the Kanto district was subjected at last to the enemy's surprise attack, with the result that army and navy planes destroyed on the ground added up to 150. Other damage inflicted on installations and vessels will be fairly big, too. It's most regrettable to see that little improvements have been made in defensive patrols and reconnaissance.[46]

17 February 1945

Early on the following morning, the Fast Carrier Task Force steamed back within striking distance of the Japanese Home Islands. Weather conditions had worsened considerably overnight. Launching before dawn, Task Group 58.5's night aircraft were the first to sortie. They were followed by combat air patrols and fighter sweeps against the Japanese airfields.[47]

At 0715, 10 of *Bunker Hill*'s VMF-451 Corsairs and nine VF-46 Hellcats from *Cowpens* were launched on a fighter sweep. Led by Major Ellis of VMF-451, the combined *Bunker Hill/Cowpens* force struggled against a 100-mile-per-hour headwind. En route, three Hellcats developed engine problems and had to return to *Cowpens*. A fourth Hellcat dropped out of formation and was never heard from again. Northwest of Tokyo, the remaining five Hellcats and 10 Corsairs encountered 30 Japanese fighters. Three "Zeke" fighters were shot down and eight other fighters were damaged.[48]

During the melee with the "Zekes," *Bunker Hill*'s Corsairs got separated from *Cowpens*'s remaining Hellcats. The Hellcats strafed Mito Airfield and destroyed two Japanese aircraft on the ground. They returned to their carrier separately. The Marine Corsairs strafed Shmomiro Airfield, damaging four enemy aircraft on the ground. Four Corsairs were hit by ground fire. Three made it back to *Bunker Hill;* one pilot ditched at sea and was rescued by a U.S. destroyer. More important than the damage inflicted, the Marine pilots discovered that flying conditions inland were dramatically better than those over the ocean.[49]

While the fighter sweeps were underway, VADM Mitscher launched air strikes against the Nakajima Tama Musashimo and the Tachikawa aircraft plants near Tokyo. The Nakajima Tama Musashimo Engine Plant was located some 12 miles northwest of Emperor Hirohito's Imperial Palace near the village of Musashi. The Nakajima Tama Musashimo Plant was one of the two largest aircraft engine plants in Japan. The complex had 51 buildings with 2.5 million square feet of total floor space. Built in 1938, the Musashimo Factory doubled Nakajima's engine production capacity when it opened. The Tama section was built in 1941. The distinctive three-story building with its seven long narrow wings was easily recognizable from the air. Together both sections were producing an estimated 1,500 engines per month, which was about 40 percent of Japan's total monthly aircraft engine production. Nakajima Tama Musashimo also produced engines for aircraft built by Mitsubishi, Kawanishi and Aichi Aircraft companies. These aircraft included the "Zeke," "Oscar," "Frank" and "Tojo" fighters and the "Frances" and "Helen" bombers.[50]

Around 0900 on the morning of 17 February 1945, Task Group 58.3 launched a major strike against the Nakajima Tama Musashimo Engine Plant. The other three task group carriers were also sending aircraft to destroy aircraft engine manufacturing facilities. *Bunker Hill* launched 12 Avengers and 10 Helldivers with 26 Corsairs as a fighter escort. *Essex* launched 18 Hellcats, eight Marine Corsairs and 14 Avengers. *Cowpens* sent seven Avengers and eight Hellcats to bomb the Nakajima plants. Many of the strike force fighters were carrying bombs or rockets. Altogether, Task Group 58.3 dispatched 103 aircraft for the raid on Nakajima Tama Musashimo. Its Action Report called the mission a "power-house strike."[51]

En route, three of the strike force's Avengers had mechanical issues and were forced to abort the mission. The remaining Task Group 58.3 aircraft continued on to the target. One hundred U.S. warbirds arrived over the two Nakajima engine factories and proceeded to pound the daylights out of them. *Essex*'s aircraft hit the Tama Plant with 11 tons of bombs. The *Cowpens*'s pilots put 90 percent of their bombs on target. Air Group 84's warbirds dropped over eight tons of bombs on the targets and fired 32 rockets at them as well. Numerous hits were observed in both factories. "As the strike began its low-level retirement to the west, heavy smoke was observed rising to 3000 feet from the flaming buildings," stated the Task Group 58.3 Action Report.[52]

"Shorty" Nist's roommate, LT(jg) Popp, flew on this strike mission. In his memoirs, he wrote of the experience: "We made at least three strafing runs dropping our bombs on our first pass, firing rockets on our second pass and using our 50 caliber machine guns with every third round being an incendiary bullet."[53]

Enemy air opposition was minimal and ineffective. "Few enemy planes were encountered and they were reluctant to engage in combat preferring to break away when our planes made an attack," stated the *Cowpens* Action Report afterward. Forty Japanese fighters attempted to intercept the Air Group 84 strike group; escorting fighters shot down five of them. "All of TOKYO's teeming population, not covered up in air raid shelters, thus has a chance to witness the impotency of Japanese aircraft against America's mighty air power," stated the Task Group 58.3 Action Report. Only one U.S. aircraft was lost, but the pilot was rescued.[54]

After the war, RADM Frederick C. Sherman wrote about his task group's air strike on the Tama Engine Plant. "One beautifully coordinated air strike from my task group pinpointed fifty 500-pound bombs, plus 42 rockets, into the Nakajima Tama Engine Plant," he wrote. "The crews had the satisfaction of observing a conflagration with smoke rising to 3,000 feet as they withdrew. Although intense flak was put up in defense of this important plant, not a single pilot or air crewman was lost."[55]

LT(jg) Nist did not participate in the Tama Engine Plant air raid. He flew an F4U-1D Corsair numbered 82214 as part of a combat air patrol for the task group. The mission lasted 4.2 hours.[56]

Combat air patrol, or CAP, was vitally important for the safety of the Fast Carrier Task Force ships steaming off the Japanese Home Islands. With acute shortages of trained pilots, the Japanese had turned to kamikaze attacks to destroy American ships. They had first employed this tactic the previous October when U.S. forces returned to the Philippines. Unable to match the quality of American pilots and aircraft, senior Japanese leaders decided to send their inadequately trained pilots crashing into American ships. The tactic was frighteningly effective and would only get worse as 1945 progressed.

Once aloft, LT(jg) Nist and the other Corsairs in his CAP team were assigned to patrol an area some distance from the task group. Radar aboard *Bunker Hill* and other ships scanned the skies for approaching enemy aircraft. If enemy aircraft were detected, then fighter direction officers would guide the CAP fighters to intercept them, but none were detected on this CAP mission.

The awful weather conditions over the Japanese Home Islands persisted throughout the day. American aircraft struggled with heavy cloud cover, low cloud ceiling and frequent squalls over the target areas. With the weather worsening, VADM Mitscher decided at 1115 to cancel all further air strikes. Throughout the afternoon, Task Force 58 aircraft completed their missions over Japan and returned to their aircraft carriers. At 1600 after all strike aircraft had been recovered, the task force retired southward. Their next mission was to support the invasion of Iwo Jima scheduled for 19 February 1945.[57]

The weather had enabled the Fast Carrier Task Force to approach the Japanese Home Islands undetected and helped hide the task force from Japanese efforts to locate it. The weather also hampered U.S. air operations over Japan and forced VADM Mitscher to cut short his air strikes. Nevertheless, despite the weather difficulties, the Fast Carrier Task Force had produced some significant results with its first naval air strikes on the Japanese Home Islands. The 10,600-ton *Yamashiro Maru* and several other Japanese vessels were sunk in Tokyo Bay. U.S. pilots claimed 341 Japanese aircraft shot down and another 190 destroyed on the ground. U.S. aircraft flew 2,761 sorties in two days of operations. Task Group 58.1 attacked Japanese airfields almost exclusively, destroying 68 aircraft on the ground and another 56 in the air. Task Group 58.2 mostly attacked airfields and also hit the Ota and Koizumi Aircraft Assembly Plants. Task Group 58.3 struck airfields and aircraft factories on both days of operations. Task Group 58.4's warbirds struck at seven Japanese airfields and the Tachikawa Aircraft Engine Plant, expending 80.10 tons of bombs and 1,148 rockets. Altogether, Task Force 58 lost 60 planes in combat and 28 for operational causes.[58]

Task Group 58.3 had done well under difficult circumstances. Its aircraft had flown 392 sorties over the targets. They destroyed 89 Japanese aircraft in the air and on the ground and damaged another 78 aircraft for a loss of 10 aircraft in combat and four aircraft to operational causes. Seven Task Group 58.3 pilots and four aircrewmen were missing or dead.[59]

RADM Frederick C. Sherman was well pleased with the performance of his Task Group 58.3. After the war, Sherman wrote, "The two days' operations demonstrated our carriers' strength and the lowly state to which the Japanese air force had sunk. They emphasized that the Rising Sun was setting."[60]

Task Group 58.3's Action Report offered high praise for the pilots and aircrewmen of this first Navy strike on the Japanese Home Islands:

It is worthy of note that in this first carrier strike on the Japanese homeland, Air Group 84 on the BUNKER HILL and Air Group 46 on the COWPENS, entered combat for the first time. Except for a nucleus of experienced pilots, this strike on TOKYO was the first action against the enemy in which these pilots participated. Their highly creditable performance, however, established them as seasoned veterans during this series of operations, and paid high tribute to the soundness of their selection, the quality of their training, and their unmistakable fighting spirit.[61]

At every level of the chain of command, Navy leaders were pleased with the results of the first Navy air strikes on the Japanese Home Islands. Fifth Fleet commander Admiral Raymond Spruance sent the following message to the Fast Carrier Task Force:

Congratulations to all hands on a superlatively well-done job. Only courage, skill and intelligent team work by every member of Task Force Fifty-Eight could have produced these historic results in spite of opposition by both enemy and weather. I know that our future operations will hurt the enemy even more.[62]

LT(jg) James Nist had performed well in his first combat missions against the Empire of Japan. He had flown three combat missions, including two over the Japanese Home Islands. He had flown one photo-strike, one target-strike and one combat air patrol for a total flight time of 12 hours. One mission was flown in an F6F-5P Hellcat and the other two missions were flown in F4U-1D Corsairs.[63]

By 18 February 1945, Japanese commanders had figured out the composition of the American carrier force. On that day, Admiral Ugaki noted (correctly) in his diary that the American force consisted of five task groups totaling 11 aircraft carriers and five converted aircraft carriers (light carriers). Tracking the U.S. carrier force, however, continued to be difficult. On the night of 17–18 February 1945, the Japanese lost track of the U.S. carrier force altogether. The next morning, the carriers were located when they transited past Chichi Jima. "They were nearly five hundred miles away from here, so we couldn't do anything about them," wrote Admiral Ugaki in his diary.[64]

Back in the United States

On 24 January 1945, Jimmy's uncle Frederick Hayes passed away at the age of 57 from stomach cancer. Uncle Frederick was one of his mother's brothers and worked in the newspaper business. Jimmy learned of his uncle's passing a couple of weeks afterward.

At the conclusion of the Navy air strikes on Japan, LT(jg) Nist found a few moments to pen a letter to his parents. "Can't say much, but Fighting 84 had it's baptism of fire recently as you undoubtedly saw headlined coast to coast," he wrote on Sunday 18 February. "I used to say we carried our colors pretty high, but I'm a-thinking we're needing a taller flagpole because we're even sharper than I thought.... And now that we've got the first one under our belt, we ought to be even better." To assuage his parents' worries, Nist added, "Just wanted you to know Lt(jg) Shorty Nist and the rest of VF-84 came through without a scratch and is now in the big leagues. Used to holler about all the training but it really paid off big."65

Soon after, Ethel and Martin Nist received a letter from their future daughter-in-law. On 22 February 1945, Alice Richards wrote to Ethel, sharing how much she was missing her fiancé. "Am certainly looking forward to next summer when he gets home," she wrote. "Sure is lonely without him here. From the newspapers and radio it looks like they are sure busy around Tokyo now."66

For security reasons, the sailors and Marines of the Fast Carrier Task Force could not provide any information about the Tokyo air strikes to the family and friends back home. However, the Public Affairs Office of the Pacific Fleet did release some information on the air strikes to the general public on 15 February 1945. Due to the International Date Line, the date was still 15 February in the U.S. when the Navy launched its first strikes on Japan. The Fleet Public Affairs communique read:

> Vice Admiral Marc A. Mitscher in command of a powerful task force of the Pacific Fleet is now attacking enemy aircraft, air bases and other military targets in and around Tokyo. This operation has long been planned and the opportunity to accomplish it fulfills the deeply cherished desire of every officer and man in the Pacific Fleet.67

Four days later, on 19 February 1945 (20 February 1945 in Tokyo), the U.S. Pacific Fleet Public Affairs Office released a communique summarizing the results of the recent air strikes on Japan. "The U.S. Pacific Fleet achieved a decisive victory over the enemy in attacks on Tokyo on February 16 and 17 (East Longitude Dates)," began the communique. The communique stated that fleet forces had approached the enemy coast under adverse weather conditions that inhibited enemy air operations and enabled the U.S. fleet to achieve tactical surprise. According to the communique, the U.S. had shot down 332 enemy aircraft, destroyed 177 enemy aircraft on the ground and probably destroyed or damaged another 159 enemy aircraft on the first day of the air strikes. In addition, an escort carrier moored at Yokohama was bombed and set afire. She subsequently rolled over on her side. Nine coastal vessels, one destroyer, two destroyer escorts and one cargo ship were also sunk and 22 coastal vessels were damaged. Pacific Fleet Public Affairs also reported that hangars and other installations at various airfields were destroyed. The Ota Aircraft Factory was damaged by bombs and the Musashine Tama and Tachigawa Engine Plants were heavily damaged as well. The U.S. forces lost 49 aircraft during the air strikes and 30 to 40 pilots. None of the U.S. ships sustained any damage."68

The full results of the 16–17 February 1945 naval air strikes on Japan would not be known until after the war when the United States Strategic Bombing Survey (USSBS) studied the air strikes as part of its investigation into the results of U.S. air power in the Pacific theater. The USSBS had been established in November 1944 within the War Department to evaluate the effectiveness of airpower and strategic bombing during the war. Exhaustive surveys were completed of both the European theater and Nazi Germany, and the Pacific Theater and Japan. In June 1947, the USSBS released a report on the Nakajima Aircraft Company that included an analysis of the various bombing raids on Nakajima's facilities. According to the report, the Nakajima Ota Plant was struck by 59 high-explosive bombs during the 16 February 1945 Navy air strikes, of which 16 bombs failed to explode.[69]

The USSBS report for Nakajima Aircraft Corporation also discussed the effects of U.S. Army Air Force and U.S. Navy air strikes on the Tama Musashimo (Musashi) Engine Plant. "Musashi was the most frequently bombed works in the Japanese aircraft industry," noted the report. The 20th U.S. Army Air Force attacked the plant 12 times, though four of those raids were unable to bomb the target because of weather conditions. Eight raids occurred prior to the Fast Carrier Task Force raid of 17 February. Bombing accuracy of the B-29s was generally poor due to weather conditions with only 15.9 tons of bombs actually striking plant buildings. The USSBS estimated that only 10 production days were lost as a result. The U.S. Navy Fast Carrier Task Force hit Tama-Musashimo Plant just once ... on 17 February 1945. "The Navy carrier-based plane attack on the morning of 17 February inflicted the heaviest damage on Musashi up to that time.... Only small bombs and rockets were used, but at low levels accuracy was good," noted the USSBS report. While the Tama section suffered only superficial damage, the Musashimo section suffered much greater damage. Twenty-five percent of the machine shop was destroyed, and 172 machine tools were destroyed or damaged. This caused some 20 production days to be lost, which equated to about 750 aircraft engines.[70]

En Route to Iwo Jima

On the night of 17–18 February 1945, the Fast Carrier Task Force steamed southward to join naval forces preparing to assault Iwo Jima. Along the way, U.S. destroyers sank three small Japanese picket boats and a larger patrol craft. The next day, the Task Force passed west of Chichi Jima and Haha Jima and launched air strikes against their airfields to prevent them from being used for air attacks on the American ships participating in the Iwo Jima invasion. Afterward, Task Groups 58.2 and 58.3 took up station west of Iwo Jima while the other three task groups refueled south of the island.[71]

The Iwo Jima Invasion

Iwo Jima was a pear-shaped volcanic island about halfway between the Marianas Islands and the Japanese Home Islands. Located astride the flight routes of U.S. B-29 Superfortresses attacking Japan from the Marianas, Iwo Jima provided early warning of U.S. air raids heading for the Home Islands. Its two airfields were used to attack those B-29s and a third airfield was under construction. Capturing the island would eliminate its use as an early warning site and for attacks on the Superfortresses. The island would also provide a convenient emergency landing field for B-29s returning from Japan with battle damage and/or running low on fuel. American long-range P-51 Mustang fighter planes based on the island could support B-29 raids on Japan. For these reasons, Iwo Jima was selected for capture by the III Amphibious Corps.[72]

Iwo Jima was barely eight square miles in size. At its southern end, Mount Suribachi rose some 528 feet. Knowing the strategic importance of the island to the defense of the Japanese Home Islands, the Japanese had been fortifying the island for over a year. Under the direction of General Tadamichi Kuribayashi, they turned the rugged volcanic island into a nearly impregnable fortress with an underground labyrinth of tunnels and fighting positions, well-concealed concrete bunkers and pillboxes, and hidden artillery and mortar positions. Some 22,000 Japanese service members were on Iwo Jima, mostly of the Imperial Japanese Army's 109th Division. Writing of Iwo Jima in his postwar memoirs, the commanding general—expeditionary troops, LT Gen. Holland M. "Howlin' Mad" Smith, USMC, wrote, "The conditions of its capture were dictated by the Japanese, not ourselves, and we took it the only possible way—by frontal attack, by interposing our own flesh and blood whenever armament did not suffice."[73]

To seize Iwo Jima, the United States Navy and Marine Corps had assembled a huge force of ships, airplanes and personnel. This included Task Force 58's 16 fleet carriers and light carriers and Task Force 51's 12 escort carriers. The Navy also provided battleships, cruisers and destroyers for naval gunfire support; logistics ships; and hundreds of amphibious assault ships and landing craft. Iwo Jima would be

February 1945 aerial photograph of Iwo Jima. Mount Suribachi is at the far left end of the island. Motoyama Airfields Numbers One and Two are in the center of the island. The invasion beaches are to the right of Mount Suribachi and below Motoyama Airfield One (Naval History and Heritage Command [Photo NH 106377]/National Archives).

A Navy TBM Avenger torpedo bomber flies over Mount Suribachi sometime after Iwo Jima's capture (Naval History and Heritage Command [Photo 80-G-412543]/National Archives).

assaulted by the three divisions of the Marine Corps' V Amphibious Corps. The Fourth and Fifth Marine Divisions would assault Iwo Jima, and Third Marine Division would serve as a floating reserve. With over 80,000 Marines committed to the invasion, this operation would be the largest Marine-only operation of World War II.

USAAF B-24 Liberator bombers operating from the Marianas had been periodically pounding Iwo Jima for the last several weeks. Beginning on 16 February, Navy warships ranging from old battleships to rocket-firing small craft and Navy, Army Air Force and Marine aircraft pounded Iwo Jima for three days. Minesweepers cleared the waters around Iwo Jima of sea mines, and underwater demolition team (UDT) swimmers reconned the landing beaches. Early on the morning of 19 February, the invasion commenced. *Essex*'s Air Group Four fighters attacked the flanks and high ground around the landing beaches with rockets and napalm bombs, then strafed the beaches themselves. *Cowpens*'s Hellcats and Avengers struck the eastern slope of Mount Suribachi with bombs and rockets. Air Group 84's aircraft attacked beach installations and gun emplacements. Altogether, 90 Task Group 58.3 warbirds pounded Iwo Jima right before the Marines hit the beaches.[74]

The first Marine waves were able to get ashore without much trouble but soon ran into difficulties with the steep slopes and loose sand of the landing beaches. Then the Japanese defenders opened up with murderous fire from concealed artillery, mortar and machine gun positions that had not been neutralized by the pre-invasion naval and aerial bombardment. Casualties quickly mounted. The beaches became congested with wrecked landing craft, amphibious assault tractors (AMTRACs) and vehicles of all kinds. Against impossible odds, individual Marines and groups of Marines pushed inland, painstakingly capturing positions. By the end of the first day, the Marines had reached the foot of Mount Suribachi and the edges of Motoyama Airfield Number One. The cost of that first awful day was high. The assaulting Marines suffered 2,420 casualties, including 501 killed. Among the dead was Gunnery Sergeant John "Manila John" Basilone of the Fifth Marine Division, whose extraordinary heroism on Guadalcanal had earned him the Medal of Honor.[75]

Overhead, Navy and Marine aircraft flew numerous sorties to help the Marines on the ground. "We flew directly over the head of the dug-in Marines and aimed our fire directly ahead of them," Fighting 84 pilot LT(jg) Wilbur Popp later wrote in his memoirs. "I can still see the dust coming up from the sand as we fired." That day, Task Group 58.3 aircraft flew 182 combat sorties in support of the Marines ashore, dropping 49 tons of bombs and 76 napalm bombs and firing 739 aerial rockets against Japanese defenses.[76]

LT(jg) Jimmy Nist of VF-84 flew two combat missions during the first days of the Iwo Jima invasion. On the first day of the invasion, he flew Corsair Number 82196 on a strike mission that lasted 3.4 hours. Two days later, he flew F6F-5P Hellcat number 72614 on a three-hour photo reconnaissance mission over Iwo Jima. These aerial photos were used to assess previous strike missions and identify targets for Air Group 84's aircraft.[77]

Ashore, U.S. Marines were encountering much heavier resistance than they had been expecting.

Airfield Number One was captured by the end of day one. Fifth Marine Division cut off Mount Suribachi from the rest of the garrison and raised U.S. flags on its summit on 23 February.

"Reports as of this time indicate that all Jap defenses on Iwo Jima were expertly planned, expertly executed and fanatically defended," recorded the War Diary of the

Commander in Chief, Pacific Fleet on 24 February 1945. "All emplacements, including block houses, pill boxes and caves, were mutually supporting and arranged in depth."[78]

American ships supporting the Iwo Jima invasion of Iwo Jima were repeatedly attacked by Japanese kamikazes based in the Home Islands. *Lunga Point* (CVE-94) was damaged by a Japanese torpedo bomber. Two kamikazes struck *Bismarck Sea* (CVE-95) and she later sank. *Saratoga* (CV-3) survived five kamikazes, but her wartime service was over.[79]

With kamikazes inflicting such damage, combat air patrols became even more vital to the defense of the fleet. On 22 February 1945, LT(jg) Jimmy Nist flew his only combat air patrol of the operation. He went up at the controls of Corsair Number 82658 for nearly four hours over Task Group 58.3.[80]

Task Group 58.3 spent only three days flying missions in support of the Iwo Jima invasion. In those three days, Task Group 58.3 flew 596 combat sorties—more than they had against the Japanese Home Islands. Task Group 58.3 fliers dropped 92 tons of bombs and 115 napalm bombs on Japanese defenses on Iwo Jima and Chichi Jima and fired 1,445 five-inch rockets.[81]

Return to Tokyo

The ferocity of Japanese kamikaze attacks on U.S. ships off Iwo Jima prompted VADM Mitscher to take his Fast Carrier Task Force back to Japanese waters for the second time in two weeks. Leaving Task Group 58.5 behind to provide night support for the invasion force, Mitscher took the rest of Task Force 58 north again to the Tokyo environs to take out the kamikazes at their source. In conjunction with these Navy air strikes, over 200 Marianas-based Superfortresses bombed Tokyo.

High winds and heavy seas delayed Task Force 58 in reaching its launching point. On the morning of 25 February 1945, Navy warbirds again took off from the task force's flight decks to pummel military and industrial targets in and around Tokyo. "Despite unfavorable weather, both in the vicinity of the Task Force and over the target, with visibility from medium to poor, planes took off the pitching flight decks on their mission," wrote RADM Frederick C. Sherman.[82]

Bunker Hill and Air Group 84's first fighter sweep was led by VF-84's commander, LCDR Roger Hedrick. The 16 VF-84 Corsairs were loaded up with external fuel tanks and five-inch aerial rockets. LT(jg) John Gildea led a division consisting of LT(jg) A.L. Brooks, LT(jg) Wilbert Popp and ENS Curtis Jefferson. Over Katori Airfield, the Corsairs encountered a large group of "Zekes," "Franks" and "Oscars" intent on fighting. LCDR Hedrick shot down two "Franks," one of which exploded in a fireball that he flew through. He also shot down a "Zeke." Hedrick's Corsair was struck nine times by ground fire. Despite the damage, Hedrick was able to get his wounded Corsair back to *Bunker Hill* with only 15 gallons of fuel remaining. Altogether, Fighting 84 claimed nine aerial victories, three of which were downed by Hedrick and two by LT W.G. Laney.[83]

While some of the VF-84 Corsairs were tangling with Japanese fighters aloft, the remaining Corsairs strafed and rocketed Katori Field. During his strafing run,

ENS Jefferson's Corsair was struck by anti-aircraft fire in his main fuel tank. His wingman, LT(jg) Popp, radioed to LT(jg) Gildea requesting that the three of them escort ENS Jefferson back to the ship. Gildea declined to do so and sent Popp back with Jefferson. "This decision on his part, in my opinion, lead to disastrous results for Jeff," Popp wrote in his memoirs. Jefferson reached the ocean but soon ran out of fuel. With Popp's guidance, Jefferson ditched his Corsair amid rough seas. He got out of his sinking plane but without his life raft. As Jefferson floated in the ocean amid dye marker, Popp radioed for other U.S. forces to rescue his downed wingman. Unfortunately, due to the low cloud ceiling, Popp's radio messages did not transmit far. Popp contacted a nearby U.S. submarine on the radio but they could not pinpoint his location. If another VF-84 Corsair had been with him, Popp could have maintained visual contact with Jefferson while the other Corsair flew higher and served as a radio relay to coordinate the rescue. When Popp's own Corsair ran low on fuel, he was forced to return to *Bunker Hill*. ENS Jefferson was never seen again. He was Fighting Squadron 84's first combat loss.[84]

Forty minutes after the fighter sweeps took off from *Essex* and *Bunker Hill*, the Task Group 58.3 carriers began launching aircraft for Strike A. Over 100 aircraft from *Essex*'s Air Group Four, *Cowpens*'s Air Group 46 and *Bunker Hill*'s Air Group 84 participated in the air strike. VMF-221 provided 20 Corsairs, each armed with a single 500-pound bomb. VB-84 sent 13 of its Helldivers, each armed with a 1,000-pound bomb and two 250-pound bombs. VT-84's contribution to the strike was 13 of its Avengers, each carrying four 500-pound bombs. To jam the enemy radar, all of the *Bunker Hill* Avengers were equipped with aluminum chaff and four Avengers were also equipped with AN/APT-1 radar jammers. Their target was the Nakajima Musashino Engine Plant near Tokyo.[85]

Fighting Squadron 84 contributed four aircraft to Task Group 58.3's strike on the Nakajima Musashino Engine Plant. Two of the aircraft were F6F-5P Hellcats sent to photograph the air strikes' results. These two photo Hellcats were piloted by LT(jg) James Nist and ENS Kenneth D. Lane. They were escorted by two Corsairs piloted by LT(jg) Willard J. Rempel and LT(jg) Lewis A. Maberry. Nist was flying Hellcat #72614. It was Nist's third time piloting this aircraft. In the last two weeks, he had flown three photo-strike combat missions, two of which were in this aircraft.[86]

Arriving over the target, Task Group 58.3's Strike A pilots discovered low-hanging clouds that precluded bombing the Musashino Plant. So, they diverted to the Nakajima Ota and Koizumi Plants instead. This was familiar territory for the American air raiders; they had just flown strikes in the vicinity the previous week. A light snow had covered the complex but left the nearby airfields and roadways visible. As the Bombing 84 Aircraft Action Report stated:

> The crazy quilt pattern of rice fields that had appeared green brown on the first flight over the area the previous week now formed tiny lines etching hollow squares in the whiteness. It was as though some giant doodler had scribbled hundreds of tick-tack-toe patterns on a freshly laid table cloth.

The American warbirds bombed the vast aircraft plants without any difficulty. "After the first few thousand-pounders slammed into the snow-covered buildings, rolling dark clouds of smoke belched upward," wrote Robert Olds in *Helldiver Squadron*. An estimated 50 500-pound bombs struck the Ota Plant, and eight 1,000-pound bombs and between 25 and 30 500-pound bombs struck the Koizumi Plant.[87]

Following the bombers, LT(jg) Nist and Ensign Lane conducted a photo run in their Hellcats over the target to record the strike results. Photo interpreters later estimated that 90 percent of the Ota Plant and 20 percent of the Koizumi Plant had been damaged or destroyed as a result of this raid and the previous ones.[88]

After the bombers worked over the Ota and Koizumi Plants, their accompanying fighters strafed the nearby Koizumi and Tatebayshi Airfields. Twelve Japanese aircraft were destroyed on the ground and six more damaged. CAPT John B. Delancey of VMF-221 put a 500-pound bomb into an aircraft hangar at Koizumi Airfield. Anti-aircraft fire was intense but inaccurate at Koizumi Airfield and none at all at Tatebayshi Airfield. There was no air opposition during the mission. The two VF-84 Hellcats and two VF-84 Corsairs strafed targets of opportunity along the coast, setting afire several fishing vessels.[89]

Throughout the morning, the weather conditions got steadily worse. At 1215, VADM Mitscher canceled further air operations for the day. Then weather forecasts indicated that the weather around Tokyo would be atrocious as well the following day. So Mitscher decided to take the Fast Carrier Task Force south and strike at Nagoya on 26 February instead.[90]

By early evening, Task Force 58 had recovered all aircraft and set a course for Nagoya.

Overnight, sea conditions worsened such that Mitscher had to reduce speed to 12 knots to avoid damage to his destroyers. At 0040, the light cruiser *Pasadena* (CL-65) and destroyer *Porterfield* (DD-682) sank a Japanese picket boat that got into the task group formation. By 0514, Mitscher realized that they were not going to reach the launching positions in time to attack Nagoya in the early morning. He canceled all further aerial operations against the Home Islands and turned the task force away to rendezvous with tankers for underway refueling. The Task Force refueled at sea on 27 February 1945. Afterward, Task Group 58.4 was sent back to Ulithi for maintenance and refit and the rest of TF 58 headed south for Okinawa.[91]

Three days after Mitscher's warbirds struck the Japanese Home Islands for a second time, the Pacific Fleet Public Affairs Office released a communique summarizing these recent operations. According to the communique, U.S. pilots destroyed 158 Japanese aircraft, including 47 in the air, and damaged another 75 on the ground. Seventeen Japanese vessels were sunk or probably sunk and 14 others were damaged. Two trains were destroyed in the vicinity of Tokyo. The Ota Aircraft Factory sustained heavy damage with 75 percent of its buildings destroyed. The Koizumi Aircraft Plant was also heavily damaged. U.S. losses were nine aircraft and four pilots. No U.S. ships were damaged by the enemy.[92]

The Fast Carrier Task Force had now struck at the Japanese Home Islands twice in two weeks. Both times the Japanese had not reacted aggressively against Mitscher's ships operating less than a hundred miles off their coast. "The enemy's policy and reaction at present are definitely passive," ADM Spruance reported shortly afterward. "He could have found us with search planes during daylight 24th [February] but there was no indication of such."[93]

RADM Frederick C. Sherman also commented on the lack of serious air opposition over Japan. "The enemy opposition was only halfhearted and Japanese planes which were not shot down seemed glad to withdraw from the scene of hostilities as swiftly and unceremoniously as possible," he wrote in *Combat Command*. "Even here, over their own capital, the enemy were notably inferior to our naval aviators in aggressiveness, tactics and determination."[94]

COM Arleigh Burke had been disappointed by the results of the first Tokyo raids but was well pleased with the second raids. Writing after the raid to his wife, Bobbi, Burke stated "The plans went much better than we thought they would. I hope that it will continue to be so—but there is a lot to do yet.... Perhaps in another six months the Japs will commence to get a taste of what war is really like, and a year from *there* [emphasis in original], perhaps they will have had enough."[95]

Task Force 58 conducted air operations over the Japanese Home Islands and the Tokyo area for three days in February 1945. During that time, TF-58 aircraft flew 2,471 sorties, dropped 377.75 tons of bombs, fired 2,910 rockets, shot down 383 enemy aircraft and destroyed an estimated 288 enemy aircraft on the ground. TF-58 lost 55 fighters and five bombers to enemy action and another 20 fighters and eight bombers to operational causes. Fifty-one pilots and aircrew were lost in combat and another 11 to operational causes. TF-58 aircraft and surface ships destroyed or sunk 48 enemy vessels. Two aircraft assembly plants and two aircraft engine plants were heavily bombed. Twenty-three Japanese airfields were attacked with varying amounts of damage inflicted on their hangars, fuel facilities, ammunition depots and support facilities.[96]

For its second visit to the Tokyo area, Task Group 58.3 performed well. During 174 sorties, TG 58.3 aircraft destroyed 20 enemy aircraft in the air and 36 on the ground. During their morning air strike, task group aircraft scored an estimated 50 bomb hits on the Ota Factory and upward of 40 bomb hits on the nearby Koizumi Factory. Both aircraft facilities were left burning. Three task group fighter aircraft were lost.[97]

Task Group 58.3 played an important role in the three days of Tokyo air strikes. TG58.3 aircraft flew 530 sorties or 21.4 percent of the total flown by TF-58. They fired 260 rockets and dropped 126.45 tons of bombs or 33.5 percent of TF-58's total bomb tonnage. TG 58.3 lost three Hellcats, six Corsairs, one Helldiver and two Avengers in combat operations and three Corsairs, a Hellcat and a Helldiver to operational causes. TG 58.3's combat losses were 20 percent of the task force's total combat losses. TG58.3 lost nine pilots and four aircrewmen in combat.[98]

James A. Nist had reported as an aviation cadet in January 1943. Two years and one month later in February 1945, LT(jg) James Nist flew his first combat missions as a naval aviator. In total, he had flown seven combat missions for a total flight time of 26.7 hours. He had attacked Japanese airfields and an aircraft factory and provided air support for the Iwo Jima invasion. By month's end, Nist had amassed some 906.5 hours of flight time as a naval aviator.[99]

Keeping in Touch

Having completed its most recent strikes on the Japanese Home Islands, *Bunker Hill* and the Fast Carrier Task Force were heading for Okinawa and the Ryukyus Island group. LT(jg) "Shorty" Nist now had some time to respond to the letters he had recently received from home. On 27 February, he received a total of 17 letters. Nine were from his fiancée, Alice, five were from his parents and three were from his sister Wootz. "Alice used to write three times a week and I promised to answer everyone one she wrote," Jimmy informed his parents on 28 February 1945. "Guess that was a big promise, because now its every day."[100]

On 28 February, Jimmy wrote a four-page letter to his parents that covered a range of topics, some of which were inspired by the letters that he had received from them. Ethel had broken her ankle earlier that year. Due to delays in getting mail out to the western Pacific, Jimmy did not find out about it until much later. Apparently, there was some speculation among the Nist family that Jimmy and Alice had gotten married before he shipped out. Jimmy put that speculation to rest. Furthermore, he promised his parents that they would meet their future daughter-in-law before he and Alice got married.[101]

There were two topics that Jimmy was surprisingly candid about in his 28 February 1945 letter to his parents. They were topics that heretofore he had not addressed in any of previous letters. Perhaps it was because entering into combat had caused him to become circumspect and reflect upon his life. The first topic was his short height. "I've learned a few things, including the fact that a few brains can make up for a few inches and then some, especially when it comes to flying." In fact, Jimmy had even given himself the nickname "Shorty" when his squadron was choosing radio call signs.[102]

The other issue was related to his rapid progression through school. Jimmy had graduated from high school at age 16 and entered Rutgers University three months before his 17th birthday. He graduated from Rutgers at age 20. To his parents, he wrote:

> The only thing ever wrong with me was an inferiority complex developed from going through school too quick and consequently with kids two or three years older all the time. It was quite a burden for a long time, but I think I can say now that that's gone over the dam and Shorty's doing okay these days. Howsomever, no kids of mine are ever going to skip grades in school and you can bet your last dollar on that.[103]

Due to the need to preserve operational security, Jimmy still could not discuss his squadron's operations or whereabouts. "I suppose you're all waiting to hear the full details on the travels of Misbehavin' Butch," he wrote to his parents. "Not quite yet, but as soon as we leave this area we're in now, we can relate our personal experiences a little as long as we don't tell too much or where we are or have been. As if you couldn't guess."[104]

Still mindful of the need for operational security, Jimmy did share a couple of details about his experiences. "Misbehavin' Butch has been on nine combat hops so far," he wrote. "As of yet, she still has to open fire on a Jap plane in the air. They don't like to get in range of a sextet of .50 caliber machine guns. She's swell and so is her pilot and I'll see that they both remain so."[105]

Here Jimmy was not being exactly truthful about his aircraft. Per standard procedures, Jimmy was not assigned to fly any particular aircraft. His assigned aircraft depended upon the mission he was flying. For combat air patrols and air strikes, Nist typically flew a Corsair. For photo and photo/strike missions, Nist flew a Hellcat equipped with aerial cameras.

Conclusion

The historic flag raisings on Mount Suribachi were far from the conclusion of the Iwo Jima invasion. The battle raged unabated for another six weeks. When TF 58 left to strike Tokyo a second time, TF51's escort carriers provided air support and old battleships and cruisers provided naval gunfire support for the Marines ashore. Mount Suribachi and Motoyama Airfield Number One were captured by the Marines within the first few days of the invasion. The rugged northern half of the island proved far more challenging and deadlier. Terrain features took on sobriquets like Bloody Gorge and the Meatgrinder, which conveyed the ferocity of the fighting. Even less ominous-sounding features like the Amphitheater and Turkey Knob were wrested from the Japanese only after vicious battles. For the only time during the Pacific War, U.S. casualties exceeded those of the Japanese. "Every cave, every pillbox, every bunker was an individual battle, where Japanese and Marine fought hand to hand to the death," wrote General Holland Smith in his postwar memoirs.[106]

The Fast Carrier Task Force played an important supporting role in the invasion. Its fighters protected the invasion force from Japanese air attack. Its fighters and bombers provided key air support for the Marines ashore. During the first days of the operation, *Bunker Hill* aircraft flew 44 percent of Task Force 58's sorties, dropped 53 percent of the bombs used against Japanese defenses and fired 67 percent of the aerial rockets fired in support of the forces ashore.[107]

Iwo Jima was finally declared secure on 26 March 1945. The cost of capturing the island had been very high, as Gen. Holland M. Smith related in his postwar memoirs:

> Iwo Jima was the most savage and the most costly battle in the history of the Marine Corps. Indeed, it has few parallels in military annals. In the first five days we suffered casualties at an average of more than 1,200 a day. One out of every three Marines who set foot on the island was killed or wounded. In the first 50 hours, our casualties were more than 3,000, and in a campaign lasting 26 days, with many more days of mopping up, our total casualties were 21,558, of whom 5,521 were killed or died of wounds. Divisions ended the battle with less than 50 percent combat efficiency.[108]

Even with the preponderance of fire support and material, the capture of Iwo Jima ultimately came down to the individual Marines who struggled daily against the tenacious Japanese defenders and their formidable fortifications. As Admiral Chester A. Nimitz succinctly stated, "Among those who served on Iwo Jima, uncommon valor was a common virtue."

7

With the Fast Carrier Task Force in March 1945

Even though the Iwo Jima invasion would continue until the end of March, the Fast Carrier Task Force's involvement was over. During the month of March 1945, the task force would get some much-needed rest and upkeep at Ulithi Atoll, strike the Japanese Home Islands several more times and conduct air strikes in preparation for the upcoming Okinawa invasion.

Preparing for the Next Invasion—Okinawa

Following the Iwo Jima invasion, the next major operation to be undertaken was the seizure of Okinawa. Located just 350 miles south of the Japanese Home Island of Kyushu, the capture of Okinawa was vitally important as a preliminary to the invasion of the Japanese Home Islands. After its capture, Okinawa would be turned into a massive staging area for the invasion.[1]

Okinawa was located in the Ryukyu group of islands southwest of the Japanese Home Islands.

The Ryukyus were further divided into three main groups or "guntos." The Amami Gunto was closest to Kyushu. The Okinawa Gunto was in the middle about 350 miles from Kyushu; its largest islands were Okinawa, the Kerama Retto and Ie Shima. The southernmost group was the Sakishima Gunto.[2]

Okinawa was 70 miles long, five to seven miles wide and encompassed 500 square miles. Much of Okinawa was rugged, hilly terrain. Southern Okinawa had wide level areas, about 80 percent of which were under agricultural cultivation. There were two large semi-protected bays on the east coast. An estimated 140,000 Japanese soldiers were defending the island. Like on Iwo Jima, the Japanese had constructed an extensive labyrinth of underground tunnels and fighting positions, and they had also converted many of Okinawa's numerous burial tombs into fighting positions.[3]

The Japanese had utilized flat areas in southern Okinawa to construct six airfields. The most important of the Japanese airfields was Naha. Located two miles southwest of Naha town on Okinawa's west coast, Naha Airfield was the oldest and most developed of the island's airfields. It was originally a civilian airfield and later taken over for military use. Naha Airfield had three intersecting runways constructed of limestone that formed a rough triangle. Support facilities included two hangars, five workshops, warehouses, barracks, radio stations, radar and direction finders. Heavy anti-aircraft guns and automatic weapons defended Naha from air attack. Okinawa's second most important airfield was Yontan Airfield, located on the central west coast of the island. Its three runways were constructed of coral; they intersected at the northeast corner of the field, forming a sort of fan configuration. The runways were encircled by 60-foot-wide taxiways. Dispersal areas and revetments were located primarily on the southern and western sides of the airfield. Support facilities included warehouses, barracks and administration buildings. Yontan Airfield was defended by seven six-gun heavy anti-aircraft gun batteries and six automatic weapons sites.[4]

Okinawa's other four airfields were smaller and less developed than Yontan and Naha. South of Naha Airfield was Itoman Airstrip. On Okinawa's southeast coast was Yonabaru Airfield, about a mile and a half northeast of the town of Yonabaru. Yonabaru Airfield had not been completed. It had a single 4,800-foot-by-400-foot runway but no support facilities or air defenses. Katena Airfield had a single coral-surfaced runway that was 4,900' in length and 265' in width. Katena had extensive dispersal areas but only four barracks and eight small support buildings. Machinato Airfield was 2½ miles northeast of Naha. Machinato had a single 4,500-foot-long-by-150-foot-wide runway that was oriented northeast-southwest and a single-loop taxiway. To the southeast, a railroad and Okinawa's main west coast highway paralleled Machinato Airfield.[5]

In addition to airfields on Okinawa, U.S. forces would have to contend with airfields located on other islands in the Ryukyus chain. The Amami group in particular was troublesome. Located between Okinawa and Kyushu, the Amami group could be used to stage kamikaze air attacks originating on Kyushu. The Amami group had several airfields with runways, fuel dumps and aviation support facilities.[6]

The Kerama group (Kerama Retto) of small islands and the island of Ie Shima were also important for the Japanese defense of Okinawa. The Kerama Retto was located off the southwest coast of Okinawa. Any invasion force assaulting the southwestern landing beaches on Okinawa would have to pass by these islands. From here, the Japanese could employ coastal guns and suicide boats against the invasion ships. Three miles off Okinawa's northwest coast was the island of Ie Shima. The oval-shaped island was five miles long by two miles wide and about 23 square miles in total area. Ie Shima had a well-developed airfield with three surfaced runways and a fourth runway under construction. The airfield's dispersal areas had 55 aircraft revetments that were connected to the runways by 35-foot-wide taxiways. Support facilities included administration buildings, a control tower, workshops, warehouses, barracks, underground storage facilities and a radio direction finder.[7]

Unlike Iwo Jima and most of the other Pacific islands that U.S. Marines and soldiers had wrested from the Japanese, Okinawa had a very large civilian population, which numbered around 445,000 persons. Most of these people, however, were not ethnically Japanese. The native population of Okinawa was an ethnicity distinct from both the Japanese and the Chinese. Japan had seized Okinawa in the 1870s. They regarded the Okinawans as their inferiors and treated them accordingly.[8]

The invasion of Okinawa was destined to become the largest and most complicated amphibious invasion of the Pacific War to date and one to rival the Normandy Invasion in the European theater. The Tenth U.S. Army with seven Army and Marine divisions was assigned to conduct the invasion, supported by the Fifth U.S. Fleet and a task group from the British Royal Navy. The invasion was scheduled for Easter Sunday, 1 April 1945.[9]

1 March 1945 Strikes on Okinawa

After hitting the Japanese Home Islands again, the Fast Carrier Task Force hit the Ryukyus and Okinawa for the first time on 1 March 1945. The targets were Okinawa's airfields, which posed a direct threat to the task force and the invasion force soon to come. Of prime importance was obtaining photographic intelligence of the island for the upcoming invasion. In addition, photographic missions were flown over Kerama Retto, Amami Oshima and Minami Daito. That meant the photo pilots were very busy on this operation. Task Group 58.3's composition remained basically the same for the first Okinawa strikes: carriers *Essex*, *Bunker Hill* and *Cowpens*, battleships *South Dakota* and *New Jersey*, three light cruisers and 19 destroyers.[10]

Task Group 58.3 launched air strikes, fighter sweeps and photographic reconnaissance missions against Japanese airfields and other installations located on southern Okinawa and Minami Daito Jima. Of the four Japanese airfields attacked that day, Naha Airfield on Okinawa was hit the hardest. Upward of 50 operational aircraft were found there. Despite the heavy anti-aircraft fire, TG58.3 attackers destroyed 16 aircraft on the ground and probably damaged another 21 aircraft. One VB-84 Helldiver was shot down but its crew was rescued. Yontan Airfield's runway was cratered by bombs and one aircraft on the ground was destroyed. Three single-engine aircraft were destroyed on the ground at Minami Daito Airfield and several support buildings were set afire. Several support buildings were set afire at Machinato Airfield.[11]

Overall, Task Group 58.3 had moderate success in its first air attacks on Okinawa and the adjacent islands. Task group aircraft flew 272 combat sorties, dropping 79 tons of bombs and 72 incendiary bombs and firing 631 aerial rockets. They damaged or destroyed 44 enemy aircraft and damaged or destroyed a number of small craft in the waters around Okinawa. Five task group aircraft were lost to enemy action, two of which were from Air Group 84, and six more were lost to operational causes. A *Bunker Hill* pilot was shot down and rescued offshore. Two *Essex* pilots and one aircrewman were lost.[12]

More important than the physical results on the ground of the air attacks were the results of the photographic reconnaissance missions. While the weather was suitable for photo reconnaissance, the intense enemy anti-aircraft fire was very challenging for the photo pilots. As the Task Group Action Report stated, "photographic pilots deserve much credit for full accomplishment of mission." The aerial photographs taken would prove invaluable as invasion planners worked to finalize the upcoming amphibious assault scheduled for 1 April 1945.[13]

One of those hardworking photo pilots was LT(jg) James A. Nist of VF-84. On 1 March, he flew F6F-5P Hellcat number 72614 on a three-hour photo reconnaissance mission over Okinawa. Six Corsairs and two photo Hellcats were used on the mission. LT(jg) J.J. Sargent flew one Hellcat and Nist flew the other one. LT(jg) Sargent was escorted by LT Helms, LT(jg) Vaughn and LT(jg) Matthews; LT(jg) Nist was escorted by LT(jg) Hutt and Ensigns Rayla and McCarthy.[14]

Air Group 84's Photo Mission #1 took off from *Bunker Hill* at 0815. Over Okinawa, Sargent and his escorting Corsairs split off from Nist and his escorts. Sargent took oblique and vertical photographs from Shima Wan to Kawata Wan. Meanwhile, Nist took aerial photographs of the beaches located west and northwest of Yontan and Katena Airfields. After completing their photographic runs, Sargent and Nist rejoined their escorting Corsairs and conducted strafing runs on targets of opportunity. LT(jg) Hutt, LT(jg) Nist and Ensigns Rayla and McCarthy strafed several fishing vessels, small villages and two factories, one of which was left burning. Both divisions returned to *Bunker Hill* independently.[15]

The First Operations of 1945 Considered

The Okinawa strikes concluded the first round of operations for Task Force 58 in 1945. The task force left Ulithi Atoll on 10 February and returned there in early March. In the interim, the task force conducted the Navy's first carrier air strikes on the Japanese Home Islands on 16–17 February, supported the invasion of Iwo Jima, returned to the Japanese Home Islands for another round of air strikes on 25 February and conducted air strikes and aerial photo reconnaissance of Okinawa, Kerama Retto and Amami Gunto in preparation for the upcoming invasion of Okinawa. During these operations, Task Force 58 aircraft flew 5,514 combat sorties, expending 1,118.65 tons of bombs, 218 napalm bombs, 12 torpedoes and 9,896 rockets. Twenty-three Japanese airfields were attacked with hangars and support facilities being destroyed or damaged. The Nakajima Koizumi Airframe Plant, the Nakajima Ota Airframe Plant and the Nakajima Tama Musashino Aircraft Engine Plants were each struck by approximately 40 tons of bombs with devastating results. Task force aircraft shot down 389 enemy aircraft, most of which were downed over the target areas. They also destroyed an estimated 266 enemy aircraft on the ground. Task force ships shot down four enemy aircraft and several Japanese vessels in surface engagements.[16]

Task Force 58 air operations had not been without cost in aircrew and aircraft. During this period, 84 aircraft were lost in combat, mostly Hellcat and Corsair fighters. A further 59 aircraft were lost for operational causes and two night Avengers were shot down by friendly anti-aircraft fire near Iwo Jima. Altogether, Task Force 58 lost 143 aircraft in combat and operational mishaps. Sixty pilots and 21 aircrew were lost in combat and another eight pilots and six aircrewmen were lost in operational mishaps.[17]

Task Group 58.3 had performed well in these two weeks of air operations against Japan. Task group pilots and aircrew had flown 1,226 combat sorties and

646 other sorties in support of combat operations for a total of 1,872 sorties. They had dropped 298 tons of bombs and 115 napalm bombs and fired 2,336 aerial rockets against ground targets. They claimed 65 enemy aircraft destroyed in the air and another 97 on the ground. They seriously damaged the Tama Musashino Engine Plants and the Ota and Koizumi Aircraft Assembly Plants in the Tokyo area. Seventeen aircraft had been lost to enemy action and 15 aircraft were lost to operational causes. Eleven pilots and five aircrewmen had been killed in action or were missing in action.[18]

Overall, VADM Mitscher was very well pleased with the performance of his pilots during the most recent air operations. In his Action Report for this period, he wrote:

> The performance of the pilots during these operations—in view of their inexperience, the nature of the target and the foul weather encountered—is considered to be of the highest order. Too much credit cannot be given to the Naval Aviation Training organization and its methods. A preliminary diagnosis of combat losses other than to anti-aircraft fire indicates that our tactics, if properly applied, will see the pilots through the most difficult tactical situation. Air combat losses in almost every case were due to pilots failing to carry out what they had been taught; namely, they did not stay together in the section.[19]

The Fast Carrier Task Force had flown combat missions over Tokyo and its region on three days during this period. The results had been surprising as the Task Group 58.3 Action Report stated:

> It was thought that the enemy air opposition in the TOKYO area would be so intense that only VF sweeps should be employed for the first day. However, it appears that even near his capital city the enemy cannot prevent us from obtaining control of the air sufficiently to employ heavy VB/VT strikes on the first day of the attack with little effective interception of these strikes by the enemy.[20]

During the Fast Carrier Task Force's first round of operations against Imperial Japan in 1945, LT(jg) James Nist had flown eight combat missions and amassed 29.7 hours of combat flight time. He had flown on two combat air patrols protecting the task group, two air support missions for the Iwo Jima invasion, one strike mission against a Japanese aircraft factory, two photo reconnaissance fighter sweeps against Japanese airfields and a photo reconnaissance/fighter sweep against airfields on Okinawa. He had flown on three combat missions over the Japanese Home Islands.[21]

Respite at Ulithi

After concluding its photo-strikes on Okinawa, the Fast Carrier Task Force headed east to the Ulithi Atoll fleet anchorage. En route, Task Group 58.3 received word of a downed B-29 Superfortress in their vicinity. Search aircraft from *Bunker Hill* located lift rafts and three hours later, USS *Preston* (DD-798) retrieved eight survivors in two rafts. *Bunker Hill* dropped anchor at Berth #9 at 1605 on 4 March. For the next 10 days, the task force performed much-needed maintenance and upkeep. Ammunition and supplies were taken aboard to replenish what was used during the recent operations. Task Force personnel enjoyed some relaxation ashore at the atoll's several recreational facilities that included swimming, sports, socializing and beer.[22]

LT(jg) Nist used the time at Ulithi to get some letters written for his loved ones back home. In one of the letters he had received, his parents had inquired about the Navy's censorship rules and what could be shared with the local newspapers. "And as for telling any of the newspapers stuff to get my name in the paper—the answer is do not—repeat NOT—tell them anything—repeat ANYTHING! [emphasis in original]" he wrote. "If you have any guesses as to where I am, keep them to strictly to yourself. Will tell all as soon as the Navy lets me."[23]

Jimmy and Alice had been making wedding plans. It is not clear whether this occurred when they had been together just prior to him shipping out or if they had been making plans through their letters to each other or a combination of the two. Regardless, Jimmy shared some of those wedding plans with his parents in his 7 March 1945 letter to them:

> When we hit New Jersey, she'll be the latest addition to the Nist Family. And I'm positive you'll find her a good addition. I expect to be in Alameda about a week waiting for my leave papers and then get those big 30 days leave. We're going to be married in St. Anne's Church in San Francisco at a Sunday morning mass which means the church will be full. And naturally it will take place as soon as possible after I get back. We'll probably stay out here for a few days and then hit the trail for New Jersey. Depending on how soon I get back, I might send home for my whites if the weather will be nice and warm. If not, it will have to be the blues. Don't know what else to say except that last September you said that seeing as how you couldn't see her, you'd trust me to pick out a nice one. Well, everybody who's seen her so far seem to agree wholeheartedly that she's very nice and in my opinion, she's perfect.[24]

While at Ulithi Atoll, Task Group 58.3 underwent a reorganization on 8 March. *Essex* was replaced by USS *Randolph* (CV-15) and *Cowpens* was replaced by *Cabot* (CVL-28). *Cabot*'s embarked air group was Carrier Light Air Group 29 with Fighting Squadron 29 and Torpedo Squadron 29. *Essex* also traded Air Group Four for Air Group 83. Air Group 83 included Fighting 83, Bombing/Fighting 83, Bombing 83 and Torpedo 83. Both VF-83's Hellcats and VBF-83's Corsairs could drop bombs as well as engage in aerial combat. In addition, Fifth Fleet's flagship USS *Indianapolis* (CA-35) joined the task group. Thus, Task Group 58.3 now had the carriers *Bunker Hill*, *Randolph* and *Cabot*; the battleships *South Dakota* and *New Jersey*; four light cruisers; and 17 destroyers.[25]

In terms of mail, 10 March 1945 was very good for LT(jg) Nist. That day, he received 16 letters from various people. The following day, he penned a reply to his parents. In it, he commented in general terms about being separated from home and loved ones due to the combat deployment. "We've been taking things easy for a while but I for one am ready to go back and get our job done and get back to San Francisco and then on to New Jersey," he wrote referring to the task force's period in Ulithi. "Never knew it was possible to miss anyone as much as I miss that girl my plane is named after."[26]

The Navy still would not let Jimmy Nist write about his war experiences. In very general terms, Jimmy commented on Fighting 84's performance thus far:

I'm not worried about the feathers in our caps any more, nor am I worried about any Japs clipping our tail feathers. The law of averages might catch up to VF-84 but I doubt it. We've done lots of bragging, but our motto is to do it scientifically instead of by blood and guts. If you stick to the things you've been taught, you'll be okay. We're a little better than the law of averages and don't forget that in the air, the average is about 15 to 1 in favor of the U.S. Navy.[27]

Despite the relaxing surroundings, the war was not far away. On 11 March, a twin-engine "Frances" kamikaze plane struck *Randolph* while she rode at anchor in the Ulithi anchorage. Twenty-seven of *Randolph*'s crew were killed and another 106 were wounded. Aboard *Bunker Hill*, the crew were watching a movie when *Randolph* was struck by the kamikaze. "Here we thought we were in a safe harbor, only to be hit at night," recalled LT(jg) Wilbert Popp. "It had a sobering effect." *Randolph* was repaired at Ulithi but would not return to action until 7 April 1945.[28]

On 14 March, the Fast Carrier Task Force weighed anchor and departed Ulithi Atoll for the next round of combat air operations. The organization of the task force had changed somewhat, in part due to *Randolph* being struck by a kamikaze. With *Essex* returning to replace *Randolph*, TG58.3 now consisted of *Essex, Bunker Hill, Cabot, New Jersey, South Dakota*, four light cruisers and 17 destroyers.[29]

Air Group 84 departed from Ulithi Atoll separate from *Bunker Hill*. LT(jg) Jimmy Nist and a number of other pilots flew a 4.5-hour training mission to practice air group tactics, then caught up with *Bunker Hill* and returned aboard. Nist flew F4U-1D Corsair number 57951 for this training flight.[30]

Nist flew again on 15 March. For 3.1 hours, Nist flew F6F-5P Hellcat number 72614 on a combat air patrol, protecting Task Group 58.3 from above. This was his fourth flight in Hellcat number 72614.[31]

On 17 March, Jimmy Nist penned another letter to his parents. In it, he expressed his mixed feelings about being on deployment:

> The second month of this cruise is drawing to a close. Only wish it were the end of the fifth one. Nothing wrong with it out here—just a little too far from San Francisco to suit my taste. If it weren't for Alice, they could leave me out here for the rest of the war, but seeing as how things stand now—take me back![32]

Jimmy Nist did have one serious complaint about being out there in the Pacific. After requesting that his parents have plenty of fresh milk on hand when he returned home, he wrote, "Haven't had any fresh milk since San Francisco two months ago. We get powdered milk which is only good for cereal and it isn't very good for that. Tastes awful."[33]

Jimmy's fiancée, Alice, and his mother were keeping in touch via letter and sharing news that they had gotten from him. On 5 March 1945 while Jimmy and the Fast Carrier Task Force were at Ulithi, Alice wrote a letter to her future mother-in-law. She hadn't received any letters from him in over two weeks and asked if Ethel had gotten any recent letters from him. At Jimmy's request, Alice was searching for records to buy and send him for the record player that his squadron had in their ready room. Alice was also starting to buy dishware in preparation for their future marriage. A local store was selling a new piece of Bluebell dishware every Thursday. The set included different size bowls, cups, a coffeepot, a pitcher, a salad set, salt and pepper shakers, custard cups and plates. "It's swell for the kitchen," she wrote.[34]

The Kyushu-Inland Sea Raids: 18–19 March 1945

On 18–19 March 1945, the Fast Carrier Task Force returned to hit the Japanese Home Islands once again. Its four task groups had 10 fleet aircraft carriers, six light aircraft carriers, eight fast battleships, two battle cruisers, 14 heavy and light cruisers and 64 destroyers.[35]

Kyushu is the third largest of Japan's five principal Home Islands. The mountainous and volcanic island encompasses some 14,202 square miles. Mount Kuju rises 5,876 feet above sea level. The island is surrounded by the Pacific Ocean to the west, the Inland Sea, the Straits of Tsushima and the East China Sea. Kyushu is the southernmost Home Island and the one closest to Okinawa. Principal cities include Fukuoka, Kitakyushu, Kumamoto, Sasebo and Nagasaki.

In March 1945, Kyushu was home to some 45 Japanese air force and navy airfields. Three Imperial Japanese Navy air fleets operated from airfields on Kyushu: Vice Admiral Kimpei Teraoka's Third Air Fleet, Vice Admiral Matome Ugaki's Fifth Air Fleet and Vice Admiral Minoru Maeda's Tenth Air Fleet. Ugaki's Fifth Air Fleet was headquartered at Kanoya Naval Air Base. The USAAF XXI Bomber Command considered Kanoya Naval Air Base to be the most important naval air base in the Japanese Empire. Kanoya was used for combat operations, flight training and aircraft repair and maintenance. Other IJN naval air bases included Kagoshima, Hakata, Omura, Hitoyoshi, Miyakonojo, Miyazaki, Kokubu, Kushira, Kasanohara, Ibusuki, Iwakawa, Tsuiki, Oita, Izumi and Usa. The Sixth Air Army of the Imperial Japanese Army also operated aircraft from Kyushu. Commanded by LT Gen. Michio Sugawara, the Sixth Air Army's airfields included Nittagahara, Chiran, Kumamoto, Kikuchi, Tachiarai, Miyakonojo and Kumanosho. The XXI Bomber Command considered Tachiarai in northern Kyushu to be the most important Japanese army air force base. With all-weather runways and extensive support facilities, Tachiarai operated fighters and medium and heavy bombers. The Sixth Air Army also operated a number of airfields in the Amami Gunto, most notably on Amami Oshima, Kikaiga Shima (Kikai) and Tokuno Shima. Japanese aircraft on Kyushu included the IJN's "Zeke" fighters, "Kate" and "Betty" bombers and the army's "Tony," "Tojo," "Oscar" and "Frank" fighters and "Sally" and "Helen" bombers. These airfields and their aircraft were critical to the defense of not only the Home Islands but Okinawa as well. Unless neutralized, Kyushu-based kamikazes could savage the U.S. fleet supporting the invasion of Okinawa.[36]

Unlike the two previous strikes on the Japanese Home Islands, the Americans were not able to achieve surprise. Japanese search planes spotted the American ships on the night of 17–18 March and shadowed them overnight, providing timely updates for their commanders ashore.

In a large predawn attack, Japanese aircraft scored minor bomb hits on USS *Intrepid* (CV-11), USS *Yorktown* (CV-10) and USS *Enterprise* (CV-6). These were the first of many kamikaze attacks that the Japanese would send against Task Force 58 over the next two days.[37]

Flight operations began early in the morning of 18 March. Task Group 58.3's carriers sent up the first sweep shortly after 0600. The task group's aircraft went after the Japanese airfields on the east coast of Kyushu as well as Hitoyoshi in central Kyushu and Kikuchi on the western side. At Tomitaka Airfield, the Americans found a large number of Japanese aircraft on the ground as well as some 30 "Zekes," "Oscars" and "Tonys" aloft looking for a fight. The Americans shot down four of the enemy fighters and probably downed two others while losing two of their own. At Izumi Airfield, six hangars were destroyed and seven more damaged.[38]

Essex's new Air Group 83 had a very busy first day of combat operations. They attacked five Japanese airfields repeatedly and conducted several combat air patrols. Air Group 83 fighter pilots downed 18 fighters and a Judy bomber and destroyed 14 Japanese aircraft on the ground. Three Corsairs and an Avenger were downed by enemy anti-aircraft fire.[39]

Bunker Hill's first operation of the day sent an eight-plane combat air patrol aloft followed by a fighter sweep of 11 Corsairs. Next, Air Group 84 sent a large strike group against the IJN's Miyazaki Airfield. The airfield was located on the southeastern coast of Kyushu and was primarily used to operate "Betty" medium bombers. It had four hangars and four support/repair buildings. Strike A took off from *Bunker Hill* starting at 0630. It consisted of 14 Helldivers, 13 Avengers and 16 Marine Corsairs from VMF-221. The light carrier *Cabot* contributed 12 Hellcats from its VF-29 and nine Avengers from its VT-29. Once over the target, the U.S. planes were greeted by moderate and inaccurate light and medium anti-aircraft fire. On the airfield itself, the U.S. pilots could see 10 or 12 "Betty" medium bombers. The Helldivers dove on the target, releasing their bombs from 1,800 feet. The Avengers attacked using the glide bombing technique. The strike force returned to the task group around 1035. Initial assessments concluded that most of the airfield's structures had been destroyed. One *Cabot* Hellcat failed to return.[40]

LT(jg) "Shorty" Nist flew one photo reconnaissance mission on 18 March 1945. Photo Mission #1 took off from *Bunker Hill* at 0631 local time. Nist was accompanied

USS *Bunker Hill* as seen from battleship USS *New Jersey* off Japan in March 1945 (Naval History and Heritage Command [Photo 80-G-373737]/National Archives).

by LT C.T. Larsen, LT(jg) G.E. Roberts, LT C. Kendall and two F6F-5P photo Hellcats each from VF-29 of USS *Cabot* and VF-4 of USS *Essex*. The distance to the search area was 190 miles. The flight reached the target area at 0745 at an altitude of 10,000 feet. For part of the way, they were followed by three single-engine Japanese fighters who wisely chose not to engage them. Photo runs were made over Japanese airfields at Kikuchi, Kikutomi and Waifu, which were all located in the center of Kyushu. Japanese anti-aircraft was meager and inaccurate and none of the American planes were hit. Next they flew southeast to the coast of Kyushu. Here they took damage photos of Miyazaki Airfield, which had just been hammered by Air Group 84's Strike Able. They observed numerous fires burning in the airfield's hangars and support buildings. Their assignment concluded, Nist and the others headed back to their respective carriers and returned aboard them around 1000. Nist and the other photo pilots' photos confirmed the preliminary assessment of Strike Able, and so a second strike mission to Miyazaki was canceled.[41]

Task Group 58.3's Action Report emphasized the importance of aerial photography for target reconnaissance. The initial fighter sweeps found few visible Japanese aircraft on Kyushu's airfields. However, aerial photographic missions showed a much different situation on the ground. "Development of photos taken during these attacks revealed literally hundreds of aircraft, mostly in revetments, and in some instances cleverly camouflaged," stated the Action Report. In this instance, the aerial cameras used by LT(jg) Nist and the other photo pilots were of greater value than their machine guns.[42]

That afternoon, *Bunker Hill* and *Cabot*'s air groups attacked the IJN's Omura seaplane station and the adjacent Omura Aircraft Factory. VB-84 sent 10 Helldivers aloft while VF-29 sent 14 Hellcats and VT-29 sent eight Avengers. "This was to be the longest overland flight over the Jap Homeland to be flown by the Bombers," recorded the Bombing 84 War History. Despite the cloud cover, the American aviators were able to successfully bomb their targets. VB-84's Helldivers hit several large hangars and the Omura Aircraft Factory. *Cabot*'s eight Avengers and 14 Hellcats destroyed or damaged 13 twin-engine aircraft on the ground. Her Hellcats shot down three Tojo fighters and four Ruff float planes. Japanese anti-aircraft fire was heavy, but fortunately no American aircraft were lost.[43]

While the Helldivers were going after the Omura seaplane station, Captain Blade Snider and his flight of 10 VMF-221 Corsairs conducted a patrol over northern Kyushu. While returning to *Bunker Hill*, the Marine aviators engaged a formation of 25 Japanese fighters. The Marines shot down 13 without any loss to themselves. CAPT Snider himself got three of the Japanese fighters.[44]

The 18 March 1945 air strikes on Kyushu's airfields were devastating. Hangars and support buildings at practically every airfield were destroyed. Two hundred seventy-five Japanese aircraft were damaged or destroyed on the ground and another 102 aircraft were shot down in the air. The American air attacks were so devastating that the Sixth Air Army relocated its aircraft to bases in Korea to prevent their destruction. Task Group 58.3's aircraft claimed 45 Japanese aircraft destroyed in the air or on the ground and another 53 damaged or probably destroyed. The task group's aircraft also dropped 77 tons of bombs and fired 704 rockets at Japanese targets.[45]

Aerial reconnaissance on 18 March 1945 discovered several Imperial Japanese Navy warships hiding at the Kobe and Kure naval bases located in the Inland Sea. Kure was Japan's largest and most important naval base and was heavily defended by anti-aircraft guns. The warships included the Japanese aircraft carrier *Ryuho*, which had survived the June 1944 Battle of the Philippine Sea. Accordingly, Mitscher shifted the air attacks of 19 March from the airfields to the remnants of the Imperial Japanese Navy. Subsequently it was discovered that the ships were largely inoperable due to lack of fuel.[46]

All three of Task Group 58.3's carriers participated in the Kure strikes. *Cabot* contributed 12 VF-29 Hellcats and seven VT-29 Avengers. *Essex* contributed 16 Corsairs, 13 Helldivers and 13 Avengers. *Bunker Hill* contributed 13 VB-84 Helldivers, 16 Avengers from VT-84, 14 VMF-451 Corsairs and a photo mission team of one photo Hellcat and three Corsairs. "Fellows, you're going to find that AA plenty heavy tomorrow ... heavier than it ever was at Truk," warned VB-84 air intelligence officer "Uncle" Charley Charles during the mission briefing. "They've got at least a hundred and sixty heavy anti-aircraft guns ringing the harbor, and Lord knows how much smaller stuff."[47]

Bunker Hill's strike on Kure Naval Base was led by the commanding officer of Air Group 84, CDR "Bunky" Ottinger. Flying an F4U Corsair, he led the force of Avengers, Helldivers and Corsairs across the island of Shikoku and the Inland Sea. The enemy flak over Kure was just as heavy as Uncle Charley had warned Bombing 84. Seven of VB-84's 13 bombers were hit.[48]

The Task Group 58.3 air raiders inflicted major damage on the Kure Naval Base. Hits were scored on a fleet aircraft carrier, two escort carriers, two battleships and a heavy cruiser. The naval base's docks, shipyard and naval arsenal were hit and fires started. The task group also lost seven of its aircraft to Japanese anti-aircraft fire. *Bunker Hill* lost two Helldivers and a Corsair to enemy action. *Essex* lost three Helldivers and an Avenger.[49]

On their way back to *Bunker Hill,* CDR Ottinger and the Air Group 84 aircrew spotted an ominous pillar of black smoke on the horizon. They soon discovered that the source of the smoke was the aircraft carrier USS *Franklin* (CV-13). She had been struck by two bomb hits that ignited huge fires. Some of the VMF-451 Corsairs broke formation and joined the fighters covering the stricken carrier for a time.[50]

While U.S. warplanes were ravaging the remnants of the Imperial Japanese Navy, Japanese kamikazes were swarming over the Fast Carrier Task Force on 18–19 March. Japanese warbirds went after American aircraft carriers in particular. *Essex* and *Bunker Hill* had near misses from Japanese Yokosuka D4Y Suisei "Judy" naval dive-bombers. Five U.S. carriers were hit by Japanese bombs. USS *Franklin* (CV-13), however, suffered the worst of all. Shortly after 0700 on 19 March, she was heavily damaged by two bomb hits that ignited serious fires that nearly sank her. LT(jg) Wilbert Popp of VF-84 flew a fighter cover mission over *Franklin* while she struggled to remain afloat. "I will never forget the sight of that black smoke rising from that glorious ship," he later wrote. "From my viewing of the scene, I didn't see how it would be possible for that ship to survive." The heroic actions and sacrifices by her crew kept her afloat. Eight hundred and thirty-two of her crew were killed and 270 wounded out of the ship's total complement of 3,000 sailors and officers. Among the numerous heroes aboard *Franklin* that day was the ship's Catholic chaplain, LCDR Joseph T. O'Callahan, whose ministry to casualties and personal direction of firefighting efforts earned him the Medal of Honor.[51]

The Fast Carrier Task Force continued to strike at Kyushu in the afternoon, even as herculean efforts were underway to save *Franklin*. Task Group 58.3 launched several fighter sweeps against Kochi, Matsuyama and Nittagahara Airfields. At Kochi, 16 aircraft were destroyed on the ground and three hangars and a fuel dump were set afire. At Nittagahara, 43 aircraft were destroyed or damaged on the ground. Task Group 58.3 pilots claimed 11 Japanese aircraft shot down. Japanese anti-aircraft fire was moderate and their air opposition was nonexistent.[52]

That afternoon, VF-84 flew a search mission to locate a battleship and possibly an aircraft carrier that were reported to be in the Kii Channel. The Kii Channel (or Strait) separated the Kii Peninsula on the island of Honshu from the island of Shikoku and connected the Inland Sea with the Pacific Ocean. Four divisions of VF-84 Corsairs armed with rockets were dispatched to search the area. A fifth division of four F6F-5N Hellcats was also sent part of the way to act as a communications link for the Corsairs. The four Corsair divisions were led by LCDR Raymond Hill, LT(jg) J.E. Gildea, LT(jg) J.J. Sargent and LT(jg) J.E. Diteman. LT(jg) James Nist was part of LT(jg) J.J. Sargent's division along with LT Caleb Kendall and LT K.C. Shaeffer. LCDR Hill's division sank three "sugar dogs" (small wooden merchant ships) and damaged three others. LT(jg) Gildea's division disabled a train. None of the reported Japanese warships were located.[53]

The U.S. Navy air attacks on Kyushu prompted Japanese army and navy leaders to work more cooperatively. The Sixth Air Army withdrew its aircraft from Kyushu to Korea but continued to use Kyushu and Amami Gunto Airfields to stage their attacks on the American fleet operating around Okinawa. On 19 March, the Sixth Air Army was placed under the authority of Admiral Soemu Toyoda, commander of the IJN Combined Fleet, to effect better coordination for air operations over Okinawa.[54]

During its third visit to the Japanese Home Islands, the Fast Carrier Task Force had inflicted significant damage on Japanese air and naval forces. Seventeen Japanese ships were hit, including the super battleship *Yamato* and the aircraft carrier *Amagi*, but none were seriously damaged. U.S. aviators claimed to have destroyed 528 aircraft on the ground and in the air. "These losses prevented heavy participation by Japanese air forces in the defense of Okinawa until 6 April," wrote historian Samuel Eliot Morison in *Victory in the Pacific* volume of the U.S. Navy's official history of its operations in World War II.[55]

Task Group 58.3's three air groups dropped 152 tons of bombs and fired off 1,243 rockets at Japanese targets. They sank five small ships; scored hits on two battleships, an aircraft carrier, two escort carriers and a heavy cruiser; and inflicted substantial damage on the Kure Naval Base. Thirty-three Japanese aircraft were destroyed on the ground, six others were downed over the target and nine aircraft were shot down over the task group.[56]

During this third U.S. Navy strike against the Japanese Home Islands, Japanese air resistance was significantly more vigorous than previously experienced. "All of our sweep and strike elements encountered the heaviest and most aggressive air opposition offered by the Nips in many months of continuous offensive operations against their inner defense 'perimeter' bases, and the Empire itself," reported the Carrier Division One (Task Group 58.3) War Diary. The task group lost 18 aircraft to enemy action; 21 pilots and aircrewmen were lost and eight were rescued by friendly forces. Three fighters were lost in operational accidents.[57]

With the second day's strikes concluded, Task Force 58 retired to rendezvous with tankers to refuel. While doing so, a large force of enemy aircraft was detected. Fighters were scrambled to augment the combat air patrol already in the air. U.S. fighters intercepted 16 single-engine fighters escorting 32 Mitsubishi "Betty" bombers. All of the Japanese aircraft were shot down at a loss of only two U.S. fighters. More significantly, however, the "Betty" bombers turned out to be carrying the new "Baka" rocket-propelled flying bombs. After being launched by the "Betty" bomber, the "Baka" was flown by a suicide pilot at over 500 mph. The appearance of the "Baka" was an ominous development in the war against the kamikazes.[58]

Japanese aircrew grossly overstated the success of their efforts against the U.S. ships. These exaggerations found their way onto the pages of Admiral Matome Ugaki's personal diary. On 21 March, he recorded that Japanese aircraft had sunk five aircraft carriers, two battleships, one heavy cruiser, two light cruisers and one other ship. In Ugaki's estimation, this left the American task force with six fleet carriers, one light carrier, eight battleships, 13 cruisers and 33 destroyers. In return, Ugaki recorded that the Japanese had lost 161 aircraft, the majority of which were on kamikaze missions. "Summing up the above, I believe we scored a good mark in this operation," he concluded.[59]

The commander of the Fifth Fleet, ADM Raymond Spruance, was pleased with the performance of his forces during the air strikes on the Japanese Home Islands. In a message sent to the members of Task Force 58, Spruance stated:

> The manner in which Task Force 58 has fought and maneuvered during the past 4 days has surpassed its own high standards. Great damage has been inflicted on both the material and morale of the enemy. Our ships damaged in action continued to fight. Our one bad cripple was repaired and brought away to safety from the enemy's nose. Our fighter and anti-aircraft protection were superb and our offensive aircraft were both savage and cruel. This has been an auspicious opening for the operations that lie ahead of us. I am very proud to have been with you again.[60]

Further Air Strikes on Okinawa

VADM Mitscher's Fast Carrier Task Force next headed for Okinawa for air strikes in preparation for Operation Iceberg, the upcoming 1 April invasion of the island group that was less than two weeks away.

LT(jg) James Nist had some time to write letters while *Bunker Hill* and the Fast Carrier Task Force were steaming for Okinawan waters. In his 21 March 1945 letter, he opined about how much about farming he had forgotten. He also noted that he had read a book on microbes and was amazed at how much he had forgotten about that subject too. This he attributed to his two years-plus of studying aviation. Significantly, he was rethinking his plan to stay in the Navy after the war. In his letter, he wrote:

> You're probably wondering what happened to the Navy idea. Well, nothing did, except that it's strictly for single guys who are out for a thrill of flying and as you have already heard, there'll be a Mrs. Jimmy Nist before too many more months. I still go for flying, but I go for Alice more than a Corsair and she doesn't think any more of my cruising around on a flattop than you do. Besides the Navy moves you around too much.[61]

During the recent operations, the Japanese had seriously damaged *Enterprise* and nearly sunk *Franklin*. Both carriers were heading back to Ulithi with several escorts as Task Group 58.2. The remaining Task Group 58.2 ships were reassigned to the other task groups of the Fast Carrier Task Force. On 22 March, Task Group 58.3 gained the fleet carrier USS *Hancock* (CV-19), the light carrier USS *Bataan* (CVL-29) and the battleships USS *Washington* (BB-56) and USS *North Carolina* (BB-55). USS *New Jersey* was detached for another assignment. *Hancock* had Air Group Six with Fighting Squadron Six, Bombing Fighting Squadron Six, Bombing Squadron Six and Torpedo Squadron Six embarked. *Bataan* had Carrier Light Air Group 47 with Fighting Squadron 47 and Torpedo Squadron 47 embarked. Task Group 58.3 now included three fleet carriers (*Essex*, *Bunker Hill* and *Hancock*), two light carriers (*Bataan* and *Cabot*), three battleships (*South Dakota*, *Washington* and *North Carolina*), the heavy cruiser *Indianapolis*, four light cruisers and 17 destroyers. Fifth Fleet commander ADM Raymond Spruance was flying his flag aboard *Indianapolis*. Task Force 58 commander VADM Mitscher was flying his flag aboard *Bunker Hill*. This impressive assemblage of naval power was greater than the entire U.S. Navy force at the epic Battles of Coral Sea and Midway in 1942 … and the Fast Carrier Task Force had two other equally powerful task groups.[62]

Mitscher's Task Force arrived off Okinawa early on the morning of 23 March and began air operations in the predawn hours. "Our pilots did a good job, and made the most of the limited opportunities afforded to them by very unfavorable weather conditions," stated the Carrier Division One War Diary. Targets included beach defenses, ground installations and airfields. *Cabot*'s aircraft struck the Unten Ko submarine base. In addition to Okinawa, airfields on Minami Daito Jima, Okino Daito Jima and Amami Shunto were attacked. Japanese anti-aircraft fire was meager and air opposition was nonexistent.[63]

The weather was uncooperative for the next day's air operations. Cloud ceilings ranged from 500 to 3,000 feet with cloud coverage varying from 5/10ths to complete overcast. The winds were consistently between 20 and 25 knots with seas running choppy and rough. Despite these challenging conditions, Task Group 58.3's carrier planes were back in action against Okinawa and nearby islands. Airfields on Miyako Shima, Minami Daito and Amami Oshima were attacked. *Bunker Hill* fighters struck Katena and Yontan Airfields and the submarine base at Unten Ko.[64]

LT(jg) Jimmy Nist of VF-84 flew two combat missions on 24 March. First, he flew Corsair Number 57823 on a three-hour mission escorting a photo reconnaissance Hellcat over Okinawa with particular emphasis on Yontan Airfield. Later that day he returned to Yontan Airfield at the controls of Hellcat Number 72582 on a photo reconnaissance mission. His total flight time for the day was 6.3 hours.[65]

Overall, 24 March 1945 was a difficult day for Task Group 58.3 in terms of weather and casualties. Seven task group aircraft were downed by Japanese anti-aircraft fire: five Corsairs, one Helldiver and one Avenger. Three pilots and two aircrewmen were rescued, but three Air Group 84 pilots were killed, including the group commander, CDR George Ottinger.[66]

CDR Ottinger was flying an F4U Corsair for *Bunker Hill*/Air Group 84's Strike A. He was leading 16 Corsairs, 13 Avengers and 13 Helldivers to attack Japanese targets on Okinawa between Point Bolo and Chatan Town. Japanese anti-aircraft fire was intense and accurate. CDR Ottinger led a flight of Corsairs to take out anti-aircraft emplacements defending Yontan Airfield. With his flight circling, Ottinger went down to draw fire from one of the emplacements. A Japanese anti-aircraft gun struck Ottinger's Corsair a lethal blow. Ottinger flew north up the west coast of Okinawa but was forced to ditch offshore. He was seen swimming in the water. Other Corsairs dropped him life rafts and dye markers. Calls for assistance were radioed. *Bunker Hill* launched four Corsairs on a rescue combat air patrol to escort a Kingfisher float plane and assist with the search. The Kingfisher located CDR Ottinger floating in the water, but the Air Group commander was dead and his body not recovered.[67]

CDR Ottinger's death was a heavy blow. "The loss of this able and gallant young officer is deeply regretted," stated the Carrier Division One War Diary. LT(jg) Wilbert Popp described his death as a "great loss." Ottinger's death required some shifting of leadership. LCDR Roger Hedrick of VF-84 was promoted to command Air Group 84 temporarily and VF-84 executive officer LCDR Raymond E. Hill stepped up to become temporary squadron commander. LT Clint Gillen became the new acting squadron executive officer. This arrangement was soon made permanent.[68]

Task Group 58.3 steamed away from Okinawa and spent the following day refueling and replenishing while underway. When air operations resumed at dawn on 26 March, the weather again was a hinderance. U.S. Navy aircrew had to contend with low cloud ceilings, scattered precipitation and widespread cloud cover. Winds initially were 25 knots. Toward the evening, the cloud cover improved and the winds subsided to 15 knots.[69]

Over the next two days, Task Group 58.3 aircraft struck numerous targets on Okinawa and other islands in the Ryukusus group. Targets included Okinawa's airfields, gun emplacements, defensive fortifications and military installations, the airfield and support facilities on Minami Daito, the airfield at Kikai Island and defensive fortifications on Ie Shima and Yoron Shima. Task Group 58.3 fighters flew combat air patrols to protect the task group ships. There was minimal enemy anti-aircraft fire and few Japanese aircraft were encountered. "The efficiency of these missions was exceedingly difficult to evaluate," noted the Task Group 58.3 After-Action Report, "since many of the targets assigned were gun positions, trenches, and caves, on which damage assessment is next to impossible."[70]

Task Group 58.3's warbirds repeatedly hit the submarine support facilities at Unten Ko and with good reason. Unten Ko was located on a small bay on Motobu

Peninsula in northern Okinawa. The Japanese were keeping a large group of mini (midget) submarines and suicide boats there to be used against the amphibious ships and landing craft that would be carrying the invasion force to Okinawa's beaches in a few days.[71]

LT(jg) Jimmy Nist flew two very different missions on 26 and 27 March. On 26 March, LT(jg) Jimmy Nist was back at the controls of F6F-5P Hellcat Number 72582. That day, he flew a 2.6-hour photo reconnaissance mission over Okinawa.[72]

LT(jg) Jimmy Nist flew one noncombat mission on 27 March. Piloting Corsair Number 57923, Nist escorted an OS2U Kingfisher float plane. The Kingfisher was carrying aerial reconnaissance photos from Task Force 58 commander VADM Marc Mitscher to Task Force 52 commander RADM William H.P. Blandy. Task Force 52 was the Amphibious Support Force and it consisted of escort aircraft carriers, destroyers, destroyer escorts and minesweepers. This escort mission was anything but routine. Some five miles east of Jima Saki, Nist and the Kingfisher spotted a downed pilot in the water. With Nist covering overhead, the Kingfisher pilot landed his aircraft near the downed pilot and effected a water rescue. The mission lasted 4.7 hours.[73]

After returning aboard *Bunker Hill*, Jimmy found some time to pen a quick letter to his parents. He wrote about a range of topics. Mail delivery out here in the western Pacific was dependent upon the fleet tankers, which brought mail as well as fuel for the ships and aircraft. The Navy still would not let them write about anything that had happened after 28 January 1945. Alice had sent his parents some photos but Jimmy was not happy with their quality. "Anyway, you can't go all by pictures, because pictures don't show that Alice is about the sweetest and swellest girl that ever put on a pair of shoes—bar none," he wrote. "I'll stack her against any one I've ever seen and just about everybody I know who have met her say the same thing." He was also hoping to get home in time to enjoy fresh watermelons. Since Jimmy was pretty tired from the day's flight operations, he kept the letter to just two pages.[74]

Task Group 58.3's next operation took it to Minami Daito Shima, located some 160 miles to the east of Okinawa. The oval-shaped coral island was roughly 4.6 square miles and home to several Japanese airfields. *Bataan*'s air group had been paying the island almost daily visits. Now the whole task group would be going after the island. After dark, Cruiser Division 17 detached from the task group and bombarded the island with naval gunfire.[75]

The weather was very good with light winds and a few scattered clouds. Sea conditions were ideal as well. All five Task Group 58.3 carriers participated in the strikes on Minami Daito. *Essex*'s flight operations were delayed by two mishaps on the slippery flight deck, one of which killed a Marine anti-aircraft gunner. The Task Group 58.3 aircraft hit Minami Daito's runways, anti-aircraft gun positions, dispersal areas, ammunition dumps and support facilities. *Hancock*'s aircraft alone dropped 23.5 tons of bombs on Japanese targets. *Bataan*'s aircraft added 6.2 tons of bombs to the aerial bombardment while *Cabot*'s aircraft dropped another 9.6 tons of bombs. *Essex*'s aircraft hit the Japanese installations with five-inch rockets and numerous bombs. The task group lost two aircraft to the intense and accurate enemy anti-aircraft fire: a VMF-451 Corsair and a VB-84 Helldiver. The Marine pilot was killed but the Helldiver crew was rescued by the destroyer USS *Waldron*. Four Corsairs were lost operationally, including the two from *Essex* mentioned previously.[76]

More Air Strikes on Japan

After completing their strikes on Minami Daito and at sea replenishment, Task Force 58 turned north again to pay another visit to Kyushu. Primary targets for this latest raid on Kyushu were the Japanese airfields and IJN warships believed to be hiding in the Inland Sea.[77]

On the morning of 29 March, TG 58.3 and TG58.4 went after the Japanese warships in the Inland Sea. Due to poor visibility and expert Japanese camouflage, the IJN warships escaped detection. So other targets were hit instead. *Hancock*'s fighters and bombers struck naval and shore facilities around Kagoshima Bay. *Bataan*'s air group hit Chiran Airfield's hangars and aircraft with 12.75 tons of bombs. *Cabot*'s Hellcats and Avengers hit a seaplane base, docks and small craft around Yamakawa Bay. *Essex*'s air group bombed, rocketed and strafed Tojimbara Airfield. Failing to find the IJN warships, *Bunker Hill*'s strike mission of Corsairs, Avengers and Helldivers attacked Kanoya Airfield, which was the headquarters of the IJN Fifth Air Fleet and home to numerous "Zeke" fighters and "Betty" bombers.[78]

The heavy cloud cover caused Air Group 84's worst air disaster of its deployment. Along the southern coast of Kyushu, a flight of VT-84 Avengers and VB-84 Helldivers flew into heavy clouds. Six aircraft collided in the clouds. Five of the aircraft subsequently crashed and one heavily damaged aircraft made it back to *Bunker Hill*. Two pilots and two aircrewmen were subsequently rescued but eight pilots and aircrewmen were killed in the tragic accident.[79]

LT(jg) "Shorty" Nist was not involved in the tragic Air Group 84 mid-air collision. On that day, "Shorty" Nist flew a photo reconnaissance/strike mission over Kyushu. He was flying Hellcat Number 72582, which he had already flown twice that month. One of the targets for this mission was the Yamakawa Airfield. Located near the city of Fukuoka, the airfield was home to the headquarters of the Japanese army's Sixth Air Army. While strafing Yamakawa Airfield, Nist destroyed a Japanese Yokosuka Navy Type 97 Flying Boat on the ground. Known to Allies as the "Cherry," the twin-engine H5Y Type 97 Flying Boat was 67' 4" long with a wingspan of 103'7". The "Cherry" had a maximum speed of 190 miles per hour and maximum range of 2,600 nautical miles. It was armed with three 7.7 mm machine guns and two 250-kilogram bombs. The mission lasted 3.6 hours and was his final mission for the month. The "Cherry" demolished by Nist was one of three Japanese aircraft destroyed on the ground that day by VF-84. LT Helms destroyed a "Jake" fighter aircraft and LT(jg) Chambers also destroyed a "Cherry."[80]

Overall, Task Group 58.3 had moderate success against the Japanese on Kyushu on 29 March 1945. TG 58.3 aviators sank four supply ships, probably sank five supply ships and damaged 22 ships. The aviators also damaged or destroyed hangars, shops, barracks, warehouses, wharves, rail lines, rail cars and seaplane facilities. One

"Emily" bomber, three "Jake" fighters, three "Cherry" flying boats and two "Ruff" float planes were destroyed and nine other aircraft were damaged on the ground. Overall, task group pilots claimed 20 enemy aircraft destroyed in the air or on the ground and 10 more either damaged or probably destroyed. The task group lost six aircraft in combat and seven more in operational accidents. Three pilots and one aircrewman were lost in combat and another three pilots and six aircrewmen were lost in operational accidents including the accident involving Air Group 84. Task Group 58.3 aircraft dropped 94 tons of bombs, launched 14 torpedoes and fired 215 rockets against enemy targets on land and on the water.[81]

Task Force 58 turned south from Kyushu and headed for Okinawa. Along the way, the Task Force would launch air strikes to neutralize the air facilities in the Amami Shunto. Amami Oshima was the largest of the group at 275 square miles. Other islands in the group included Kikai to the east and Tokuno Shima, Yoro Shima, Uke Shima and Kakero Shima to the southwest. An estimated 20,000 Japanese service members were stationed in the Amami Shunto. The Amami Shunto's location between Kyushu and Okinawa made it ideal for supporting the defense of the latter. Kamikaze aircraft originating on Kyushu could stage through the Amami Shunto for attacks on the U.S. fleet supporting the invasion of Okinawa.[82]

Task Group 58.3 spent several hours getting its planes and aircrews ready for the 1400 Amami Strike. With aircraft fully armed and ready to launch, the strike mission was abruptly scrubbed by the Task Force 58 commander. Instead, the task force proceeded directly to Okinawa without delay.[83]

With the invasion of Okinawa scheduled for 1 April 1945 (Easter Sunday), Task Force 58's operations on 30 and 31 March were directed at softening up Okinawa and other islands in the Rykukus group for the invasion. Throughout these two days, flight operations were hindered by cloud cover and intermittent rain squalls. Targets included airfields, anti-aircraft guns, fortifications and military installations on Okinawa and Minami Daito. Eight Corsairs, 12 *Essex* Helldivers and 10 Avengers plastered the Unten Ko submarine pens and support facilities with 16 tons of bombs on 30 March. On 31 March, VF-84's LT(jg) Billie Carroll shot down a "Frank" near Naha Airfield—the squadron's first aerial victory in five weeks. Eleven *Bunker Hill* Corsairs strafed and rocketed Tokuno Airfield, hitting a "Kate" torpedo bomber, a "Francis" bomber and four other aircraft in their protective revetments. Altogether, Task Group 58.3 lost at least 10 aircraft to operational and combat causes. Task Group 58.3 aircraft inflicted heavy damage on a midget submarine pen, runways, anti-aircraft guns, fuel dumps and communications installations. In addition, 10 Japanese aircraft were shot down. LT(jg) Jimmy Nist did not fly any missions on these two days.[84]

The Month of March 1945

Thus ended another successful month for the Fast Carrier Task Force. The development of the Ulithi Atoll advanced naval base was invaluable for Fifth Fleet and its task forces. The Fast Carrier Task Force was able to conduct major maintenance, resupply and enjoy a recreation period at a location within several sailing days of its area of operations. In addition, logistics vessels were able to keep the task force resupplied while underway. Before and after its time at Ulithi, Task Force 58 conducted numerous air strikes on Kyushu in the Japanese Home Islands and against targets in the Ryukyus in preparation for the Okinawa invasion.

LT(jg) James Nist of VF-84 flew 11 missions in March 1945, nine of which were combat missions. His missions were nearly equally split between the F4U-1D Corsair and the F6F-5P photo Hellcat. He flew a total of 37.3 hours that month, bringing his total Navy flight time to 943.8 hours; 19.3 hours were flown in Hellcats and 18 hours were in Corsairs. He flew one fighter sweep, one combat air patrol, one combat search mission, one photo escort, one OS2U aircraft escort, one target combat air patrol and four photo-strikes. Eight of the missions were over enemy territory: one over Honshu, two over Kyushu and five over Okinawa. Nist assisted in the rescue of a downed American pilot from the waters near Jima Saki. While strafing Yamakawa Airfield on Kyushu, LT(jg) Nist destroyed one "Cherry" flying boat on the ground.[85]

8

The Invasion of Okinawa

The seizure of Okinawa was vitally important for the later invasion of the Japanese Home Islands. Previously, U.S. ground, air and naval forces had overcome determined, often fanatical, Japanese resistance in the Marianas, Peleliu, the Philippines, Iwo Jima and various other places across the Pacific theater. Above, around and on Okinawa, U.S. service members would be tested like no other previous operation.

The Invasion of Okinawa

The U.S. invasion of Okinawa was going to be one of the most complicated and longest amphibious operations in World War II. Ultimately, capturing Okinawa and adjacent islands would involve 318 combatant vessels, 1,139 auxiliary vessels, hundreds of landing craft and over 548,000 personnel. The naval forces were commanded by Fifth U.S. Fleet commander ADM Raymond Spruance and also included a British Royal Navy carrier task force. The land forces were part of Tenth U.S. Army, commanded by General Simon Bolivar Buckner, USA. Tenth Army consisted of the U.S. Army's XXIV Corps with four infantry divisions and the III Amphibious Corps with three Marine divisions. The forces required for this massive invasion were assembled from all across the Pacific theater and from as far away as the West Coast of the United States. Preinvasion operations included aerial bombardment by the Fast Carrier Task Force aircraft, naval gunfire bombardment, minesweeping and the seizure of several outlying island groups, including Kerama Retto and Keise Shima.[1]

The mission of the Fast Carrier Task Force was to protect the invasion ships from air attack and to provide air support for the U.S. forces struggling to overcome the Japanese defenders ashore. "In accomplishing its mission, the American fleet was to suffer the heaviest punishment it had ever taken," wrote Rear Admiral Frederick C. Sherman later. "We had experienced Japanese suicide attacks before, but they had never approached in magnitude the effort put out in defense of Okinawa."[2]

The invasion of Okinawa commenced on the morning of 1 April 1945—Easter Sunday. In most previous invasions, the Japanese had fiercely contested the Americans literally from the water's edge. However, here on Okinawa, Japanese resistance was sporadic and minimal. Within several hours, U.S. forces were firmly established ashore and pushing inland. By nightfall, U.S. forces had overrun and occupied Yontan and Kadena Airfields. Immediately, combat engineers began repairing battle damage and preparing the airfields for operations by the new owners. Not until several days into the invasion did U.S. forces discover that the Japanese had established a series of heavily fortified defensive lines that they had skillfully constructed using the natural terrain to maximize their lethality.[3]

Task Group 58.3's air operations in support of the invasion began in the pre-dawn hours. Before dawn, Air Group 84 night fighters shot down three Japanese aircraft. In the hour preceding the landing, *Bunker Hill* and *Essex* aircraft bombed, strafed and rocketed the invasion beaches. Once the Marines and soldiers were ashore, aircraft from all five Task Group 58 carriers flew support missions all across Okinawa. Over the course of the day, four task group aircraft were shot down and two were lost in operational crashes. Three pilots were killed and seven personnel were rescued. "It was again difficult to assess the effectiveness of any one of these missions or of their cumulative total, although in the aggregate the damage done was undoubtedly very substantial," noted the Task Group 58.3 Action Report.[4]

On the day of the invasion, LT(jg) Jimmy Nist flew F6F-5P Hellcat number 72614 on an early morning photo reconnaissance/strike mission over Okinawa. This was his sixth time piloting number 72614 on a combat mission. The mission lasted about three hours. This was one of three photo/strikes flown by Air Group 84 that day.[5]

Late in the day on Easter Sunday, LT(jg) Jimmy Nist took a few moments to write a letter to his parents. "Today was or rather is Easter," he wrote. "Was flying early this morning from 0615 'til about 0930 and just got back in time for church. They didn't have Communion like they usually do for some reason. Was going to Catholic Mass this afternoon but I missed that. So I guess this is one Easter I miss Communion."[6]

Jimmy then proceeded to relate an incident that happened aboard ship a few days prior. He wrote:

> We have jeeps aboard to tow planes around the deck. Well, the flight deck is pretty big and you can get up quite a bit of speed in a jeep. This joker is tearing down the flight deck in a jeep but he was going too fast to stop. So over the side he goes with the jeep. It hit a catwalk and in so doing knocked off a life raft. So when the jeep hits the water (after a fall of some 65 feet) he calmly climbs out, swims about six strokes, climbs into the life raft and waits for a destroyer to pick him up. Believe it or not![7]

Task Group 58.3 retired from the area on the evening of 1 April and steamed toward a resupply rendezvous. That night, the winds increased to 30 knots and the seas became rough.[8]

The weather got progressively worse during Monday, 2 April. The task group experienced periodic squalls, reduced visibility and a low cloud ceiling with winds of 35 knots and gusts to 45 knots. The larger ships were able to refuel but the destroyers would have to wait. Rearming was postponed due to the heavy seas. After refueling, Task Group 58.3 headed back north toward Okinawa.[9]

Task Group 58.3 was back in action on 3 April 1945 and weather conditions were much improved. *Hancock*'s and *Essex*'s aircraft flew support missions for the soldiers and Marines advancing on Okinawa. *Essex*'s and *Bataan*'s aircraft attacked Ie Shima. While attacking Kikai Island's airfield in the Amami Oshima group, *Bataan*'s Hellcats damaged two aircraft on the ground and shot down four "Zeke" and three "Tojo" fighters. Two Hellcats were lost but one of the downed pilots was rescued. *Cabot*'s aircraft bombed Japanese military targets on Okinawa and Amami Oshima. While attacking Tokuno Shima's airfield, *Essex*'s fighters shot down 16 Japanese aircraft and destroyed four more on the ground. *Bunker Hill*'s air group hit targets on Amami Oshima, Kikai, Ie Shima and Okinawa. *Bunker Hill* pilots also shot down a "Zeke" and three "Judy" bombers while flying combat air patrols.[10]

Bunker Hill's fliers hit the Amami Gunto twice on 3 April 1945. In the early morning, eight VF-84 Corsairs strafed Japanese aircraft at Amami Oshima's airfield and bombed two ships in the vicinity. LT(jg) John Pini's VF-84 Corsair got hit by a 7.7 mm round in the oil cooler. Unable to reach *Bunker Hill*, he landed aboard *Cabot* and his irreparable Corsair was pushed over the side.[11]

Air Group 84's afternoon return to Amami Oshima proved even more eventful. Seven VMF-451 Corsairs, a VF-84 photo section and 10 VF-29 Hellcats from *Cabot* bombed and strafed the Japanese airfields on Amami Oshima. After attacking the airfields, the Navy and Marine fliers were ambushed by more than 15 Japanese fighters over Kikai. The Marine pilots shot down 10 of their attackers in what historians Barrett Tillman and Jan Jacobs called a "mini turkey shoot." The VF-29 pilots shot down a "Jill" and seven "Zekes." One U.S. pilot was shot down but rescued the following morning by a Navy flying boat.[12]

LT(jg) "Shorty" Nist flew his 20th mission on 3 April 1945. At the controls of F4U-1D Corsair number 57808, Nist flew a combat air patrol over the task group that was 3.8 hours in duration.[13]

4 April 1945

For Task Group 58.3, Wednesday, 4 April 1945, was scheduled to be another day of air support missions in support of the Marines and soldiers battling on Okinawa, strike missions against Japanese military targets, fighter sweeps to destroy Japanese aircraft on the ground, combat air patrols to counter the growing threat from Japanese kamikazes and photo reconnaissance missions. Over the course of the day, Task Group 58.3 fliers would range from Okinawa and Ie Shima, and north to the Amami Shunto.

The task group's day began at 0100 when *Bunker Hill* launched one of its night fighter Hellcats on a combat air patrol. That night fighter shot down a "Betty" medium bomber. Around 0725, four VF-84 Corsairs intercepted four "Zeke" fighters at 11,000 feet, shooting down two and probably destroying a third "Zeke." Task Group 58.3 aircraft conducted combat missions against Okinawa, Ie Shima, Yoron Shima and Tsuken Shima. *Bataan* and *Bunker Hill* sent fighters on sweeps against Amami Oshima and Kikai in the morning and afternoon. Meanwhile, constant combat air patrols covered the task group from Japanese kamikazes. Flight operations for the day ended when night fighters returned aboard their carriers by 2100.[14]

TBM Avengers from USS *Hancock* fly a support mission on 4 April 1945 against targets on Okinawa (Naval History and Heritage Command [Photo 80-G-319244]/National Archives).

Amami Gunto

On the fourth day of the Okinawa invasion, Air Group 84 was tasked with striking Japanese airfields in the Amami Oshima group (Gunto). Located between Kyushu and Okinawa, Amami Oshima was being used as a staging area for kamikazes attacking the U.S. ships supporting the invasion. Amami Oshima was the largest island in the group and also the seventh-largest island in the archipelago that makes up Japan. Amami Oshima lies 210 nautical miles south of Kyushu and about 130 nautical miles north of Okinawa. To the east is the Pacific Ocean; to the west is the East China Sea. In area, the volcanic island encompasses 275 square miles. Amami Oshima was a lush, tropical island of incredible beauty with rainforests, waterfalls, offshore coral reefs and numerous flowering plants. The other islands of the Amami Gunto were Edateku to the west; Yoroshima, Ukejima and Kakeromajima to the south; and Kikai some 16 miles to the east of Amami Oshima. Kikai encompassed just under 22 square miles and was mostly low and flat. Kikai had an airfield with a single runway on its southwestern coast and one other minor airfield.

On 4 April 1945, *Bunker Hill*'s Air Group 84 and *Bataan*'s Carrier Light Air Group 47 were tasked to attack and destroy Japanese airpower in the Amami Gunto. In the morning, eight *Bunker Hill* Corsairs and eight *Bataan* Hellcats conducted a fighter sweep of the Amami Gunto. The Corsairs strafed Tokuno Airfield, destroying several Japanese aircraft on the ground and starting fires in a nearby town. Only one Japanese heavy anti-aircraft battery fired at the attacking American planes. *Bataan*'s Hellcats also strafed and rocketed Tokuno Airfield and attacked Kikai's airfield as well. They hit two aircraft on Kikai and three aircraft on Tokuno. All 16 American fighters safely returned to their carriers.[15]

The afternoon fighter sweep of Kikai Shima in the Amami Shunto was another combined effort between *Bunker Hill*/Air Group 84 and *Bataan*/Carrier Light Air Group 47. This time, VF-84 provided three photo Hellcats and seven Corsairs armed with bombs. *Bataan*'s VF-47 provided seven Hellcats, each of which was armed with a single 1,000-pound bomb. LT C.J. (Cy) Chambers led the VF-84 raiders, which included LT(jg) Jimmy Nist. Having originally trained as an SBD Dauntless dive-bomber pilot, Nist was very proficient in dive-bombing. Their target was Kikai Airfield on Kikai island. Anti-aircraft guns ringed the airfield. The two air groups conducted their attacks independently. *Bataan*'s Hellcats did not suffer any casualties, but three Fighting 84 Corsairs were struck by anti-aircraft fire. Coke Coconougher's Corsair was hit and sustained damage to the hydraulic system that also dropped his landing gear. LT "Sarge" Sargent's Corsair was struck in the wing and windshield, wounding the pilot in the face. Assessing the damage, Coconougher and Chambers decided that Sergeant could not make it back to *Bunker Hill*. Apprising the carrier of the situation, Coconougher elected to escort Sargent to Yontan Airfield on Okinawa, which was now in American hands. Cocanougher guided his wounded squadron mate the hundred miles south to Yontan. He landed first, then talked Sargent down over radio. Sargent landed his damaged Corsair. Then his aircraft ground-looped and burst into flames. Coconougher and a Marine sergeant rushed to Sargent's burning plane and pulled him free. The two VF-84 pilots then spent four days on Okinawa before returning to *Bunker Hill*.[16]

One other VF-84 Corsair was struck by Japanese anti-aircraft fire over Kikai on Wednesday, 4 April 1945. Corsair Number 57835 piloted by LT(jg) James A. Nist was hit while diving on the airfield. Later that day, another VF-84 pilot wrote in Nist's Logbook: "FAILED TO RETURNED [sic] FROM MISSION."[17]

9

The War Goes On

LT(jg) James Nist's squadron mates from Fighting 84 returned to *Bunker Hill* without him. Nist was reported as missing in action and notifications were made through the standard channels of communication. Later that month, word reached Martin and Ethel Nist and family back in the United States via a Western Union telegram. They in turn notified Jimmy's fiancée, Alice. Now began a prolonged period of uncertainty and anguish.

April and May 1945

The war continued on without "Shorty" Nist. Two days after his disappearance, the super battleship *Yamato* sortied forth with the light cruiser *Yahagi* and eight destroyers on a surface kamikaze mission to punish the U.S. fleet invading Okinawa. They came nowhere near accomplishing their mission. Carrier aircraft from *Bunker Hill*, *Cabot*, *Essex*, *Bataan* and other Task Force 58 carriers found *Yamato* on 7 April and sent her to the bottom of the Pacific Ocean along with *Yahagi* and four of the escorting destroyers. LT(jg) Wilbert Popp witnessed *Yamato*'s death throes. "As it sank a great geyser of water shot up into the air as the ammo aboard the ship or its boilers exploded. It looked like Old Faithful erupting," he wrote in his memoirs. At VADM Mitscher's personal request, LCDR Hedrick remained behind to assess the results of the air attacks.[1]

Practically tied to Okinawa to support the grueling campaign to wrest her from Japanese control, the Fifth U.S. Fleet was daily being struck by waves of kamikaze attacks launched from the Japanese Home Islands. The first major kamikaze raid came on 6 April 1945. TF-58 claimed 300 aircraft shot down, with *Bunker Hill* pilots accounting for 15 of them. *Cabot* avoided a kamikaze but was struck by its bomb. Destroyers set up as pickets to provide early warning of impending attacks were savaged by kamikazes. The next day, Task Group 58.3 combat air patrols knocked down 15 Japanese aircraft but one got through and dropped a bomb on *Hancock*'s forward flight deck. Twenty-eight sailors were killed, 52 were wounded and 15 were reported missing. Two days later, *Hancock* was sent back to the United States for extensive repairs along with *Cabot*, which was due for an overhaul. That left TG58.3 with two fleet carriers (*Essex* and *Bunker Hill*) and one light carrier (*Bataan*).[2]

On 12 April, the Japanese launched their second-largest kamikaze attack of the war. Around 200 kamikazes were shot down by task force pilots and anti-aircraft gunners. Task Group 58.3 claimed 104 Japanese aircraft shot down by fighters and two more by ships' anti-aircraft fire. Air Group 84 accounted for 32 of the kamikazes downed. VMF-451 pilots shot down 16, VMF-221 pilots shot down nine and VF-84 pilots shot down eight. LT(jg) Wilbert Popp shot down an Aichi Val dive-bomber—his third and final aerial victory of the war. Among the several American ships damaged by kamikazes was the battleship USS *Tennessee* (BB-43), survivor of the 7 December 1941 Pearl Harbor attack.[3]

That same day, President Franklin D. Roosevelt died of a cerebral hemorrhage at Warm Springs, Georgia. His long declining health had been a closely guarded secret skillfully kept from the public, much like the crippling effects of his bout with polio back in 1921. Upon his death, Vice President Harry S. Truman became president.

With kamikaze attacks coming frequently and at all hours of the day, the fighter pilots of Air Group 84 were both busy and successful. On the night of 21–22 April, the night fighter detachment shot down four Japanese aircraft. They got two more on the night of 27–28 April. West of Okinawa later that day, 15 VF-84 Corsairs on a combat air patrol intercepted a large group of "Nate," "Frank" and "Tony" fighters and shot down 18 of them. LT Doris "Chico" Freeman and LT(jg) J.M. Smith earned "ace" status with their respective aerial victories that day. Another Air Group 84 combat air patrol consisting of 16 Corsairs intercepted 20 incoming Japanese aircraft over Amami Oshima. Two "Zekes," 13 "Nates," four "Franks" and one "Tojo" were shot down without any loss to the Americans. On 3 May, VF-84 pilots shot down three enemy aircraft over Kikai Airfield in the Amami Shunto.[4]

The high tempo of operation and Japanese defenses took a toll on men and machines alike. LT(jg) A.S. Bearwa crashed into the sea and was killed during the strike on *Yamato* and her escorts on 7 April. LT E.J. Littlejohn and LT(jg) J.C. Dixon of VF-84 were shot down during a 16 April 1945 raid on Nagoya and Nagoya East Airfields on the Home Island of Honshu. Littlejohn was killed; Dixon was captured and survived the war. The next day, LT(jg) Leroy L. Wallet of VF-84 shot up a "Betty" bomber but was killed when the "Betty" and the Baka flying bomb that it was carrying exploded. On 3 May, CAPT John B. Delancey of VMF-221 was shot down and killed while attacking Inujo Airfield on Tanega Shima.[5]

LT(jg) Wallet's death was particularly hard on LT(jg) Wilbert Popp. "Like Nist whom we lost earlier Wally was my roommate on the carrier," he wrote in his 2004 memoirs. "It was sad and gloomy having lost both of my roomies."[6]

11 May 1945

On the morning of 11 May, Air Group 84 returned to the skies over Amami Oshima with LCDR Hedrick in command of the sweep. Between 0730 and 0900, the air group fighter pilots shot down 15 enemy aircraft of various types. Near Kikai Airfield, eight VF-84 Corsairs surprised a group of 30 "Nates" and "Zekes" and shot down 11 of them. LT "Chico" Freeman and LT(jg) John Smith each shot down their seventh Japanese aircraft. VMF-451's First LT J.S. Norris, Jr., shot down a "Zeke" near Amami Oshima. While defending the destroyer USS *Hugh W. Hadley*

(DD-774), seven VMF-221 Corsairs led by Capt. James Swett shot down three enemy bombers; Swett shot down one of them, thus earning his 15th aerial victory. During this battle, *Hugh W. Hadley* was struck by a Baka suicide bomb and two kamikazes but continued fighting on, shooting down 23 Japanese aircraft.[7]

By 0900, the aircraft of LCDR Hedrick's morning sweep were back aboard *Bunker Hill*. At 1005, *Bunker Hill* was preparing to launch another strike mission. Thirty-four Corsairs, Avengers and Helldivers were on the flight deck awaiting launch. Among those pilots waiting in their cockpits to take off was LCDR Raymond Hill, LT(jg) John Pini, LT(jg) M.T. "Mac" Daniel and LT(jg) "Dusty" Miller of VF-84. Many other Air Group 84 aircrews were in their squadron ready rooms awaiting their next missions. LT(jg) Wilbert Popp was scheduled for a 1200 mission and so was taking a nap on a couch in the wardroom. Capt. Swett's Marines were overhead returning from their morning mission. Fast Carrier Task Force commander VADM Marc Mitscher; his chief of staff, COM Arleigh Burke; and the vice admiral's staff were in the flag plot in *Bunker Hill*'s island coordinating the task force's operations.[8]

Without warning, a Japanese "Zeke" piloted by Sub Lieutenant (junior grade) Yasunori Seizō dropped out of the low clouds and dove on *Bunker Hill*. There was no time to react. The "Zeke" dropped a 550-pound bomb that hit the flight deck, penetrated through the ship and exploded in the water. The "Zeke" then struck *Bunker Hill*'s crowded flight deck near the number 3 elevator with devastating results. Thirty seconds later, a second "Zeke" piloted by Ensign Ogawa Kiyoshi approached unseen from *Bunker Hill*'s stern. In a near vertical dive, Kiyoshi dropped a 550-pound bomb that struck the air combat intelligence office and the signal bridge and caused major destruction to the air group ready rooms and hangar deck. Kiyoshi's "Zeke" was hit by a 40 mm anti-aircraft shell that failed to stop the kamikaze from striking the flight deck near the island. A huge conflagration ensued that threatened to destroy the ship.[9]

Seizō's kamikaze struck the aircraft on *Bunker Hill*'s flight deck two rows in front of LT(jg) Pini and LT(jg) Daniel's Corsairs. Somehow, they managed to escape from their planes and make their way to the fantail where the light cruiser USS *Wilkes-Barre* (CL-103) rescued them. LCDR Roger Hedrick and VT-84's commanding officer, LCDR Chandler Swanson, were working on the upcoming flight schedule below deck. They both survived along with LCDR Raymond Hill. Being in the wardroom at the time of the attack, LT(jg) Popp escaped the fate of so many of his colleagues in the ready rooms and on the flight deck. He assisted with firefighting on the flight deck.[10]

Overhead, Capt. Swett and his pilots were unable to prevent the catastrophe. "We watched the planes dive on CV-17, but could do nothing but scream over our radio that *kamikazes* were diving on *Viceroy* base. We had no ammo after chasing Japs all over the sky," he later recalled. He and his Marines landed aboard USS *Enterprise*.[11]

The kamikaze strikes created an inferno amid the fully armed and fueled aircraft on the flight deck and throughout the hangar deck below. Fires raged throughout the ship, trapping men and generating toxic smoke that killed many. Nearby escorting ships such as USS *Wilkes-Barre*; the destroyers USS *English* (DD-696), USS

Stembel (DD-644) and USS *The Sullivans* (DD-537); and the submarine tender USS *Sperry* (AS-12) closed in to render assistance and protect the stricken carrier from further kamikazes lurking about. A Japanese Yokosuka D4Y3 "Judy" dive-bomber attempted to crash on *Bunker Hill* but one of her Marine anti-aircraft gun crews shot it down before it had a chance to add to the destruction. Down in the engineering spaces, the ship's chief engineer, CDR Joseph R. Carmichael, Jr., and his crew valiantly kept the ship's systems operating despite horrendous smoke and heat conditions. At a critical time in the ship's survival, CAPT George A. Seitz ordered a crucial hard turn to port, which sent much of the burning fuel and debris over the side and into the sea.[12]

The cost was enormous, exceeded only by USS *Franklin*'s March 1945 ordeal. Vice Admiral Mitscher and COM Burke escaped from the flag plot, but three officers and 10 enlisted sailors died in the attack. For his bravery in evacuating his personnel, Burke was awarded the Silver Star. *Bunker Hill* suffered a total of 389 dead or missing and another 264 wounded. Air Group 84 lost 103 officers and enlisted killed. Of these, VT-84 had 26 killed, VB-84 had 21 killed, VF-84 had 22 killed, the two Marine squadrons lost 30 killed and four from the Air Group staff were killed. The air group's losses represented 33 percent of its 431-man roster at the time of its embarkation aboard *Bunker Hill* in January 1945. Many of the air group pilots and

Bunker Hill on fire after being struck by two Japanese kamikazes on 11 May 1945 (Naval History and Heritage Command [Photo 80-G-274266]/National Archives).

aircrew in the ready rooms were killed in the initial explosion. The survivors were trapped by the resultant fires and died afterward from smoke inhalation.[13]

Like its sister squadrons, Fighting Squadron 84 was hit hard by the kamikaze attacks. The squadron's dead included LT(jg) John Gildea, LT(jg) "Dusty" Miller, LT(jg) Gene Powell, LT(jg) Caleb Kendall, LT(jg) Doris Freeman, LT(jg) John Sargent and flight surgeon LT Paul Schroeder. LT(jg) Kendall's wife had just given birth to their son Timothy the day before. He found out about the birth of his son the night before the fateful day. LT(jg) Miller's wife was expecting their first child.[14]

Later when it was safe to do so, LT(jg) Popp and several others from VF-84 went below to assess the damage in their squadron ready room. There Popp found the lifeless bodies of his best friend, LT(jg) John Sargent; LT(jg) Doris Freeman; and the other pilots of VF-84. The following day, Popp supervised a group of 45 enlisted sailors in recovering bodies from the damaged areas of the ship. The bodies were brought to elevators and then lifted up to the hangar deck for identification and eventual burial at sea.[15]

Mitscher and his staff transferred to *Enterprise*. Three days later, *Enterprise* was struck by a kamikaze and they had to transfer again. USS *Randolph* thus became the new flagship for the Fast Carrier Task Force.[16]

On the afternoon of the kamikaze attack, the ship's surviving crew members undertook the grim task of recovering the bodies of their fallen shipmates from the damaged spaces. Nearly 400 of *Bunker Hill*'s crew had been killed by fire, smoke or physical trauma resulting from the two kamikazes. Many of the bodies had been horribly burned. Recovering the bodies was a dangerous undertaking as many of the ship's spaces had been heavily damaged by the impact of the kamikazes and by explosions. Recovery teams had to contend with lingering smoke, water, heat and debris. Bodies were first brought to the portside hangar deck for identification. Medical personnel used dog tags, uniform name stencils and dental records to identify the bodies. If those methods failed, then they searched for clues in the deceased's clothing that could help identify him.[17]

After identification, the bodies were then brought up to the flight deck and prepared for burial at sea. Each body was sewn into a white canvas burial shroud. To weigh the body down so that it would sink, a 55-pound, five-inch projectile was tied to the deceased's chest and another one was tied to his legs.[18]

At three minutes past noon on 12 May, *Bunker Hill*'s crew began one of the longest burials at sea in U.S. Navy history. The ship's officers and men gathered on the flight deck. Her commanding officer, CAPT George Seitz, presided over the service. In his remarks, he praised the ship's company for saving the ship and honored the dead. Three Navy chaplains—a rabbi, a Protestant minister and a Catholic priest—participated in the service. The Catholic and Protestant chaplains offered scripture, prayers and eulogy. The Navy Hymn was sung and a bugler played "Taps." *Bunker Hill* had three burial chutes available to commit the deceased to the deep. With so many *Bunker Hill* crewmembers requiring burial at sea, three olive drab stretchers were pressed into service as an expedient. The bodies of six crewmembers were placed upon the burial chutes at a time. If the decedent's religious preference was known, then the appropriate chaplain offered prayers for him. If no religious preference was known, then all three chaplains prayed for him. All three chaplains also prayed for the 24 unidentified crewmembers. Then their bodies were committed to the deep. At the end of the ceremony, a Marine honor guard fired a 21-gun rifle salute. The ceremony ended at around 2000. During the emotionally grueling eight-hour ceremony, 352 *Bunker Hill* crewmembers were committed to the deep. This included LT(jg) "Dusty" Miller, LT(jg) Gene Powell and Steward's Mate First Class Norman "Coca" Cola.[19]

Bunker Hill began the long, painful voyage back to the United States. Escorted by the destroyers USS *Ault* (DD-698) and USS *Waldron* (DD-699), *Bunker Hill* returned to the fleet anchorage at Ulithi, arriving there on 14 May. Soon after, the body of one of the missing sailors was discovered. He was interred ashore on one of Ulithi's islets. Accompanied by USS *Langley* (CVL-27), *Bunker Hill* departed Ulithi on 17 May and arrived at Pearl Harbor on 25 May. Three days later, *Bunker Hill* left Pearl Harbor on her own headed for Naval Station Puget Sound, arriving there on 1 June. She went into drydock at Bremerton on 4 June to begin extensive repairs that lasted until 22 July. Meanwhile, her surviving crew were granted 30 days of "survivor's leave."[20]

Catholic Memorial Mass held on *Bunker Hill*'s Hangar Deck on 20 May 1945 in remembrance of the sailors and Marines killed during the 11 May 1945 kamikaze attack (Naval History and Heritage Command [Photo 80-G-323704]/National Archives).

After nearly three grueling months, the Okinawa campaign came to a conclusion. The invasion cost the lives of 7,213 service members ashore and wounded another 31,081. In supporting the invasion, the Navy suffered 4,907 killed and 4,824 wounded. Thirty-six ships were sunk and another 388 ships were damaged. Major damage was sustained by 10 battleships; 13 carriers, including *Bunker Hill*; five cruisers; and 67 destroyers. In all, 763 aircraft were lost, including an F4U Corsair piloted by LT(jg) James A. Nist on 4 April 1945. The Japanese suffered far greater losses—131,000 Japanese were killed on Okinawa and a surprising 7,400 were captured. Deaths among the Okinawan civilians were also very high. Sixteen Japanese warships, including the super battleship *Yamato*, were sunk at sea and over 7,800 aircraft were destroyed in the air or on the ground.[21]

During her three years of wartime service, *Bunker Hill* and her embarked air groups contributed mightily to the victory in the Pacific. Her aircraft sank 162,000 tons of enemy shipping, damaged another 454,075 tons, destroyed 230 enemy aircraft on the ground and shot down 475 enemy aircraft. Of these, 169 aerial victories occurred on her final war cruise. Her anti-aircraft gunners shot down 20 enemy aircraft. On her final deployment, she brought the war to the skies of the Japanese Home Islands.[22]

In their one and only wartime cruise, Air Group 84 amassed an impressive record of achievement. The Air Group 84 flight crews performed 5,920 sorties, sinking four enemy vessels and downing 192 Japanese aircraft. They assisted in sinking the Japanese super battleship *Yamato*. VF-84 shot down 92 Japanese aircraft and VMF-221 and VMF-451 shot down 66 Japanese aircraft and 34 Japanese aircraft, respectively. Nine AG-84 pilots became aces. LT(jg) J.M. Smith, LT Doris Freeman, LT(jg) John Gildea and 1stLt D Caswell each shot down seven aircraft. Including their aerial victories with VF-17, LT(jg) Smith had a total of 10 aerial victories and LT Freeman had a total of nine aerial victories. From VMF-221, Capt. W.M. Snider earned 6.5 aerial victories, and 1stLt J McManus earned six aerial victories. Capt. James E. Swett increased his aerial victories to 15.5. Major A.G. Donahue of VMF-451 shot down five Japanese aircraft, adding to his nine victories with VMF-112 in 1943. LT W.G. Laney and LT(jg) L.A. Maberry both shot down five Japanese aircraft. Another 42 Japanese aircraft were destroyed on the ground, including one by LT(jg) James A. Nist of VF-84.[23]

Air Group 84's aerial victories were impressive but even more so when compared with their combat losses. Only four Air Group 84 Corsairs were lost to Japanese fighters, which amounted to a 48-to-1 kill ratio. Equally important, the Corsairs did a phenomenal job in protecting the air group's bombers from enemy fighters. During 547 combat missions, only two VT-84 Avengers were lost to enemy fighters. Both were shot down on the air group's first bombing mission over Japan. "I hasten to say that our VF squadrons generally were great," said VT-84's commanding officer, LCDR Chandler Swanson, afterward.[24]

Prior to the 11 May 1945 kamikaze attack on *Bunker Hill*, Air Group 84 lost 39 aircraft. Twelve were lost to operational causes, split equally among Corsairs, Helldivers and Avengers. Twenty-one aircraft were lost to anti-aircraft fire: 15 Corsairs, five Helldivers and one Avenger. Only six aircraft were lost in aerial combat.[25]

10

Missing in Action

LT(jg) James Nist failed to return from a strike mission on Kikai Airfield in the Amami Shunto on 4 April 1945. He was officially listed as missing in action. The war in the Pacific continued on without him.

Back at Home

None of this was known to Jimmy's loved ones back home in the United States. They continued on with their lives completely unaware that Jimmy was missing in action. Life continued in San Francisco and Squankum.

During this time, Ethel Nist sent three letters to her forward-deployed son. On 17 April, Ethel sent a letter to him in which she commented on news about the war and updated Jimmy on what was happening back home. She informed him that Bill Marks and his wife had had a baby girl and Milton and Margorie Estelle had had a baby boy whom they named Milton after his father. Marge Estelle was the younger sister of Walter Dickerson, husband of Martin and Ethel's daughter Kathryn and Jimmy's older sister. She also made mention of the recent deaths of President Franklin D. Roosevelt and war correspondent Ernie Pyle.[1]

A week later, Ethel sent another letter to her forward-deployed son. Most of the letter contained a description of a recent medical emergency that their neighbors the Fitzpatricks had experienced. She and Martin went over there and helped out. Mrs. Fitzpatrick ended up being taken to the hospital.[2]

Ethel sent her final letter to her son on 25 April 1945. Martin had begun the spring planting on the Nist farm. Ethel believed that two recent rounds of frost had killed off their strawberry crop for the year and possibly the huckleberry crop as well. Her letter contained some hometown news. Walter Dickerson's other sister, Gladys, was getting married on 12 May. The wedding was going to be a small-scale affair and children were not invited to the reception.[3]

Ethel and Martin's daughter Kathryn and her family had come by for a visit on the previous Sunday evening and Ethel described the visit for her son. Kathryn's eldest son, Walt, Jr. (a.k.a. Dickie), had helped his grandfather milk the cow. Ethel devoted most of her account of the visit to her grandson Ronnie/Jim's namesake. Ronnie (James Ronald) was now 19 months old. Ethel wrote:

> Ronnie hasn't learned to say Uncle Jim yet but he still climbs even worse than ever. Nobody can be on the floor one second before he is on their back and Kathryn says Dickie called her

one day to take him down. She found him standing up on Dickie's back and he didn't dare move. Another pet trick is to climb up on the window sill behind the couch and lay there. I told her she had better get a rope and teach him tight rope walking. I think he could do it. Some nephew you got.[4]

On 23 April 1945, Alice wrote a letter to Ethel Nist. She mentioned that her younger brother had shipped out for duty in the Pacific theater with the Marines. She asked how Ethel's ankle was healing and how her gardening was doing. She wrote about receiving several letters from Jim in the last two weeks but lamented that Jim was still unable to share anything about what they had been doing.[5]

In recent weeks, Alice had been very busy planning the wedding. Jimmy wanted to get married as soon as he got back from his deployment. Alice wrote:

> Jim wants to spend his leave with you folks and I think its swell—so we will see you then, but I think it would be wonderful if you and Dad could come to San Francisco for our wedding. Do you think you could—then we could all go back together. We would love to have you here. I've been planning on a white wedding with three bridesmaids and a maid of honor all in white with colored flowers. I'm going to wear a white satin dress with a fingertip vail. Have some of the dress already and am very busy with other arrangements trying to get things ready so when Jim gets home we can be married as soon as possible; his friends will also want to start for home quickly. I don't think Jim has made up his mind whether they will wear their blues or whites but I'm sure either of them will look grand.[6]

Alice also wrote about how much she was missing Jimmy and how much she was looking forward to his return:

> I'm looking forward so much to his homecoming as I know you are too—Today its been three months since he left here but it seems like ages to me—Perhaps two more months will find him homeward bound—that's what they seem to think and I've also heard from other people who have relatives in Task Force 58 that they expected the fellows back home in June.[7]

Official Notification

After he failed to return from the Kikai mission, LT(jg) Nist was listed as missing in action by Air Group 84/USS *Bunker Hill*. It took some time for notification of LT(jg) Nist's status to work its way through the Navy's casualty reporting system. On 26 April 1945, Martin and Ethel Nist received the following Western Union telegram from Vice Admiral Randall Jacobs, chief of naval personnel:

> THE NAVY DEPARTMENT DEEPLY REGRETS TO INFORM YOU THAT YOUR SON LIEUTENANT (JG) JAMES ARTHUR NIST USNR IS MISSING FOLLOWING ACTION. WHILE IN THE SERVICE OF HIS COUNTRY. THE DEPARTMENT APPRECIATES YOUR GREAT ANXIETY BUT DETAILS NOT NOW AVAILABLE AND DELAY IN RECEIPT THEREOF MUST NECESSARILY BE EXPECTED. TO PREVENT POSSIBLE AID TO OUR ENEMIES PLEASE DO NOT DIVULGE THE NAME OF HIS SHIP OR STATION.[8]

Prior to deploying, LT(jg) Nist had requested that his fiancée, Alice Richards, be notified in the event of him becoming a casualty. However, the Navy Department did not immediately notify her. Instead, Alice learned that her fiancé was missing from a telegram that Ethel and Martin sent her.[9]

On 28 April 1945, Alice sent her future in-laws a letter in reply to the telegram that they had sent. "As I start this letter out, I don't know what to say," she wrote. "Only that we're all sharing the same feeling, hope and waiting and we must keep our chin up, Jimmy always told me to do that."[10]

In her letter, Alice tried to be hopeful and strong. She wrote:

> I'm sure we'll have some good news very soon so let's have faith that all is well. I love Jimmy so much and in the short time we knew each other were the happiest times I have ever had and I know God will bring him back to us.[11]

Over the last few months, Alice had become friends with Lois Miller, the wife of Jimmy's best friend, LT(jg) Dusty Miller. Lois lived in Santa Rosa, about 60 miles north of San Francisco. She and Dusty were expecting their first child. Lois had heard from Dusty and called Alice. Dusty was supposed to have flown on the same mission that Jimmy failed to return from. Dusty had flown a mission in the morning and when he got back from that mission, he had been dropped from the afternoon mission that Jimmy flew on.[12]

The Western Union telegram was followed up four days later by a letter from the Navy Bureau of Personnel's Casualty Notification and Processing Section. In his letter, LT W.J. McNicol, Jr., wrote, "It is with regret that this Bureau confirms the report that your son, Lieutenant (junior grade) James Arthur Nist, U.S. Naval Reserve, is missing in action as of 4 April 1945. Detailed information in connection with his disappearance has not been received in this Bureau." Along with the letter, LT McNicol included a booklet that provided information on naval personnel who were in a missing status.[13]

After receiving official word of his status, Martin and Ethel Nist and their extended family and Alice and her family agonized for months before Jimmy's fate was definitively known.

On 9 May 1945, the Navy Department finally notified Alice Richards that her fiancé was missing in action. The Navy Department telegram was essentially the same that Martin and Ethel Nist had received a couple of weeks prior. That same day, Alice penned a letter to Ethel Nist and told her about the Navy Department telegram. She was surprised to have received the telegram, apparently unaware that Jimmy had directed that she be notified in the event of him becoming a casualty.[14]

In her letter, Alice told Ethel about her recent trip up to Santa Rosa to visit with Lois Miller. Lois had heard from Dusty again. Dusty could not provide any details about Jimmy but he suggested that Alice write to one of *Bunker Hill*'s chaplains.[15]

Alice had also contacted the Red Cross for advice on how to find out more about Jimmy's situation. The Red Cross advised her to write to Jimmy's commanding officer or chaplain. Out of respect for her future mother-in-law, Alice refrained from sending any letters out and instead asked Ethel if it was all right for her to do so.[16]

Overall, Alice was trying to remain hopeful and optimistic. To Ethel, she wrote:

> I have been feeling much better and have faith and hope. I have been keeping busy at work and it helps a lot. It was such an awful shock I didn't know which way to turn but I know that if we all hope and pray our prayers will be answered soon.[17]

Two days after Alice sent that letter, *Bunker Hill* was struck by the two kamikazes that caused such devastating results. Among the dead was Lois Miller's husband,

Dusty. Lois received the dreadful news on 28 May. He had been buried at sea along with the other dead from the kamikaze attack. "Mom I felt so badly as she is expecting a baby next month," Alice wrote to Ethel on 3 June 1945. Alice was beginning a two-week vacation so she was going to take a few days and visit with Lois up in Santa Rosa. Lois had given Alice the name of one of *Bunker Hill*'s chaplains, LCDR R.E. Delaney, and Alice shared his name with Ethel.[18]

Word of LT(jg) Nist's disappearance during combat operations was steadily circulating through the U.S. Navy. The Headquarters of the Commandant Third Naval District in New York City received word in early May. The district chaplain, CDR John F. Hagen, sent Martin Nist a letter on 15 May 1945 offering his prayers and sympathies. "We sincerely hope and reverently pray that your dear one may eventually be found, while we, his comrades, will go on with the struggle to preserve the good and noble we hold precious in our nation's life," he wrote.[19]

On 22 May 1945, the deputy chief of naval operations (Air), Vice Admiral Aubrey W. Fitch, sent a letter to Martin Nist about his son being missing in action. "I fully realize your anxiety and want you to know that you have my heartfelt sympathy," VADM Fitch wrote. He continued:

> It is my earnest hope that the knowledge you have of your son's loyalty to our country and his patriotic participation in the essential work of the aviation branch of its defense forces will sustain you during this trying time, and give you strength and fortitude. His unfaltering courage and devotion to duty will serve as an inspiration to all of us.[20]

As the weeks progressed, a few details emerged about the fate of their son. Ethel Nist wrote to the commanding officer of USS *Bunker Hill*, CAPT George Seitz, to learn more about what had happened. She also wrote to the squadron chaplain of VF-84 on 25 June 1945. It would be several months before Ethel Nist received replies to her letters.

On 24 June 1945, Alice again wrote to her future-in-laws. She had gotten a letter from LT Abele. By now, *Bunker Hill* had returned to the United States and LT Abele was on leave. He had been berthed in a room adjacent to Jimmy's. In his letter, LT Abele explained what had happened to Jimmy on his final mission. Alice did not summarize and relate any details from it for Ethel and Martin. Instead she included the letter with her own letter. "My feeble attempt at writing is not very comforting but please be brave and have courage and even though the story is there for us to read, I can't believe it and I will go on day after day hoping and praying for his safety," Alice wrote. She also provided LT Abele's home address in New Orleans, Louisiana. Unfortunately, LT Abele's letter was not included in Jimmy's personal papers that were given to the author by Jimmy's sister Kathryn/the author's grandmother.[21]

Further confirmation about Jimmy's fate came directly from *Bunker Hill*'s commanding officer, CAPT George Seitz, a couple of weeks later. On 16 July 1945, Ethel and Martin Nist received a letter from CAPT Seitz via the Casualty Section of the Bureau of Naval Personnel. CAPT Seitz had written a letter to them on 9 April 1945 but it had taken a long time to work its way through channels to BUPERS and hence on to them. He acknowledged that James was officially declared missing in action by the Navy. "However, I regret to have to inform you that this 'missing' status is merely a technicality, since his body was not recovered, and that actually there can be little question concerning his death," he wrote.[22]

In his letter of 9 April 1945 to Martin and Ethel Nist, CAPT Seitz described LT(jg) Nist's final mission:

> Your son was pilot of one of our aircraft launched on a fighter sweep against a vitally important Japanese airfield. In the course of his bombing run on the target, his plane was hit at an altitude of approximately 2,500 feet by a burst of enemy heavy anti-aircraft fire and was observed to crash in flames. It is the opinion of the pilot who was the closest witness of it that your son's plane was hit in the area of the cockpit and that consequently his death was instantaneous and without suffering.[23]

CAPT Seitz then went on to praise James Nist as a naval aviator. He wrote:

> Considered one of the best pilots and most outstanding photographers in the Task Force, your son's loss is keenly felt. In recent weeks he had brought back photographs which had tremendous value in correctly assessing enemy installations and dispositions and in appraising damage to them. He always carried out these vitally important missions in complete disregard of his own personal safety and with an aggressiveness and enthusiasm which won him the high respect of his shipmates just as his friendly, cheerful personality won him their affection.[24]

Then CAPT Seitz offered his sympathies and tried to provide some measure of solace to the grieving parents. He wrote:

> Although I fully realize that there is little I can say which will help to alleviate your natural grief at a time like this, I do want to assure you of the very deep sympathy of every officer and man aboard this ship. We too share your sorrow in a very real sense, for we have lost a very fine shipmate who we shall greatly miss. Please try to take at least some measure of comfort in your sorrow in the thought that your son died as only a brave man can, fighting for those ideals and values and verities which we believe to be more important that even life itself. I can assure you that we who have been granted the opportunity to carry on the fight for him are determined that his death shall not have been in vain.[25]

Around the time that Ethel Nist received CAPT Seitz's letter of 9 April 1945, she received a letter from Miss Martha Deckard of San Diego, California. She and Jimmy had been friends while he was stationed at NAS North Island and she frequently cooked spaghetti dinners for him. She had last seen him before he and VF-84 went north to NAS Alameda to meet up with their new aircraft carrier. She had learned of *Bunker Hill* and VF-84's ordeal and about Jimmy's being missing in action and presumed dead. "Being a Christian and looking at it from that standpoint it is his [God's] gain and our loss," she wrote sympathetically. "Jimmy was a very dear friend of mine and I'll never forget the fun we had together." She regretted that she did not have a photo of him. "If you have one that I could have, I would enjoy having it," she wrote.[26]

As Navy aviation squadrons typically did not have a specific chaplain assigned to them, Ethel Nist's June 1945 letter to VF-84's squadron chaplain was forwarded to LT Thomas J. Mullins at U.S. Naval Auxiliary Air Station, Los Alamitos, California. Upon receipt of Ethel's letter, Chaplain Mullins spoke with James's roommate, LT(jg) Wilbert P. Popp. Nist's other roommate, LT(jg) Leroy Wallet, had also been killed in action. Chaplain Mullins replied to Ethel's 25 June 1945 letter on 21 August 1945. In his reply to her, Chaplain Mullins relayed what he had learned from LT(jg) Popp:

> Your son, Lt.(jg) James A. Nist, was killed on a strafing run on Kikai, which is off the tip Amami O-Shima in the Southern Ryuku Islands. He was killed instantly according to the reports of those who saw the crash.

In closing, Chaplain Mullins wrote that LT(jg) Popp would be contacting them and he offered his sympathies on their loss.[27]

The Empire of Japan formally surrendered to the Allied Powers on the deck of the battleship USS *Missouri* in Tokyo Bay on 2 September 1945. The long Pacific War had finally come to an end. For Alice Richards, the Nist family and others who had lost ones during the war, it was a bittersweet day. The war was over, but their loved ones would not be coming home alive. "It was a bright day for some people but brought sadness to us and others for those we have lost," Alice wrote later that month.[28]

On 29 September 1945, Alice wrote a lengthy letter to Ethel Nist. Ethel had previously shared the contents of CAPT Seitz's 9 April 1945 letter and Chaplain Mullins's letter of 21 August 1945 with Alice. Alice informed Jimmy's mother that CAPT Seitz had also written her a letter on 9 April 1945 about her fiancé. That letter was essentially the same as the one that he had sent to Jimmy's parents. Like his letter to the Nists, his letter to Alice had taken several months to reach her. "It made me feel blue but also proud to know of the wonderful work and flying he did," Alice wrote to Ethel, "and that his friends thought the world of him."[29]

As she told Jimmy's mother, Alice was still having trouble dealing with his presumed death. Though CAPT Seitz's and LT Abele's letters had provided many details about his final mission, Alice was still holding out some hope that he might be found alive in a Japanese prisoner of war camp. She quit her job in August and went to the country with a friend for two months. The time away was good for her and she was planning on going back to work in a few weeks. She also visited with Lois Miller, who by now had given birth to a son. According to Alice, the baby looked just like his dad. Alice also mentioned that her baby brother was now walking.[30]

Ethel Nist did not get a reply to her June 1945 letter to CAPT Seitz until October 1945. There was some delay in getting her a reply as both CAPT Seitz and Air Group 84 had been transferred to other duty. The ship's new commanding officer, CAPT H.L. Meadow, replied to Ethel Nist on 28 October 1945. Though he did not know her son personally, CAPT Meadow apparently did some research because he sent her a detailed summary of Nist's service aboard *Bunker Hill*. Regarding James's last mission, CAPT Meadow wrote:

> On April 4th he was participating in an attack on Omami Gunto when in the course of a bombing run on Kikai Airfield, while flying at 2500 feet, he was hit by a burst of enemy anti-aircraft fire and was killed. One of the pilots flying in the same formation witnessed the attack. He made no attempt to get out of the plane, the conclusion being that he was killed by the shell fire.[31]

In preparing his reply to Ethel Nist, CAPT Meadow had talked with several other officers aboard *Bunker Hill*. To her, he wrote:

The Air Group has left the ship, but many of our officers knew your son. They all speak highly of him, his sense of humor and his ability to mix with his fellow-officers. To them he was known as "Shorty," a nickname by which he was always addressed. As a pilot he was one of the best, his lack of fear and his desire to do the job ahead was evidence of his courage. I need not tell you that in the raids in which he took part were some of the most important of the war. He was engaged very often in taking the pictures of enemy defenses and installations, said pictures were of inestimable value in planning future operations.[32]

In conclusion, CAPT Meadow tried to offer some words of consolation: "I realize that his loss has been a deep and tragic wound to you, but may you find some measure of consolation in that he died as only a brave man can die, sacrificing himself for his home and country."[33]

In December 1945, Lois Miller received an invitation from CAPT Meadows to come visit *Bunker Hill,* which was now at NAS Alameda. Lois in turn called Alice and invited her to come along for the visit. On Saturday 8 December, Lois Miller and Alice Richards went out NAS Alameda to visit the aircraft carrier aboard which their loved ones had served and spent their final days. ENS Jack Burness met Lois and Alice at the main gate and escorted them to the ship. Alice informed ENS Burness that she was Jimmy's fiancée and asked if he knew him. "I never saw such a surprised person when I told him who I was," Alice wrote to Jimmy's mother two days later, "as he roomed right across from Jim and heard him speak all the time of home and all. He knew Jim very well and told us how all the fellows liked him so much and he was always laughing and kidding—I was so glad to talk to someone who knew him."[34]

Aboard ship, ENS Burness took Lois and Alice to get some coffee and continue the conversation. After learning that the carrier's chaplain had not replied to her letters, ENS Burness went and brought the chaplain to see her. The chaplain told her that he had written two letters to her in April 1945 but apparently Alice had not received them. Fortunately, he had the carbon copy of his 13 April letter. He went back to his room and quickly returned with the carbon copy for Alice to read. They then talked at length about Jimmy's time aboard ship and he shared what he knew about Jimmy's final mission. According to the chaplain, Jimmy's services as a photo pilot were in high demand but he preferred to fly fighter missions. On one of his later photo missions that occurred in either late March or early April, Jimmy had returned to *Bunker Hill* with 96 holes in his plane, the result of intense anti-aircraft fire. His colleagues didn't know how he managed to bring his plane home in that condition.[35]

Following their lengthy conversation with the chaplain, another *Bunker Hill* officer, ENS Wallace, escorted Lois and Alice on a tour of the ship. They got to see Dusty and Jimmy's berthing rooms, the squadrons' ready rooms, the flight deck and the hangar deck. By now, most of the damage from the May 1945 kamikaze attacks had been repaired. "It was a nice trip but it left me with a very odd feeling," Alice wrote to Ethel. "But it is something I won't forget."[36]

The remainder of Alice's 10 December letter covered several other topics. She was back working for an insurance company. Not happy with her job, she was considering finding a new one in the new year. She would be remembering Jimmy on his upcoming birthday that would occur in a few days. She wished Martin and Ethel a merry Christmas and happy new year.[37]

Sometime in late 1945, Robert Olds published an updated edition of his book, *Helldiver Squadron*. Originally published in 1944, *Helldiver Squadron* related the story of Bombing Squadron 17 during its operations aboard *Bunker Hill*. The updated version included chapters on Bombing Squadron 84 and Air Group 84 during their 1945 operations in the western Pacific. Though not identified by name, LT(jg) Nist's death was briefly described in Robert Olds's updated edition of *Helldiver Squadron*. "Coke Cocanougher [sic] winced," he wrote. "The Corsair ahead of him began to smoke, then exploded." Three VF-84 Corsairs were struck by anti-aircraft fire that fateful day. Since Olds identified the pilots of two of them (Coconougher and LT "Sarge" Sergeant), that third Corsair could only be "Shorty" Nist's.[38]

In late January 1946, Martin and Ethel Nist received a letter from Jimmy's former Rutgers roommate Alfred Messer. At this time, Messer was a Navy lieutenant (junior grade) serving aboard USS *LCS(L)-19* in Sasebo, Japan. "I have recently learned that Jim is listed as missing in action out here," he wrote. "It was tragic news to me, and I cannot help but feel a great personal loss, as I know you do. Please accept my deepest sympathies."[39]

Messer then went on to describe having visited with Jimmy in San Diego in the fall of 1944. "I had occasion to meet many of his fellow pilots, and I felt sure that they were just as proud to call him their friend and shipmate as I am," he wrote. "I have met many fine people in my time, but none better than Jim."[40]

In the middle of April 1946, the Nists received official notification that James Nist's status had been changed from missing in action to killed in action. Having reliable witnesses from VF-84 and in accordance with applicable federal laws and Navy regulations, the Navy declared him dead as of 5 April 1946. On 12 April 1946, Secretary of the Navy James Forrestal wrote:

> In view of the strong probability that your son lost his life when the plane he was piloting crashed and exploded, because no official or unconfirmed reports have been received that he survived, because his name has not appeared on any lists or reports of personnel liberated from Japanese prisoner of war camps, and in view of the length of time that has elapsed since he was reported to be missing in action, I am reluctantly forced to the conclusion that he is deceased. In compliance with Section 5 of Public Law 490, 77th Congress, as amended, the death of your son is, for the purposes of termination of pay and allowances, settlement of accounts, and payment of death gratuities, presumed to have occurred on 5 April 1946, which is the day following the expiration of twelve months in the missing status.[41]

Recognizing the finality of this notification, Secretary Forrestal concluded his letter with these following words in an effort of sympathy and consolation:

> I know what little solace the formal and written word can be to help meet the burden of your loss, but in spite of that knowledge, I cannot refrain from saying very simply, that I am sorry. It is hoped that you may find comfort in the thought that your son gave his life for his country, upholding the highest traditions of the Navy.[42]

Soon after the war ended, a U.S. Navy unit landed on Kikai to accept the surrender of the Japanese garrison. Other U.S. forces landed on Amami Oshima and Kikai Jima at various times between September 1945 and April 1946, but did not locate LT(jg) Nist's crash site or remains.

Several American aircraft had been shot down and crashed on the island. The

Japanese had respectfully recovered the bodies of the American aviators and given them proper burials. This included LT(jg) James Nist of VF-84; and Second LT Owen R. Baird, USMCR; Staff Sergeant Frederick E. Johnson, USMCR; and Sergeant Clyde B. Hight, Jr., of Marine Torpedo Squadron 232 (VMTB-232). At some point between mid–April 1946 and early June 1946, U.S. Army Graves Registration Services personnel had located and disinterred their bodies for repatriation. "Shorty" Nist's body was temporarily relocated to Okinawa and reinterred in the Island Command Cemetery, Plot 4, Row 24, Grave 757.[43]

Alice Richards wrote to Ethel Nist on 4 June 1946 to see how the family was doing. She had not heard anything further about Jimmy since her visit to *Bunker Hill* the preceding December. She was still in touch with Lois Miller. She had a suitcase of Jimmy's clothes. With Ethel's permission, Alice had kept a few items and then shipped the rest back home to the Nists. In closing, Alice was hoping that she would be able to meet Ethel and Martin in person.[44]

Six days later, Martin and Ethel Nist received a letter from CDR H.B. Atkinson of the Navy Bureau of Personnel. In his letter, CDR Atkinson informed the Nists that their son's body had been located by U.S. Army Graves Registration Services personnel and reinterred in the Island Command Cemetery on Okinawa. From the tone of the letter, it sounds like BUPERS had only recently learned of this fact.[45]

Alice wrote again to Ethel on 18 August 1946. In the interim, the suitcase of Jim's belongings had successfully made the long trip from San Francisco, California, to Howell, New Jersey. Alice had received a letter from the Navy Department similar to the one that Ethel and Martin had received regarding the change of Jimmy's status from missing in action to killed in action. Alice now had a toy fox terrier and was enjoying spending time with her younger brother, Paul. Lois Miller had remarried in July. Her new husband was a man from her hometown. While Alice indicated her desire to continue corresponding with Ethel, there are no further letters from her in Jimmy's personal papers.[46]

In 1947, Rutgers published its first yearbook following the end of World War II. This edition was also a memorial to the 183 Rutgers University graduates and former students who had died during the war. On page 35, James A. Nist '42 was honored with a photo and a description of his wartime service. In a letter that accompanied the yearbook, Rutgers University President Robert C. Clothier wrote, "No tribute can ever express, in full, the depth of gratitude we all have in our hearts for these men who joined the other men of Rutgers who, in earlier wars, similarly gave their lives for the nation's welfare."[47]

Coming Home

On 16 February 1949, the U.S. Army Quartermaster Corps sent a Western Union telegram to Martin and Ethel Nist informing them that their son's remains were en route back to the United States and would be arriving at New York, New York, in the coming weeks. The telegram confirmed that C.H.T. Clayton and Son Funeral Home in Adelphia, New Jersey, would be accepting Jimmy's remains. More details would be provided as they became available. The Nists were advised to confirm receipt of the telegram within 48 hours.[48]

James Arthur Nist's remains were shipped back to the United States on the U.S. Army transport SS *Dalton Victory* and arrived in New York in March 1949. On 15 March 1949, New York City Mayor William O'Dwyer sent a letter of condolence to Martin Nist.

Accompanied by a military escort, LT(jg) Nist's remains were placed aboard Jersey Central Lines Railroad train number 3305 in Jersey City. Train 3305 left Jersey City at 0830 on 29 March and traveled south to Lakewood, arriving there at approximately 1035. Representatives of C.H.T. Clayton and Son Funeral Home then accepted Nist's remains and brought them to their funeral home in Adelphia. LT(jg) Nist's body lay in state on the night of Wednesday, 30 March 1949. Frank Wrobel, Robert Morris and Robert Reese of American Legion Post No. 166 stood as an honor guard next to his casket.[49]

Around this time the Township Committee of Lakewood, New Jersey, issued a proclamation in honor of LT(jg) Nist. In their proclamation, the Township Committee honored the sacrifice of LT(jg) Nist and requested that all businesses and homes display the U.S. flag at half-mast in his honor on the day of his funeral.[50]

On Thursday, 31 March 1949, a funeral service was held for LT(jg) Nist at the C.H.T. Clayton and Son Funeral Home at 2 p.m. The service was conducted by the Rev. William I. Lockwood, pastor of All Saints Episcopal Church in Lakewood. Post Commander Lee Hurlburt, Arthur LaVinge, Gene Anthony, Frank Wrobel, Theodore Schwartz and Carl Evertz of American Legion Post No. 166 served as pallbearers. Afterward, LT(jg) James A. Nist, USNR, was buried with full military honors in the Nist family plot of the Woodlawn Cemetery, Lakewood. The military funeral honors were performed by a detachment from Naval Air Station Lakehurst. The

James A. Nist's funeral on 31 March 1949 (Dickerson Family Photograph).

graveside service was officiated by the Reverend Lockwood and Chaplain McQueen from NAS Lakehurst. James Whatoff, Robert Reese, Joseph Barchi and Robert Morris of Post No. 166 provided a color guard and Dale Debow sounded "Taps." Navy sailors fired rifle volleys over the grave and LT(jg) Nist was committed to the earth. In time, James would be joined in the Nist family plot by his great-aunts Wilhemina and Margaretha; mother, Ethel; father, Martin; sister Kathryn; and brother-in-law Walter.[51]

11

Honors and Tributes

In the months and years that followed James Nist's death in the skies over Amami Oshima, numerous tributes and honors were bestowed upon him posthumously.

Sometime following his death, the Township Committee of James's hometown of Howell, New Jersey, honored his memory with a memorial certificate. The certificate read:

> In Memoriam from all the people of Howell Township, in memory of our friend and good neighbor James Nist who paid the supreme sacrifice in World War II, that we may continue to live our lives in freedom and independence. In his passing, our people, our municipality, our state and our nation have lost a good soldier and a true citizen. May his sacrifice forever inspire us to defend and cherish the ideals for which he died.[1]

After LT(jg) Nist's status was changed from missing in action to killed in action, the *Rutgers Alumni Monthly* magazine printed an announcement about this change in status in its June 1946 edition along with a photo of him in his dress whites. The following year, James A. Nist was honored in the Rutgers yearbook along with the other 182 Rutgers University graduates and former students who died during the war.[2]

On 8 May 1946, the chief of naval personnel, VADM Louis Denfield, sent Martin and Ethel Nist the temporary citations for their son's Distinguished Flying Cross and Air Medal. Both medals had been issued by the commander of the First Carrier Task Force, Pacific, Vice Admiral Marc A. Mitscher, to which *Bunker Hill* and Air Group 84 belonged during the operations in the western Pacific. The Distinguished Flying Cross temporary citation read as follows:

> For distinguishing himself by heroism and extraordinary achievement while participating in an aerial flight in operations against the enemy in the Tokyo area on 17 February 1945. As a member of a carrier based fighter escort for a group of bombers he aided in escorting the formation over 120 miles of vigorously defended enemy territory. Over the target, an aircraft engine plant, he delivered a rocket and strafing attack in the face of intense and accurate antiaircraft fire, and then helped successfully escort the bombers back to the carrier. The latter part of the flight and his landing were made in extremely hazardous weather conditions. In defending the bombers and in delivering his attack his courage and determination were at all times in keeping with the highest traditions of the United States Naval Service.

While the DFC was awarded specifically for the 17 February 1945 air strikes on Tokyo, LT(jg) Nist was awarded the Air Medal for multiple missions conducted

11. Honors and Tributes

between 16 February and 1 March 1945. The Air Medal temporary citation read as follows:

> For distinguishing himself by meritorious achievement while participating in aerial flights as pilot of a carrier based fighter plane in attacks against the enemy in the Tokyo, Iwo Jima, and Okinawa areas during the period 16 February 1945 to 1 March 1945. During these attacks he carried out his duties as a fighter photographic pilot and in escorting groups of our own bombers in an outstanding manner. His courage was at all times in keeping with the highest traditions of the United States Naval Service.[3]

A month later, the Bureau of Naval Personnel informed the Nists that James had been awarded the Purple Heart posthumously. The Purple Heart was awarded to LT(jg) Nist by Secretary of the Navy James Forrestal and the Chief of Naval Personnel VADM Louis Denfeld "For Military Merit and For Wounds Received in Action resulting in his death."[4]

On 11 October 1946, VADM James L. Kauffman, commandant of the Fourth Naval District, presented the citation for LT(jg) James Nist's Gold Star in Lieu of Second Air Medal to his parents. The citation read as follows:

> For meritorious achievement in aerial flight as Pilot of a Fighter Plane in Fighting Squadron EIGHTY-FOUR, attached to the U.S.S. BUNKER HILL, during operations against Japanese forces at Amami Shima on April 4, 1945. Flying wing during a fighter sweep against Kikai airfield, Lieutenant, Junior Grade, Nist daringly plunged through intense and accurate hostile antiaircraft fire to drop his bombs directly on the runway and cause extensive damage. His superb airmanship and courageous initiative in the face of grave peril contributed materially to the success of his squadron's aerial offensive against the Japanese and reflect the highest credit upon Lieutenant, Junior Grade, Nist and the United States Naval Service.[5]

On 17 January 1947, the chief of naval personnel awarded LT(jg) James Nist the World War II Victory Medal in recognition of his part in the defeat of the Japanese Empire. The World War II Victory Medal had been established by President Franklin D. Roosevelt on November 6, 1942, via Executive Order No. 9265 and subsequently amended by another executive order issued

Ethel Nist receives one of her son's awards posthumously during a ceremony held at Navy Yard Philadelphia in October 1946 (Dickerson Family Photograph).

by President Harry S. Truman March 15, 1946. President Truman's order specified the time period for those eligible for the medal.[6]

Later that year, on 4 November 1947, CAPT W.C. Thomas, director—medals and awards for the Bureau of Naval Personnel, sent the Permanent Citation for LT(jg) Nist's Air Medal to his father. The citation read as follows:

> For meritorious achievement in aerial flight as a Photographic Pilot of a Fighter Plane in Fighting Squadron EIGHTY-FOUR, attached to the U.S.S. BUNKER HILL, in action Against enemy Japanese forces in the vicinity of Tokyo, Iwo Jima, and Okinawa, from February 16 to March 1, 1945. Participating in five combat missions during this period, Lieutenant, Junior Grade, Nist capably carried out his duties as a fighter photographic pilot and rendered invaluable service in escorting groups of friendly bombers on attack missions. His airmanship and courage under enemy fire were in keeping with the highest traditions of the United States Naval Service.[7]

Two months later, on 9 January 1948, the Navy Bureau of Personnel sent the Permanent Citation for LT(jg) Nist's Distinguished Flying Cross to his parents. The citation read as follows:

> For heroism and extraordinary achievement in aerial flight as Pilot of a Fighter Plane in Fighting Squadron Eighty Four, attached to the U.S.S. Bunker Hill, in action against enemy Japanese forces in the Tokyo Area on February 17, 1945. flying cover for a bomber formation over 120 miles of enemy territory, vigorously defended by intense and accurate anti-aircraft fire, Lieutenant, Junior Grade, Nist delivered a rocket and strafing attack on an aircraft engine plant and assisted in successfully escorting the bombers back to their carrier through extremely hazardous weather. His skilled airmanship and courageous devotion to duty were in keeping with the highest Traditions of the United States Naval Service.

The award was issued on behalf of President Truman by Navy Secretary John L. Sullivan.[8]

Nearly six years after his death, LT(jg) James Nist received another posthumous honor. In January 1951, President Harry S. Truman awarded the Presidential Unit Citation to USS *Bunker Hill* and its attached Air Groups 17, Eight, Four, and 84. The Presidential Unit Citation was awarded to *Bunker Hill* and her air groups for operations against Rabaul, Nauru, Kavieng and Truk Island and the Gilberts, the Marshalls and the Marianas island groups from November 1943 to February 1944; Palau, Hollandia and Truk in March and April 1944; the Marianas, Bonin Islands and Palau from June to August 1944; the Philippines, Palau, Yap, the Ryukyus Islands and Formosa in September and October 1944; Luzon in November 1944; and the Japanese Home Islands, the Bonins and the Ryukyus from February to May 1945. Nist was awarded the PUC "by virtue of his service in the U.S.S. Bunker Hill or her attached Air Groups during whole or part of the period cited," wrote LCDR Christopher J. Kersting, director of medals and awards for BUPERS. In part, the citation read "Daring and dependable in combat, the BUNKER HILL with her gallant officers and men rendered loyal service in achieving the ultimate defeat of the Japanese Empire."[9]

Nearly 50 years after his death in the western Pacific, LT(jg) James A. Nist was remembered by one of his former Rutgers classmates. On the occasion of Memorial Day 1993, former classmate Thomas A. Kindre included him in a column titled

"Memorial Day Reopens the Corridors of Memory" that was published in the *Asbury Park Press*. Thomas A. Kindre had graduated with Nist as part of the Class of 1942 and subsequently served as an infantry officer with the U.S. Army in Italy. In his column, Kindre wrote:

> When we graduated in May, we went in all directions and ended up fighting on land, sea and in the air in places we'd never heard of—like Iwo Jima, Monte Cassino, Normandy Beach, Guadalcanal, Anzio, Eniwetok and Okinawa. Most of us didn't get back for 3 ½ to four years. Twenty-one of us didn't get back at all.

Kindre then offered his memories of several of his Rutgers Class of '42 classmates who did not return from the war, including James Nist. Of Nist, Kindre wrote, "Jimmy Nist, in a pilot's helmet, about to take off for a training flight in a Waco biplane at the old Hadley Field."[10]

Now in 2023, James A. Nist's great-nephew offers this book as a memorial tribute to his late great-uncle who gave his life for our country three decades before his great-nephew was born.

Eternal rest grant unto him, Lord, and may his soul and the souls of all the faithfully departed through the mercy of God, rest in peace. Amen.

> "The souls of the righteous are in the hand of God, and no torment shall touch them.
> They seemed, in the view of the foolish, to be dead; and their passing away was thought an affliction and their going forth from us, utter destruction. But they are in peace."
> —The Book of Wisdom,
> Chapter 3, Verses 1–3

12

Shorty Nist's Final Mission

LT(jg) James "Shorty" Nist was killed in his final mission as a naval aviator while conducting a dive-bombing attack on an airfield on the Japanese island of Kikai in the Amami Shunto group of islands. For many months, he was listed as missing in action before his remains were located on Kikai and properly interred temporarily on Okinawa. For his fiancée, parents, family and friends, there would be agonizing months before some details of his final mission would be learned.

Many decades would pass before a more complete account of "Shorty" Nist's final mission would be compiled by his great-nephew based upon official U.S. Navy records. What follows is a detailed description of "Shorty" Nist's final mission and his death in the skies over Kikai Island. It has been compiled from official U.S. Navy correspondence to Nist's parents, mission reports for Navy Fighting Squadron 84 and Navy Fighting Squadron 47, the war diaries of USS *Bunker Hill* and USS *Bataan* and other official U.S. Navy documents obtained from the National Archives repository in College Park, Maryland.

Located as it was between the Japanese Home Island of Kyushu and Okinawa, the Amami Shunto group of islands was vitally important for Japanese air attacks on the U.S. fleet supporting the invasion of Okinawa. The several airfields located in these islands were heavily used for staging kamikaze attacks on those U.S. ships off Okinawa. Neutralizing these airfields and intercepting Japanese aircraft coming down from Kyushu was a high priority for the Fast Carrier Task Force and specifically Task Group 58.3. Throughout the Okinawa Campaign, the Amami Shunto was frequently bombed and strafed by American carrier aircraft as well as American aircraft based on Okinawa after its airfields were captured.

During the morning of 4 April 1945, Task Group 58.3 warbirds had attacked the Amami islands. At around 1200, Task Group 58.3 ordered a second mission against Amami Shunto. Fighter-bombers from USS *Bunker Hill*/Air Group 84 and USS *Bataan*/Carrier Light Air Group 47 were tasked to conduct a fighter sweep of the Amami Shunto with takeoff time scheduled for 1500. This combined afternoon fighter sweep would consist of seven F4U Corsairs from *Bunker Hill*'s Fighting Squadron 84 and eight F6F Hellcats from *Bataan*'s Fighting Squadron 47. *Bunker Hill* would also send along three photo F6F Hellcats.[1]

VF-84's Corsairs were organized into two divisions. LT(jg) Cy Chambers led a division that included LT(jg) W.J. Rempie and LT(jg) R.J. Vaughn. LT(jg) R.K. Coconougher led the other division, which included LT(jg) John J. Sargent, ENS

K.D. Lane and LT(jg) Jimmy Nist. The photo Hellcats were piloted by Laurie, Ecksberg and Packard from the Air Group 84 staff. For this mission, Nist would fly Corsair Number 57835.[2]

For the fighter sweep of Amami Shunto, the *Bunker Hill* and *Bataan* fighter-bombers were armed with bombs. *Bunker Hill*'s Corsairs were each armed with two 500-pound bombs. *Bataan*'s Hellcats were each armed with a single 1,000-pound bomb, these being the only ones that were available aboard ship.[3]

Bunker Hill's and *Bataan*'s fighters launched from their flight decks starting at 1500 local time. They launched from the vicinity of longitude 129 degrees 16 minutes east, latitude 26 degrees 16 minutes north. After assembling the two carriers' fighter planes, the combined *Bataan*/*Bunker Hill* fighter sweep proceeded north toward the Amami Shunto. The skies were overcast and visibility was from 10 to 12 nautical miles.[4]

Arriving in the Amami Shunto, the *Bunker Hill*/*Bataan* fighters first scouted the Tokuno Airfield on Tokuno Island, which was south of Amami Oshima. Finding no operational aircraft on the airfield, they headed toward Kikai, which was about 70 miles to the northeast.[5]

At some point en route to Kikai, the *Bataan* and *Bunker Hill* fighters split up. The sky was overcast at 1,000 feet with heavy haze.

There were two airfields located on Kikai Island. Wan Airfield was located on the western side of the island and Shitooke Airfield was located on the eastern side. Neither had established airfield facilities but both were defended with many anti-aircraft guns. As Kikai had two airfields, this may explain why Fighting 47 and Fighting 84 split up before launching their attacks.[6]

VF-47 and VF-84 made their attacks on Kikai separately. The VF-84 and VF-47 Action Reports do not indicate which squadron attacked Wan first. Regardless of who attacked first, VF-47's pilots were near enough to observe VF-84's attacks.

The VF-47 flight leader brought his Hellcats directly over Wan Airfield and led them on a high-altitude 60-degree dive-bombing attack with all aircraft attacking together. As aimed, all of their bombs struck the southeastern end of the airfield. Two of the bombs hit the takeoff area. The intention was to destroy enemy anti-aircraft positions and aircraft hidden in the trees in this area. One Japanese plane attempted to maneuver into takeoff position and was promptly strafed by the VF-47 Hellcats. The enemy anti-aircraft fire was intense but none of the VF-47 aircraft was hit.[7]

LT(jg) Cy Chambers led the *Bunker Hill* fighters across the southern tip of Kikai island at around 6,000 feet. LT(jg) Chambers and his division were in the lead followed by LT(jg) Coconougher's division, including LT(jg) Shorty Nist. Chambers initially intended to attack Shitooke Airfield but found that it was nonoperational. So instead, Chambers brought his flight back around to attack Wan Airfield.[8]

Japanese anti-aircraft defenses were ready for the American fighters. The Japanese sent up a moderate amount of heavy and medium anti-aircraft fire. After-Action Reports for the units involved described the anti-aircraft fire as "very accurate." Heavy anti-aircraft fire exploded close by but without inflicting any damage. They circled around to the north of the island and climbed to an attack altitude.

A break in the clouds appeared over the airfield and Chambers led his division down through the break on a 45-degree dive-bombing attack that began at 11,000 feet. Japanese anti-aircraft fire targeted the diving Corsairs but failed to hit Chambers and his other two Corsairs.[9]

LT(jg) Shorty Nist had originally trained as a dive-bomber pilot using the famed Douglas Dauntless dive-bomber and had served with Bombing Squadron 303 prior to being assigned to Fighting Squadron 84. Both in the Dauntless and in the Corsair, Nist was a proficient and very capable dive-bomber.

With LT(jg) Coconougher leading, Nist, Sargent and Lane followed the preceding division down through the break. This time, Japanese anti-aircraft fire was more accurate. LT(jg) Coke Coconougher's Corsair was hit and sustained damage to the hydraulic system, which caused his landing gear to lower. Sargent's Corsair was struck in the cockpit, wing and the hydraulic system. The wing began to smoke from the anti-aircraft hit. His aircraft was heavily damaged and he was wounded in the face.[10]

At an altitude of approximately 2,500 feet, Shorty Nist's Corsair was struck in the cockpit by Japanese anti-aircraft fire. In the opinion of nearby pilots who witnessed it, Nist was killed instantly. He made no effort to escape his stricken aircraft and the Corsair crashed into the ground with him still aboard. According to *Bunker Hill*'s War Diary, "Three planes were hit, one VF, piloted by Lt. (jg) J.A. Nist (A1), USNR, of VF84 crashed on the island exploding on impact. Pilot went in with aircraft."[11]

VF-84's fighters came off the target and reformed for the return to *Bunker Hill*. During the attack run on Kikai's Wan Airfield, three of the squadron's Corsairs had been hit by Japanese anti-aircraft fire. All three Corsairs were from Coconougher's division. LT(jg) Nist had been killed and his Corsair had crashed on Kikai. LT(jg) Coconougher's Corsair was damaged with its landing gear stuck in the lowered position. LT(jg) J.J. "Sarge" Sargent was wounded and his Corsair had suffered serious damage. Assessing the damage, Coconougher and LT(jg) Chambers decided that Sargent could not make it back to *Bunker Hill*. Apprising the carrier of the situation, Coconougher elected to escort Sargent to Yontan Airfield on Okinawa, which was now in American hands. Coconougher guided his wounded squadron mate the hundred miles south to Yontan. He landed first, then talked Sargent down over radio. Sargent attempted to land the damaged Corsair, but his aircraft ground-looped and burst into flames. Coconougher and a Marine sergeant pulled Sargent free from the burning plane. After spending four days on Okinawa, Cocanougher and Sargent returned to *Bunker Hill*.[12]

With the exception of Sargent, Coconougher and Nist, *Bunker Hill*'s Corsairs and photo Hellcats and *Bataan*'s Hellcats returned to their respective carriers and recovered aboard by 1820.[13]

The VF-47 Action Report for the afternoon Kikai mission was critical of the VF-84 flight leader's tactics for attacking the airfield amid significant anti-aircraft fire. "It is felt that the loss and damage to Bunker Hill planes on this attack could have been avoided," stated the Action Report. "The Bunker Hill flight leader lead [sic] his flight in from a position which forced his planes to fly over almost the entire length of the island before reaching the field, and in a 45 degree dive. His planes were hit before they reached the field."[14]

In contrast, as the Action Report noted, the VF-47 flight leader approached the airfield directly and began their attack from a higher altitude. The VF-47 Hellcats then dove on the target at a much steeper angle (60 degrees vs. 45 degrees) than their VF-84 colleagues. No VF-47 aircraft was hit by enemy anti-aircraft fire. "When the weather allows, it is recommended that nothing short of a 60 degree dive be used," stated the Action Report.[15]

Thus, James Arthur Nist's naval career and his young life came to a violent end over the skies of an obscure Japanese island in the western Pacific while serving his country in the most horrendous war ever experienced by humankind.

Epilogue

On the afternoon of 4 April 1945, LT(jg) James Nist strapped into his F4U Corsair, took off from USS *Bunker Hill*'s flight deck and headed up into the skies over the western Pacific Ocean on his 21st combat mission against the Japanese Empire.

In just 24 years, "Shorty" Nist had had an extraordinary life. Raised on a farm in central New Jersey, Nist had graduated from high school at age 16. He had earned a bachelor's degree from Rutgers University and a private pilot's license, too. Joining the Navy as an aviation cadet, he had earned an officer's commission in the Naval Reserve and his naval aviator wings. After becoming a proficient pilot of three of the Navy's high-performance combat aircraft (SBD Dauntless, F6F Hellcat and F4U Corsair), Nist had deployed to the western Pacific as part of Fighting Squadron 84. He had flown combat missions over Japan, Iwo Jima and Okinawa with skill and bravery.

As he flew north to the Amami Shunto islands, Nist had much to look forward to in the future. He looked forward to the inevitable defeat of Imperial Japan and the end of World War II. He looked forward to returning home and marrying the love of his life, Alice. He looked forward to reuniting with his family and meeting his nephew and namesake for the first time.

Instead, Jimmy Nist's 21st mission would end in eternity.

Now may Jimmy be forever blessed with fair winds and following seas in the company of our Heavenly Father.

Appendix
Nist Chronology

14 December 1921	Born in Lakewood, New Jersey.
14 June 1934	Graduated from Farmingdale (NJ) Grammar School.
17 June 1938	Graduated from Lakewood (NJ) High School.
10 May 1942	Graduated from Rutgers University with a BS in biology.
7 October 1942	Enlisted in the U.S. Naval Reserve as an aviation cadet.
6 January 1943	Reported for active duty as an aviation cadet in New York.
7 January 1943	Arrived at University of North Carolina at Chapel Hill for pre-flight training and assigned to 17th Battalion.
22 March 1943	Completed pre-flight school and graduated with 16th Battalion.
24–25 March 1943	Transferred to Naval Air Station Glenview, IL, to begin flight training.
On or about 6 June 1943	Transferred to Naval Air Station Corpus Christi, TX, for flight training.
24 September 1943	Enlisted service as an aviation cadet terminated so as to accept commission as an ensign, USNR.
25 September 1943	Commissioned as an ensign, USNR and executed oath of office. Rank dated from 1 September 1943.
	Detached from Naval Air Training Center, NAS Corpus Christi, TX, and ordered to NAS Miami, FL, for flying duty under instruction.
2 October 1943	Reported to NAS Miami, FL, for flying duty under instruction.
22 October 1943	Detached from NAS Miami, FL, and ordered to NAS Daytona Beach, FL, for flying duty under instruction.
23 October 1943	Reported to NAS Daytona Beach, FL, for flying duty under instruction.
27 December 1943	Detached from NAS Daytona Beach, FL, and ordered to Carrier Qualification Training Unit, NAS Glenview, IL, for flying duty under instruction.

Appendix

29 December 1943	Reported to Carrier Qualification Training Unit, NAS Glenview, IL, for flying duty under instruction.
4 January 1944	Detached from Carrier Qualification Training Unit, NAS Glenview, IL, and ordered to Fleet Air, West Coast, NAS San Diego, CA, for further assignment for flying duty. Granted leave.
26 January 1944	Reported to Fleet Air, West Coast, NAS San Diego, CA, for flying duty.
27 January 1944	Ordered to Carrier Aircraft Service Unit Five for temporary flying duty. Reported same day.
9 February 1944	Detached Carrier Aircraft Service Unit Five and ordered to Fleet Air, West Coast, for further assignment involving flying duty. Reported same day.
10 February 1944	Ordered to Fleet Air, Alameda, NAS Alameda, CA, for flying duty with Carrier Aircraft Service Unit Six in conjunction with the fitting out of Bombing Squadron 303 and flying duty with that squadron when it was commissioned.
11 February 1944	Reported to Fleet Air, Alameda.
12 February 1944	Reported to Carrier Aircraft Service Unit Six, NAS Alameda, CA.
15 March 1944	Detached from Carrier Aircraft Service Unit Six and ordered to Bombing Squadron 303 for flying duty. Reported same day.
4 May 1944	Detached from Bombing Squadron 303 as part of squadron decommissioning. Ordered to Fleet Air, West Coast, NAS San Diego, CA, for further assignment.
12 May 1944	Reported to Fleet Air, West Coast, NAS San Diego.
13 May 1944	Ordered to Fighting Squadron 84, NAS San Diego, for flying duty. Reported same day.
1 December 1944	Appointed lieutenant (junior grade) A-V(N), rank effective this date.
12 December 1944	Classification changed to (A1)L.
Late December 1944	Attended and completed photo reconnaissance school.
January 1945	Embarked aboard USS *Bunker Hill* as part of Air Group 84.
16–17 February 1945	Tokyo air strikes.
19–23 February 1945	Supported Iwo Jima invasion.
25 February 1945	Second Tokyo air strikes.
1 March 1945	First photo-strike on Okinawa.
18–19 March 1945	Strikes on Kyushu, Japanese Home Islands.
24–27 March 1945	Photo-strikes on Okinawa, combat air patrol, escort mission.

Nist Chronology

29 March 1945	Photo-strike on Kyushu; destroyed one aircraft on ground.
1 April 1945	Okinawa invasion day; photo-strike.
3 April 1945	Combat air patrol off Okinawa.
4 April 1945	Shot down by anti-aircraft fire and killed while flying on an air strike against Wan Airfield, Kikai Island, Amami Shunto.
26 April 1945	Martin and Ethel Nist informed via telegram of Jimmy being missing in action.
28 June 1945	Classification changed to (A1).
12 April 1946	Nist's status changed from missing in action to killed in action.
January 1948	Awarded the Distinguished Flying Cross for air strike on Tokyo 17 February 1945.
29 March 1949	Nist's remains arrived in Lakewood, NJ.
31 March 1949	Funeral service for James A. Nist and interment at Woodlawn Cemetery, Lakewood, NJ.

Chapter Notes

Chapter 1

1. Kathryn Louise Nist Dickerson. "The Story of My Life." Unpublished memoirs written in 2007. Copy in possession of the author: pg1 [hereafter cited as "The Story of My Life"]; The Nist Family history section of this chapter is based primarily upon the genealogical research of my late uncle, Dr. Richard Conrad. An expert in genealogy, Uncle Richard passed away in August 2020 at age 79.
2. *Ibid.*
3. Kathryn Dickerson, "The Story of My Life," pp. 1–2.
4. Kathryn Dickerson, "The Story of My Life," pp. 1–2.
5. Kathryn Dickerson, "The Story of My Life," p. 2.
6. Kathryn Dickerson, "The Story of My Life," p. 2.
7. Kathryn Dickerson, "The Story of My Life," p. 3.
8. Kathryn Dickerson, "The Story of My Life," p. 3.
9. Kathryn Dickerson, "The Story of My Life," p. 3.
10. Farmingdale Grammar School, Farmingdale, New Jersey, Annual Commencement, 14 June 1934. James A. Nist Papers, held by the author [hereafter cited as "Nist Papers"].
11. James Arthur Nist Certificate for Sacrament of Confirmation, 9 May 1938, issued by All Saints Episcopal Church, Lakewood, NJ. Nist Papers.
12. James Arthur Nist School Record, Lakewood High School, Lakewood, NJ. Nist Papers.
13. *Ibid; The Pine Needle 1938.* Privately published by Lakewood High School in June 1938. Copy in possession of the author. See page 18 for the quote; Rutgers University, New Brunswick, NJ. Transcript for James Arthur Nist. Copy provided to the author by the Office of the Registrar, Rutgers University, on 21 December 2017 [hereafter cited as "James Nist Rutgers Transcript"]. His college transcript included a summary of his high school classes.
14. Lakewood High School, Lakewood, NJ, Commencement Class of 1938, 17 June 1938, Program. Nist Papers.
15. Thomas B. Harper, County Superintendent, Department of Public Instruction, County of Monmouth, NJ. Letter to James A. Nist, 2 August 1938. Nist Papers.
16. James Nist Rutgers Transcript.
17. Dr. Walter T. Marvin, Dean, College of Arts and Sciences, Rutgers University. Letter to Mr. Martin Nist, 23 February 1939.
18. James Nist Rutgers Transcript.
19. James Nist Rutgers Transcript.
20. Charles Prout, Ed. *The Scarlett Letter 1941* (privately published for the Scarlett Letter Council by Haddon Craftsmen of Camden, NJ, in 1941). See page 128.
21. James Nist Rutgers Transcript.
22. *The Scarlett Letter 1942* (privately published for the Scarlett Letter Council by Country Life Press of Garden City, NY, in 1942). See pages 95, 257, 285.
23. LT(jg) Alfred Messer, USNR, Letter to Martin and Ethel Nist, 24 January 1946.
24. Most of the information on James Nist's collegiate wrestling career was derived from newspaper clippings preserved (presumably) by him in a scrapbook. Most of these clippings do not include the bibliographical information for proper citation. Wherever possible, full citations will be given in the footnotes. However, when full citations are not available, then the record will be cited as "Nist Scrapbook."
25. Rutgers University Department of Physical Education Certificate, Wrestling 1938–1939, Awarded to James A. Nist. Nist Papers.
26. *The Scarlett Letter 1940* (privately published for the Scarlett Letter Council by the Haddon Craftsmen of Camden, NJ, in 1940). "Matmen Drop Match to Army as Cook Takes Fourteenth." Found in Nist Scrapbook.
27. Dick Nelson. "Wrestlers Stage Clinic" (*The Targum*). Found in Nist Scrapbook.
28. Rutgers University Department of Physical Education Certificate, Wrestling 1938–1939, Awarded to James A. Nist. Nist Scrapbook; *The Scarlett Letter 1941*, p. 156.
29. "Rutgers and Montclair Matmen in Deadlock." *The Sunday Times* (New Brunswick, NJ). 15 December 1940, p. 1+. Found in Nist Scrapbook. Other unidentifiable press clippings mention the other wrestling results.

30. "Rutgers and Montclair Matmen in Deadlock." Middle Atlantic Collegiate Wrestling Association, Sixth Annual Championship Meet, 7-8 March 1941, Memorial Gymnasium, Lafayette College, Easton, PA. Official Program. The program contained a scorecard of wrestling matches. "Rutgers and Montclair Matmen in Deadlock." *The Sunday Times* (New Brunswick, NJ). 15 December 1940, p. 1+. Found in Nist Scrapbook.

31. *The Scarlett Letter 1942*, p. 285.

32. Middle Atlantic Collegiate Wrestling Association, Seventh Annual Championship Meet, 6-7 March 1941, Gettysburg College, Gettysburg, PA, Official Program. The program contained a scorecard of wrestling matches. The Nist Scrapbook also contained an itinerary of the wrestlers' trip to Gettysburg.

33. *The Scarlett Letter 1942*, p. 214.

34. U.S. Department of Commerce, Civil Aeronautics Administration, Form ACA-551 (CPT41) Student Pilot Rating Book. James Arthur Nist. Certificate #5214709. Hereafter cited as "Nist Student Pilot Rating Book."

35. Nist Student Pilot Rating Book.

36. Nist Student Pilot Rating Book. See entry for 14 March 1941.

37. Nist Student Pilot Rating Book. See entry for 9 April 1941 for completion of Stage A.

38. Nist Student Pilot Rating Book. See entry for 18 April 1941.

39. Nist Student Pilot Rating Book. See entry for 15 May 1941.

40. Nist Student Pilot Rating Book. See entry for 20 May 1941.

41. Nist Student Pilot Rating Book. See entry for 20 May 1941.

42. Nist Student Pilot Rating Book. See entry for 7 June 1941.

43. Rutgers University 176th Anniversary Baccalaureate Service, 3 May 1942. Program. Nist Papers.

44. Rutgers University 176th Anniversary Commencement, 10 May 1942. Program. Nist Papers. James was not the first in the Nist Family to graduate from higher education. Older sister Kathryn had attended and graduated from nursing school in 1934.

Chapter 2

1. James Arthur Nist Draft Registration Card, Number 11,352. I found a digital copy of his draft card on www.fold3.com.

2. U.S. Department of the Navy, Bureau of Naval Personnel. Record of Service, Lieutenant (Junior Grade) James A. Nist (A1)L, United States Naval Reserve, Active, Deceased. 10 May 1946. Nist Papers [hereafter cited as "Nist Record of Service"]; U.S. Navy. "Preliminary Application for Flight Training in the U.S. Naval Reserve and Marine Corps Reserve." 2 September 1942. Nist Papers.

3. Aviation Cadet James A. Nist. Letter to Martin and Ethel Nist. 7 January 1943. Nist Papers [hereafter cited as "Nist Letter. 7 January 1943"].

4. *Ibid.* Rear Admiral Randall Jacobs, USN, Chief of Naval Personnel, Bureau of Naval Personnel, Department of the Navy, Washington, DC. To Ensign James A. Nist, A-V(N) USNR. Subject: Orders to Active Duty. 28 August 1943. Nist Papers; Aviation Cadet James A. Nist. Letter to Martin and Ethel Nist. 23 January 1943. Nist Papers [hereafter cited as "Nist Letter. 23 January 1943"].

5. Nist Letter. 23 January 1943; Jack Hackett. "Sachsel '44, Wrestling Champion, Loses Life Training with Navy," *Daily Targum*, 12 March 1943. This was included in a letter that James Nist sent home to his parents on 14 March 1943. See Aviation Cadet James A. Nist. Letter to Martin and Ethel Nist. 14 March 1943. Nist Papers [hereafter cited as "Nist Letter. 14 March 1943"]; "Richard Rudolph Sachsel," *Rutgers Alumni Monthly*, October 1945, p. 32.

6. Nist Letter. 7 January 1943; Aviation Cadet James A. Nist. Letter to Martin and Ethel Nist. 9 January 1943. Nist Papers [hereafter cited as "Nist Letter. 9 January 1943"].

7. Matt Portz, Captain, USN (Ret.). "Aviation Training and Expansion—Part 1." *Naval Aviation News*, July-August 1990, pp. 22–27.

8. Matt Portz, Captain, USN (Ret.). "Aviation Training and Expansion—Part 2," *Naval Aviation News*, September-October 1990, pp. 22–27.

9. Nist Letter. 9 January 1943.

10. Nist Letter. 9 January 1943; Aviation Cadet James A. Nist. Letter to Martin and Ethel Nist. 10 January 1943. Nist Papers [hereafter cited as "Nist Letter. 10 January 1943"]; Aviation Cadet James A. Nist. Letter to Martin and Ethel Nist. 16 January 1943. Nist Papers [hereafter cited as "Nist Letter. 16 January 1943"]; Nist Letter. 23 January 1943.

11. Nist Letter. 10 January 1943; Aviation Cadet James A. Nist. Letter to Martin and Ethel Nist. 17 January 1943. Nist Papers [hereafter cited as "Nist Letter. 17 January 1943"]; Nist Letter. 23 January 1943.

12. Nist Letter. 16 January 1943.

13. Nist Letter. 9 January 1943; Nist Letter. 17 January 1943; Nist Letter. 23 January 1943; Nist Letter. 31 January 1943.

14. Aviation Cadet James A. Nist. Letter to Martin and Ethel Nist. 24 January 1943. Nist Papers [hereafter cited as Nist Letter. 24 January 1943]; Aviation Cadet James A. Nist. Letter to Martin and Ethel Nist. 27 January 1943. Nist Papers [hereafter cited as Nist Letter. 27 January 1943]; Aviation Cadet James A. Nist. Letter to Martin and Ethel Nist. 31 January 1943. Nist Papers [hereafter cited as "Nist Letter. 31 January 1943"]; Aviation Cadet James A. Nist. Letter to Martin and Ethel Nist. 8 February 1943. Nist Papers [hereafter cited as "Nist Letter. 8 February 1943]"

15. Nist Letter. 31 January 1943; Nist Letter. 8 February 1943.

16. Nist Letter. 31 January 1943.
17. Aviation Cadet James A. Nist. Letter to Martin and Ethel Nist. 3 March 1943. Nist Papers [Hereafter cited as "Nist Letter. 3 March 1943"].
18. The text of the Letter of Commendation was taken from a news clipping that Nist sent home to his parents. See Aviation Cadet James A. Nist. Letter to Martin and Ethel Nist. 17 March 1943. Nist Papers [hereafter cited as "Nist Letter. 17 March 1943"].
19. Aviation Cadet James A. Nist. Letter to Martin and Ethel Nist. 11 March 1943. Nist Papers [hereafter cited as "Nist Letter. 11 March 1943"].
20. Nist Letter. 17 March 1943; Nist Letter. 14 March 1943.
21. Aviation Cadet James A. Nist. Letter to Martin and Ethel Nist. 19 March 1943. Nist Papers; Aviation Cadet James A. Nist. Letter to Martin and Ethel Nist. 20 March 1943. Nist Papers.
22. Aviation Cadet James A. Nist. Letter to Martin and Ethel Nist. 23 March 1943. Nist Papers.
23. Jonathan Zamaites. "Naval Air Station Glenview," 21 October 2017. Published on the Military History of the Upper Great Lakes website and accessed on 7 December 2018 at https://ss.sites.mtu.edu/mhugl/2017/10/21/naval-air-station-glenview/; U.S. Navy. Bureau of Yards and Docks. *Building the Navy's Bases in World War II. History of the Bureau of Yards and Docks and the Civil Engineer Corps 1940–1946.* Printed in 1946. See Volume 1, pp. 227, 235. Accessed on 13 August 2019 at https://www.history.navy.mil/content/history/nhhc/research/library/online-reading-room/title-list-alphabetically/b/building-the-navys-bases.html [hereafter cited as *Building the Navy's Bases in World War II*].
24. Aviation Cadet James A. Nist. Letter to Martin and Ethel Nist. 12 April 1943. Nist Papers. [Hereafter cited as "Nist Letter. 12 April 1943."]
25. Aviation Cadet James A. Nist. Letter to Martin and Ethel Nist. 30 March 1943. Nist Papers [hereafter cited as Nist Letter. 30 March 1943]; Aviation Cadet James A. Nist. Letter to Martin and Ethel Nist. 3 April 1943. Nist Papers [hereafter cited as "Nist Letter. 3 April 1943"].
26. "N3N: The Original 'Yellow Peril.'" 4 September 2014. Accessed on the National Naval Aviation Museum website on 24 December 2018 at https://www.navalaviationmuseum.org/history-up-close/n3n-original-yellow-peril/nggallery/image/richard-fleming-in-n3n/.
27. U.S. Navy. Aviator's Flight Logbook. Nist, J.A. Included in Nist Papers. See entries for 28, 29 and 31 March 1943 [hereafter cited as J.A. Nist Flight Logbook].
28. Nist Letter. 30 March 1943.
29. Nist Letter. 30 March 1943; Aviation Cadet James A. Nist. Letter to Martin and Ethel Nist. 1 April 1943. Nist Papers [hereafter cited as Nist Letter. 1 April 1943].
30. Nist Letter. 30 March 1943.
31. Nist Letter. 1 April 1943; J.A. Nist Flight Logbook. See entries for 1 and 2 April 1943.
32. Nist Letter. 3 April 1943; J.A. Nist Flight Logbook. See entry for 2 April 1943.
33. Nist Letter. 3 April 1943.
34. Aviation Cadet James A. Nist. Letter to Martin and Ethel Nist. 11 April 1943. Nist Papers [hereafter cited as "Nist Letter. 11 April 1943"].
35. Nist Letter. 3 April 1943.
36. Nist Letter. 11 April 1943.
37. Nist Letter. 11 April 1943; Aviation Cadet James A. Nist. Letter to Martin and Ethel Nist. 16 April 1943. Nist Papers [hereafter cited as "Nist Letter. 16 April 1943"].
38. Aviation Cadet James A. Nist. Letter to Martin and Ethel Nist. 12 April 1943; Aviation Cadet James A. Nist. Letter to Martin and Ethel Nist. 20 April 1943. Nist Papers [hereafter cited as "Nist Letter. 20 April 1943].
39. Nist Letter. 16 April 1943.
40. Nist Letter. 20 April 1943.
41. Nist Letter. 20 April 1943.
42. Aviation Cadet James A. Nist. Letter to Martin and Ethel Nist. 23 April 1943. Nist Papers [hereafter cited as "Nist Letter. 23 April 1943"].
43. Nist Letter. 23 April 1943.
44. Nist Letter. 23 April 1943.
45. Nist Letter. 23 April 1943.
46. Aviation Cadet James A. Nist. Letter to Martin and Ethel Nist. 26 April 1943. Nist Papers [hereafter cited as "Nist Letter. 26 April 1943"].
47. "Hotel Sherman," posted on the "Jazz Age Chicago" website. Accessed on 13 March 2019 at https://jazzagechicago.wordpress.com/hotel-sherman/. The hotel closed in 1973 and was torn down in 1980.
48. Nist Letter. 26 April 1943.
49. Nist Letter. 26 April 1943.
50. Nist Letter. 26 April 1943.
51. Nist Letter. 26 April 1943.
52. Aviation Cadet James A. Nist. Letter to Martin and Ethel Nist. 28 April 1943. Nist Papers [hereafter cited as "Nist Letter. 28 April 1943"].
53. Aviation Cadet James A. Nist. Letter to Martin and Ethel Nist. 30 April 1943. Nist Papers [hereafter cited as "Nist Letter. 30 April 1943"].
54. J.A. Nist Flight Logbook. See entries for April 1943; Nist Letter. 30 April 1943.
55. Aviation Cadet James A. Nist. Letter to Martin and Ethel Nist. 2 May 1943. Nist Papers [hereafter cited as "Nist Letter. 2 May 1943"].
56. Nist Letter. 2 May 1943.
57. Nist Letter. 2 May 1943.
58. Aviation Cadet James A. Nist. Letter to Martin and Ethel Nist. 5 May 1943. Nist Papers [hereafter cited as "Nist Letter. 5 May 1943"].
59. Nist Letter. 5 May 1943.
60. Aviation Cadet James A. Nist. Letter to Martin and Ethel Nist. 8 May 1943. Nist Papers [hereafter cited as "Nist Letter. 8 May 1943"]; J.A. Nist Flight Logbook. See entries for 6, 7 and 8 May 1943.
61. Nist Letter. 8 May 1943; J.A. Nist Flight Logbook. See entry for 8 May 1943.
62. Nist Letter. 8 May 1943.

63. Aviation Cadet James A. Nist. Letter to Martin and Ethel Nist. 10 May 1943. Nist Papers [hereafter cited as "Nist Letter. 10 May 1943"].

64. Aviation Cadet James A. Nist. Letter to Martin and Ethel Nist. 14 May 1943. Nist Papers [hereafter cited as "Nist Letter. 14 May 1943"].

65. Nist Letter. 14 May 1943. Nist's letters are frequently not dated beyond the day of the week so following the sequence can be difficult at times.

66. Nist Letter. 14 May 1943.

67. Aviation Cadet James A. Nist. Letter to Martin and Ethel Nist. 16 May 1943. Nist Papers [hereafter cited as "Nist Letter. 16 May 1943"]. Dottie Schultz was not mentioned anymore in his correspondence.

68. Nist Letter. 16 May 1943.

69. Aviation Cadet James A. Nist. Letter to Martin and Ethel Nist. 20 May 1943. Nist Papers.

70. J.A. Nist Flight Logbook. See entry for 26 May 1943.

71. Norman C. Delaney. "Corpus Christi's 'University of the Air,'" *Naval History Magazine*, June 2013. Accessed on 16 November 2018 at https://www.usni.org/magazines/navalhistory/2013-05/corpus-christis-university-air; *Handbook of Texas Online*, Art Leatherwood, "NAVAL AIR STATION, CORPUS CHRISTI," accessed 5 April 2019, http://www.tshaonline.org/handbook/online/articles/qbn01; For the 2019 cost of NAS Corpus Christi construction, I used CNN Money's inflation calculator: https://money.cnn.com/calculator/pf/inflation-adjustment/; See Volume 1, pp. 228-231, of *Building the Navy's Bases in World War II*; U.S. Department of the Navy, Bureau of Aeronautics. "Corpus is University of the Air." *Bureau of Aeronautics News Letter*, 1 June 1944, pp. 28-35.

72. *Handbook of Texas Online*, Art Leatherwood, "NAVAL AIR STATION, CORPUS CHRISTI." Accessed 5 April 2019, http://www.tshaonline.org/handbook/online/articles/qbn01; *Building the Navy's Bases in World War II*, p.238. "Corpus is University of the Air," p. 31.

73. "USS Hornet (CV-8)." *Dictionary of American Naval Fighting Ships*. Accessed on the Naval History and Heritage Command website on 27 June 2019 at https://www.history.navy.mil/research/histories/ship-histories/danfs/h/hornet-vii.html; The citation for his Navy Cross is posted on the Military Times Hall of Valor website, https://valor.militarytimes.com/hero/20661, accessed on 27 June 2019.

74. Aviation Cadet James A. Nist. Letter to Martin and Ethel Nist. 11 June 1943. Nist Papers [hereafter cited as "Nist Letter. 11 June 1943"].

75. Nist Letter. 11 June 1943.

76. Nist Letter. 11 June 1943.

77. Aviation Cadet James A. Nist. Letter to Martin and Ethel Nist. 12 June 1943. Nist Papers.

78. Aviation Cadet James A. Nist. Letter to Martin and Ethel Nist. 16 June 1943. Nist Papers [hereafter cited as "Nist Letter. 16 June 1943"].

79. "Corpus Christi's 'University of the Air.'"; Nist Letter. 16 May 1943.

80. J.A. Nist Flight Logbook. See entries for 8 May and 14, 15 and 16 June 1943; Nist Letter. 16 June 1943.

81. Nist Letter. 16 June 1943.

82. J.A. Nist Flight Logbook. See entries for June 1943; Aviation Cadet James A. Nist. Letter to Martin and Ethel Nist. 20 June 1943. Nist Papers [hereafter cited as "Nist Letter. 20 June 1943"].

83. Aviation Cadet James A. Nist. Letter to Martin and Ethel Nist. 19 June 1943. Nist Papers [hereafter cited as "Nist Letter. 19 June 1943"].

84. Nist Letter. 19 June 1943.

85. Nist Letter. 19 June 1943.

86. Aviation Cadet James A. Nist. Letter to Martin and Ethel Nist. 25 June 1943. Nist Papers [hereafter cited as "Nist Letter. 25 June 1943"].

87. Nist Letter. 25 June 1943.

88. Nist Letter. 25 June 1943.

89. Aviation Cadet James A. Nist. Letter to Martin and Ethel Nist. 29 June 1943. Nist Papers.

90. Aviation Cadet James A. Nist. Letter to Martin and Ethel Nist. 2 July 1943. Nist Papers [hereafter cited as "Nist Letter. 2 July 1943"].

91. J.A. Nist Flight Logbook. See entries for June 1943; Nist Letter. 20 June 1943.

92. Nist Letter. 2 July 1943; According to the Federal Bureau of Labor Statistics Consumer Price Index inflation calculator, that would be $14.53 and $43.58 in 2019 dollars; Aviation Cadet James A. Nist. Letter to Martin and Ethel Nist. 3 July 1943. Nist Papers [hereafter cited as "Nist Letter. 3 July 1943"].

93. "The Link Flight Trainer: A Historic Mechanical Engineering Landmark." Privately published by the Roberson Museum and Science Center, Binghamton, NY. 10 June 10, 2000.

94. Nist Letter. 3 July 1943.

95. Nist Letter. 3 July 1943.

96. Aviation Cadet James A. Nist. Letter to Martin and Ethel Nist. 6 July 1943. Nist Papers [hereafter cited as "Nist Letter. 6 July 1943"].

97. Nist Letter. 6 July 1943.

98. Nist Letter. 6 July 1943. Author's note: "Dickie" is my father's older brother/my uncle.

99. Aviation Cadet James A. Nist. Letter to Martin and Ethel Nist. 10 July 1943. Nist Papers [hereafter cited as "Nist Letter. 10 July 1943"].

100. Nist Letter. 10 July 1943.

101. Nist Letter. 10 July 1943.

102. Nist Letter. 10 July 1943.

103. Aviation Cadet James A. Nist. Letter to Martin and Ethel Nist. 17 July 1943. Nist Papers; J. A. Nist Flight Logbook. See entries for July 1943.

104. Aviation Cadet James A. Nist. Letter to Martin and Ethel Nist. 27 July 1943. Nist Papers [hereafter cited as "Nist Letter. 27 July 1943"].

105. J.A. Nist Flight Logbook. See entries for 27 July 1943; Nist Letter 27 July 1943.

106. Nist Letter. 27 July 1943.

107. Nist Letter. 27 July 1943.

108. Howard C. Sumner. "North Atlantic Hurricanes and Tropical Disturbances of 1943," *Monthly Weather Review*, November 1943.

Accessed on 29 April 2019 at https://www.aoml.noaa.gov/general/lib/lib1/nhclib/mwreviews/1943.pdf; U.S. Department of Commerce, National Oceanic and Atmospheric Administration, National Weather Service, Weather Prediction Center. David Roth. "Texas Hurricane History," 17 January 2010. Accessed on 30 April 2019 at https://www.wpc.ncep.noaa.gov/research/txhur.pdf; U.S. Department of Commerce, National Oceanic and Atmospheric Administration, Office of Oceanic and Atmospheric Research, Atlantic Oceanographic and Meteorological Laboratory, Hurricane Research Division. "Seventy-fifth Anniversary of first hurricane eye penetration." 27 July 2018. Accessed online on 30 April 2019 at https://noaahrd.wordpress.com/2018/07/27/seventy-fifth-anniversary-of-first-hurricane-eye-penetration/.

109. Aviation Cadet James A. Nist. Letter to Martin and Ethel Nist. 31 July 1943. Nist Papers [hereafter cited as Nist Letter. 31 July 1943"].

110. Nist Letter. 31 July 1943.

111. Nist Letter. 31 July 1943.

112. Nist Letter. 31 July 1943.

113. Nist Letter. 31 July 1943.

114. Aviation Cadet James A. Nist. Letter to Martin and Ethel Nist. 1 August 1943. Nist Papers [hereafter cited as "Nist Letter. 1 August 1943"].

115. *Jane's Fighting Aircraft of World War II* (London: Random House, 1989). Reprint of the 1945–46 edition, p.251; Mike Lombardi and Erik Simonsen. "The High and the Mighty." *Boeing Frontiers*. (Dec 2009—Jan 2010), pp. 54–57; Norm Goyer. "The T-6 Texan: The world's best advanced trainers and beyond." *Flying*. (12 August 2011). Accessed online on 8 May 2019 at https://www.flyingmag.com/aircraft/pistons/t-6-texan; Paul Glenshaw. "The Best-Built Airplane That Ever War." *Air & Space Magazine*. (December 2015). Accessed online on 8 May 2019 at https://www.airspacemag.com/history-of-flight/best-airplane-that-ever-was-t6-texan-180957294/; Nist Letter. 1 August 1943.

116. Nist Letter. 1 August 1943.

117. Aviation Cadet James A. Nist. Letter to Martin and Ethel Nist. 2 August 1943. Nist Papers [hereafter cited as "Nist Letter. 2 August 1943"].

118. Ensign James A. Nist, USNR. Letter to Martin and Ethel Nist. 25 November 1943 [hereafter cited as "Nist Letter. 25 November 1943]"

119. Nist Letter. 2 August 1943.

120. Aviation Cadet James A. Nist. Letter to Martin and Ethel Nist. 3 August 1943. Nist Papers [hereafter cited as "Nist Letter. 3 August 1943"].

121. U.S. Navy. Naval Air Station Kingsville. NAS Kingsville Public Affairs. "NAS Kingsville—Flying for the Future for 60 Years." 6 August 2002. Accessed on 8 May 2019 online at https://www.navy.mil/submit/display.asp?story_id=2988.

122. Nist Letter. 3 August 1943.

123. Nist Letter. 3 August 1943.

124. Nist Letter. 3 August 1943.

125. Aviation Cadet James A. Nist. Letter to Martin and Ethel Nist. 7 August 1943. Nist Papers [hereafter cited as "Nist Letter. 7 August 1943"].

126. Nist Letter. 7 August 1943.

127. Aviation Cadet James A. Nist. Letter to Martin and Ethel Nist. 11 August 1943. Nist Papers [hereafter cited as "Nist Letter. 11 August 1943"].

128. Nist Letter. 11 August 1943.

129. Aviation Cadet James A. Nist. Letter to Martin and Ethel Nist. 15 August 1943. Nist Papers.

130. Aviation Cadet James A. Nist. Letter to Martin and Ethel Nist. 19 August 1943. Nist Papers [hereafter cited as "Nist Letter. 19 August 1943"].

131. Nist Letter. 19 August 1943.

132. Aviation Cadet James A. Nist. Letter to Martin and Ethel Nist. 22 August 1943. Nist Papers [hereafter cited as "Nist Letter. 22 August 1943"].

133. Nist Letter. 22 August 1943.

134. Nist Letter. 22 August 1943.

135. Aviation Cadet James A. Nist. Letter to Martin and Ethel Nist. 24 August 1943. Nist Papers [hereafter cited as "Nist Letter. 24 August 1943"].

136. Nist Letter. 24 August 1943.

137. Nist Letter. 24 August 1943.

138. Nist Letter. 24 August 1943.

139. Aviation Cadet James A. Nist. Letter to Martin and Ethel Nist. 28 August 1943. Nist Papers [hereafter cited as "Nist Letter. 28 August 1943"].

140. Nist Letter. 28 August 1943.

141. Nist Letter. 28 August 1943.

142. Nist Letter. 28 August 1943.

143. Rear Admiral Randall Jacobs, USN, Chief of Naval Personnel, Bureau of Naval Personnel, Department of the Navy, Washington, DC. To Ensign James A. Nist, A-V(N) USNR. Subject: Orders to Active Duty. 28 August 1943. Nist Papers.

144. Aviation Cadet James A. Nist. Letter to Martin and Ethel Nist. 29 August 1943. Nist Papers.

145. Aviation Cadet James A. Nist. Letter to Martin and Ethel Nist. 1 September 1943. Nist Papers [hereafter cited as "Nist Letter. 1 September 1943"].

146. See Nist Flight Log entries for August 1943; Nist Letter. 1 September 1943.

147. Aviation Cadet James A. Nist. Letter to Martin and Ethel Nist. 4 September 1943. Nist Papers. *Hosho* was a Japanese light aircraft carrier.

148. Aviation Cadet James A. Nist. Letter to Martin and Ethel Nist. 8 September 1943. Nist Papers [hereafter cited as "Nist Letter. 8 September 1943"].

149. Nist Letter. 8 September 1943.

150. Aviation Cadet James A. Nist. Letter to Martin and Ethel Nist. 12 September 1943. Nist Papers [hereafter cited as "Nist Letter. 12 September 1943"].

151. Nist Letter. 12 September 1943.

152. Nist Letter. 12 September 1943.

153. Nist Letter. 12 September 1943.

154. Aviation Cadet James A. Nist. Letter

to Martin and Ethel Nist. 15 September 1943. Nist Papers [hereafter cited as "Nist Letter. 15 September 1943"].

155. Howard C. Sumner. "North Atlantic Hurricanes and Tropical Disturbances of 1943." pp. 180, 183.

156. Aviation Cadet James A. Nist. Letter to Martin and Ethel Nist. 17 September 1943. Nist Papers [hereafter cited as "Nist Letter. 17 September 1943"].

157. Nist Letter. 17 September 1943.

158. Nist Letter. 17 September 1943.

159. Aviation Cadet James A. Nist. Letter to Martin and Ethel Nist. 20 September 1943. Nist Papers [hereafter cited as "Nist Letter. 20 September 1943"].

160. Nist Letter. 17 September 1943.

161. Nist Letter. 17 September 1943.

162. Howard C. Sumner. "North Atlantic Hurricanes and Tropical Disturbances of 1943." pp. 180, 183.

163. Nist Letter. 20 September 1943.

164. Nist Letter. 20 September 1943.

165. Nist Letter. 20 September 1943.

166. Nist Letter. 20 September 1943.

167. See Nist Flight Log for September 1943.

168. Nist Record of Service; C.P. Mason. Rear Admiral, USN. Commandant. Naval Air Training Center, Naval Air Station Corpus Christi, Texas. To Ensign James A. Nist, A-V(N), U.S.N.R. Subj: Orders to Active Duty. 25 September 1943. Nist Papers; C.P. Mason. Rear Admiral, USN. Commandant. Naval Air Training Center, Naval Air Station Corpus Christi, Texas. To Aviation Cadet James A. Nist, V-5, U.S.N.R. Subject: Appointment as Ensign in the United States Naval Reserve. 25 September 1943. Nist Papers; C.P. Mason. Rear Admiral, USN. Commandant. Naval Air Training Center, Naval Air Station Corpus Christi, Texas. To Ensign James A. Nist, A-V(N), U.S.N.R. Subject: Naval Aviator Designation. 25 September 1943. Nist Papers; C.P. Mason. Rear Admiral, USN. Commandant. Naval Air Training Center, Naval Air Station Corpus Christi, Texas. To Ensign James A. Nist, A-V(N), U.S.N.R. Subject: Change of Duty. 25 September 1943. Nist Papers; Ensign James A. Nist. Statement of Travel. 25 September 1943. Nist Papers.

169. Nist Record of Service; C.P. Mason. Rear Admiral, USN. Commandant. Naval Air Training Center, Naval Air Station Corpus Christi, Texas. To Ensign James A. Nist, A-V(N), U.S.N.R. Subject: Change of Duty. 25 September 1943. Nist Papers; Ensign James A. Nist. Statement of Travel. 25 September 1943. Nist Papers.

Chapter 3

1. Nist Record of Service; C.P. Mason. Rear Admiral, USN. Commandant, Naval Air Training Center, Naval Air Station Corpus Christi, Texas. To Ensign James A. Nist, A-V(N), U.S.N.R. Subject: Change of Duty. 25 September 1943. Nist Papers; Ensign James A. Nist. Statement of Travel. 25 September 1943. Nist Papers.

2. Ensign James A. Nist, USNR. Letter to Martin and Ethel Nist. 1 October 1943 [hereafter cited as "Nist Letter. 1 October 1943"].

3. Nist Letter. 1 October 1943.

4. "NAS Miami: Opa-Locka Airport." Museum of Florida History website. Accessed online on 25 June 2019 at http://www.museumoffloridahistory.com/exhibits/permanent/wwii/sites.cfm?PR_ID=191.

5. Nist Record of Service; C.P. Mason. Rear Admiral, USN. Commandant, Naval Air Training Center, Naval Air Station Corpus Christi, Texas. To Ensign James A. Nist, A-V(N), U.S.N.R. Subject: Change of Duty. 25 September 1943. Nist Papers; Ensign James A. Nist. Statement of Travel. 25 September 1943. Nist Papers; Ensign James A. Nist, USNR. Letter to Martin and Ethel Nist. 6 October 1943 [hereafter cited as "Nist Letter. 6 October 1943"].

6. Nist Letter. 6 October 1943.

7. Nist Letter. 6 October 1943.

8. Nist Letter. 6 October 1943.

9. Nist Letter. 6 October 1943.

10. Nist Letter. 6 October 1943.

11. See Nist's Flight Log for October 1943.

12. Ensign James A. Nist, USNR. Letter to Martin and Ethel Nist. 9 October 1943 [hereafter cited as "Nist Letter. 9 October 1943"].

13. James R. Dickerson is the author's father; This paragraph is derived from two of Nist's letters: Nist Letter. 9 October 1943. Jimmy's prediction about his namesake proved incorrect. After graduating from college, James Dickerson served in the U.S. Army during the Vietnam era. James's son/Jimmy's grand-nephew (the author) did go the Navy route, serving as a Navy Reserve religious program specialist during Operation Iraqi Freedom; Ensign James A. Nist, USNR. Letter to Martin and Ethel Nist. 14 October 1943 [hereafter cited as "Nist Letter. 14 October 1943"].

14. Nist Letter. 14 October 1943.

15. Nist Letter. 14 October 1943.

16. Nist Letter. 14 October 1943.

17. Ensign James A. Nist, USNR. Letter to Martin and Ethel Nist. 18 October 1943.

18. Nist Record of Service; C.P. Mason. Rear Admiral, USN. Commandant, Naval Air Training Center, Naval Air Station Corpus Christi, Texas. To Ensign James A. Nist, A-V(N), U.S.N.R. Subject: Change of Duty. 25 September 1943. Nist Papers; Ensign James A. Nist. Statement of Travel. 25 September 1943. Nist Papers; H.D. Felt. Captain, USN. Commanding Officer. Naval Air Station Miami, Florida. To Ensign James A. Nist, A-V(N), U.S.N.R. Subject: Change of Duty. 22 October 1943. Nist Papers.

19. "NAS Daytona Beach/Daytona Beach International Airport." Posted on the Museum of Florida History website and accessed on 28 June 2019 at http://www.museumoffloridahistory.

com/exhibits/permanent/wwii/sites.cfm?PR_ID=79; See also "Historical Information" posted on the Daytona Beach International Airport website. Accessed on 28 June 2019 at http://www.flydaytonafirst.com/about-dab/historical-information.stml.

20. "Adm. W. E. Cleaves, Bendix Executive; Combat Leader in WWII Is Dead at 62." *New York Times* (13 May 1962). Accessed online on 23 October 2018 at https://www.nytimes.com/1964/05/14/archives/adm-we-cleaves-bedix-executive-combat-leader-in-world-war-ii-is.html; For *Casco*, see https://www.history.navy.mil/research/histories/ship-histories/danfs/c/casco-iii.html, accessed online on 23 October 2018.

21. *Jane's Fighting Aircraft of World War II*, p.227.

22. Ensign James A. Nist, USNR. Letter to Martin and Ethel Nist. 29 October 1943 [hereafter cited as "Nist Letter. 29 October 1943"].

23. Ensign James A. Nist, USNR. Letter to Martin and Ethel Nist. 27 October 1943 [hereafter cited as "Nist Letter. 27 October 1943"].

24. Nist Letter. 27 October 1943; Ian W. Toll. "Rear Seat Gunners at Midway." *Naval History Magazine* (May 2013). Accessed online on 9 July 2019 at https://www.usni.org/magazines/naval-history-magazine/2013/may/rear-seat-gunners-midway; Ensign James A. Nist, USNR. Letter to Martin and Ethel Nist. 30 October 1943 [hereafter cited as "Nist Letter. 30 October 1943"].

25. Nist Letter. 29 October 1943.

26. Nist Letter. 30 October 1943.

27. Ensign James A. Nist, USNR. Letter to Martin and Ethel Nist. 2 November 1943 [hereafter cited as "Nist Letter. 2 November 1943"].

28. Nist Letter. 2 November 1943.

29. Ensign James A. Nist, USNR. Letter to Martin and Ethel Nist. 4 November 1943.

30. Ensign James A. Nist, USNR. Letter to Martin and Ethel Nist. 5 November 1943 [hereafter cited as "Nist Letter. 5 November 1943"].

31. Ensign James A. Nist, USNR. Letter to Martin and Ethel Nist. 7 April 1944 [hereafter cited as "Nist Letter. 7 April 1944"]. Author's Note: P-10 was a Dauntless that Nist had regularly flown at the time of the letter being written.

32. Nist Letter. 5 November 1943.

33. Ensign James A. Nist, USNR. Letter to Martin and Ethel Nist. 10 November 1943.

34. Ensign James A. Nist, USNR. Letter to Martin and Ethel Nist. 14 November 1943 [hereafter cited as "Nist Letter. 14 November 1943"].

35. Nist Letter. 14 November 1943.

36. Ensign James A. Nist, USNR. Letter to Martin and Ethel Nist. 16 November 1943 [hereafter cited as "Nist Letter. 16 November 1943"]; See Nist Flight Log entry for 16 November 1943.

37. Ensign James A. Nist, USNR. Letter to Martin and Ethel Nist. 20 November 1943 [hereafter cited as "Nist Letter. 20 November 1943"].

38. Nist Letter. 20 November 1943.

39. Nist Letter. 20 November 1943.

40. Ensign James A. Nist, USNR. Letter to Martin and Ethel Nist. 22 November 1943 [hereafter cited as "Nist Letter. 22 November 1943"].

41. Nist Letter. 22 November 1943.

42. Nist Letter. 22 November 1943.

43. Ensign James A. Nist, USNR. Letter to Martin and Ethel Nist. 25 November 1943 [hereafter cited as "Nist Letter. 25 November 1943].

44. Nist Letter. 25 November 1943.

45. Ensign James A. Nist, USNR. Letter to Martin and Ethel Nist. 27 November 1943 [hereafter cited as "Nist Letter. 27 November 1943"].

46. Nist Letter. 27 November 1943.

47. Ensign James A. Nist, USNR. Letter to Martin and Ethel Nist. 4 December 1943 [hereafter cited as "Nist Letter. 4 December 1943"].

48. Nist Letter. 4 December 1943.

49. Nist Letter. 4 December 1943.

50. Nist Letter. 4 December 1943.

51. Nist Letter. 4 December 1943.

52. Ensign James A. Nist, USNR. Letter to Martin and Ethel Nist. 13 December 1943 [hereafter cited as "Nist Letter. 13 December 1943"].

53. Ensign James A. Nist, USNR. Letter to Martin and Ethel Nist. 7 December 1943; Nist Flight Log. See entry for 7 December 1943. Ensign James A. Nist, USNR. Letter to Martin and Ethel Nist. 10 December 1943 [hereafter cited as "Nist Letter. 10 December 1943"]; Nist Flight Log. See entry for 9 December 1943; Nist Flight Log. See entry for 10 December 1943.

54. Nist Letter. 10 December 1943.

55. Nist Record of Service; Chief of Naval Air Operational Training, Naval Air Station Jacksonville, Florida. To: Ensign James A. Nist. Subject: Change of Duty. 13 December 1943. Nist Papers.

56. Ensign James A. Nist, USNR. Letter to Martin and Ethel Nist. 19 December 1943 [hereafter cited as "Nist Letter. 19 December 1943"].

57. Nist Letter. 19 December 1943.

58. This paragraph was pieced together from scraps of information scattered amid a half dozen Nist letters written over the course of nearly a year. Eventually Nist and McChesney would reconnect at NAS San Diego nearly a year later when the latter was reassigned to that air station.

59. Nist Letter. 22 December 1943.

60. Ensign James A. Nist, USNR. Letter to Martin and Ethel Nist. 22 December 1943 [hereafter cited as "Nist Letter. 22 December 1943"].

61. Nist Letter. 22 December 1943.

62. Nist Record of Service; Chief of Naval Air Operational Training, Naval Air Station Jacksonville, Florida. To: Ensign James A. Nist. Subject: Change of Duty. 13 December 1943.

Nist Papers; Willis E. Cleaves. Captain. USN. Commanding Officer. Naval Air Station Daytona Beach, Florida. 27 December 1943. To: Ensign James A. Nist Subject: Change of Duty. Nist Papers.

63. Nist Record of Service; J.O. Vosseller. Commander, USN. Commanding Officer, Carrier Qualification Training Unit, Naval Air Station Glenview, Illinois. To: Ensign James A. Nist Subj: Change of Duty. 29 December 1943. Nist Papers.

64. This brief description of *Sable* and *Wolverine* was obtained from the Naval History and Heritage Command's *Dictionary of American Naval Fighting Ships*. See entry for *Sable* accessed online on 23 July 2019 at https://www.history.navy.mil/research/histories/ship-histories/danfs/s/sable.html and *Wolverine* accessed online on 23 July 2019 at https://www.history.navy.mil/research/histories/ship-histories/danfs/w/-wolverine-ii.html.

65. Ensign James A. Nist, USNR. Letter to Martin and Ethel Nist. 2 January 1944 [hereafter cited as "Nist Letter. 2 January 1944"].

66. Nist Letter. 2 January 1944.

67. Nist Flight Log. See entry for 4 January 1944.

68. Nist Record of Service; J.O. Vosseller. Commander, USN. Commanding Officer, Carrier Qualification Training Unit, Naval Air Station Glenview, Illinois. To: Ensign James A. Nist Subj: Change of Duty. 4 January 1944. Nist Papers.

69. Ensign James A. Nist, USNR. Letter to Martin and Ethel Nist. 8 February 1944 [hereafter cited as "Nist Letter. 8 February 1944"]; Ensign James A. Nist, USNR. Letter to Martin and Ethel Nist. 15 February 1944 [hereafter cited as "Nist Letter. 15 February 1944"].

70. Ensign James A. Nist, USNR. Letter to Martin and Ethel Nist. 25 January 1944 [hereafter cited as "Nist Letter. 25 January 1944"].

71. Nist Letter. 2 January 1944.

72. U.S. Navy. Commander, Naval Installations Command, Naval Base Coronado. "Naval Air Station North Island." Accessed online on 18 September 2019 at https://www.cnic.navy.mil/regions/cnrsw/installations/navbase_coronado/about/installations/nas_north_island.html.

73. Nist Record of Service; William K. Harrill. Rear Admiral, USN. Commanding Officer, Fleet Air, West Coast. U.S. Naval Air Force. United States Pacific Fleet. Naval Air Station San Diego, California. To: Ensign James A. Nist Subj: Change of Duty. 27 January 1944. Nist Papers; T.F. Carlin. Commanding Officer, Carrier Aircraft Service Unit Five, Fleet Air, West Coast. U.S. Naval Air Force. United States Pacific Fleet. Naval Air Station San Diego, California. To: Ensign James A. Nist. Subj: Change of Duty. 27 January 1944. Nist Papers; Ensign James A. Nist, USNR. Letter to Martin and Ethel Nist. 28 January 1944 [hereafter cited as "Nist Letter. 28 January 1944"].

74. U.S. Navy, United States Pacific Fleet, Naval Air Forces, Carrier Aircraft Service Unit Five (CASU-5). "History of Carrier Aircraft Service Unit Five—21 July 1942 to 31 December 1944." Written by LCDR T. A. Reeves, USNR, Historian. 31 January 1945. RG38, NARA, Archives II, College Park, MD. Digital copy posted online at www.fold3.com; U.S. Department of the Navy, Bureau of Aeronautics. "CASU: Carrier Aircraft Service Unit." *Bureau of Aeronautics News Letter* (1 September, 1944), pp. 13–21.

75. Nist Letter. 28 January 1944; Ensign James A. Nist, USNR. Letter to Martin and Ethel Nist. 31 January 1944 [hereafter cited as "Nist Letter. 31 January 1944"]; Ensign James A. Nist, USNR. Letter to Martin and Ethel Nist. 2 February 1944.

76. Ensign James A. Nist, USNR. Letter to Martin and Ethel Nist. 5 February 1944; Ensign James A. Nist, USNR. Letter to Martin and Ethel Nist. 6 February 1944 [hereafter cited as "Nist Letter. 6 February 1944"].

77. Nist Letter. 6 February 1944.

78. Nist Record of Service; William K. Harrill, Rear Admiral, USN. Commanding Officer, Fleet Air, West Coast. U.S. Naval Air Forces. United States Pacific Fleet. Naval Air Station San Diego, California. To: Ensign James A. Nist Subj: Change of Duty. 10 February 1944. Nist Papers.

79. Ensign James A. Nist, USNR. Letter to Martin and Ethel Nist. 14 February 1944 [hereafter cited as "Nist Letter. 14 February 1944"]; Nist Letter. 6 February 1944; Nist Record of Service; United States Pacific Fleet, Commander Fleet Air Alameda, Naval Air Station Alameda, California. To: Ensign James A. Nist. Subj: Change of Duty. 12 February 1944. Nist Papers. These orders were signed with "By Direction" authority by Garth V. Lacey; J.T. Sunderman, Lieutenant Commander, USN. Commanding Officer, Carrier Aircraft Service Unit Six, U.S. Naval Air Forces, United States Pacific Fleet. To: Ensign James A. Nist. Subj: Change of Duty. 12 February 1944. Nist Papers.

80. *Building the Navy's Bases in World War II.*, pp. 232. 238, 244-45; *Cultural Landscape Report for Naval Air Station Alameda*. Prepared for Naval Facilities Engineering Command Southwest by JRP Historical Consulting LLC and PGAdesign Inc. April 2012., pp. 17-32.

81. U.S. Navy, United States Pacific Fleet, Naval Air Forces, Carrier Aircraft Service Unit Six (CASU-6). "Unit History." Written by LT Walter M. Miller, USNR, Historical Officer. 1 December 1944. RG38, NARA, Archives II, College Park, MD [hereafter cited as "CASU-6 Unit History"]. Digital copy posted online at www.fold3.com.

82. Ensign James A. Nist, USNR. Letter to Martin and Ethel Nist. 14 February 1944.

83. Ensign James A. Nist, USNR. Letter to Martin and Ethel Nist. 15 February 1944 [hereafter cited as "Nist Letter. 15 February 1944"].

84. Nist Letter. 15 February 1944.

85. Ensign James A. Nist, USNR. Letter to Martin and Ethel Nist. 17 February 1944.

86. Ensign James A. Nist, USNR. Letter to Martin and Ethel Nist. 19 February 1944.

87. Ensign James A. Nist, USNR. Letter to Martin and Ethel Nist. 21 February 1944.
88. Ensign James A. Nist. Letter to Mrs. Roscoe Estelle, Jr. 23 February 1944.
89. See *Dictionary of American Naval Fighting Ships* entry for USS *Lexington*, accessed online on 26 July 2019 at https://www.history.navy.mil/research/histories/ship-histories/danfs/l/-lexington-cv-16-v.html; Ensign James A. Nist. Letter to Mrs. Roscoe Estelle, Jr. 23 February 1944; Ensign James A. Nist. Letter to Mr. and Mrs. Martin Nist. 24 February 1944.
90. Ensign James A. Nist. Letter to Mr. and Mrs. Martin Nist. 4 March 1944 [hereafter cited as "Nist Letter. 4 March 1944"].
91. Nist Letter. 4 March 1944.
92. Ensign James A. Nist. Letter to Mr. and Mrs. Martin Nist. 6 March 1944 [hereafter cited as "Nist Letter. 6 March 1944"]; For more about *The Song of Bernadette*, see the International Movie Database at https://www.imdb.com/title/tt0036377/plotsummary?ref_=tt_ov_pl.
93. Nist Letter. 6 March 1944.
94. Ensign James A. Nist. Letter to Mr. and Mrs. Martin Nist. 8 March 1944 [hereafter cited as "Nist Letter. 8 March 1944"].
95. Nist Letter. 8 March 1944.
96. Ensign James A. Nist. Letter to Mr. and Mrs. Martin Nist. 13 March 1944 [hereafter cited as "Nist Letter. 13 March 1944"].
97. Nist Letter. 13 March 1944.
98. Nist Record of Service; John R. McCarthy, Lieutenant Commander, USN. Commander, Bombing Squadron Three Hundred Three, U.S. Naval Air Forces, United States Pacific Fleet. To: Ensign James A. Nist Subj: Change of Duty. 15 March 1944. Nist Papers; U.S. Department of the Navy, Deputy Chief of Naval Operations (Air), Location of Naval Aircraft. Report 12–44. 21 March 1944. Accessed online at https://www.history.navy.mil/research/histories/naval-aviation-history/involvement-by-conflict/world-war-ii/location-of-us-naval-aircraft-world-war-ii/1944/21-mar-1944.html; CASU-6 Unit History, p.A-6; Ensign James A. Nist. Bombing Squadron Three Hundred Three. Letter to Mr. and Mrs. Martin Nist. 15 March 1944.
99. Walter Lord, *Day of Infamy*. Sixtieth Anniversary Edition (NY: Henry Holt, 2001), pp. 121, 161; Robert J. Cressman and J. Michael Wenger. "This is No Drill: U.S. Naval Aviation and Pearl Harbor, December 7, 1941," *Naval Aviation News* (November-December 1991), pp. 20–25.
100. "John Reginald McCarthy." Citation for Navy Cross posted on The Military Times Hall of Valor. Accessed on 27 August 2019 at https://valor.militarytimes.com/hero/21362; "Accounts—John McCarthy." Posted on the website of the USS *Enterprise* (CV-6) Association, www.cv6.0rg/company/accounts/jmccarthy/. Accessed on 27 August 2019.
101. R. Elmer Miller, Jr. Draft Registration Card. Number 13,156. I found a digital copy of his draft card on www.fold3.com.
102. Gene Scruggs Powell. Draft Registration Card. Number 10,945. I found a digital copy of his draft card on www.fold3.com.
103. Ensign James A. Nist. Bombing Squadron Three Hundred Three. Letter to Mr. and Mrs. Martin Nist. 18 March 1944 [hereafter cited as "Nist Letter. 18 March 1944"]; U.S. Department of the Navy, Deputy Chief of Naval Operations (Air), Location of Naval Aircraft. Report 13–44, 29 March 1944. Accessed online on 8 August 2019 at https://www.history.navy.mil/research/histories/naval-aviation-history/involvement-by-conflict/world-war-ii/location-of-us-naval-aircraft-world-war-ii/1944/29-mar-1944.html. Apparently there was some lag time in reporting because the 29 March 1944 report still had VB-303 at 6 SBD-5s. The next report had the proper aircraft number for VB-303. See U.S. Department of the Navy, Deputy Chief of Naval Operations (Air), Location of Naval Aircraft. Report 14–44, 4 April 1944. Accessed online on 8 August 2019 at https://www.history.navy.mil/research/histories/naval-aviation-history/involvement-by-conflict/world-war-ii/location-of-us-naval-aircraft-world-war-ii/1944/4-apr-1944.html.
104. Nist Letter. 18 March 1944; See Nist Flight Log. Entry for 18 March 1944.
105. Ensign James A. Nist. Letter to Mr. and Mrs. Martin Nist. 21 March 1944 [hereafter cited as "Nist Letter. 21 March 1944"].
106. Nist Flight Log. See Entry for 20 March 1944; Nist Letter. 21 March 1944.
107. Nist Letter. 21 March 1944.
108. Nist Letter. 21 March 1944.
109. Nist Letter. 21 March 1944.
110. Ensign James A. Nist. Letter to Mr. and Mrs. Martin Nist. 30 March 1944 [hereafter cited as "Nist Letter. 30 March 1944"].
111. Nist Letter. 30 March 1944.
112. Nist Letter. 30 March 1944.
113. Ensign James A. Nist. Letter to Mr. and Mrs. Martin Nist. 30 March 1944 [hereafter cited as "Nist Letter. 30 March 1944"]; "SNAFU"—Situation Normal All Fouled Up. "TARFU"—Things Are Really Fouled Up. The "Fouled Up" was often substituted for a much stronger F—word.
114. Ensign James A. Nist. Letter to Mr. and Mrs. Martin Nist. 2 April 1944 [hereafter cited as "Nist Letter. 2 April 1944"].
115. Nist Letter. 2 April 1944.
116. Nist Letter. 2 April 1944.
117. Ensign James A. Nist. Letter to Martin and Ethel Nist. 7 April 1944.
118. Nist Letter. 7 April 1944.
119. Ensign James A. Nist. Letter to Mr. and Mrs. Martin Nist. 13 April 1944.
120. Ensign James A. Nist. Letter to Mr. and Mrs. Martin Nist. 16 April 1944.
121. Ensign James A. Nist. Letter to Mr. and Mrs. Martin Nist. 23 April 1944.
122. Ensign James A. Nist. Letter to Mr. and

Mrs. Martin Nist. 26 April 1944 [hereafter cited as "Nist Letter. 26 April 1944"].

123. Nist Letter. 26 April 1944.

124. Nist Letter. 26 April 1944.

125. Ensign James A. Nist. Letter to Mr. and Mrs. Martin Nist. 1 May 1944 [hereafter cited as "Nist Letter. 1 May 1944"]; "Scuttlebutt" was Navy slang for rumor.

126. Nist Letter. 1 May 1944.

127. Ensign James A. Nist. Letter to Mr. and Mrs. Martin Nist. 2 May 1944 [hereafter cited as "Nist Letter. 2 May 1944"].

128. Nist Letter. 2 May 1944; I deduced who the seven VB-303 pilots that were transferred to VF-84 by comparing the VB-303 Squadron photo with names found in VF-84 documents. I also found LCDR McCarthy's name on a roster of VB-84.

129. Nist Letter. 2 May 1944.

130. Nist Letter. 2 May 1944.

131. Ensign James A. Nist. Letter to Mr. and Mrs. Martin Nist. 7 May 1944.

132. Nist Record of Service; John R. McCarthy, Lieutenant Commander, USN. Commander, Bombing Squadron Three Hundred Three, U.S. Naval Air Forces, United States Pacific Fleet. To: Ensign James A. Nist Subj: Change of Duty. 4 May 1944. CO VB303 Orders P16–4/00. Nist Papers; J. T. Sunderman. Lieutenant Commander, USN. Commanding Officer, Carrier Aircraft Service Unit Six, U.S. Naval Air Forces, United States Pacific Fleet. To: Ensign James A. Nist Subj: Change of Duty. 4 May 1944. Nist Papers. This is the First Endorsement on Nist's Change of Duty Orders (CO VB303 Orders P16–4/00) from VB-303 dated 4 May 1944.

133. Nist Letter. 7 May 1944; Ensign James A. Nist, USNR. Letter to Martin and Ethel Nist. 29 July 1944 [hereafter cited as Nist Letter 29 July 1944]. Probably because of his engagement to June, Jimmy did not share the full story about Alice until the end of July 1944.

134. Nist Letter. 29 July 1944.

135. Nist Letter. 9 May 1944.

136. Nist Letter. 29 July 1944.

137. Ensign James A. Nist. Letter to Mr. and Mrs. Martin Nist. 9 May 1944 [hereafter cited as "Nist Letter. 9 May 1944"].

Chapter 4

1. Nist Letter. 9 May 1944; Ensign James A. Nist. Letter to Mr. and Mrs. Martin Nist. 14 May 1944 [hereafter cited as "Nist Letter. 14 May 1944"].

2. Nist Record of Service; Frederick C. Sherman, Rear Admiral, USN. Commanding Officer, Fleet Air, West Coast. U.S. Naval Air Forces. United States Pacific Fleet. Naval Air Station San Diego, California. To: Ensign James A. Nist Subj: Change of Duty. 13 May 1944. Third Endorsement on CO VB303 Orders P16–4/00. Nist Papers; Roger Hedrick. Lieutenant Commander, USN. Commander, Navy Fighting Squadron Eighty-Four. Fleet Air, West Coast. U.S. Naval Air Forces. U.S. Pacific Fleet. To: Ensign James A. Nist Subj: Change of Duty. 13 May 1944. Fourth Endorsement on CO VB303 P16–4/00. Nist Papers; Nist Letter 14 May 1944.

3. U.S. Navy. United States Pacific Fleet Air Force. Fighting Squadron Eighty-Four. War Diary 1 May 1944 through 30 June 1944. LCDR Roger Hedrick, USN. 1 July 1944. RG38, NARA, Archives II [hereafter cited as "VF-84 War Diary May-June 1944"]; U.S. Navy. United States Pacific Fleet Air Force. Fighting Squadron Eighty-Four. History of Fighting Squadron Eighty Four 1 May 1944 through 1 January 1945. LCDR Roger Hedrick, USN. 1 January 1945. RG38, NARA, Archives II [hereafter cited as "VF-84 History 1944"]; Both of these documents are also found on www.fold3.com.

4. Tom Blackburn with Eric Hammel. *The Jolly Rogers: The Story of Tom Blackburn and Navy Fighting Squadron VF-17*. (St Paul, MN: Zenith P, 1998); "Roger R. Hedrick." Obituary. *Orange County Register*. (1 February 2006). Accessed online on 30 August 2019 at https://obits.ocregister.com/obituaries/orangecounty/obituary.aspx?n=roger-r-hedrick&pid=16567690 [hereafter cited as "Hedrick Obituary"]; VF-84 History 1944. See Appendix for Squadron Biographies. Also found on www.fold3.com.

5. Tom Blackburn. *The Jolly Rogers*, p.258; U.S. Navy. United States Pacific Fleet Air Force. Fighting Squadron Seventeen. War Diary. 1 FEB 1944 to 29 FEB 1944. RG38. NARA. Archives II [hereafter cited as VF-17 War Diary FEB 1944]. Also found on www.fold3.com; Popp, *The Survival of a WWII Navy Fighter Pilot*, p. 146.

6. VF-84 History 1944; "Wilbert P. Popp." *Association of Naval Aviation*. Published for the association by Turner Publishing, Paducah, Kentucky in 2003. See page 117; Tom Blackburn, *The Jolly Rogers*, p.258; Maxwell Taylor Kennedy. *Danger's Hour: The Story of USS Bunker Hill and the Kamikaze Pilot Who Crippled Her*. (NY: Simon & Schuster, 2008), p. 75; Wilbert P. "Beads" Popp, LCDR, USNR (Ret). *The Survival of a WWII Navy Fighter Pilot* (privately published by Wilbert P. Popp in 2004). Author's note: this privately published memoir was extremely difficult to find. I was able to locate only two copies. One is held by the Library of Congress and the other is held by the Schuyler Otis Bland Memorial Library at the U.S. Merchant Marine Academy. My great appreciation to LT Jeremy R. Lauber, USMS, and Stephanie Apperio of the library for providing me with digital copies of key portions of Popp's memoirs.

7. VF-84 History 1944, p. 3; Tom Blackburn, *The Jolly Rogers*, p.258.

8. Ensign James A. Nist. Letter to Mr. and Mrs. Martin Nist. 16 May 1944 [hereafter cited as "Nist Letter. 16 May 1944"].

9. VF-84 History 1944, pp. 1–5; Popp, *The Survival of a WWII Navy Fighter Pilot*, p. 146.

10. VF-84 History 1944, pp. 1–5; Maxwell Taylor Kennedy. *Danger's Hour: The Story of USS Bunker Hill and the Kamikaze Pilot Who Crippled Her*, p. 75.

11. VF-84 History 1944; See entry for USS *Liscome Bay* in the *Dictionary of American Naval Fighting Ships* accessed online on 23 September 2019 at https://www.history.navy.mil/research/histories/ship-histories/danfs/l/liscome-bay.html; *I-175* was later sunk on 4 February 1944.

12. Jan Jacobs and Barrett Tillman. "The Wolf Gang: A History of Carrier Air Group 84." *The Hook. (World War II Special)* (Summer 1990), pp. 78–87. My thanks to Cyndi T. Deppe, Mark Aldrich and Janet Warren of the Tailhook Association for providing me with a digital copy of this article [hereafter cited as "The Wolf Gang"]; George M. Ottinger, Commander, USN. Commander Air Group Eighty-Four. United States Pacific Fleet Air Force. United States Pacific Fleet. To: The Commander in Chief, U.S. Fleet. Subject: War Diary from 1 May 1944 through 30 June 1944. 1 July 1944. RG38. National Archives and Records Administration. Archives II, College Park, Maryland. This record has also been digitized by www.fold3.com and is available on their website; VF-84 History 1944, p. 1.

13. "The Wolf Gang," pp. 78–9; U.S. Navy. United States Pacific Fleet Air Force. Air Group Eighty-Four. War History. 1944. RG38. Archives II, NARA. Also found on www.fold3.com.

14. "George M. Ottinger." USNA Virtual Memorial Hall. Accessed online on 4 September 2019 at https://usnamemorialhall.org/index.php/GEORGE_M._OTTINGER,_CDR,_USN.

15. Nist Letter. 16 May 1944.

16. Gregory "Pappy" Boyington, Colonel, USMC. *Baa Baa Black Sheep*. (NY: Bantam Books, 1958), p. 115.

17. Tom Blackburn with Eric Hammel. *The Jolly Rogers*, pp. 43–5, 75–6.

18. Ensign James A. Nist. Letter to Mr. and Mrs. Martin Nist. 18 May 1944; Nist Flight Log. See entries for 18 May 1944.

19. Ensign James A. Nist. Letter to Mr. and Mrs. Martin Nist. 21 May 1944; Nist Flight Log. See entries for 19 and 21 May 1944.

20. Ensign James A. Nist. Letter to Mr. and Mrs. Martin Nist. 24 May 1944.

21. Popp. *The Survival of a WWII Navy Fighter Pilot*, pp. 149–50; VF-84 War Diary May–June 1944.

22. Popp. *The Survival of a WWII Navy Fighter Pilot*, pp. 149–50.

23. Popp. *The Survival of a WWII Navy Fighter Pilot*, pp. 149–50.

24. Popp. *The Survival of a WWII Navy Fighter Pilot*, p. 150.

25. Stanley Switlik, Switlik Parachute Company. Letter to LT(jg) Wilbert P. Popp. 11 October 1944. Included in Popp. *The Survival of a WWII Navy Fighter Pilot*.

26. Ensign James A. Nist. Letter to Mr. and Mrs. Martin Nist. 28 May 1944 [hereafter cited as "Nist Letter. 28 May 1944"]; See Nist Flight Log for May 1944.

27. Nist Letter. 28 May 1944.

28. VF-84 War Diary May–June 1944.

29. Ensign James A. Nist. Letter to Mr. and Mrs. Martin Nist. 2 June 1944 [hereafter cited as "Nist Letter. 2 June 1944]; See Nist Flight Log for 2 June 1944.

30. Nist Letter. 2 June 1944.

31. Nist Letter. 2 June 1944; Dave LeMieux. "Lookback: 'Ike' Kepford was Muskegon's top gun during World War II." April 22, 2013. Accessed online on 7 October 2019 at https://www.mlive.com/news/muskegon/2013/04/lookback_ike_kepford_was_muske.html; Tom Blackburn. *The Jolly Rogers*, pp. 144–45.

32. Ensign James A. Nist. Letter to Mr. and Mrs. Martin Nist. 6 June 1944.

33. Ensign James A. Nist. Letter to Mr. and Mrs. Martin Nist. 10 June 1944 [hereafter cited as "Nist Letter. 10 June 1944"].

34. Nist Letter. 10 June 1944.

35. Nist Letter. 10 June 1944.

36. Nist Letter. 10 June 1944.

37. Nist Letter. 10 June 1944.

38. Nist Letter. 10 June 1944.

39. Ensign James A. Nist. Letter to Mr. and Mrs. Martin Nist. 12 June 1944 [hereafter cited as "Nist Letter. 12 June 1944"].

40. Ensign James A. Nist. Letter to Mr. and Mrs. Martin Nist. 14 June 1944 [hereafter cited as "Nist Letter. 14 June 1944"].

41. Nist Letter. 14 June 1944.

42. Ensign James A. Nist. Letter to Mr. and Mrs. Martin Nist. 18 June 1944.

43. VF-84 History 1944, pp. 1–2.

44. Nist Flight Log. See entries for June 1944.

45. Nist Letter. 12 June 1944.

46. Nist Letter. 12 June 1944.

47. Nist Letter. 12 June 1944.

48. Nist Letter. 29 July 1944.

49. Nist Letter. 14 June 1944.

50. Ensign James A. Nist. Letter to Mr. and Mrs. Martin Nist. 25 June 1944.

51. Ensign James A. Nist. Letter to Mr. and Mrs. Martin Nist. 30 June 1944.

52. Ensign James A. Nist. Letter to Mr. and Mrs. Martin Nist. 5 July 1944 [hereafter cited as "Nist Letter. 5 July 1944"].

53. Nist Letter. 5 July 1944.

54. VF-84 History 1944, pp. 1–2; U.S. Navy. United States Pacific Fleet Air Force. Fighting Squadron Eighty-Four. War Diary 1 July 1944 through 31 July 1944. LCDR Roger Hedrick, USN. 1 August 1944. RG38, NARA, Archives II [hereafter cited as "VF-84 War Diary July 1944"]; Ensign James A. Nist. Letter to Mr. and Mrs. Martin Nist. 10 July 1944 [hereafter cited as "Nist Letter. 10 July 1944"]; Popp, *The Survival of a WWII Navy Fighter Pilot*, p. 155; Ensign James A. Nist. Letter to Mr. and Mrs. Martin Nist. 19 July 1944 [hereafter cited as "Nist Letter. 19 July 1944"].

55. Popp. *The Survival of a WWII Navy Fighter Pilot*, p. 155.
56. Nist Letter 10 July 1944; SNAFU (Situation Normal All Fouled Up). Another word is frequently used for the letter F in these delightful acronyms.
57. Nist Letter. 10 July 1944; Ensign James A. Nist. Letter to Mr. and Mrs. Martin Nist. 14 July 1944.
58. Nist Letter. 17 July 1944.
59. Nist Letter. 17 July 1944.
60. VF-84 History 1944, pp. 1–2; VF-84 War Diary July 1944; Ensign James A. Nist. Letter to Mr. and Mrs. Martin Nist. 19 July 1944 [hereafter cited as "Nist Letter. 19 July 1944"].
61. Nist Letter. 19 July 1944.
62. Ensign James A. Nist. Letter to Mrs. Roscoe Estelle, Jr. 27 July 1944 [hereafter cited as "Nist Letter to Wootz. 27 July 1944"].
63. Nist Letter. 19 June 1944.
64. Ensign James A. Nist. Letter to Mr. and Mrs. Martin Nist. 24 July 1944 [hereafter cited as "Nist Letter. 24 July 1944"]; Nist Letter to Wootz. 27 July 1944.
65. VF-84 War Diary July 1944; Nist Letter. 24 July 1944; Ensign James A. Nist. Letter to Mr. and Mrs. Martin Nist. 27 July 1944 [hereafter cited as "Nist Letter. 27 July 1944"]; Popp. *The Survival of a WWII Navy Fighter Pilot*, p. 157.
66. VF-84 War Diary July 1944; Nist Flight Log. See entries for July 1944; Nist Letter 27 July 1944.
67. Ensign James A. Nist. Letter to Mr. and Mrs. Martin Nist. 18 August 1944 [hereafter cited as "Nist Letter. 18 August 1944"].
68. VF-84 War Diary August 1944; AG84 War Diary July 1944; VF-84 History 1944, p. 2; Ensign James A. Nist. Letter to Mr. and Mrs. Martin Nist. 12 August 1944 [hereafter cited as "Nist Letter. 12 August 1944"]; U.S. Navy. United States Pacific Fleet Air Force. Air Group Eighty-Four. War Diary 1 August to 31 August 1944. CDR George M. Ottinger. 9 September 1944. RG38. Archives II. NARA [hereafter cited as "AG84 War Diary September 1944."] Also found on www.fold3.com.
69. Nist Letter .12 August 1944; Nist Flight Log. See entry for 11 August 1944.
70. Nist Letter. 18 August 1944.
71. Ensign James A. Nist. Letter to Mr. and Mrs. Martin Nist. 23 August 1944 [hereafter cited as "Nist Letter. 23 August 1944"]; The identity of the groom was not provided in this letter but did appear in a later letter.
72. U.S. Navy. United States Pacific Fleet Air Force. Fighting Squadron Eighty-Four. War Diary 1 August 1944 through 31 August 1944. LCDR Roger Hedrick, USN. 1 September 1944. RG38, NARA, Archives II [hereafter cited as "VF-84 War Diary August 1944"]; U.S. Navy. United States Pacific Fleet Air Force. Air Group Eighty-Four. War Diary 1 July to 31 July 1944. CDR George M. Ottinger. 9 August 1944. RG38. Archives II. NARA [hereafter cited as "AG84 War Diary July 1944"]. Also found on www.fold3.com; VF-84 History 1944, p. 2.
73. Nist Letter. 23 August 1944.
74. Ensign James A. Nist. Letter to Mr. and Mrs. Martin Nist. 29 August 1944 [hereafter cited as "Nist Letter. 29 August 1944"].
75. VF-84 War Diary August 1944.
76. VF-84 War Diary August 1944; Nist Flight Log. See entries for August 1944.
77. Nist Letter 29 August 1944; VF-84 War Diary August 1944; AG84 War Diary July 1944; VF-84 History 1944, p. 2; Ensign James A. Nist. Letter to Mr. and Mrs. Martin Nist. 1 September 1944 [hereafter cited as "Nist Letter. 1 September 1944"].
78. Nist Letter. 1 September 1944; Ensign James A. Nist. Letter to Mr. and Mrs. Martin Nist. 6 September 1944.
79. U.S. Navy. United States Pacific Fleet Air Force. Fighting Squadron Eighty-Four. War Diary 1 September 1944 through 30 September 1944. LCDR Roger Hedrick, USN. 1 October 1944. RG38, NARA, Archives II [hereafter cited as "VF-84 War Diary September 1944"].
80. VF-84 History 1944.
81. Nist Letter. 29 September 1944.
82. VF-84 War Diary September 1944; U.S. Navy. United States Pacific Fleet Air Force. Air Group Eighty-Four. War Diary 1 September to 30 September 1944. CDR George M. Ottinger. 5 October 1944. RG38. Archives II. NARA [hereafter cited as "AG84 War Diary September 1944"]. Also found on www.fold3.com; Nist Flight Log. See Entries for September 1944.
83. Ensign James A. Nist. Letter to Mr. and Mrs. Martin Nist. 29 September 1944 [hereafter cited as "Nist Letter. 29 September 1944"]; Ensign James A. Nist. Letter to Mr. and Mrs. Martin Nist. 3 October 1944 [hereafter cited as "Nist Letter. 3 October 1944"]; Miss Alice M. Richards. Letter to Ethel Nist. 21 November 1944 [hereafter cited as "Richards Letter. 21 November 1944"].
84. Sister Mary Victorine Richards. Obituary. *San Francisco Chronicle* (21 June 1976); Bertram Richards. Obituary. *San Francisco Chronicle* (2 August 1976).
85. Nist Letter. 29 September 1944.
86. Nist Letter. 29 September 1944.
87. Nist Letter. 3 October 1944.
88. Nist Letter. 29 September 1944; Ensign James A. Nist. Letter to Mr. and Mrs. Martin Nist. 11 October 1944 [hereafter cited as "Nist Letter. 11 October 1944"].
89. Nist Letter. 11 October 1944.
90. VF-84 History 1944, p. 3.
91. Ensign James A. Nist. Letter to Mr. and Mrs. Martin Nist. 21 October 1944; Ensign James A. Nist. Letter to Mr. and Mrs. Martin Nist. 26 October 1944 [hereafter cited as "Nist Letter. 26 October 1944"]; Nist Flight Log. See entries for October 1944.
92. Popp. *The Survival of a WWII Navy Fighter Pilot*, p. 157.
93. Nist Flight Log. See October 1944 entries.
94. Ensign James A. Nist. Letter to Mr. and Mrs. Martin Nist. 21 October 1944; Ensign James

A. Nist. Letter to Mr. and Mrs. Martin Nist. 12 November 1944 [hereafter cited as "Nist Letter. 12 November 1944"]; Miss Alice M. Richards. Letter to Ethel Nist. 21 November 1944 [hereafter cited as "Richards Letter. 21 November 1944."]

95. *Ibid.*
96. *Ibid.*
97. Richards Letter. 21 November 1944.
98. Popp. *The Survival of a WWII Navy Fighter Pilot,* p. 157.
99. Gosson, Louis C., Thomas F. Fitzgerald, F. L Lundy, and New Jersey Legislature. *Manual of the Legislature of New Jersey* (Trenton, NJ: E. J. Mullin, 1945), pp. 678–681; National Archives and Records Administration. U.S. Electoral College. "Historic Election Results: Electoral Votes for President and Vice President 1941–1953." Accessed online on 22 October 2019 at https://www.archives.gov/federal-register/electoral-college/votes/1941_1953.html#1944; Dave Leip's Atlas of U.S. Elections. Accessed online on 22 October 2019 at https://uselectionatlas.org/RESULTS/national.php?year=1944&off=0&elect=0.
100. Nist Letter. 12 November 1944.
101. Ensign James A. Nist. Letter to Mr. and Mrs. Martin Nist. 21 October 1944; Ensign James A. Nist. Letter to Mr. and Mrs. Martin Nist. 19 November 1944 [hereafter cited as "Nist Letter. 19 November 1944"].
102. Ensign James A. Nist. Letter to Mr. and Mrs. Martin Nist. 20 November 1944 [hereafter cited as "Nist Letter. 20 November 1944"].
103. VF-84 History 1944 Chronology; VF-84 History 1944, p. 3; U.S. Navy. United States Pacific Fleet. USS *Takanis Bay* (CVE-89). War Diary. 1 November to 30 November 1944. CAPT A. R. Brady, commanding. RG38, Archives II, NARA [hereafter cited as "USS *Takanis Bay* War Diary"]. Also found on www.fold3.com; See entry for USS *Takanis Bay* in the *Dictionary of American Naval Fighting Ships* accessed online on 3 October 2019 at https://www.history.navy.mil/research/histories/ship-histories/danfs/t/takanis-bay.html.
104. Nist Letter. 19 November 1944.
105. Nist Letter. 20 November 1944.
106. Ensign James A. Nist. Letter to Mr. and Mrs. Martin Nist. 26 November 1944 [hereafter cited as "Nist Letter. 26 November 1944"]; Nist Flight Log. See entries for 20 and 22 November 1944; U.S. Navy. United States Pacific Fleet. USS *Ranger* (CV-4). War Diary. November 1944. CAPT Arthur Gavin, commanding. 14 March 1945. RG38, Archives II, NARA. Found also on www.fold3.com [hereafter cited as "*Ranger* War Diary NOV 1944"]; Nist's comments on VF-12 were confirmed by *Ranger*'s War Diary.
107. Nist Letter. 26 November 1944.
108. VF-84 History 1944 Chronology; VF-84 History 1944, p. 3; USS *Takanis Bay* War Diary.
109. Nist Letter. 26 November 1944.
110. Nist Letter. 26 November 1944.
111. VF-84 History 1944 Chronology; VF-84 History 1944, p. 3; USS *Takanis Bay* War Diary.
112. Nist Letter. 26 November 1944.
113. See USS *Ranger* entry in the *Dictionary of American Naval Fighting Ships*. Accessed online at https://www.history.navy.mil/research/histories/ship-histories/danfs/r/ranger-ix.html.
114. Nist Flight Log. See entries for November and December 1944; Ensign James A. Nist. Letter to Martin and Ethel Nist. 3 December 1944 [hereafter cited as "Nist Letter. 3 December 1944"].
115. VF-84 History 1944 Chronology; VF-84 History 1944, p. 3; *Ranger* War Diary NOV 1944; U.S. Navy. United States Pacific Fleet. USS *Ranger* (CV-4). War Diary. December 1944. CAPT Arthur Gavin, commanding. 14 March 1945. RG38, Archives II, NARA. Found also on www.fold3.com [hereafter cited as "*Ranger* War Diary DEC 1944"]; Popp. *The Survival of a WWII Navy Fighter Pilot,* p. 157.
116. Nist Letter. 3 December 1944.
117. Ensign James A. Nist. Letter to Martin and Ethel Nist. 5 December 1944 [hereafter cited as "Nist Letter. 5 December 1944"].
118. Nist Letter. 5 December 1944.
119. Nist Letter. 5 December 1944.
120. Lieutenant (junior grade) James A. Nist. Letter to Martin and Ethel Nist. 15 December 1944 [hereafter cited as "Nist Letter. 15 December 1944"].
121. For a comprehensive biography of Mitscher, see Theodore Taylor's *The Magnificent Mitscher* (Annapolis MD: Bluejacket Books, 2006).
122. Nist Letter. 5 December 1944.
123. Lieutenant (junior grade) James A. Nist. Letter to Martin and Ethel Nist. 3 February 1945 [hereafter cited as "Nist Letter. 3 February 1945"].
124. U.S. Navy. United States Pacific Fleet Air Force. Fighting Squadron Eighty-Four. War Diary 1 December 1944 through 31 December 1944. LCDR Roger Hedrick, USN. 1 January 1945. RG38, NARA, Archives II [hereafter cited as "VF-84 War Diary December 1944"]; Ensign James A. Nist. Letter to Martin and Ethel Nist. 10 December 1944 [hereafter cited as "Nist Letter. 10 December 1944"]; U.S. Navy. United States Pacific Fleet Air Force. Air Group Eighty-Four. War Diary. 1 December 1944 to 31 December 1944. CDR George M. Ottinger. 11 January 1945. RG38. Archives II. NARA [hereafter cited as "AG84 War Diary December 1944"]. Also found online on www.fold3.com; VF-84 War Diary December 1944; VF-84 History 1944 Chronology; VF-84 History 1944, p. 4; Nist Letter. 15 December 1944.
125. Nist Letter. 15 December 1944.
126. AG-84 War Diary December 1944; Robert Sherrod. *History of Marine Corps Aviation in World War II* (Washington DC: Combat Forces P, 1952), pp.462–3; U.S. Marine Corps. Marine Aircraft Group 42/Carrier Air Group Eighty-Four. Marine Fighting Squadron Four Fifty One. War Diary. 19 December to 31 December 1944. Major H.A. Ellis, Commanding. 10 January 1945. RG127, Archives II, NARA. Also found on www.fold3.com; U.S. Marine Corps. Marine Aircraft

Group 42/Carrier Air Group Eighty-Four. Marine Fighting Squadron Two Twenty One. War Diary. 19 December to 31 December 1944. Major Edwin S. Roberts Jr., Commanding. 11 January 1945. RG127, Archives II, NARA. Also found on www.fold3.com; Jan Jacobs and Barrett Tillman, "The Wolf Gang: A History of Carrier Air Group 84," p.79.

127. *Ibid*; *Ranger* War Diary DEC 1944.

128. VF-84 War Diary December 1944; VF-84 History 1944 Chronology; VF-84 History 1944, p. 4; LT(jg) James A. Nist. Letter to Martin and Ethel Nist. 22 December 1944 [hereafter cited as "Nist Letter. 22 December 1944"].

129. Nist Letter. 22 December 1944.

130. LT(jg) James A. Nist. Letter to Martin and Ethel Nist. 28 December 1944 [hereafter cited as "Nist Letter. 28 December 1944]; LT(jg) James A. Nist. Letter to Martin and Ethel Nist. 2 January 1945 [hereafter cited as "Nist Letter. 2 January 1945"].

131. VF-84 War Diary December 1944; VF-84 History 1944 Chronology; VF-84 History 1944, p. 4.

132. Nist Flight Log. See entries for December 1944.

133. VF-84 War Diary December 1944.

134. Nist Letter. 22 December 1944.

135. Nist Letter. 28 December 1944.

136. Nist Letter. 2 January 1945.

137. Alice Richards. Letter to Martin and Ethel Nist. 8 January 1945 [hereafter cited as "Richards Letter. 8 January 1945"].

138. U.S. Navy. United States Pacific Fleet Air Force. Air Group Eighty-Four. Fighting Squadron Eighty-Four. History of Fighting Squadron Eighty-Four 1 January 1945 to 1 June 1945. LCDR Roger Hedrick. RG38. Archives II. NARA [hereafter cited as "VF-84 History Jan-Jun 1945"]. Also found online at www.fold3.com; U.S. Navy. United States Pacific Fleet. USS *Ranger* (CV-4). War Diary. January 1945. CAPT Arthur Gavin, commanding. 14 March 1945. RG38, Archives II, NARA.

139. Nist Letter. 2 January 1945.

140. Nist Flight Log. See entries for January 1945.

141. VF-84 History Jan-Jun 1945, p. 1; LT(jg) James A. Nist. Letter to Martin and Ethel Nist. 5 January 1945 [hereafter cited as "Nist Letter. 5 January 1945"].

142. Nist Letter. 5 January 1945.

143. Nist Letter. 5 January 1945.

144. Richards Letter. 8 January 1945.

145. Richards Letter. 8 January 1945.

146. LT(jg) James A. Nist. Letter to Martin and Ethel Nist. 17 January 1945 [hereafter cited as "Nist Letter. 17 January 1945"].

147. Nist Letter. 17 January 1945.

148. Nist Letter. 17 January 1945.

149. Nist Letter. 17 January 1945.

150. Nist Letter. 17 January 1945.

151. VF-84 History Jan-Jun 1945, p. 1; Nist Letter. 17 January 1945.

152. Nist Flight Log. See entries for January 1945.

153. Miss Alice Richards. Letter to Martin and Ethel Nist. January 25, 1945 [hereafter cited as "Richards Letter. January 25, 1945"].

154. LT(jg) James A. Nist. Letter to Martin and Ethel Nist. 27 January 1945 [hereafter cited as "Nist Letter. 27 January 1945"].

155. Richards Letter. January 25, 1945.

156. Nist Letter. 27 January 1945.

157. Nist Letter. 27 January 1945.

Chapter 5

1. Evans, Mark L., and Guy J. Nasuti. "Bunker Hill I (CV-17) 1943–1966." 25 March 2020. Naval History and Heritage Command. *Dictionary of American Naval Fighting Ships*. Accessed online on 20 April 2020 at https://www.history.navy.mil/research/histories/ship-histories/danfs/b/bunker-hill-i.html [hereafter cited as "Evans and Nasuti. 'Bunker Hill I (CV-17) 1943–1966,' *DANFS*]. See Chapter Four of Maxwell Taylor Kennedy's *Danger's Hour: The Story of USS* Bunker Hill *and the Kamikaze Pilot Who Crippled Her*. (NY: Simon & Schuster, 2008.)

2. Evans and Nasuti. "Bunker Hill I (CV-17) 1943–1966," *DANFS*; See Chapter Four of Maxwell Taylor Kennedy's *Danger's Hour: The Story of USS* Bunker Hill *and the Kamikaze Pilot Who Crippled Her*; Captain John Moore, RN. Editor. *Jane's American Fighting Ships of the 20th Century*. (NY: Mallard P, 1991), p. 63.

3. See Chapter Four of Maxwell Taylor Kennedy's *Danger's Hour: The Story of USS* Bunker Hill *and the Kamikaze Pilot Who Crippled Her*.

4. See Chapter Four of Maxwell Taylor Kennedy's *Danger's Hour: The Story of USS* Bunker Hill *and the Kamikaze Pilot Who Crippled Her*.

5. See Chapter Four of Maxwell Taylor Kennedy's *Danger's Hour: The Story of USS* Bunker Hill *and the Kamikaze Pilot Who Crippled Her*.

6. See Chapter Four of Maxwell Taylor Kennedy's *Danger's Hour: The Story of USS* Bunker Hill *and the Kamikaze Pilot Who Crippled Her*.

7. See Chapter Four of Maxwell Taylor Kennedy's *Danger's Hour: The Story of USS* Bunker Hill *and the Kamikaze Pilot Who Crippled Her*.

8. Moore. *Jane's American Fighting Ships of the 20th Century*, p. 63; U.S. Navy. USS Bunker Hill. (CV-17). *The U.S.S.* Bunker Hill *November 1943–November 1944: The record of a carrier's combat actions against the Axis Nations in the Pacific*. Edited by LT Wallace C. Mitchell, USNR, and LT Eugene F. Brissie, USNR. (Chicago, IL: Privately published for the ship by Rogers Printing Company, 1945), pp. 47–53; Norman Friedman, "The Ubiquitous 5-inch/38." *Naval History Blog*. U.S. Naval Institute. 16 November 2015. Accessed online on 13 January 2020 at https://www.navalhistory.org/2015/11/16/the-ubiquitous-5-inch38.

9. Evans and Nasuti. "Bunker Hill I (CV-17) 1943-1966," *DANFS*.
10. *The U.S.S. Bunker Hill November 1943–November 1944*, pp. 47–53.
11. *The U.S.S. Bunker Hill November 1943–November 1944*, pp. 28–65.
12. *The U.S.S. Bunker Hill November 1943–November 1944*, pp. 28–65.
13. U.S. Navy. USS *Bunker Hill* (CV-17). War Diary. January 1945. RG38, NARA. Archives II. See entries for 1 to 20 January 1945 [hereafter cited as "*Bunker Hill* War Diary JAN 1945"]; Evans and Nasuti. "Bunker Hill I (CV-17) 1943–1966," *DANFS*.
14. *Bunker Hill* War Diary JAN 1945, p. 3; Evans and Nasuti, "Bunker Hill I (CV-17) 1943–1966," *DANFS*. For approximate distances, I referred to U.S. Department of Commerce. National Oceanic and Atmospheric Administration. National Ocean Service. *Distance Between United States Ports 2019* (13th Edition). Accessed online on 31 January 2020 at https://nauticalcharts.noaa.gov/publications/docs/distances.pdf.
15. Maxwell Taylor Kennedy. *Danger's Hour: The Story of USS* Bunker Hill *and the Kamikaze Pilot Who Crippled Her*, pp. 75, 82–83; *Bunker Hill* War Diary JAN 1945, p. 3.
16. *Bunker Hill* War Diary JAN 1945, p. 4.
17. Richards Letter. 25 January 1945; Nist Letter. 27 January 1945.
18. Popp. *The Survival of a WWII Navy Fighter Pilot*, pp. 159–60.
19. Popp. *The Survival of a WWII Navy Fighter Pilot*, p. 160. In his memoirs, Popp identified Cola as Seaman Second Class Cola. A search of *Bunker Hill*'s rosters posted on www.fold3.com filled in the missing information about Norman Cola.
20. Nist Letter. 27 January 1945; *Bunker Hill* War Diary JAN 1945, p. 4. The storm was not mentioned in the War Diary but Nist provided details in his 27 January 1945 letter to his parents.
21. Popp. *The Survival of a WWII Navy Fighter Pilot*, p. 160.
22. Nist Letter. 27 January 1945.
23. *Bunker Hill* War Diary JAN 1945, p. 5; For the World War Two layout of Pearl Harbor, I referred to the "Pearl Harbor, Oahu, T.H. Mooring & Berthing Plan" posted on the Naval History and Heritage Command website https://www.history.navy.mil/content/history/nhhc/research/archives/digitized-collections/action-reports/wwii-pearl-harbor-attack/pearl-harbor-mooring-and-berthing-plans.html; Popp. *The Survival of a WWII Navy Fighter Pilot*, p. 161.
24. Ibid.
25. Popp. *The Survival of a WWII Navy Fighter Pilot*, p. 161; LT(jg) James A. Nist. Letter to Martin and Ethel Nist. 3 March 1945.
26. *Bunker Hill* War Diary JAN 1945, pp. 5–6; Jan Jacobs and Barrett Tillman, "The Wolf Gang: A History of Carrier Air Group 84," p.79.
27. Popp. *The Survival of a WWII Navy Fighter Pilot*, p. 161. "Zeros, Haps, etc." were Japanese Navy and Army fighter planes.
28. *Bunker Hill* War Diary JAN 1945, pp. 6–7; U.S. Navy. USS *Bunker Hill* (CV-17). War Diary. February 1945. RG38, NARA. Archives II. See entries for 1 to 6 February 1945 [hereafter cited as "*Bunker Hill* War Diary FEB 1945"].
29. Alan P. Rems. "Two Birds with One Hailstone." *Naval History Magazine*. (January 2014.) Accessed online on 4 February 2020 at https://www.usni.org/magazines/naval-history-magazine/2014/january/two-birds-one-hailstone; Evans and Nasuti. "Bunker Hill I (CV-17) 1943-1966," *DANFS*.
30. *Bunker Hill* War Diary FEB 1945, p. 3.
31. *Bunker Hill* War Diary FEB 1945, p. 3; Popp. *The Survival of a WWII Navy Fighter Pilot*, p. 161.
32. U.S. Department of the Navy. *Building the Navy's Bases in World War II: History of the Bureau of Yards and Docks and the Civil Engineer Corps 1940–1946. Volume II of II.* (Washington DC: GPO, 1947), pp. 332–5. Accessed online on 13 August 2019 at https://www.history.navy.mil/content/history/nhhc/research/library/online-reading-room/title-list-alphabetically/b/building-the-navys-bases.html; Evans and Nasuti, "Bunker Hill I (CV-17) 1943–1966," *DANFS*.
33. Popp. *The Survival of a WWII Navy Fighter Pilot*, p. 161.
34. *Bunker Hill* War Diary FEB 1945, p. 4; Evans and Nasuti. "Bunker Hill I (CV-17) 1943-1966," *DANFS*.
35. U.S. Navy. Naval History and Heritage Command. "Admiral Arleigh A. Burke. Fifteenth Chief of Naval Operations August 17th, 1955—August 1, 1961." Accessed online on 4 February 2020 at https://www.history.navy.mil/browse-by-topic/people/chiefs-of-naval-operations/admiral-arleigh-a—burke.html; Jones, Ken, and Hubert Kelly, Jr. *Admiral Arleigh (31-Knot) Burke: The Story of a Fighting Admiral*. (NY: Bantam Books, 1985.)
36. U.S. Navy. United States Pacific Fleet. Fifth Fleet. Commander, First Carrier Task Force Pacific. Action Report 10 February–4 March 1945. 13 March 1945. RG 38, NARA, Archives II [hereafter cited as "TF-58 Action Report 10 FEB–4 MAR 1945"]. See page 1.
37. Nist Letter. 27 January 1945; Nist Letter. 3 February 1945; Lieutenant (junior grade) James A. Nist. Letter to Martin and Ethel Nist. 7 February 1945 [hereafter cited as "Nist Letter. 7 February 1945"]; Lieutenant (junior grade) James A. Nist. Letter to Martin and Ethel Nist. 13 February 1945 [hereafter cited as "Nist Letter. 13 February 1945"].
38. Nist Letter. 7 February 1945.
39. USS *Bunker Hill* War Diary FEB 1945, p. 4.
40. Nist Letter. 13 February 1945.
41. Frederick C. Sherman, Admiral, USN (Ret.). *Combat Command*. (NY: Bantam Books, 1982.)
42. U.S. Navy. USS *Essex* (CV-9). Action Report Operations in Support of Occupation of Iwo Jima 10 February to 4 March 1945. 12 March 1945. RG38, NARA, Archives II [hereafter cited as "*Essex* Action Report 12 MAR 1945"]; See *Dictionary of*

American Naval Fighting Ships entries for *Essex* https://www.history.navy.mil/research/histories/ship-histories/danfs/e/essex-iv.html and *Cowpens* https://www.history.navy.mil/research/histories/ship-histories/danfs/c/cowpens.html accessed on 21 February 2020; U.S. Navy. USS *Cowpens* (CVL-25). Report of Air Operations Against Japan, Bonins and Ryukus 2/16/45 to 3/1/45. 4 March 1945 [hereafter cited as "*Cowpens* Report of Air Operations 4 MAR 1945"].

43. USS *Bunker Hill* (CV-17) War Diary FEB 1945, p. 5; Samuel Eliot Morison. *Victory in the Pacific*. Volume 14 In the series *History of United States Naval Operations in World War II*. (Chicago IL: U of Illinois P, 2002), p. 21. This is a reprint of the original 1960 edition published by Little, Brown and Company; U.S. Navy. United States Pacific Fleet. Commander, Fifth Fleet. War Diary 1–28 February 1945. RG38, NARA, Archives II. Also found online on www.fold3.com [hereafter cited as "COM Fifth Fleet War Diary FEB 1945"].

44. Morison. *Victory in the Pacific*, p. 21; TF-58 Action Report 10 FEB–4 MAR 1945, p. 2; Robert Sherrod, *History of Marine Corps Aviation in World War II*, p. 343.

45. USS *Bunker Hill* (CV-17) War Diary FEB 1945, p. 6; Nist Flight Log. See entry for 11 February 1945; Morison. *Victory in the Pacific*, pp. 21–3.

46. USS *Bunker Hill* (CV-17) War Diary FEB 1945, p. 6; Nist Flight Log. See entry for 12 February 1945; Morison. *Victory in the Pacific*, pp. 21–3.

47. USS *Bunker Hill* (CV-17) War Diary FEB 1945, p. 7; COM Fifth Fleet War Diary FEB 1945, pp. 4–5.

48. Morison. *Victory in the Pacific*, pp. 21–3; COM Fifth Fleet War Diary FEB 1945, pp. 6–7; Evans and Nasuti. "Bunker Hill I (CV-17) 1943-1966," *DANFS*.

Chapter 6

1. U.S. Army Air Forces. Headquarters, U.S. Army Air Forces. Joint Target Group. *Air Target System Folder—Japanese Aircraft*. 6 January 1945. See the General Analysis section pages 3–4. This document was obtained on www.fold3.com.

2. Joint Target Group. *Air Target System Folder—Japanese Aircraft*, p. 4.

3. "Interrogation Nav No. 28 USSBS No. 112—Major Toga, Hiroshi, Imperial Japanese Army—23 October 1945." Included on pages 117–121 of U.S. Strategic Bombing Survey (Pacific). Naval Analysis Division. *Interrogation of Japanese Officials*. Washington, DC: GPO, 1946. Accessed online on 8 June 2020 at https://www.history.navy.mil/research/library/online-reading-room/title-list-alphabetically/i/interrogations-japanese-officials-voli.html; U.S. Department of the Navy. Bureau of Aeronautics. "Jap Antiaircraft." *Naval Aviation News*. (March 1, 1945), pp. 1–7.

4. Chris Chant, *Aircraft of World War II* (NY: Metro Books, 1999), p. 235, 255–7; Rene J. Francillon, *Japanese Aircraft of the Pacific War* (Annapolis, MD: Naval Institute Press, 1995), p. 250; U.S. Department of the Navy. Bureau of Aeronautics. "Japanese Fighter Aircraft," *Bureau of Aeronautics News Letter* (15 April 1943), pp. 1–3; *Jane's Fighting Aircraft of World War II*, p. 187–90.

5. Morison. *Victory in the Pacific*, pp. 22–3.

6. Olds, Robert. *Helldiver Squadron: The Story of Carrier Bombing Squadron 17 With Task Force 58*. 2nd edition (NY: Dodd, Mead & Company, 1945), p. 226.

7. U.S. Navy. United States Pacific Fleet. Fifth Fleet. Commander, First Carrier Task Force Pacific. Memorandum. To: Task Force FIFTY-EIGHT Pilots. Subject: Air Combat Notes for Pilots. February 1945. RG38, NARA, Archives II [hereafter cited as "Air Combat Notes for Pilots"]; U.S. Navy. United States Pacific Fleet. Fifth Fleet. Commander, First Carrier Task Force Pacific. Memorandum For Commander Task Groups 58.1, 58.2, 58.3, 58.4, and 58.5. Subject: Recommended Procedure for VF Sweeps in Tokyo Area. 6 February 1945. RG38, NARA, Archives II [hereafter cited as "Recommended Procedure for VF Sweeps in Tokyo Area"]; U.S. Navy. United States Pacific Fleet. Fifth Fleet. Commander, First Carrier Task Force Pacific. Memorandum. To: All Aviators. Subject: Flak Evasion. 5 February 1945. RG38, NARA, Archives II [hereafter cited as "Flak Evasion"].

8. Flak Evasion.

9. Flak Evasion.

10. Recommended Procedure for VF Sweeps in Tokyo Area.

11. Recommended Procedure for VF Sweeps in Tokyo Area.

12. Air Combat Notes for Pilots.

13. Air Combat Notes for Pilots.

14. Air Combat Notes for Pilots.

15. Air Combat Notes for Pilots.

16. Air Combat Notes for Pilots.

17. Air Combat Notes for Pilots.

18. Air Combat Notes for Pilots.

19. USS *Bunker Hill* War Diary FEB 1945, p. 9; Morison, *Victory in the Pacific*, p. 22; U.S. Navy. USS *Essex* (CV-9). War Diary. Month of February 1945. RG38, NARA. Archives II. See entries for 15 to 17 February 1945 [hereafter cited as "*Essex* War Diary FEB 1945"]; *Essex* Action Report 12 MAR 1945, Part III, page 4.

20. Morison, *Victory in the Pacific*, pp. 22–3; U.S. Navy. United States Pacific Fleet. Fifth Fleet. First Carrier Task Force Pacific. Commander, Carrier Division One/Task Group 58.3. Action Report 10 February–4 March 1945. 28 March 1945. RG38, NARA, Archives II [hereafter cited as "TG58.3 Action Report FEB–MAR 1945"].

21. Sherman, Frederick C. *Combat Command*, p. 286.

22. *Essex* Action Report 12 MAR 1945. See

Table 4a. Enemy planes destroyed in combat on land or water and enemy ships sunk, probably sunk and damaged by strikes; John Pomeroy Condon, Major General, USMC (dec.) *Corsairs and Flattops: Marine Carrier Air Warfare 1944- 1945* (Annapolis, MD: U.S. Naval Institute P, 1997), p. 27; John DeChant, "Devil Birds: With the Fast Carrier Task Forces." *Marine Corps Gazette* (September 1947), pp. 36-45; *Cowpens* Report of Air Operations 4 MAR 1945, pp. 7-8; TG58.3 Action Report FEB-MAR 1945, pp. 2-3.

23. USS *Bunker Hill* War Diary FEB 1945, p. 8; U.S. Navy. Air Group Eighty-Four. ACA-1 Report, First and Second Strikes on Tokyo and Support of Capture of Iwo, 10 February to 5 March 1945. 13 March 1945. RG38, NARA, Archives II. See Table of Damage to Enemy [hereafter cited as "AG84 Report FEB-MAR 1945"]; Robert Olds, *Helldiver Squadron*, p. 226; Jacobs, Jan, and Barrett Tillman. "The Wolf Gang: A History of Carrier Air Group 84," p. 80; John Pomeroy Condon, *Corsairs and Flattops*, p. 33; Evans and Nasuti. "Bunker Hill I (CV-17) 1943-1966," *DANFS*.

24. Popp. *The Survival of a WWII Navy Fighter Pilot*, p. 162.

25. USS *Bunker Hill* War Diary FEB 1945, p. 8; AG84 Report FEB-MAR 1945. See Table of Damage to Enemy and VF-84 Aircraft Action Report No. 1; Nist Flight Log. See Entry for 16 February 1945; Jacobs, Jan, and Barrett Tillman. "The Wolf Gang: A History of Carrier Air Group 84," p. 80; Evans and Nasuti. "Bunker Hill I (CV-17) 1943-1966," *DANFS*.

26. *Ibid.*

27. USS *Bunker Hill* War Diary FEB 1945, p. 8; AG84 Report FEB-MAR 1945. See Table of Damage to Enemy and VF-84 Aircraft Action Report No. 1; Nist Flight Log. See Entry for 16 February 1945; Jacobs, Jan, and Barrett Tillman. "The Wolf Gang: A History of Carrier Air Group 84," p. 80; Evans and Nasuti. "Bunker Hill I (CV-17) 1943-1966," DANFS.

28. USS *Bunker Hill* War Diary FEB 1945, p. 8; AG84 Report FEB-MAR 1945. See Table of Damage to Enemy and VF-84 Aircraft Action Report No. 1; Nist Flight Log. See Entry for 16 February 1945; Jacobs, Jan, and Barrett Tillman. "The Wolf Gang: A History of Carrier Air Group 84," p. 80; Evans and Nasuti. "Bunker Hill I (CV-17) 1943-1966," *DANFS*.

29. USS *Bunker Hill* War Diary FEB 1945, p. 8; AG84 Report FEB-MAR 1945. See Table of Damage to Enemy; AG84 Report FEB-MAR 1945. See VF-84 Aircraft Action Report No. 2; Jacobs, Jan, and Barrett Tillman. "The Wolf Gang: A History of Carrier Air Group 84," p. 80; Evans and Nasuti. "Bunker Hill I (CV-17) 1943-1966," *DANFS*; John DeChant, "Devil Birds: With the Fast Carrier Task Forces," pp. 36-45.

30. USS *Bunker Hill* War Diary FEB 1945, pp. 8-9; AG84 Report FEB-MAR 1945. See Table of Damage to Enemy; John Pomeroy Condon, *Corsairs and Flattops*, pp. 33, 35. Jacobs, Jan, and Barrett Tillman. "The Wolf Gang: A History of Carrier Air Group 84," p. 80; Evans and Nasuti. "Bunker Hill I (CV-17) 1943-1966," *DANFS*; Brown remains listed as Missing in Action to this day.

31. Morison. *Victory in the Pacific*, pp. 24-5.

32. U.S. Department of War. U.S. Strategic Bombing Survey. Aircraft Division. "Nakajima Aircraft Company, L.T.D.—Corporation Report No. II (Airframes and Engines)." June 1947. Record Group 243. National Archives and Records Administration. Archives II, College Park, Maryland. See pages 1-3, 5 [hereafter cited as "USSBS Nakajima Report"].

33. USS *Bunker Hill* War Diary FEB 1945, p. 9; U.S. Navy. United States Pacific Fleet Air Force. Air Group Eighty-Four. CVG 84 Report No. 1. 16 FEB 1945. RG38. NARA. Archives II [hereafter cited as "CVG 84 Report No. 1"]. Also found on www.fold3.com; Morison. *Victory in the Pacific*, pp. 24-5; Olds, Robert. *Helldiver Squadron*, p. 232; U.S. Army Air Forces. Headquarters, U.S. Army Air Forces. Joint Target Group. *Air Target System Folder—Japanese Aircraft*. January 1945. See Table 1, "Principal Japanese Operational Aircraft, Their Producers and Engines," for production figures. See "Target Information Sheet No. 90.13-1544-T1/2 Date 8 Feb. 1945" for a detailed description of Nakajima Ota; "USSBS Nakajima Report," pp. 1-2; Author's Note: After the Japanese surrender, Nakajima Corporation renamed itself Fuji Industrial Company, LTD.

34. USS *Bunker Hill* War Diary FEB 1945, p. 9; U.S. Navy. United States Pacific Fleet Air Force. Air Group Eighty-Four. CVG 84 Report No. 1. 16 FEB 1945. RG38. NARA. Archives II [hereafter cited as "CVG 84 Report No. 1"]. Also found on www.fold3.com; Morison. *Victory in the Pacific*, pp. 24-5; Olds, Robert. *Helldiver Squadron*, p. 232; U.S. Army Air Forces. Headquarters, U.S. Army Air Forces. Joint Target Group. *Air Target System Folder -Japanese Aircraft*. January 1945. See Table 1, "Principal Japanese Operational Aircraft, Their Producers and Engines," for production figures; "USSBS Nakajima Report," pp. 1-2.

35. Morison. *Victory in the Pacific*, pp. 24-5; *Cowpens* Report of Air Operations 4 MAR 1945, p. 8; *Essex* Action Report 12 MAR 1945, Part III, page 4; TG58.3 Action Report FEB-MAR 1945, p. 3.

36. USS *Bunker Hill* War Diary FEB 1945, p. 9; CVG 84 Report No. 1. This report includes Bombing Squadron Eighty-Four's narrative of the mission. U.S. Navy. United States Pacific Fleet Air Force. Air Group Eighty-Four. Bombing Squadron Eighty-Four. Aircraft Action Report No. 1. 16 February 1945. RG38, NARA, Archives II [hereafter cited as "VB-84 Report No. 1"]; Robert Olds, *Helldiver Squadron*, p. 227; Nist Flight Log. See entry for 16 February 1945.

37. Nist Flight Log. See entry for 16 February 1945; Nist was later awarded the Distinguished Flying Cross for this mission.

38. *Essex* Action Report 12 MAR 1945, Part III, page 4. See also Table 4.a. and Table 4.b. Damage to land targets; TG58.3 Action Report FEB–MAR 1945, p. 3.

39. USS *Bunker Hill* War Diary FEB 1945, p. 9; CVG 84 Report No. 1; VB-84 Report No. 1; Robert Olds, *Helldiver Squadron*, p. 228.

40. USS *Bunker Hill* War Diary FEB 1945, p. 9; CVG 84 Report No. 1; AG84 Report FEB–MAR 1945. See Table of Damage to Enemy; VB-84 Report No. 1; Robert Olds, *Helldiver Squadron*, p. 228; Condon, John Pomeroy. *Corsairs and Flattops*, p. 33. Pemble's remains were recovered after the war and he was interred in a cemetery in Indianola, Iowa according to the Find A Grave website. https://www.findagrave.com/memorial/28869863/william-m-pemble; Jacobs, Jan, and Barrett Tillman. "The Wolf Gang: A History of Carrier Air Group 84," p. 80.

41. AG84 Report FEB–MAR 1945. See Table of bombs, rockets, torpedoes and mines dropped at the target by strike (including strafing sorties); VB-84 Report No. 1; Olds, Robert. *Helldiver Squadron*, pp. 228–9; Evans and Nasuti. "Bunker Hill I (CV-17) 1943–1966," *DANFS*.

42. Nist Flight Log. 16 February 1945.

43. USS *Bunker Hill* War Diary FEB 1945, p. 9; CVG 84 Report No. 1; VB-84 Report No. 1; Olds, Robert. *Helldiver Squadron*, p. 229; Condon, John Pomeroy. *Corsairs and Flattops*, p. 33; Jacobs, Jan, and Barrett Tillman. "The Wolf Gang: A History of Carrier Air Group 84," p. 80.

44. USS *Bunker Hill* War Diary FEB 1945, p. 9; Morison. *Victory in the Pacific*, pp. 24–5; TG58.3 Action Report FEB–MAR 1945, p. 3.

45. USS *Bunker Hill* War Diary FEB 1945, p. 9; Morison. *Victory in the Pacific*, pp. 24–5.

46. Ugaki, Matome. *Fading Victory: The Diary of Admiral Matome Ugaki 1941-1945.* trans. by Masataka Chihaya. ed. by Donald M. Goldstein and Katherine V. Dillon (Pittsburgh, PA: U of Pittsburgh P, 1991), p. 538. Ugaki never intended for his diary to be published. Fortunately for history, those entrusted to destroy his diary after his death did not carry out his wishes. Ugaki died on 15 August 1945 while participating in a final kamikaze attack on the U.S. fleet off Japan.

47. Morison. *Victory in the Pacific*, pp. 24–5.

48. USS *Bunker Hill* War Diary FEB 1945, p. 10; AG84 Report FEB–MAR 1945. See Table of Damage to Enemy; Robert Olds, *Helldiver Squadron*, p. 229; *Cowpens* Report of Air Operations 4 MAR 1945, p. 8.

49. USS *Bunker Hill* War Diary FEB 1945, p. 10; AG84 Report FEB–MAR 1945. See Table of Damage to Enemy; Robert Olds, *Helldiver Squadron*, p. 229; *Cowpens* Report of Air Operations 4 MAR 1945, p. 8.

50. Morison. *Victory in the Pacific*, pp. 24–5. Joint Target Group. *Air Target System Folder—Japanese Aircraft*, p. 4. See also "Table 1—Principal Japanese Operational Aircraft, Their Producers and Engines—15 December 1944," and "Table 2—Principal Japanese Engines, Their Producers and Planes Using Them—November 1944."; "USSBS Nakajima Report," pp. 1–2.

51. Robert Olds, *Helldiver Squadron*, p. 230; USS *Bunker Hill* War Diary FEB 1945, p. 10; AG84 Report FEB–MAR 1945; *Essex* Action Report 12 MAR45; *Cowpens* Report of Air Operations 4 MAR 1945, p. 8; TG58.3 Action Report FEB–MAR 1945, p. 4.

52. USS *Bunker Hill* War Diary FEB 1945, p. 10; *Essex* Action Report 12 MAR45. See Table 4b. Damage to land targets; *Cowpens* Report of Air Operations 4 MAR 1945, p. 8; AG84 Report FEB–MAR 1945. See Table of Damage to Enemy and Table of bombs, rockets, torpedoes, and mines dropped at the target by strike (including strafing sorties); Olds, Robert. *Helldiver Squadron*, pp. 230–1; Jacobs, Jan, and Barrett Tillman, "The Wolf Gang: A History of Carrier Air Group 84," p. 80; TG58.3 Action Report FEB–MAR 1945 p. 4; *Essex* Action Report 12 MAR45; *Cowpens* Report of Air Operations 4 MAR 1945, p. 8.

53. Popp. *The Survival of a WWII Navy Fighter Pilot*, p. 163.

54. *Cowpens* Report of Air Operations 4 MAR 1945, p. 8. USS *Bunker Hill* War Diary FEB 1945, p. 10; TG58.3 Action Report FEB–MAR 1945 p. 4; USS *Bunker Hill* War Diary FEB 1945, p. 10; AG84 Report FEB–MAR 1945. See Table of Damage to Enemy and Table of bombs, rockets, torpedoes, and mines dropped at the target by strike (including strafing sorties); Olds, Robert. *Helldiver Squadron*, pp. 230–1; Jacobs, Jan, and Barrett Tillman, "The Wolf Gang: A History of Carrier Air Group 84," p. 80; TG58.3 Action Report FEB–MAR 1945 p. 4.

55. Sherman, Frederick C. *Combat Command*, p. 286.

56. Nist Flight Log. See entry for 17 February 1945.

57. Morison. *Victory in the Pacific*, pp. 24–5; Evans and Nasuti. "Bunker Hill I (CV-17) 1943-1966," *DANFS*; USS *Bunker Hill* War Diary FEB 1945, p. 10; Morison. *Victory in the Pacific*, pp. 24–5; TG58.3 Action Report FEB–MAR 1945 p. 4.

58. Morison. *Victory in the Pacific*, pp. 24–5; U.S. Navy. United States Pacific Fleet and Pacific Ocean Areas. Headquarters, Commander in Chief. CinCPac War Diary for the period 27 January 1945-28 February 1945. 10 March 1945. The results of the Tokyo Air Raids were recorded in the War Diary on 19 February 1945 on page 28 [hereafter cited as "CinCPac War Diary 27 JAN to 28 FEB 1945"]; U.S. Department of the Navy. Office of Public Information. *Navy Department Communiques 301-600 And Pacific Fleet Communiques March 6, 1943 to May 24, 1945* (Washington DC: GPO, June 15, 1945). Accessed online on 2 February 2020 at www.history.navy.mil/research/library/online-reading-room/title-list-alphabetically/n/navy-depart-communiques-301-660.hmtl. See "CINCPOA

Communique No. 263, February 19, 1945," pg. 347; Morison's statistics for the 16–17 February 1945 air strikes are slightly different from those released by Commander in Chief Pacific Fleet Public Affairs Office on 19 February 1945; U.S. Navy. United States Pacific Fleet. Fifth Fleet. First Carrier Task Force Pacific. Commander, Carrier Division Five/Task Group 58.1. Report of Operations of Task Group Fifty-Eight Point One (Fast Carrier Group One) in Support of Landings at Iwo Jima 10 February to 4 March (East Longitude Dates) including Actions against Tokyo, Chichi Jima, Okinawa and the Nansei Shoto, Second Action Against Tokyo and Operations in Direct Support of the Landings at Iwo Jima. 15 March 1945. RG38, NARA, Archives II [hereafter cited as "TG58.1 Report of Operations 10 FEB to 4 MAR 1945"]. See Enclosure B; U.S. Navy. United States Pacific Fleet. Fifth Fleet. First Carrier Task Force Pacific. Commander, Carrier Division Two/Task Group 58.2. Action Report—Operations in Tokyo Area, Support Of Landing on Iwo Jima And Strikes in Nansei Shoto. 10 February through 1 March, 1945. 12 March 1945. RG38, NARA, Archives II [hereafter cited as "TG58.2 Action Report 10 FEB to 1 MAR 1945"]; U.S. Navy. United States Pacific Fleet. Fifth Fleet. First Carrier Task Force Pacific. Commander, Carrier Division Six/Task Group 58.4. Action Report—10 February 1945 to 1 March 1945. 1 March 1945. RG38, NARA, Archives II [hereafter cited as "TG58.4 Action Report 10 FEB to 1 MAR 1945"].

59. TG58.3 Action Report FEB–MAR 1945 p. 5.
60. Sherman, Frederick C. *Combat Command*, p. 287.
61. TG58.3 Action Report FEB–MAR 1945 p. 14.
62. "CINCPOA Communique No. 263, February 19, 1945," found on page 347 of *Navy Department Communiques 301–600 And Pacific Fleet Communiques March 6, 1943 to May 24, 1945*.
63. See Nist Flight Log for 16–17 February 1945.
64. Ugaki, Matome. *Fading Victory*, p. 539.
65. Lieutenant (junior grade) James A. Nist. Letter to Martin and Ethel Nist. 18 February 1945.
66. Miss Alice Richards. Letter to Ethel Nist. 22 February 1945.
67. "CINCPOA Communique No. 259, February 15, 1945," found on page 345 of *Navy Department Communiques 301–600 And Pacific Fleet Communiques March 6, 1943 to May 24, 1945*.
68. "CINCPOA Communique No. 263, February 19, 1945," found on pages 347–8 of *Navy Department Communiques 301–600 And Pacific Fleet Communiques March 6, 1943 to May 24, 1945*.
69. "USSBS Nakajima Report." See "Bomb Plot Raid of 16 Feb. 1945."
70. "USSBS Nakajima Report," pp. 100–101.
71. Morison. *Victory in the Pacific*, p. 25.
72. Alexander, Colonel Joseph H., USMC (Ret.). *Closing In: Marines in the Seizure of Iwo Jima*. In the *Marines in World War II Commemorative Series* (Washington, DC: History and Museums Division, Headquarters U.S. Marine Corps, 1994); Ross, Bill D. *Iwo Jima: Legacy of Valor* (NY: Vanguard P, 1985).
73. Smith, General Holland M. USMC (Ret.), and Percy Finch. *Coral and Brass*. FMFRP 12-37 (Washington DC: Headquarters—U.S. Marine Corps, 1989).
74. Condon, John Pomeroy. *Corsairs and Flattops*, pp. 37–8; DeChant, John. "Devil Birds: With the Fast Carrier Task Forces," pp. 36–45; *Cowpens* Report of Air Operations 4 MAR 1945, p. 10; *Essex* Action Report 12 MAR 1945. Table 4.b. Damage to land targets; Evans and Nasuti, "Bunker Hill I (CV-17) 1943-1966," *DANFS*; TG58.3 Action Report FEB–MAR 1945 p. 5; CinCPac War Diary 27 JAN to 28 FEB 1945. See entries for 16, 17 and 18 February 1945, pages 23–28.
75. Alexander, Colonel Joseph H., USMC (Ret.). *Closing In: Marines in the Seizure of Iwo Jima*, p. 19.
76. Popp. *The Survival of a WWII Navy Fighter Pilot*, p. 163; TG58.3 Action Report FEB–MAR 1945 p. 5.
77. Nist Flight Log. See entries for 19 and 21 February 1945.
78. CinCPac War Diary 27 JAN to 28 FEB 1945. See entry for 24 February 1945, page 42.
79. Sherman, Frederick C. *Combat Command*, p. 290.
80. Nist Flight Log. See entry for 22 February 1945.
81. TG58.3 Action Report FEB–MAR 1945 p. 7.
82. Sherman, Frederick C. *Combat Command*, p. 291; TG58.3 Action Report FEB–MAR 1945 p. 7.
83. Jacobs, Jan, and Barrett Tillman. "The Wolf Gang: A History of Carrier Air Group 84," p. 81; *Evans and Nasuti*, "Bunker Hill I *(CV-17) 1943-1966*," *DANFS*.
84. *Ibid;* Popp. *The Survival of a WWII Navy Fighter Pilot*, pp. 166–68; 171–2.
85. TG58.3 Action Report FEB–MAR 1945 p. 7; Jacobs, Jan, and Barrett Tillman. "The Wolf Gang: A History of Carrier Air Group 84," p. 81; U.S. Navy. USS *Bunker Hill* (CV-17). Air Group Eighty-Four. Aircraft Action Report No. 8. 25 February 1945. RG38, NARA, Archives II [hereafter cited as "AG84 AAR No. 8"]; Nist Flight Log. See entry for 25 February 1945.
86. *Ibid.*
87. TG58.3 Action Report FEB–MAR 1945 p. 7; *Essex* Action Report 12 MAR 1945. Table 4.b. Damage to Land Targets; AG84 AAR No. 8.
88. *Ibid.*
89. *Cowpens* Report of Air Operations 4 MAR 1945, p. 11; *Essex* Action Report 12 MAR 1945. Table 4.b. Damage to Land Targets; TG58.3 Action Report FEB–MAR 1945 p. 8; AG84 AAR No. 8.
90. Sherman, Frederick C. *Combat Command*, p. 291; Evans and Nasuti. "Bunker Hill I (CV-17) 1943-1966," *DANFS*; Morison. *Victory in the Pacific*, p. 58; TG58.3 Action Report FEB–MAR 1945, p. 8. See also Action Report's Chronology, p. 11.

91. Sherman, Frederick C. *Combat Command*, p. 291; Evans and Nasuti. "Bunker Hill I (CV-17) 1943-1966," *DANFS*; Morison. *Victory in the Pacific, p. 58;* TG58.3 Action Report FEB-MAR 1945, p. 8.

92. "CINCPAO Communique No. 281, February 27, 1945," found on page 357 in *Navy Department Communiques 301-600 And Pacific Fleet Communiques March 6, 1943 to May 24, 1945;* CinCPac War Diary 27 JAN to 28 FEB 1945. See entry for 27 February 1945 on pages 48-9; Sherman, Frederick C. *Combat Command*, p. 291.

93. Admiral Raymond Spruance quoted in CinCPac War Diary 27 JAN to 28 FEB 1945, page 49.

94. Sherman, Frederick C. *Combat Command*, p. 291.

95. Burke quoted in Jones and Kelley, *Admiral Arleigh (31-Knot) Burke*, pp. 188-9.

96. TF-58 Action Report 10 FEB—4 MAR 1945, pp. 5-6; Morison. *Victory in the Pacific*, p. 59. Morison has slightly different figures but he included operations in support of the Iwo Jima invasion.

97. TG58.3 Action Report FEB—MAR 1945, p. 8.

98. TF-58 Action Report 10 FEB—4 MAR 1945, p. 5.

99. Nist Flight Log. See entries for Month of February 1945.

100. Lieutenant (junior grade) James A. Nist. Letter to Martin and Ethel Nist. 28 February 1945 [hereafter cited as "Nist Letter. 28 February 1945"].

101. Nist Letter. 28 February 1945.
102. Nist Letter. 28 February 1945
103. Nist Letter. 28 February 1945.
104. Nist Letter. 28 February 1945.
105. Nist Letter. 28 February 1945.
106. Gen. Holland M. Smith, *Coral and Brass*, p. 269.
107. Robert Olds, *Helldiver Squadron*, p. 232.
108. Gen. Holland M. Smith, *Coral and Brass*, p. 236.

Chapter 7

1. Sherman, Rear Admiral Frederick C. *Combat Command*, pp. 293-5; Morison. *Victory in the Pacific*, pp. 79-86.

2. Morison. *Victory in the Pacific*, pp. 79-81.

3. Sherman, Rear Admiral Frederick C. *Combat Command*, pp. 293-5; U.S. Department of the Navy. Bureau of Aeronautics. "Okinawa." *Naval Aviation News* (15 June 1945), pp. 1-7; Morison. *Victory in the Pacific*, pp. 79-86.

4. "Okinawa." *Naval Aviation News* (15 June 1945), pp. 2-4.

5. "Okinawa." *Naval Aviation News* (15 June 1945), pp. 2-4.

6. "Okinawa." *Naval Aviation News* (15 June 1945), pp. 2-4.

7. "Okinawa." *Naval Aviation News* (15 June 1945), p. 5.

8. Sherman, Rear Admiral Frederick C. *Combat Command*, pp. 293-5; Morison. *Victory in the Pacific*, pp. 80-81.

9. For a detailed description of preparations for the Okinawa invasion, see Chapter 6 of Samuel Eliot Morison's *Victory in the Pacific*.

10. Jacobs, Jan, and Barrett Tillman. "The Wolf Gang: A History of Carrier Air Group 84," p. 81; Evans and Nasuti, "Bunker Hill I (CV-17) 1943-1966," *DANFS*; TG58.3 Action Report FEB-MAR 1945 pp. 9-10; Morison. *Victory in the Pacific*, p. 58; U.S. Navy. USS *Bunker Hill* (CV-17). War Diary. March 1945. RG38, NARA. Archives II, p. 1 [hereafter cited as "*Bunker Hill* War Diary MAR 1945"]; U.S. Navy. United States Pacific Fleet. Fifth Fleet. First Carrier Task Force Pacific. Commander, Carrier Division One/Task Group 58.3. War Diary. 1 March 1945 to 31 March 1945. RG38, NARA, Archives II. See entry for 18 March 1945 [hereafter cited as "CARDIVONE War Diary MAR 1945"].

11. Olds, Robert. *Helldiver Squadron*, p. 233; Jacobs, Jan, and Barrett Tillman. "The Wolf Gang: A History of Carrier Air Group 84," p. 81; TG58.3 Action Report FEB-MAR 1945 pp. 9-10; *Bunker Hill* War Diary MAR 1945, p. 1; CARDIVONE War Diary MAR 1945, p. 1.

12. TG58.3 Action Report FEB-MAR 1945 pp. 9-10; *Bunker Hill* War Diary MAR 1945, p. 1; CARDIVONE War Diary MAR 1945, p. 3.

13. TG58.3 Action Report FEB-MAR 1945 pp. 9-10.

14. Nist Flight Log. See entry for 1 March 1945; U.S. Navy. United States Pacific Fleet Air Force. Air Group Eighty-Four. Fighting Squadron Eighty-Four. Aircraft Action Report No. 11. 1 March 1945. RG38, NARA, Archives II [hereafter cited as "VF-84 Action Report No. 11"].

15. Nist Flight Log. See entry for 1 March 1945; VF-84 Action Report No. 11.

16. TF-58 Action Report 10 FEB-4 MAR 1945, pp. 2-9; Morison. *Victory in the Pacific*, p. 59.

17. TF-58 Action Report 10 FEB-4 MAR 1945, pp. 2-3; Morison. *Victory in the Pacific*, p. 59; *Bunker Hill* War Diary MAR 1945, p. 2; CARDIVONE War Diary MAR 1945, P.4.

18. TG58.3 Action Report FEB-MAR 1945 pp. 10-11.

19. TF-58 Action Report 10 FEB-4 MAR 1945, p. 25.

20. TG58.3 Action Report FEB-MAR 1945 p. 12.

21. Nist Flight Log. See entries for February and March 1945.

22. Jacobs, Jan, and Barrett Tillman. "The Wolf Gang: A History of Carrier Air Group 84," p. 81; Evans and Nasuti, "Bunker Hill I (CV-17) 1943-1966," *DANFS*; *Bunker Hill* War Diary MAR 1945, pp. 3-4; CARDIVONE War Diary MAR 1945, p. 4; TF-58 Action Report 10 FEB-4 MAR 1945, pp. 2-3; Morison. *Victory in the Pacific*, p. 59.

23. LT(jg) James A. Nist. Letter to Martin and

Ethel Nist. 7 March 1945 [hereafter cited as "Nist Letter. 7 March 1945"].

24. Nist Letter. 7 March 1945.

25. CARDIVONE War Diary MAR 1945, p. 8.

26. LT(jg) James A. Nist. Letter to Martin and Ethel Nist. 11 March 1945 [hereafter cited as "Nist Letter. 11 March 1945"].

27. Nist Letter. 11 March 1945.

28. Jacobs, Jan, and Barrett Tillman. "The Wolf Gang: A History of Carrier Air Group 84," p. 81; CARDIVONE War Diary MAR 1945, pp. 8–9; Popp, *The Survival of a WWII Navy Fighter Pilot*, p. 174.

29. *Bunker Hill* War Diary MAR 1945, pp. 4–5; CARDIVONE War Diary MAR 1945, p. 11; U.S. Navy. United States Pacific Fleet. Fifth Fleet. First Carrier Task Force Pacific. Commander, Carrier Division One/Task Group 58.3./38.3 Action Report 14 March–1 June 1945. 18 June 1945. RG38, NARA, Archives II [hereafter cited as "TG 58.3 Action Report MAR–UN 1945"].

30. Nist Flight Log. See entry for 14 March 1945.

31. Nist Flight Log. See entry for 15 March 1945.

32. LT(jg) James A. Nist. Letter to Martin and Ethel Nist. 17 March 1945 [hereafter cited as "Nist Letter. 17 March 1945"].

33. Nist Letter. 17 March 1945.

34. Miss Alice Richards. Letter to Ethel Nist. 5 March 1945.

35. Morison. *Victory in the Pacific*, pp. 94–100; U.S. Navy. United States Pacific Fleet. Fifth Fleet. First Carrier Task Force Pacific. Commander, Carrier Division One/Task Group 58.3./38.3 Action Report 14 March–1 June 1945. June 1945. RG38, NARA, Archives II [hereafter cited as "TG 58.3 Action Report MAR–JUN 1945"].

36. Reilly, Robin L. *Kamikazes, Corsairs, and Picket Ships: Okinawa, 1945* (Drexel Hill, PA: Casemate, 2008), pp. 84–91.

37. Morison. *Victory in the Pacific*, pp. 94–100; U.S. Navy. United States Pacific Fleet. Fifth Fleet. First Carrier Task Force Pacific. Commander, Carrier Division One/Task Group 58.3./38.3 Action Report 14 March–1 June 1945. June 1945. RG38, NARA, Archives II [hereafter cited as "TG 58.3 Action Report MAR—JUN 1945"]; Sherman, Rear Admiral Frederick C. *Combat Command*, p. 301; CARDIVONE War Diary MAR 1945, pp. 13–4.

38. TG 58.3 Action Report MAR–JUN 1945, p. 7.

39. U.S. Navy. USS *Essex*. (CV-9). Action Report—Support of Occupation of Okinawa: 14 March–1 June 1945. 7 June 1945. RG38. NARA. Archives II [hereafter cited as "*Essex* Action Report Okinawa"]. See Part III—Chronological Account of Action, pp. 1–2; Part III—Table 2.a Table of Bombs and Rockets Dropped at Target, p. 5; Part IV—Table 3.a Own Losses, p. 42 ; Part IV—Table 4.a Enemy Planes Destroyed and Ship Losses, p. 59; and Part IV—Table 4.b Damage to Enemy Land Targets, p. 68.

40. U.S. Navy. United States Pacific Fleet Air Force. Air Group Eighty-Four. Bombing Squadron Eighty-Four. Aircraft Action Report No. 11. 18 March 1945. RG38, NARA, Archives II; U.S. Navy. United States Pacific Fleet Air Force. Air Group Eighty-Four. Torpedo Squadron Eighty-Four. Aircraft Action Report No. 10. 18 March 1945. RG38, NARA, Archives II; *Bunker Hill* War Diary MAR 1945, p. 7; Reilly. *Kamikazes, Corsairs, and Picket Ships*, See Appendix IV; U.S. Navy. USS *Cabot*. (CVL-28). Action Report. 14 March–11 April 1945. 12 April 1945. RG-38, NARA, Archives II [hereafter cited as "*Cabot* Action Report"]. See Enclosure C, pages 1–2; U.S. Navy. United States Pacific Fleet Air Force. Air Group Eighty-Four. Bombing Squadron Eighty-Four. War History. Second Cruise. 14 March 1945 to 28 May 1945. RG38, NARA, Archives II [hereafter cited as "VB-84 War History 2nd Cruise"]. See VB-84 Report No.11.

41. U.S. Navy. United States Pacific Fleet Air Force. Air Group Eighty-Four. Fighting Squadron Eighty-Four. Aircraft Action Report No. 15. 18 March 1945. RG38, NARA, Archives II; Nist Flight Log. See entry for 18 March 1945.

42. TG 58.3 Action Report MAR–JUN 1945. See Part III, paragraph 103.

43. Olds, Robert. *Helldiver Squadron*, p. 234; Jacobs, Jan, and Barrett Tillman, "The Wolf Gang: A History of Carrier Air Group 84," p. 81; *Cabot* Action Report, Enclosure C, pages 1–2, and Enclosure F, pages 2, 8 and 9; VB-84 War History 2nd Cruise. See VB-84 Report No.12.

44. Olds, Robert. *Helldiver Squadron*, p. 235; Jan Jacobs and Barrett Tillman, "The Wolf Gang: A History of Carrier Air Group 84," p. 81.

45. Sherman, Rear Admiral Frederick C. *Combat Command*, p. 301; Reilly. *Kamikazes, Corsairs, and Picket Ships*, p. 89; TG 58.3 Action Report MAR–JUN 1945. See Part III, Paragraph 15.

46. Sherman, Rear Admiral Frederick C. *Combat Command*, p. 301; Olds, Robert. *Helldiver Squadron*, p. 235; USS *Drum* is currently a museum in Mobile, Alabama; Morison. *Victory in the Pacific*, p. 94.

47. *Cabot* Action Report, Enclosure F, pages 2 and 9; *Essex* Action Report Okinawa. See Part III—Chronological Account of Action, pp. 3–4; Part III—Table 2.a Table of Bombs and Rockets Dropped at Target, pp. 6–7; Part IV—Table 3.a Own Losses, p. 42 ; Part IV—Table 4.a Enemy Planes Destroyed and Ship Losses, p. 59; and Part IV—Table 4.b Damage to Enemy Land Targets, p. 68; *Bunker Hill* War Diary MAR 1945, p. 8; Uncle Charley quoted in Robert Olds, *Helldiver Squadron*, p. 235.

48. Olds, Robert. *Helldiver Squadron*, pp. 236–7; Jacobs, Jan, and Barrett Tillman. "The Wolf Gang: A History of Carrier Air Group 84," p. 81; DeChant, John. "Devil Birds: With the Fast Carrier Task Forces," pp. 36–45; *Bunker Hill* War Diary MAR 1945, p. 8; VB-84 War History 2nd Cruise. See VB-84 Report No.16; TG 58.3 Action Report

MAR-JUN 1945. See Part III, Paragraphs 20 and 21.

49. TG 58.3 Action Report MAR-JUN 1945. See Part III, Paragraphs 20 and 21; *Essex* Action Report Okinawa. See Part IV—Table 3.a Own Losses, p. 42 ; Part IV—Table 4.a Enemy Planes Destroyed and Ship Losses, p. 59; and Part IV—Table 4.b Damage to Enemy Land Targets, p. 68.

50. Olds, Robert. *Helldiver Squadron*, pp. 236-7; Jacobs, Jan, and Barrett Tillman. "The Wolf Gang: A History of Carrier Air Group 84," p. 81.

51. Sherman, Rear Admiral Frederick C. *Combat Command*, pp. 301-3; Jacobs, Jan, and Barrett Tillman. "The Wolf Gang: A History of Carrier Air Group 84," p. 81; Morison. *Victory in the Pacific*, pp. 94-100; Popp. *The Survival of a WWII Navy Fighter Pilot*, p. 175; *Bunker Hill* War Diary. See entry for 18 March 1945; *Essex* Action Report Okinawa. See Part III—Chronological Account of Action, pp. 3-4.

52. TG 58.3 Action Report MAR-JUN 1945. See Part III, Paragraphs 27-29; *Cabot* Action Report, Enclosure C, page 2, and Enclosure F, pages 8-9; *Essex* Action Report Okinawa. See Part III—Chronological Account of Action, pp. 3-4; Part III—Table 2.a Table of Bombs and Rockets Dropped at Target, pp. 6-7; Part IV—Table 3.a Own Losses, p. 42 ; Part IV—Table 4.a Enemy Planes Destroyed and Ship Losses, p. 60; and Part IV—Table 4.b Damage to Enemy Land Targets, p. 68.

53. U.S. Navy. United States Pacific Fleet Air Force. Air Group Eighty-Four. Fighting Squadron Eighty-Four. Aircraft Action Report No. 19. 19 March 1945. RG38, NARA, Archives II; See Nist Flight Log for 19 March 1945; *Bunker Hill* War Diary MAR 1945, pp. 8-9; Nist Flight Log. See entry for 19 March 1945.

54. Reilly. *Kamikazes, Corsairs, and Picket Ships*, pp. 86-92.

55. Morison. *Victory in the Pacific*, p. 100; CARDIVONE War Diary MAR 1945, pp. 15-6.

56. CARDIVONE War Diary MAR 1945, p. 16; TG 58.3 Action Report MAR-JUN 1945. See Part III, Paragraph 29.

57. CARDIVONE War Diary MAR 1945, p. 16; TG 58.3 Action Report MAR-JUN 1945. See Part III, Paragraph 29.

58. Sherman, Rear Admiral Frederick C. *Combat Command*, pp. 302-3; Morison. *Victory in the Pacific*, pp. 99-100; *Bunker Hill* War Diary MAR 1945, p. 10; CARDIVONE War Diary MAR 1945, p. 16.

59. Ugaki, Matome. *Fading Victory*, p. 559; Morison. *Victory in the Pacific*, pp. 99-100.

60. Reprinted in CARDIVONE War Diary MAR 1945, p. 21.

61. LT(jg) James A. Nist. Letter to Martin and Ethel Nist. 21 March 1945.

62. CARDIVONE War Diary MAR 1945, p. 17; *Bunker Hill* War Diary MAR 1945, p. 19; U.S. Navy. USS *Hancock* (CV-19). Action Report. 14 March 1945 to 11 April 1945. RG38, NARA, Archives II [hereafter cited as "*Hancock* Action Report"]; U.S. Navy. USS *Bataan* (CVL-29). Action Report. 14 March 1945 to 29 May 1945. RG38, NARA, Archives II. See entry for 22 March 1945 [hereafter cited as "*Bataan* Action Report"].

63. Sherman, Rear Admiral Frederick C. *Combat Command*, p. 302; Jacobs, Jan, and Barrett Tillman. "The Wolf Gang: A History of Carrier Air Group 84," p. 82; *Bunker Hill* War Diary MAR 1945, p. 12; CARDIVONE War Diary MAR 1945, p. 22; *Cabot* Action Report, Enclosure F, page 2; *Hancock* Action Report, pp. 13-14, and Table 2—Bombs, Rockets, Torpedoes and Mines Dropped at the Target by Strikes and Sweeps; *Bataan* Action Report. See entry for 23 March 1945; *Essex* Action Report Okinawa. See Part III—Chronological Account of Action, pp. 7-8; Part III—Table 2.a Table of Bombs and Rockets Dropped at Target, p. 7; *Bunker Hill* War Diary MAR 1945, p. 13; *Cabot* Action Report, Enclosure F, page 2; *Essex* Action Report Okinawa. See Part III—Chronological Account of Action, pp. 7-8; Part III—Table 2.a Table of Bombs and Rockets Dropped at Target, p. 7.

64. *Bunker Hill* War Diary MAR 1945, p. 13; *Cabot* Action Report, Enclosure F, page 2; *Hancock* Action Report, pp. 14-5, and Table 2—Bombs, Rockets, Torpedoes and Mines Dropped at the Target by Strikes and Sweeps; *Bataan* Action Report. See entry for 24 March 1945; *Essex* Action Report Okinawa. See Part III—Chronological Account of Action, pp. 8-9; Part III—Table 2.a Table of Bombs and Rockets Dropped at Target, pp. 8-9; and Part IV—Table 4.b Damage to Enemy Land Targets, p. 69.

65. Nist Flight Log. See entry for 24 March 1945.

66. CARDIVONE War Diary MAR 1945, p. 23; Jacobs, Jan, and Barrett Tillman. "The Wolf Gang: A History of Carrier Air Group 84," p. 82; *Bunker Hill* War Diary MAR 1945, p. 14.

67. *Bunker Hill* War Diary MAR 1945, p. 14; CARDIVONE War Diary MAR 1945, p. 23. Some sources have CDR Ottinger listed as missing. Both the *Bunker Hill* War Diary and the Carrier Division One War Diary stated that CDR Ottinger's body was found floating in the ocean.

68. Olds, Robert. *Helldiver Squadron*, p. 239; *Bunker Hill* War Diary MAR 1945, p. 14; CARDIVONE War Diary MAR 1945, p. 23; Popp. *The Survival of a WWII Navy Fighter Pilot*, p. 175.

69. *Bunker Hill* War Diary MAR 1945, pp. 15-6; CARDIVONE War Diary MAR 1945, p. 24.

70. TG 58.3 Action Report MAR-JUN 1945. See Part III, Paragraphs 27-29; *Cabot* Action Report, Enclosure F, page 2; *Hancock* Action Report, pp. 16-7; *Essex* Action Report Okinawa. See Part III—Chronological Account of Action, pp. 9-10; Jacobs, Jan, and Barrett Tillman. "The Wolf Gang: A History of Carrier Air Group 84," p. 82; *Bunker Hill* War Diary MAR 1945, pp. 16-18. *Bataan* Action Report. See entries for 26-27 March 1945.

71. Marines from 2nd Battalion/29th Marine Regiment/6th Marine Division captured Unten Ko on 9 April 1945. See Benis M. Frank and Henry I.

Shaw Jr. *Victory and Occupation: Volume V of the History of U.S. Marine Corps Operations in World War II* (Washington, DC: Historical Branch, G-3 Division, Headquarters, U.S. Marine Corps, 1968), p. 139.

72. Nist Flight Log. See entry for 26 March 1945.
73. Nist Flight Log. See entry for 27 March 1945.
74. LT(jg) James A. Nist, USNR. Letter to Martin and Ethel Nist. 27 March 1945.
75. *Bunker Hill* War Diary MAR 1945, p. 18; CARDIVONE War Diary MAR 1945, pp. 27–8; *Cabot* Action Report, Enclosure F, page 11.
76. Jacobs, Jan, and Barrett Tillman. "The Wolf Gang: A History of Carrier Air Group 84," p. 82; CARDIVONE War Diary MAR 1945, p. 29; *Hancock* Action Report, p. 20, and Table 2—Bombs, Rockets, Torpedoes and Mines Dropped at the Target by Strikes and Sweeps; *Cabot* Action Report, Part III—p. 10, and Enclosure F, p. 3; *Essex* Action Report Okinawa. See Part III—Chronological Account of Action, p. 12; Part III—Table 2.a Table of Bombs and Rockets Dropped at Target, p. 12; and Part IV—Table 4.b Damage to Enemy Land Targets, p. 69; CARDIVONE War Diary MAR 1945, pp. 27–8; *Essex* Action Report Okinawa. See Part III—Chronological Account of Action, p. 12; Part III—Table 2.a Table of Bombs and Rockets Dropped at Target, p. 11; and Part IV—Table 4.b Damage to Enemy Land Targets, p. 69; *Bunker Hill* War Diary MAR 1945, p. 19; VB-84 War Diary. 2nd Cruise. See VB-84 Report No. 22. *Bataan* Action Report. See entry for 28 March 1945, and see Part VI-B-2 Table of Bombs, Rockets, Torpedoes & Mines Dropped at Targets.
77. *Bunker Hill* War Diary MAR 1945, p. 19.
78. *Hancock* Action Report, pp. 21–2; CARDIVONE War Diary MAR 1945, p. 29. *Bataan* Action Report. See entry for 29 March 1945; *Essex* Action Report Okinawa. See Part III—Chronological Account of Action, pp. 13–14; *Bataan* Action Report. See entry for 29 March 1945; *Cabot* Action Report, Part III—p. 10., and Enclosure F, p. 3; *Essex* Action Report Okinawa. See Part III—Chronological Account of Action, pp. 13–14; *Bunker Hill* War Diary MAR 1945, p. 20; Rear Admiral Frederick C. Sherman. *Combat Command*, pp. 302–3; Morison. *Victory in the Pacific*, pp. 112–3; Reilly. *Kamikazes, Corsairs, and Picket Ships*. See Appendix IV; CARDIVONE War Diary MAR 1945, p. 29.
79. Olds, Robert. *Helldiver Squadron*, p. 240; Jacobs, Jan, and Barrett Tillman. "The Wolf Gang: A History of Carrier Air Group 84," p. 82; *Bunker Hill* War Diary MAR 1945, p. 20; CARDIVONE War Diary MAR 1945, p. 30; VB-84 War Diary 2nd Cruise. See VB-84 Report No. 23.
80. Nist Flight Log. See entry for 29 March 1945; Reilly. *Kamikazes, Corsairs, and Picket Ships*. See Appendix IV; The VF-84 Historical Report lists the aircraft destroyed by the Squadron on that day in Appendix 2; For details about the "Cherry," see www.combinedfleet.com/ijna/h5y.htm.

81. CARDIVONE War Diary MAR 1945, pp. 30–1; TG 58.3 Action Report MAR–JUN 1945. See Part III, Paragraphs 27–29. See Part III, Paragraphs 33 and 37.
82. "Okinawa." *Naval Aviation News* (June 15, 1945), pp. 2–4.
83. *Bunker Hill* War Diary MAR 1945, pp. 21–2; CARDIVONE War Diary MAR 1945, p. 31.
84. *Hancock* Action Report, pp. 22–5; *Bataan* Action Report. See entries for 30–31 March 1945.; *Cabot* Action Report, Part III—p. 10., and Enclosure F, p. 3; *Essex* Action Report Okinawa. See Part III—Chronological Account of Action, pp. 14–16, Part III—Table 2.a Table of Bombs and Rockets Dropped at Target, p. 12, and Part IV—Table 4.b Damage to Enemy Land Targets, p. 71; *Bunker Hill* War Diary MAR 1945, pp. 22–4; Jacobs, Jan, and Barrett Tillman. "The Wolf Gang: A History of Carrier Air Group 84," p. 82; CARDIVONE War Diary MAR 1945, pp. 31–2; U.S. Navy. Air Group Eighty-Three. Bombing Squadron Eighty-Three. History of Bombing Squadron Eighty-Three. 1 January 1945 to 21 September 1945. RG38, NARA, Archives II.
85. Nist Flight Log. See March 1945.

Chapter 8

1. Sherman, Rear Admiral Frederick C. Sherman. *Combat Command*, pp. 293–5; For a detailed discussion of the events leading up to the invasion of Okinawa, see Chapter 7 of Samuel Eliot Morison's *Victory in the Pacific*.
2. Sherman, Rear Admiral Frederick C. *Combat Command*, pp. 300–1.
3. In Chapters 9 and 11 of his *Victory in the Pacific*, Samuel Eliot Morison details the landings on Okinawa and the first five days of fighting ashore.
4. Evans and Nasuti. "Bunker Hill I (CV-17) 1943–1966," *DANFS*; U.S. Navy. USS *Bunker Hill* (CV-17). War Diary. April 1945. RG38, NARA. Archives II, pp. 1–2 [hereafter cited as "*Bunker Hill* War Diary APR 1945"]; *Essex* Action Report Okinawa. See Part III—Chronological Account of Action, pp. 16–17; *Cabot* Action Report, Part III—p. 10; *Hancock* Action Report, pp. 24–5; *Bataan* Action Report. See entry for 1 April 1945; TG 58.3 Action Report MAR–JUN 1945. See Part III, Paragraph 77.
5. Nist Flight Log. See entry for 1 April 1945; *Bunker Hill* War Diary APR 1945, p. 2.
6. LT(jg) James A. Nist. Letter to Martin and Ethel Nist. 1 April 1945 [hereafter cited as Nist Letter 1 April 1945].
7. Nist Letter. 1 April 1945.
8. *Bunker Hill* War Diary APR 1945, p. 2.
9. Jacobs, Jan, and Barrett Tillman. "The Wolf Gang: A History of Carrier Air Group 84," p. 82; Evans and Nasuti. "Bunker Hill I (CV-17) 1943–1966," *DANFS*; *Bunker Hill* War Diary APR 1945, p. 3; *Hancock* Action Report, p. 25; *Essex* Action

Report Okinawa. See Part III—Chronological Account of Action, p. 17.

10. *Hancock* Action Report, pp. 26-7, and Table 2—Bombs, Rockets, Torpedoes and Mines Dropped at the Target by Strikes and Sweeps; *Bataan* Action Report. See entry for 3 April 1945, and see Part VI-B-2 Table of Bombs, Rockets, Torpedoes & Mines Dropped at Targets; *Cabot* Action Report, Part III—p.10, and Enclosure F, p. 3; *Essex* Action Report Okinawa. See Part III—Chronological Account of Action, pp. 17-18; Part III—Table 2.a Table of Bombs and Rockets Dropped at Target, pp. 15-16; Part IV Table 4.a Enemy planes destroyed in combat on land or water and enemy ships sunk, probably sunk and damaged by strikes, and Part IV—Table 4.b Damage to Enemy Land Targets, p. 73.

11. Jacobs, Jan. and Barrett Tillman. "The Wolf Gang: A History of Carrier Air Group 84," p. 82; *Bunker Hill* War Diary APR 1945, p. 4; DeChant, John. "Devil Birds: With the Fast Carrier Task Forces," pp. 36-45; Rielly. *Kamikazes, Corsairs, and Picket Ships*, p. 105.

12. Jacobs, Jan, and Barrett Tillman. "The Wolf Gang: A History of Carrier Air Group 84," p. 82; DeChant, John. "Devil Birds: With the Fast Carrier Task Forces," pp. 36-45; Rielly. *Kamikazes, Corsairs, and Picket Ships*, p. 105; *Bunker Hill* War Diary APR 1945, p. 4; *Cabot* Action Report, Enclosure F, pages 8, 12, and Enclosure C, page 6.

13. Nist Flight Log. See Entry for 3 April 1945.

14. *Bunker Hill* War Diary APR 1945, pp. 5-6; *Cabot* Action Report, Enclosure F, p. 12; *Hancock* Action Report, pp. 27-8, and Table 2—Bombs, Rockets, Torpedoes and Mines Dropped at the Target by Strikes and Sweeps; *Bataan* Action Report. See entry for 4 April 1945, and see Part VI-B-2 Table of Bombs, Rockets, Torpedoes & Mines Dropped at Targets; Rielly. *Kamikazes, Corsairs, and Picket Ships*, p. 107; *Essex* Action Report Okinawa. See Part III—Chronological Account of Action, pp. 19-20; Part III—Table 2.a Table of Bombs and Rockets Dropped at Target, pp. 17-18; and Part IV—Table 4.b Damage to Enemy Land Targets, p. 74.

15. *Bataan* Action Report. See entry for 4 April 1945, and see Part VI-B-2 Table of Bombs, Rockets, Torpedoes & Mines Dropped at Targets; *Bunker Hill* War Diary APR 1945, pp. 5-6;

16. Olds, Robert. *Helldiver Squadron*, pp. 240-1; Jacobs, Jan, and Barrett Tillman. "The Wolf Gang: A History of Carrier Air Group 84," p. 82; Evans and Nasuti. "Bunker Hill I (CV-17) 1943-1966," *DANFS*; *Bunker Hill* War Diary APR 1945, p. 6; *Bataan* Action Report. See entry for 4 April 1945, and see Part VI-B-2 Table of Bombs, Rockets, Torpedoes & Mines Dropped at Targets.

17. Nist Flight Log. See Entry for 4 April 1945; Jacobs, Jan, and Barrett Tillman. "The Wolf Gang: A History of Carrier Air Group 84," p. 82; Evans and Nasuti, "Bunker Hill I (CV-17) 1943-1966," *DANFS*; *Bunker Hill* War Diary APR 1945, p. 6.

Chapter 9

1. Jones and Kelley. *Admiral Arleigh (31-Knot) Burke*, pp. 192-5; Sherman, Rear Admiral Frederick C. Sherman. *Combat Command*, pp. 306-7; Olds, Robert. *Helldiver Squadron*, pp. 241-3; Evans and Nasuti. "Bunker Hill I (CV-17) 1943-1966," *DANFS*; DeChant, John. "Devil Birds: With the Fast Carrier Task Forces," pp. 36-45; Morison. *Victory in the Pacific*, pp. 199-209; *Bunker Hill* War Diary APR 1945, p. 10; Popp, *The Survival of a WWII Navy Fighter Pilot*, pp. 178-9; TG 58.3 Action Report MAR-JUN 1945. See Part III, Paragraphs 38-49; *Bataan* Action Report. See entry for 7 April 1945, and see Part VI-B-2 Table of Bombs, Rockets, Torpedoes & Mines Dropped at Targets; *Essex* Action Report Okinawa. See Part III—Chronological Account of Action, p. 21; Part III—Table 2.a Table of Bombs and Rockets Dropped at Target, p. 19.

2. Jacobs, Jan, and Barrett Tillman. "The Wolf Gang: A History of Carrier Air Group 84," p. 83; Evans and Nasuti, "Bunker Hill I (CV-17) 1943-1966," DANFS; DeChant, John. "Devil Birds: With the Fast Carrier Task Forces," pp. 36-45; See Chapter 12 of Morison's *Victory in the Pacific*; Rielly. *Kamikazes, Corsairs, and Picket Ships*, p. 124; *Bunker Hill* War Diary APR 1945, pp. 8-10; TG 58.3 Action Report MAR-JUN 1945. See Part III, Paragraph 74; *Hancock* Action Report, p. 32.

3. Jacobs, Jan, and Barrett Tillman. "The Wolf Gang: A History of Carrier Air Group 84," p. 83; DeChant, John. "Devil Birds: With the Fast Carrier Task Forces," pp. 36-45; See Chapter 14 of Morison's *Victory in the Pacific*; *Bunker Hill* War Diary APR 1945, p. 16; Popp. *The Survival of a WWII Navy Fighter Pilot*, p. 184; TG 58.3 Action Report MAR-JUN 1945. See Part II, page 2.

4. Jacobs, Jan, and Barrett Tillman. "The Wolf Gang: A History of Carrier Air Group 84," p. 84; *Bunker Hill* War Diary APR 1945, p. 30; TG 58.3 Action Report MAR-JUN 1945. See Part II, page 2.

5. Jacobs, Jan, and Barrett Tillman. "The Wolf Gang: A History of Carrier Air Group 84," p. 84; *Bunker Hill* War Diary APR 1945, pp. 19-20, 21; U.S. Navy. USS *Bunker Hill* (CV-17). War Diary. May 1945. RG38, NARA. Archives II, p. 3 [hereafter cited as "*Bunker Hill* War Diary MAY 1945"].

6. Popp. *The Survival of a WWII Navy Fighter Pilot*, p. 185.

7. Jacobs, Jan, and Barrett Tillman. "The Wolf Gang: A History of Carrier Air Group 84," p. 84; Evans and Nasuti. "Bunker Hill I (CV-17) 1943-1966," *DANFS*; DeChant, John. "Devil Birds: With the Fast Carrier Task Forces," pp. 36-45; Rielly. *Kamikazes, Corsairs, and Picket Ships*, pp. 248-9; *Bunker Hill* War Diary MAY 1945, p. 10.

8. Jacobs, Jan, and Barrett Tillman. "The Wolf Gang: A History of Carrier Air Group 84," p. 84; Evans and Nasuti. "Bunker Hill I (CV-17) 1943-1966," *DANFS*; Morison, *Victory in the Pacific*, pp. 262-4.

9. Jones and Kelley. *Admiral Arleigh (31-Knot) Burke,* p. 195; Olds, Robert. *Helldiver Squadron,* pp. 243–55; Jacobs, Jan, and Barrett Tillman. "The Wolf Gang: A History of Carrier Air Group 84," p. 84; Evans and Nasuti. "Bunker Hill I (CV-17) 1943–1966," *DANFS*; Morison. *Victory in the Pacific,* pp. 262–4; *Bunker Hill* War Diary MAY 1945, pp. 11–12.

10. Jacobs, Jan, and Barrett Tillman. "The Wolf Gang: A History of Carrier Air Group 84," p. 84; Evans and Nasuti. "Bunker Hill I (CV-17) 1943-1966," *DANFS*; Popp. *The Survival of a WWII Navy Fighter Pilot,* p. 189.

11. Jones and Kelley. *Admiral Arleigh (31-Knot) Burke,* p. 195; Olds, Robert. *Helldiver Squadron,* pp. 243–55; Jacobs, Jan, and Barrett Tillman. "The Wolf Gang: A History of Carrier Air Group 84," p. 84; Rielly. *Kamikazes, Corsairs, and Picket Ships,* pp. 249–51.

12. Jacobs, Jan, and Barrett Tillman. "The Wolf Gang: A History of Carrier Air Group 84," p. 84; Evans and Nasuti. "Bunker Hill I (CV-17) 1943-1966," *DANFS*; Morison. *Victory in the Pacific,* pp. 262–4; *Bunker Hill* War Diary MAY 1945, pp. 11-13.

13. Jones and Kelley. *Admiral Arleigh (31-Knot) Burke,* p. 195; Olds, Robert. *Helldiver Squadron,* pp. 243–55; Jacobs, Jan, and Barrett Tillman. "The Wolf Gang: A History of Carrier Air Group 84," p. 84; Evans and Nasuti. "Bunker Hill I (CV-17) 1943-1966," *DANFS*; DeChant, John. "Devil Birds: With the Fast Carrier Task Forces," pp. 36–45; Morison. *Victory in the Pacific,* pp. 262–4; *Bunker Hill* War Diary MAY 1945, pp. 11–13.

14. Popp. *The Survival of a WWII Navy Fighter Pilot,* p. 168.

15. Popp. *The Survival of a WWII Navy Fighter Pilot,* p. 191.

16. Jones and Kelley. *Admiral Arleigh (31-Knot) Burke,* p. 195; Evans and Nasuti. "Bunker Hill I (CV-17) 1943-1966," *DANFS*; Morison. *Victory in the Pacific,* pp. 262–4.

17. Nasuti, Gary. "A Ceremony for the Fallen: Aftermath of a Kamikaze Attack." U.S. Naval History and Heritage Command. April 2020. Accessed online on 24 June 2021 at www.history.navy.mil/browse-by-topic/wars-conflicts-and-operations/world-war-ii/1945/battle-of-okinawa/ceremony-for-fallen.html.

18. Nasuti, Gary. "A Ceremony for the Fallen: Aftermath of a Kamikaze Attack."

19. Popp. *The Survival of a WWII Navy Fighter Pilot,* p. 192; Nasuti, Gary. "A Ceremony for the Fallen: Aftermath of a Kamikaze Attack."

20. Evans and Nasuti. "Bunker Hill I (CV-17) 1943-1966," *DANFS*; *Bunker Hill* War Diary MAY 1945, pp. 13-18; U.S. Navy. USS *Bunker Hill* (CV-17). War Diary. June 1945. RG38, NARA. Archives II, pp. 1–2; U.S. Navy. USS *Bunker Hill* (CV-17). War Diary. July 1945. RG38, NARA. Archives II, p. 1; U.S. Navy. USS *Bunker Hill* (CV-17). War Diary. August 1945. RG38, NARA. Archives II, pp. 1

21. Sherman, Rear Admiral Frederick C. *Combat Command,* p. 309; Morison. *Victory in the Pacific,* p. 282.

22. Evans and Nasuti. "Bunker Hill I (CV-17) 1943-1966," *DANFS*.

23. Jacobs, Jan, and Barrett Tillman. "The Wolf Gang: A History of Carrier Air Group 84," p. 87.

24. Jacobs, Jan, and Barrett Tillman. "The Wolf Gang: A History of Carrier Air Group 84," p. 87.

25. Jacobs, Jan, and Barrett Tillman. "The Wolf Gang: A History of Carrier Air Group 84," p. 87.

Chapter 10

1. Ethel Nist. Letter to LT(jg) James A. Nist, USNR. 17 April 1945.

2. Ethel Nist. Letter to LT(jg) James A. Nist, USNR. 23 April 1945.

3. Ethel Nist. Letter to LT(jg) James A. Nist, USNR. 25 April 1945.

4. *Ibid.* Author's Note: These three letters were returned unopened to Ethel Nist in late June 1945. These letters remained sealed and unopened for 76 years until the author opened them while writing this chapter.

5. Miss Alice Richards. Letter to Ethel Nist. 23 April 1945.

6. *Ibid.*

7. *Ibid.*

8. U.S. Navy. Bureau of Naval Personnel. Chief of Naval Personnel. Vice Admiral Randall Jacobs, USN. Telegram (Western Union) to Mr. and Mrs. Martin Nist, RD#1 Box 435 Lakewood NJ. April 26, 1945. Nist Papers.

9. Alice M. Richards. Letter to Martin and Ethel Nist. 28 April 1945 [hereafter cited as "Alice Letter. 28 April 1945"].

10. Alice Letter. 28 April 1945.

11. Alice Letter. 28 April 1945.

12. Alice Letter. 28 April 1945.

13. U.S. Navy. Bureau of Personnel. Casualty Notification and Processing Section. LT W.J. McNichol, Jr., Assistant Officer in Charge. Letter to Mr. and Mrs. Martin Nist. 30 April 1945. Nist Papers.

14. Alice M. Richards. Letter to Ethel Nist. 9 May 1945 [hereafter cited as "Alice Letter. 9 May 1945"].

15. Alice Letter. 9 May 1945.

16. Alice Letter. 9 May 1945.

17. Alice Letter. 9 May 1945.

18. Alice M. Richards. Letter to Ethel Nist. 9 June 1945.

19. U.S. Navy. Third Naval District. Headquarters, Commandant. District Chaplain's Office. CDR John F. Hagen, CHC, USN. Letter to Martin Nist. 15 May 1945. Nist Papers.

20. U.S. Navy Deputy Chief of Naval Operations (Air). Vice Admiral Aubrey W. Fitch, USN. Letter to Martin Nist. 22 May 1945. Nist Papers.

21. Alice M. Richards. Letter to Martin and Ethel Nist. 24 June 1945.

22. W.J. McNicol, Jr. Lieutenant, USNR. Acting

Officer in Charge. Casualty Section. Bureau of Naval Personnel. Navy Department. Letter to Mr. and Mrs. Martin Nist. 16 July 1945. Nist Papers; George A. Seitz. Captain, USN. Commanding Officer. USS *Bunker Hill* (CV-17). Fast Carrier Task Force. Fifth U.S. Fleet. U.S. Pacific Fleet. U.S. Navy. Letter to Mr. and Mrs. Nist. 9 April 1945. Nist Papers.

23. *Ibid.*
24. *Ibid.*
25. *Ibid.*
26. Martha Deckard. Letter to Martin and Ethel Nist. 12 July 1945.
27. Thomas J. Mullins, Lieutenant, CHC, USN. Chaplain. U.S. Naval Auxiliary Air Station. Los Alamitos, California. Letter to Mrs. Martin Nist. 21 August 1945. Nist Papers. Chaplain Mullins was a Roman Catholic priest and a January 1943 graduate of the Navy Chaplain School. Author's Note: I do not know if LT(jg) Popp ever contacted his roommate's parents. I did not find any correspondence from Popp included in my great-uncle's papers and personal effects.
28. Alice M. Richards. Letter to Ethel Nist. 29 September 1945 [hereafter cited as "Alice Letter. 29 September 1945"].
29. Alice Letter. 29 September 1945.
30. Alice Letter. 29 September 1945.
31. H.L. Meadow. Captain. USN. Commanding Officer. USS *Bunker Hill* (CV-17). Letter to Mrs. Martin Nist. 28 October 1945. Nist Papers.
32. *Ibid.*
33. *Ibid.*
34. Alice M. Richards. Letter to Ethel Nist. 10 December 1945 [hereafter cited as "Alice Letter. 10 December 1945"].
35. Alice Letter. 10 December 1945. Author's Note: Jimmy's flight log records that he flew a photo mission over Kyushu on 29 March and a photo mission over Okinawa on 1 April. The chaplain was probably referring to one of these missions.
36. Alice Letter. 10 December 1945.
37. Alice Letter. 10 December 1945.
38. Olds, Robert. *Helldiver Squadron*, pp. 240-1.
39. LT(jg) Alfred Messer, USNR. Letter to Martin and Ethel Nist. 24 January 1946.
40. LT(jg) Alfred Messer, USNR. Letter to Martin and Ethel Nist. 24 January 1946.
41. James Forrestal. Secretary of the Navy. Letter to Mr. and Mrs. Martin Nist. 12 April 1946. Nist Papers.
42. *Ibid.*
43. Author's Note: My grandmother (Jimmy's older sister) told me about the circumstances of the recovery of his body; In his memoirs, *Flights of Passage,* Samuel Hynes recounted the death and burial of Second LT Baird and his crew of VMTB-232. See pages 259-260; U.S. Marine Corps. Marine Torpedo Bombing Squadron Two Hundred Thirty-Two. War Diary. 7/1/1945 to 7/31/1945. RG38, NARA, Archives II; U.S. Navy Department. Bureau of Personnel. Casualty Section. H. B. Atkinson, Commander, USNR. Officer in Charge. Letter to Mr. & Mrs. Martin Nist. 10 June 1946. Nist Papers.

44. Alice M. Richards. Letter to Ethel Nist. 4 June 1946.
45. U.S. Navy. Bureau of Personnel. Casualty Section. H.B. Atkinson, Commander, USNR. Officer in Charge. Letter to Mr. & Mrs. Martin Nist. 10 June 1946. Nist Papers.
46. Alice M. Richards. Letter to Ethel Nist. 18 August 1946.
47. *The Scarlett Letter 1947.* Memorial 73rd Edition. (Privately published for the Scarlett Letter Council by Conway Printing Company of NY in 1947.) See page 35; Robert C. Clothier. President. Rutgers University. Letter to Mr. and Mrs. Martin Nist. July 25, 1947. Nist Papers.
48. Western Union. Telegram. From U.S. Army Quartermaster Corps to Martin Nist. 16 February 1949. Nist Papers.
49. The details of the funeral service were provided by newspaper clippings saved by Ethel Nist. She did not record the names of the newspapers nor the issue dates; City of New York, New York. Office of the Mayor. William O'Dwyer, Mayor. Letter to Martin Nist. 15 March 1949. Nist Papers; Western Union. Telegram. From Colonel G.H. Bare, U.S. Army Quartermaster Corps. 23 March 1949. Nist Papers.
50. Township of Lakewood, New Jersey. Township Committee. Edward K. Burdge, Chairman. Proclamation in Honor of LT(jg) James A. Nist. Nist Papers.
51. "Lt. J. A. Nist Buried With Full Military Rites Here." *Lakewood Daily Times* (1 April 1949). Nist Papers.

Chapter 11

1. Township of Howell, New Jersey. Township Committee. Memoriam Certificate for James Nist. Undated. Nist Papers.
2. "Military Intelligence." *Rutgers Alumni Monthly* (June 1946), pp. 14-15; *The Scarlett Letter 1947.* See page 35; Robert C. Clothier. President. Rutgers University. Letter to Mr. and Mrs. Martin Nist. July 25, 1947. Nist Papers.
3. Louis Denfeld. Vice Admiral, USN. Chief of Naval Personnel. Bureau of Naval Personnel. Navy Department. Letter to Mr. and Mrs. Martin Nist. 8 May 1946. Nist Papers; Vice Admiral Marc A. Mitscher, USN. Commander First Carrier Task Force, Pacific. United States Pacific Fleet. U.S. Navy. Citation for Distinguished Flying Cross for LT(jg) James Arthur Nist, USNR. Nist Papers; Vice Admiral Marc A. Mitscher, USN. Commander First Carrier Task Force, Pacific. United States Pacific Fleet. U.S. Navy. Citation for Air Medal for LT(jg) James Arthur Nist, USNR. Nist Papers.
4. Purple Heart. Citation. Awarded to LT(jg) James A. Nist, USNR. 11 June 1946 Nist Papers;

L.C. Thompson. Lieutenant Commander, USNR. Medals and Awards Section. Bureau of Naval Personnel. Navy Department. Letter to Mr. and Mrs. Martin Nist. 11 June 1946. Nist Papers.

5. J.L. Kauffman, Vice Admiral, USN. Commandant, Fourth Naval District. U.S. Naval Base Philadelphia, Pennsylvania. U.S. Navy. Letter to Mr. Martin Nist. 11 October 1946. Nist Papers; U.S. Navy. Secretary of the Navy. James Forrestal. Citation for Gold Star in Lieu of the Second Air Medal for Lieutenant Junior Grade James Arthur Nist, USNR. Nist Papers.

6. Assistant to Director. Medals and Awards. Bureau of Naval Personnel. Navy Department. Letter to Mr. Martin Nist. 17 January 1947. Nist Papers. The letter's signatory's name was illegible. The Presidential Executive Orders were attached.

7. W.C. Thomas, Captain, USN (Ret.). Director, Medals & Awards. Bureau of Naval Personnel. Navy Department. Letter to Mr. Martin Nist. 4 November 1947. Nist Papers; U.S. Navy. Secretary of the Navy. James Forrestal. Citation for the Air Medal for Lieutenant Junior Grade James Arthur Nist, USNR. Nist Papers.

8. K. Steen, Lieutenant Commander, USN. Assistant Director, Medals & Awards. Bureau of Naval Personnel. Navy Department. Letter to Mr. Martin Nist. 9 January 1946. Nist Papers; U.S. Navy. Secretary of the Navy. John L. Sullivan. Citation for Distinguished Flying Cross for Lieutenant Junior Grade James Arthur Nist, USNR. Nist Papers. There is a typo in the original citation in which the word "plant" was spelled as "plane." I have corrected it above.

9. Christopher J. Kersting, Lieutenant Commander, USN. Director, Medals and Awards. Bureau of Naval Personnel. Department of the Navy. Letter to Mr. Martin Nist. 11 January 1951. Nist Papers. The letter included a facsimile copy of the PUC citation; U.S. Navy. Secretary of the Navy. James Forrestal. Presidential Unit Citation. Awarded to U.S.S. Bunker Hill and her attached Air Groups. Nist Papers.

10. Thomas A. Kindre. "Memorial Day Reopens the Corridors of Memory." *Asbury Park Press* (May 30, 1993), p. C3.

Chapter 12

1. U.S. Navy. USS *Bataan* (CVL-29). Carrier Light Air Group 47. Fighting Squadron 47. Aircraft Action Report Number 36. 4 April 1945. RG38, NARA, Archives II [hereafter cited as "VF-47 Action Report 36"]. Also found online on www.fold3.com; U.S. Navy. USS *Bunker Hill* (CV-17). Air Group Eighty-Four. Fighting Squadron Eighty-Four. Aircraft Action Report Number 36. 4 April 1945. RG38, NARA, Archives II [hereafter cited as "VF-84 Action Report 36"].

2. VF-84 Action Report 36.

3. VF-47 Action Report 36.

4. VF-47 Action Report 36; USS *Bataan* (CVL-29). Operations Report for Period 14 March 1945 to 22 May 1945. 29 May 1945. RG38. Archives II. NARA. See page 16; *Bunker Hill* War Diary for April 1945. See entry for 4 April 1945; VF-84 Action Report No. 36.

5. VF-84 Action Report No. 36.

6. VF-84 Action Report No. 36.

7. VF-47 Action Report No. 36.

8. VF-84 Action Report No. 36.

9. VF-84 Action Report No. 36; *Bunker Hill* War Diary for April 1945.

10. VF-84 Action Report No. 36; *Bunker Hill* War Diary for April 1945.

11. *Bunker Hill* War Diary for April 1945. See entry for 4 April 1945.

12. Olds, Robert. *Helldiver Squadron*, pp. 240–1; Jacobs, Jan, and Barrett Tillman. "The Wolf Gang: A History of Carrier Air Group 84," p. 82; Evans and Nasuti. "Bunker Hill I (CV-17) 1943–1966," *DANFS*; *Bunker Hill* War Diary APR 1945, p. 6; USS *Bataan*. Operations Report for Period 14 March 1945 to 22 May 1945. See entry for 4 April 1945, and see Part VI-B-2 Table of Bombs, Rockets, Torpedoes & Mines Dropped at Targets; *Bunker Hill* War Diary for April 1945. See entry for 4 April 1945.

13. USS *Bataan*. Operations Report for Period 14 March 1945 to 22 May 1945. See page 16.

14. VF-47 Action Report No. 36.

15. VF-47 Action Report No. 36.

Bibliography

Family Records

Dickerson, Kathryn Louise Nist. "The Story of My Life." Unpublished memoirs written in 2007.

James Arthur Nist Personal Papers

These documents are in the personal possession of the author. They were originally compiled by James Nist and his mother, Ethel, and passed down to his sister Kathryn. Prior to her death, Kathryn passed them down to her grandson (the author).

All Saints Episcopal Church. Lakewood, New Jersey. Certificate for Sacrament of Confirmation for James A. Nist. 9 May 1938.

Assistant to Director. Medals and Awards. Bureau of Naval Personnel. Navy Department. Letter to Mr. Martin Nist. 17 January 1947.

Carlin, T.F. Commanding Officer. Carrier Aircraft Service Unit Five. Fleet Air, West Coast. U.S. Naval Air Force. United States Pacific Fleet. Naval Air Station San Diego, California. To: Ensign James A. Nist. Subj: Change of Duty. 27 January 1944.

Chief of Naval Air Operational Training. Naval Air Station Jacksonville, Florida. To: Ensign James A. Nist. Subject: Change of Duty. 13 December 1943.

City of New York, New York. Office of the Mayor. William O'Dwyer, Mayor. Letter to Martin Nist. 15 March 1949.

Cleaves, Willis. E. Captain. USN. Commanding Officer. Naval Air Station Daytona Beach, Florida. 27 December 1943. To: Ensign James A. Nist Subject: Change of Duty.

Clothier, Robert C. President. Rutgers University. Letter to Mr. and Mrs. Martin Nist. 25 July 1947.

Denfeld, Louis. Vice Admiral, USN. Chief of Naval Personnel. Bureau of Naval Personnel. Navy Department. Letter to Mr. and Mrs. Martin Nist. 8 May 1946.

Farmingdale Grammar School. Farmingdale, New Jersey. Annual Commencement. 14 June 1934.

Felt, H.D. Captain, USN. Commanding Officer. Naval Air Station Miami, Florida. To Ensign James A. Nist, A-V(N), U.S.N.R. Subject: Change of Duty. 22 October 1943.

Forrestal, James. Secretary of the Navy. Citation for the Air Medal for Lieutenant Junior Grade James Arthur Nist, USNR.

———. Citation for Gold Star in Lieu of the Second Air Medal for Lieutenant Junior Grade James Arthur Nist, USNR.

———. Letter to Mr. and Mrs. Martin Nist. 12 April 1946.

———. Presidential Unit Citation. Awarded to U.S.S. Bunker Hill and her attached air groups.

Hackett, Jack. "Sachsel '44, Wrestling Champion, Loses Life Training with Navy." *Daily Targum.* March 12, 1943.

Harper, Thomas B. County Superintendent. Department of Public Instruction. County of Monmouth, New Jersey. Letter to James A. Nist. 2 August 1938.

Harrill, William K. Rear Admiral, USN. Commanding Officer. Fleet Air, West Coast. U.S. Naval Air Force. United States Pacific Fleet. Naval Air Station San Diego, California. To: Ensign James A. Nist Subj: Change of Duty. 27 January 1944.

———. To: Ensign James A. Nist Subj: Change of Duty. 10 February 1944.

Hedrick, Roger. Lieutenant Commander, USN. Commander, Navy Fighting Squadron Eighty-Four. Fleet Air, West Coast. U.S. Naval Air Forces. U.S. Pacific Fleet. To: Ensign James A. Nist Subj: Change of Duty. 13 May 1944. Fourth Endorsement on CO VB303 P16-4/00.

Jacobs, Randall. Rear Admiral, USN. Chief of Naval Personnel. Bureau of Naval Personnel. Department of the Navy. Washington, D.C. To Ensign James A. Nist, A-V(N) USNR. Subject: Orders to Active Duty. 28 August 1943.

Kauffman, J.L. Vice Admiral, USN. Commandant, Fourth Naval District. U.S. Naval Base Philadelphia, Pennsylvania. U.S. Navy. Letter to Mr. Martin Nist. 11 October 1946.

Kersting, Christopher J. Lieutenant Commander, USN. Director, Medals and Awards. Bureau of Naval Personnel. Department of the Navy. Letter to Mr. Martin Nist. 11 January 1951.

Kindre, Thomas A. "Memorial Day reopens The Corridors of Memory." *Asbury Park Press.* (May 30, 1993), p.C3.

Lakewood High School. Lakewood, New Jersey. Commencement Class of 1938. 17 June 1938. Program.

_____. School Record for James A. Nist.

_____. *The Pine Needle 1938*. Privately published by Lakewood High School in June 1938.

"Lt. J.A. Nist Buried With Full Military Rites Here." *Lakewood Daily Times*. 1 April 1949.

Marvin, Dr. Walter T. Dean. College of Arts and Sciences. Rutgers University. Letter to Mr. Martin Nist. 23 February 1939.

Mason, C.P. Rear Admiral, USN. Commandant. Naval Air Training Center, Naval Air Station Corpus Christi, Texas. To Aviation Cadet James A. Nist, V-5, U.S.N.R. Subject: Appointment as Ensign in the United States Naval Reserve. 25 September 1943.

_____. To Ensign James A. Nist, A-V(N), U.S.N.R. Subject: Change of Duty. 25 September 1943.

_____. To Ensign James A. Nist, A-V(N), U.S.N.R. Subject: Naval Aviator Designation. 25 September 1943.

_____. To Ensign James A. Nist, A-V(N), U.S.N.R. Subject: Orders to Active Duty. 25 September 1943.

McCarthy, John R. Lieutenant Commander, USN. Commander. Bombing Squadron Three Hundred Three. U.S. Naval Air Forces. United States Pacific Fleet. To: Ensign James A. Nist Subj: Change of Duty. 15 March 1944.

_____. To: Ensign James A. Nist Subj: Change of Duty. 4 May 1944. CO VB303 Orders P16–4/00.

Meadow, H.L. Captain. USN. Commanding Officer. *USS Bunker Hill* (CV-17). Letter to Mrs. Martin Nist. 28 October 1945.

Messer, Alfred. LT(jg) USNR. Letter to Martin and Ethel Nist. 24 January 1946. Middle Atlantic Collegiate Wrestling Association. Sixth Annual Championship Meet. 7–8 March 1941. Memorial Gymnasium, Lafayette College, Easton, Pennsylvania. Official Program.

_____. Seventh Annual Championship Meet. 6–7 March 1941. Gettysburg College, Gettysburg, Pennsylvania. Official Program.

"Military Intelligence." *Rutgers Alumni Monthly*. (June 1946), pp.14–15.

Mitscher, Marc A. Vice Admiral, USN. Commander First Carrier Task Force, Pacific. United States Pacific Fleet. U.S. Navy. Citation for Air Medal for LT(jg) James Arthur Nist, USNR.

_____. Citation for Distinguished Flying Cross for LT(jg) James Arthur Nist, USNR.

Mullins, Thomas J. Lieutenant, CHC, USN. Chaplain. U.S. Naval Auxiliary Air Station. Los Alamitos, California. Letter to Mrs. Martin Nist. 21 August 1945.

Nist, James A. Ensign, USNR. Statement of Travel. 25 September 1943.

Nist, James A. Letters to His Parents—Martin and Ethel Nist. 7 January 1943 to April 1945.

Nist, James A. Letters to His Sister—Mrs. Roscoe Estelle, Jr. January to December 1944.

Nist, James A. Scrapbook. Undated.

Prout, Charles. Ed. *The Scarlett Letter 1941*. Privately published for the Scarlett Letter Council by Haddon Craftsmen of Camden, NJ, in 1941.

Purple Heart. Citation. Awarded to LT(jg) James A. Nist, USNR. 11 June 1946.

"Richard Rudolph Sachsel." *Rutgers Alumni Monthly*. (October 1945), p.32.

Richards, Alice. Letters to Mr. and Mrs. Martin Nist. January to December 1946.

"Rutgers and Montclair Matmen in Deadlock." *The Sunday Times* (New Brunswick, NJ). 15 December 1940, p.1+.

Rutgers University. New Brunswick, New Jersey. 176th Anniversary Baccalaureate Service. 3 May 1942. Program.

_____. 176th Anniversary Commencement. 10 May 1942. Program.

_____. Transcript for James Arthur Nist. Copy provided to the author by the Office of the Registrar, Rutgers University, on 21 December 2017.

Rutgers University. New Brunswick, New Jersey. Department of Physical Education. Certificate. Wrestling 1938–1939. Awarded to James A. Nist.

Seitz, George A. Captain, USN. Commanding Officer. *USS Bunker Hill* (CV-17). Fast Carrier Task Force. Fifth U.S. Fleet. U.S. Pacific Fleet. U.S. Navy. Letter to Mr. and Mrs. Nist. 9 April 1945.

Sherman, Frederick C. Rear Admiral, USN. Commanding Officer. Fleet Air, West Coast. U.S. Naval Air Forces. United States Pacific Fleet. Naval Air Station San Diego, California. To: Ensign James A. Nist Subj: Change of Duty. 13 May 1944. Third Endorsement on CO VB303 Orders P16-4/00.

Steen, K. Lieutenant Commander, USN. Assistant Director, Medals & Awards. Bureau of Naval Personnel. Navy Department. Letter to Mr. Martin Nist. 9 January 1946.

Sullivan, John L. Secretary of the Navy. Citation for Distinguished Flying Cross for Lieutenant Junior Grade James Arthur Nist, USNR.

Sunderman, J.T. Lieutenant Commander, USN. Commanding Officer. Carrier Aircraft Service Unit Six. U.S. Naval Air Forces. United States Pacific Fleet. To: Ensign James A. Nist. Subj: Change of Duty. 12 February 1944.

_____. To: Ensign James A. Nist Subj: Change of Duty. 4 May 1944. *The Scarlett Letter 1940*. Camden, NJ: Privately published for the Scarlett Letter Council by The Haddon Craftsmen, 1940.

The Scarlett Letter 1942. Garden City, NY: Privately published for the Scarlett Letter Council by Country Life Press, 1942.

The Scarlett Letter 1947. Memorial 73rd Edition. Privately published for the Scarlett Letter Council by Conway Printing Company of NY in 1947.

Thomas, W.C. Captain, USN (Ret.). Director, Medals & Awards. Bureau of Naval Personnel. Navy Department. Letter to Mr. Martin Nist. 4 November 1947.

Thompson, L.C. Lieutenant Commander, USNR. Medals and Awards Section. Bureau of Naval Personnel. Navy Department. Letter to Mr. and Mrs. Martin Nist. 11 June 1946.

Township of Howell, New Jersey. Township

Committee. Memoriam Certificate for James Nist. Undated.

Township of Lakewood, New Jersey. Township Committee. Edward K. Burdge, Chairman. Proclamation in Honor of LT(jg) James A. Nist. Undated.

U.S. Department of Commerce. Civil Aeronautics Administration. Form ACA-551(CPT41) Student Pilot Rating Book. James Arthur Nist. Certificate #5214709.

U.S. Navy. Aviator's Flight Logbook. Nist, J.A.

U.S. Navy. Bureau of Personnel. Casualty Section. H.B. Atkinson, Commander, USNR. Officer in Charge. Letter to Mr. & Mrs. Martin Nist. 10 June 1946.

U.S. Navy. Bureau of Personnel. Casualty Notification and Processing Section. LT W.J. McNichol, Jr. Assistant Officer in Charge. Letter to Mr. and Mrs. Martin Nist. 30 April 1945.

_____. LT W.J. McNichol, Jr. Assistant Officer in Charge. Letter to Mr. and Mrs. Martin Nist. 16 July 1945.

U.S. Navy. Bureau of Naval Personnel. Chief of Naval Personnel. Vice Admiral Randall Jacobs, USN. Telegram (Western Union) to Mr. and Mrs. Martin Nist, RD#1 Box 435 Lakewood, NJ. 26 April 1945.

U.S. Navy. Bureau of Naval Personnel. Record of Service. Lieutenant (Junior Grade) James A. Nist (A1)L, United States Naval Reserve, Active, Deceased. 10 May 1946.

U.S. Navy Deputy Chief of Naval Operations (Air). Vice Admiral Aubrey W. Fitch, USN. Letter to Martin Nist. 22 May 1945.

U.S. Navy. "Preliminary Application for Flight Training in the U.S. Naval Reserve and Marine Corps Reserve." James A. Nist. 2 September 1942.

U.S. Navy. Third Naval District. Headquarters, Commandant. District Chaplain's Office. CDR John F. Hagen, CHC, USN. Letter to Martin Nist. 15 May 1945.

U.S. Navy. United States Pacific Fleet. Commander Fleet Air Alameda. Naval Air Station Alameda, California. To: Ensign James A. Nist. Subj: Change of Duty. 12 February 1944.

Vosseller, J.O. Commander, USN. Commanding Officer. Carrier Qualification Training Unit. Naval Air Station Glenview, Illinois. To: Ensign James A. Nist Subj: Change of Duty. 29 December 1943.

_____. To: Ensign James A. Nist Subj: Change of Duty. 4 January 1944.

Western Union. Telegram. From U.S. Army Quartermaster Corps to Martin Nist. 16 February 1949.

_____. From Colonel G.H. Bare, U.S. Army Quartermaster Corps. 23 March 1949.

Official U.S. Navy Documents

These records are maintained as part of Record Group 38 at the National Archives II, College Park, Maryland. Digital copies of many of these documents are also posted online by www.fold3.com.

United States Pacific Fleet Air Force. Air Group Eighty-Four. Bombing Squadron Eighty-Four. Aircraft Action Report No. 11. 18 March 1945.

United States Pacific Fleet Air Force. Air Group Eighty-Four. Bombing Squadron Eighty-Four. War History. Second Cruise. 14 March 1945 to 28 May 1945.

United States Pacific Fleet Air Force. Air Group Eighty-Four. Fighting Squadron Eighty-Four. Aircraft Action Report No. 11. 1 March 1945.

United States Pacific Fleet Air Force. Air Group Eighty-Four. Fighting Squadron Eighty-Four. Aircraft Action Report No. 15. 18 March 1945.

United States Pacific Fleet Air Force. Air Group Eighty-Four. Fighting Squadron Eighty-Four. Aircraft Action Report No. 19. 19 March 1945.

United States Pacific Fleet Air Force. Air Group Eighty-Four. Fighting Squadron Eighty-Four. History of Fighting Squadron Eighty-Four 1 May 1944 through 1 January 1945. LCDR Roger Hedrick, USN. 1 January 1945.

United States Pacific Fleet. Commander, Fifth Fleet. War Diary 1–28 February 1945.

United States Pacific Fleet. Fifth Fleet. Commander, First Carrier Task Force Pacific. Action Report 10 February––4 March 1945. 13 March 1945.

United States Pacific Fleet. Fifth Fleet. Commander, First Carrier Task Force Pacific. Memorandum fFor Commander Task Groups 58.1, 58.2, 58.3, 58.4, and 58.5. Subject: Recommended Procedure for VF Sweeps in Tokyo Area. 6 February 1945.

United States Pacific Fleet. Fifth Fleet. Commander, First Carrier Task Force Pacific. Memorandum. To: All Aviators. Subject: Flak Evasion. 5 February 1945.

United States Pacific Fleet. Fifth Fleet. Commander, First Carrier Task Force Pacific. Memorandum. To: Task Force FIFTY-EIGHT Pilots. Subject: Air Combat Notes for Pilots. February 1945.

United States Pacific Fleet. Fifth Fleet. First Carrier Task Force Pacific. Commander, Carrier Division Five / Task Group 58.1. Report of Operations of Task Group Fifty-Eight Point One (Fast Carrier Group One) in Support of Landings at Iwo Jima 10 February to 4 March (East Longitude Dates) including Actions against Tokyo, Chichi Jima, Okinawa and the Nansei Shoto, Second Action Against Tokyo and Operations in Direct Support of the Landings at Iwo Jima. 15 March 1945.

United States Pacific Fleet. Fifth Fleet. First Carrier Task Force Pacific. Commander, Carrier Division Two / Task Group 58.2. Action Report—Operations in Tokyo Area, Support of Landing on Iwo Jima And Strikes in Nansei Shoto. 10 February through 1 March, 1945. 12 March 1945.

United States Pacific Fleet. Fifth Fleet. First Carrier Task Force Pacific. Commander, Carrier

Division One / Task Group 58.3. Action Report 10 February—4 March 1945. 28 March 1945.

United States Pacific Fleet. Fifth Fleet. First Carrier Task Force Pacific. Commander, Carrier Division One / Task Group 58.3. / 38.3 Action Report 14 March—1 June 1945. June 1945.

United States Pacific Fleet. Fifth Fleet. First Carrier Task Force Pacific. Commander, Carrier Division One / Task Group 58.3. War Diary. 1 March 1945 to 31 March 1945.

United States Pacific Fleet. Fifth Fleet. First Carrier Task Force Pacific. Commander, Carrier Division Six / Task Group 58.4. Action Report—10 February 1945 to 1 March 1945. 1 March 1945.

United States Pacific Fleet. Naval Air Forces. Air Group Eighty-Four. ACA-1 Report, First and Second Strikes on Tokyo and Support of Capture of Iwo, 10 February to 5 March 1945. 13 March 1945.

United States Pacific Fleet. Naval Air Forces. Air Group Eighty-Four. CVG 84 Report No. 1. 16 FEB 1945.

United States Pacific Fleet. Naval Air Forces. Air Group Eighty-Four. Commander Air Group Eighty-Four. To: The Commander in Chief, U.S. Fleet. Subject: War Diary from 1 May 1944 through 30 June 1944. 1 July 1944.

United States Pacific Fleet. Naval Air Forces. Air Group Eighty-Four. Commander Air Group Eighty-Four. To: The Commander in Chief, U.S. Fleet. Subject: War Diary from 1 July 1944 through 31 July 1944. 9 August 1944.

United States Pacific Fleet. Naval Air Forces. Air Group Eighty-Four. Commander Air Group Eighty-Four. To: The Commander in Chief, U.S. Fleet. Subject: War Diary from 1 August 1944 through 31 August 1944. 9 September 1944.

United States Pacific Fleet. Naval Air Forces. Air Group Eighty-Four. Commander Air Group Eighty-Four. To: The Commander in Chief, U.S. Fleet. Subject: War Diary from 1 September 1944 through 30 September 1944. 5 October 1944.

United States Pacific Fleet. Naval Air Forces. Air Group Eighty-Four. Commander Air Group Eighty-Four. To: The Commander in Chief, U.S. Fleet. Subject: War Diary from 1 December 1944 through 31 December 1944. 11 January 1945.

United States Pacific Fleet. Naval Air Forces. Air Group Eighty-Four. Aircraft Action Report No. 8. 25 February 1945.

United States Pacific Fleet. Naval Air Forces. Air Group Eighty-Four. War History. 1944. Undated.

United States Pacific Fleet. Naval Air Forces. Air Group Eighty-Four. Bombing Squadron Eighty-Four. Aircraft Action Report No. 1. 16 February 1945.

United States Pacific Fleet. Naval Air Forces. Air Group Eighty-Four. Fighting Squadron Eighty-Four. War Diary 1 May 1944 through 30 June 1944. LCDR Roger Hedrick, USN. 1 July 1944.

United States Pacific Fleet. Naval Air Forces. Air Group Eighty-Four. Fighting Squadron Eighty-Four. War Diary 1 July 1944 through 31 July 1944. LCDR Roger Hedrick, USN. 1 August 1944.

United States Pacific Fleet. Naval Air Forces. Air Group Eighty-Four. Fighting Squadron Eighty-Four. War Diary 1 August 1944 through 31 August 1944. LCDR Roger Hedrick, USN. 1 September 1944.

United States Pacific Fleet. Naval Air Forces. Air Group Eighty-Four. Fighting Squadron Eighty-Four. War Diary 1 September 1944 through 30 September 1944. LCDR Roger Hedrick, USN. 1 October 1944.

United States Pacific Fleet. Naval Air Forces. Air Group Eighty-Four. Fighting Squadron Eighty-Four. War Diary 1 December 1944 through 31 December 1944. LCDR Roger Hedrick, USN. 1 January 1945.

United States Pacific Fleet. Naval Air Forces. Air Group Eighty-Four. Fighting Squadron Eighty-Four. History of Fighting Squadron Eighty-Four 1 January 1945 to 1 June 1945. LCDR Roger Hedrick. 1 June 1945.

United States Pacific Fleet. Naval Air Forces. Air Group Eighty-Four. Torpedo Squadron Eighty-Four. Aircraft Action Report No. 10. 18 March 1945.

United States Pacific Fleet. Naval Air Forces. Carrier Aircraft Service Unit Five (CASU-5). History of Carrier Aircraft Service Unit Five—21 July 1942 to 31 December 1944. Written by LCDR T.A. Reeves, USNR, Historian. 31 January 1945.

United States Pacific Fleet. Naval Air Forces. Carrier Aircraft Service Unit Six (CASU-6). Unit History. Written by LT Walter M. Miller, USNR, Historical Officer. 1 December 1944.

United States Pacific Fleet. Naval Air Forces. Fighting Squadron Seventeen. War Diary. 1 FEB 1944 to 29 FEB 1944.

USS *Bataan*. (CVL-29). Action Report. 14 March 1945 to 22 May 1945. 29 May 1945.

USS *Bataan* (CVL-29). Carrier Light Air Group 47. Fighting Squadron 47. Aircraft Action Report Number 36. 4 April 1945.

USS *Bunker Hill* (CV-17). Air Group 84. Fighting Squadron 84. Aircraft Action Report Number 36. 4 April 1945.

USS *Bunker Hill* (CV-17). Air Group Eighty-Four. Aircraft Action Report Number 8. 25 February 1945.

USS *Bunker Hill* (CV-17). War Diaries. January through December 1945.

USS *Cabot*. (CVL-28). Action Report. 14 March—11 April 1945. 12 April 1945.

USS *Cowpens* (CVL-25). Report of Air Operations Against Japan, Bonins and Ryukus 2/16/45 to 3/1/45. 4 March 1945.

USS *Essex* (CV-9). Action Report Operations in Support of Occupation of Iwo Jima 10 February to 4 March 1945. 12 March 1945.

USS *Essex*. (CV-9). Action Report—Support of

Occupation of Okinawa: 14 March–1 June 1945. 7 June 1945.

USS *Essex* (CV-9). War Diary. Month of February 1945.

USS *Hancock* (CV-19). Action Report. 14 March 1945 to 11 April 1945.

USS *Ranger* (CV-4). War Diaries. November 1944, December 1944, and January 1945. CAPT Arthur Gavin, commanding. 14 March 1945.

USS *Takanis Bay* (CVE-89). War Diary. 1 November to 30 November 1944. CAPT A.R. Brady, commanding.

Official U.S. Marine Corps Documents

These records are maintained as part of Record Group 127 at the National Archives II, College Park, Maryland. Digital copies of many of these documents are also posted online by www.fold3.com.

Marine Aircraft Group 42/Carrier Air Group Eighty-Four. Marine Fighting Squadron Two Twenty-One. War Diary. 19 December to 31 December 1944. Major Edwin S. Roberts, Jr., Commanding. 11 January 1945.

Marine Aircraft Group 42/Carrier Air Group Eighty-Four. Marine Fighting Squadron Four Fifty-One. War Diary. 19 December to 31 December 1944. Major H.A. Ellis, Commanding. 10 January 1945.

Marine Torpedo Bombing Squadron Two Hundred Thirty-Two. War Diary. 7/1/1945 to 7/31/1945.

Other Primary Sources

"Accounts—John McCarthy." Posted on the website of the *USS Enterprise* (CV-6) Association www.cv6.0rg/company/accounts/jmccarthy/. Accessed on 27 August 2019.

"Adm. W.E. Cleaves, Bendix Executive; Combat Leader in WWII Is Dead at 62." *New York Times*. (13 May 1962.) Accessed online on 23 October 2018 at https://www.nytimes.com/1964/05/14/archives/adm-we-cleaves-bendix-executive-combat-leader-in-world-war-ii-is.html.

"Bertram Richards." Obituary. *San Francisco Chronicle* (2 August 1976).

Blackburn, Tom, with Eric Hammel. *The Jolly Rogers: The Story of Tom Blackburn and Navy Fighting Squadron VF-17*. St Paul, MN: Zenith P, 1998.

Boyington, Gregory "Pappy," Colonel, USMC. *Baa Baa Black Sheep*. NY: Bantam Books, 1958.

DeChant, John. "Devil Birds: With the Fast Carrier Task Forces." *Marine Corps Gazette*. (September 1947), pp.36–45.

Gosson, Louis C., Thomas F. Fitzgerald, F.L. Lundy, and New Jersey Legislature. *Manual of the Legislature of New Jersey*. Trenton, NJ: E.J. Mullin 1945.

Gunnison, Herbert Foster. *A Visitor's Guide to the greater New York, Jersey City and suburbs*. Brooklyn, NY: Eagle P, 1896. Accessed online at https://archive.org/details/visitorsguidetog00gunno on 28 August 2018.

Hynes, Samuel. *Flights of Passage: Reflections of a World War II Aviator*. (Annapolis, MD: U.S. Naval Institute P, 1988.)

"Interrogation Nav No. 28 USSBS No. 112—Major Toga, Hiroshi, Imperial Japanese Army—23 October 1945." Included on pages 117–121 of U.S. Strategic Bombing Survey (Pacific). Naval Analysis Division. *Interrogation of Japanese Officials*. Washington, D.C.: GPO, 1946. Accessed online on 8 June 2020 at https://www.history.navy.mil/research/library/online-reading-room/title-list-alphabetically/i/interrogations-japanese-officials-voli.html.

Killenberger's Pocket Gazetteer of the State of New Jersey. New Brunswick, NJ: New Jersey Publishing Company, 1887. Accessed online at https://archive.org/details/fkillenbergerspo00kill on 28 August 2018.

Miller, R. Elmer, Jr. Draft Registration Card. Number 13,156. Found on www.fold3.com.

Nist, James Arthur. Draft Registration Card. Number 11,352. Found on www.fold3.com.

Popp, Wilbert P. "Beads" LCDR, USNR (Ret). *The Survival of a WWII Navy Fighter Pilot*. Privately published by Wilbert P. Popp in 2004.

Powell, Gene Scruggs. Draft Registration Card. Number 10,945. Found on www.fold3.com.

Richards, Sister Mary Victorine. Obituary. *San Francisco Chronicle*. (21 June 1976.)

"Roger R. Hedrick." Obituary. *Orange County Register*. (1 February 2006.) Accessed online on 30 August 2019 at https://obits.ocregister.com/obituaries/orangecounty/obituary.aspx?n=roger-r-hedrick&pid=16567690.

Scott, J. Davis. "Strike One!" *Marine Corps Gazette*. (October 1945), pp.43–4.

Sherman, Frederick C. Admiral, USN (Ret.). *Combat Command*. NY: Bantam Books, 1982.

Smith, Holland M., General, USMC (Ret.), and Percy Finch. *Coral and Brass*. FMFRP 12–37. Washington, D.C.: Headquarters—U.S. Marine Corps, 1989.

Sumner, Howard C. "North Atlantic Hurricanes and Tropical Disturbances of 1943." *Monthly Weather Review*. November 1943. Accessed online on 29 April 2019 at https://www.aoml.noaa.gov/general/lib/lib1/nhclib/mwreviews/1943.pdf.

Ugaki, Matome. *Fading Victory: The Diary of Admiral Matome Ugaki 1941–1945*. Trans. by Masataka Chihaya. Ed. by Donald M. Goldstein and Katherine V. Dillon. Pittsburgh, PA: U of Pittsburgh P, 1991.

U.S. Army Air Forces. Headquarters, U.S. Army Air Forces. Joint Target Group. *Air Target System Folder—Japanese Aircraft*. January 1945.

U.S. Department of Commerce. National Oceanic and Atmospheric Administration. National Ocean Service. *Distance Between United States*

Ports 2019 (13th Edition). Accessed online on 31 January 2020 at https://nauticalcharts.noaa.gov/publications/docs/distances.pdf.

U.S. Department of the Navy. Bureau of Aeronautics. "CASU: Carrier Aircraft Service Unit." *Bureau of Aeronautics News Letter.* (September 1, 1944), pp.13–21.

———. "Corpus is University of the Air." *Bureau of Aeronautics News Letter.* (June 1, 1944), pp.28–35.

———. "Jap Antiaircraft." *Naval Aviation News.* (March 1, 1945), pp.1–7.

———. "Japanese Fighter Aircraft," *Bureau of Aeronautics News Letter.* (April 15, 1943), pp.1–3.

———. "Okinawa." *Naval Aviation News.* (June 15, 1945), pp.1–7.

U.S. Department of the Navy. Deputy Chief of Naval Operations (Air). Location of Naval Aircraft. Report 12–44. 21 March 1944. Accessed online at https://www.history.navy.mil/research/histories/naval-aviation-history/involvement-by-conflict/world-war-ii/location-of-us-naval-aircraft-world-war-ii/1944/21-mar-1944.html.

———. Location of Naval Aircraft. Report 13–44. 29 March 1944. Accessed online on 8 August 2019 at https://www.history.navy.mil/research/histories/naval-aviation-history/involvement-by-conflict/world-war-ii/location-of-us-naval-aircraft-world-war-ii/1944/29-mar-1944.html.

———. Location of Naval Aircraft. Report 14–44. 4 April 1944. Accessed online on 8 August 2019 at https://www.history.navy.mil/research/histories/naval-aviation-history/involvement-by-conflict/world-war-ii/location-of-us-naval-aircraft-world-war-ii/1944/4-apr-1944.html.

U.S. Department of the Navy. Office of Public Information. *Navy Department Communiques 301–600 and Pacific Fleet Communiques March 6, 1943 to May 24, 1945.* (Washington, D.C.: GPO, June 15, 1945.) Accessed online on 2 February 2020 at www.history.navy.mil/research/library/online-reading-room/title-list-alphabetically/n/navy-depart-communiques-301-660.hmtl.

U.S. Navy. Naval Station Pearl Harbor, Oahu, Hawaii. "Pearl Harbor, Oahu, T.H. Mooring & Berthing Plan" posted on the Naval History and Heritage Command website, https://www.history.navy.mil/content/history/nhhc/research/archives/digitized-collections/action-reports/wwii-pearl-harbor-attack/pearl-harbor-mooring-and-berthing-plans.html.

U.S. Navy. United States Pacific Fleet and Pacific Ocean Areas. Headquarters, Commander in Chief. CinCPac War Diary for the period 27 January 1945–28 February 1945. 10 March 1945.

U.S. Navy. *USS Bunker Hill (CV-17). The U.S.S. Bunker Hill November 1943—November 1944: The record of a carrier's combat actions against the Axis Nations in the Pacific.* Edited by LT Wallace C. Mitchell, USNR, and LT Eugene F. Brissie, USNR. Chicago, IL: Privately published for the ship by Rogers Printing Company, 1945.

U.S. Strategic Bombing Survey. Aircraft Division. "Nakajima Aircraft Company, L.T.D.—Corporation Report No. II (Airframes and Engines)." June 1947. Record Group 243. National Archives and Records Administration. Archives II, College Park, Maryland.

Secondary Sources

Alexander, Joseph H., Colonel, USMC (Ret.). *Closing In: Marines in the Seizure of Iwo Jima.* In the Marines in World War II Commemorative Series. Washington, D.C.: History and Museums Division, Headquarters U.S. Marine Corps, 1994.

Chant, Chris. *Aircraft of World War II.* NY: Metro Books, 1999.

Condon, John Pomeroy. Major General, USMC (dec.) *Corsairs and Flattops: Marine Carrier Air Warfare 1944–1945.* Annapolis, MD: U.S. Naval Institute P, 1997.

Cressman, Robert J., and J. Michael Wenger. "This Is No Drill: U.S. Naval Aviation and Pearl Harbor, December 7, 1941." *Naval Aviation News.* (November-December 1991), pp.20–25.

Cultural Landscape Report for Naval Air Station Alameda. Prepared for Naval Facilities Engineering Command Southwest by JRP Historical Consulting LLC and PGAdesign Inc. April 2012.

Dave Leip's Atlas of U.S. Elections. Accessed online on 22 October 2019 at https://uselectionatlas.org/RESULTS/national.php?year=1944&off=0&elect=0.

Delaney, Norman C. "Corpus Christi's 'University of the Air.'" *Naval History Magazine* (June 2013). Accessed online on 16 November 2018 at https://www.usni.org/magazines/navalhistory/2013-05/corpus-christis-university-air.

Dictionary of American Naval Fighting Ships. Accessed online at https://www.history.navy.mil/research/histories/ship-histories/danfs.

Evans, Mark L., and Guy J. Nasuti. "Bunker Hill I (CV-17) 1943–1966." 25 March 2020. Naval History and Heritage Command. *Dictionary of American Naval Fighting Ships.* Accessed online on 20 April 2020 at https://www.history.navy.mil/research/histories/ship-histories/danfs/b/bunker-hill-i.html.

Francillon, Rene J. *Japanese Aircraft of the Pacific War.* (Annapolis, MD: Naval Institute Press), 1995.

Frank, Benis M., and Henry I. Shaw Jr. *Victory and Occupation: Volume V of the History of U.S. Marine Corps Operations in World War II.* Washington, D.C.: Historical Branch, G-3 Division, Headquarters, U.S. Marine Corps, 1968.

Friedman, Norman. "The Ubiquitous 5-inch/38." *Naval History Blog.* U.S. Naval Institute. November 16, 2015. Accessed online on 13 January 2020 at https://www.navalhistory.org/2015/11/16/the-ubiquitous-5-inch38.

"George M. Ottinger." USNA Virtual Memorial Hall. Accessed online on 4 September 2019 at https://usnamemorialhall.org/index.php/GEORGE_M._OTTINGER,_CDR,_USN.

Glenshaw, Paul. "The Best-Built Airplane That Ever Was." *Air & Space Magazine*. (December 2015.) Accessed online on 8 May 2019 at https://www.airspacemag.com/history-of-flight/best-airplane-that-ever-was-t6-texan-180957294/.

Goyer, Norm. "The T-6 Texan: The world's best advanced trainers and beyond." *Flying*. (August 12, 2011.) Accessed online on 8 May 2019 at https://www.flyingmag.com/aircraft/pistons/t-6-texan.

Handbook of Texas Online, Art Leatherwood, "NAVAL AIR STATION, CORPUS CHRISTI," accessed April 05, 2019 at http://www.tshaonline.org/handbook/online/articles/qbn01.

"Historical Information" posted on the Daytona Beach International Airport website. Accessed on 28 June 2019 at http://www.flydaytonafirst.com/about-dab/historical-information.stml.

"Hotel Sherman" posted on the "Jazz Age Chicago" website. Accessed online on 13 March 2019 at https://jazzagechicago.wordpress.com/hotel-sherman/.

Jacobs, Jan, and Barrett Tillman, "The Wolf Gang: A History of Carrier Air Group 84." *The Hook. (World War II Special)* (Summer 1990), pp.78–87.

Jane's Fighting Aircraft of World War II. London: Random House, 1989. Reprint of the 1945–46 edition.

John Bryan Grimes Papers. Collection Guide. East Carolina University. Accessed online on 30 November 2018 at http://digital.lib.ecu.edu/special/ead/findingaids/0054/.

"John Reginald McCarthy." Citation for Navy Cross posted on The Military Times Hall of Valor. Accessed on 27 August 2019 at https://valor.militarytimes.com/hero/21362.

Jones, Ken, and Hubert Kelly, Jr. *Admiral Arleigh (31-Knot) Burke: The Story of a Fighting Admiral.* NY: Bantam Books, 1985.

Kennedy, Maxwell Taylor. *Danger's Hour: The Story of USS* Bunker Hill *and the Kamikaze Pilot Who Crippled Her.* NY: Simon & Schuster, 2008.

LeMieux, Dave. "Lookback: 'Ike' Kepford was Muskegon's top gun during World War II." April 22, 2013. Accessed online on 7 October 2019 at https://www.mlive.com/news/muskegon/2013/04/lookback_ike_kepford_was_muske.html.

"The Link Flight Trainer: A Historic Mechanical Engineering Landmark." Privately published by the Roberson Museum and Science Center, Binghamton, NY. June 10, 2000.

Lombardi, Mike, and Erik Simonsen. "The High and the Mighty." *Boeing Frontiers*. (Dec 2009–Jan 2010), pp.54–57.

Lord, Walter. *Day of Infamy*. Sixtieth Anniversary Edition. NY: Henry Holt, 2001.

Moore, John. Captain, RN. Editor. *Jane's American Fighting Ships of the 20th Century*. NY: Mallard P, 1991.

Morison, Samuel Eliot. *Victory in the Pacific*. Volume 14 in the series *History of United States Naval Operations in World War II*. Chicago IL: U of Illinois P, 2002.

"N3N: The Original 'Yellow Peril.'" 4 September 2014. Accessed on the National Naval Aviation Museum website on 24 December 2018 at https://www.navalaviationmuseum.org/history-up-close/n3n-original-yellow-peril/nggallery/image/richard-fleming-in-n3n/.

"NAS Daytona Beach / Daytona Beach International Airport." Posted on the Museum of Florida History website and accessed on 28 June 2019 at http://www.museumoffloridahistory.com/exhibits/permanent/wwii/sites.cfm?PR_ID=79.

"NAS Miami: Opa-Locka Airport." Museum of Florida History website. Accessed online on 25 June 2019 at http://www.museumoffloridahistory.com/exhibits/permanent/wwii/sites.cfm?PR_ID=191.

Nasuti, Gary. "A Ceremony for the Fallen: Aftermath of a Kamikaze Attack." U.S. Naval History and Heritage Command. April 2020. Accessed online on 24 June 2021 at www.history.navy.mil/browse-by-topic/wars-conflicts-and-operations/world-war-ii/1945/battle-of-okinawa/ceremony-for-fallen.html.

National Archives and Records Administration. U.S. Electoral College. "Historic Election Results: Electoral Votes for President and Vice President 1941-1953." Accessed online on 22 October 2019 at https://www.archives.gov/federal-register/electoral-college/votes/1941_1953.html#1944.

Olds, Robert. *Helldiver Squadron: The Story of Carrier Bombing Squadron 17 With Task Force 58.* 2nd edition. NY: Dodd, Mead & Company, 1945.

Portz, Matt. Captain, USN (Ret.). "Aviation Training and Expansion—Part 1." *Naval Aviation News*. (July-August 1990), pp.22–27.

_____. "Aviation Training and Expansion—Part 2." *Naval Aviation News*. (September-October 1990), pp.22–27.

Quatman, G. William. *A Young General and the Fall of Richmond. The Life and Career of Godfrey Weitzel*. Athens, OH: Ohio U P, 2015.

Rems, Alan P. "Two Birds with One Hailstone." *Naval History Magazine*. (January 2014.) Accessed online on 4 February 2020 at https://www.usni.org/magazines/naval-history-magazine/2014/january/two-birds-one-hailstone.

Rielly, Robin L. *Kamikazes, Corsairs, and Picket Ships: Okinawa 1945*. Drexel Hill, PA: Casemate, 2008.

Ross, Bill D. *Iwo Jima: Legacy of Valor*. NY: Vanguard P, 1985.

Sherrod, Robert. *History of Marine Corps Aviation in World War II*. Washington, D.C.: Combat Forces P, 1952.

Strand, George, and Truman R. Strobridge. *Western Pacific Operations*. Volume IV of *History of U.S. Marine Corps Operations in World War II*. Washington, D.C.: Historical Division, Headquarters, U.S. Marine Corps, 1971.

Taylor, Theodore. *The Magnificent Mitscher*. Annapolis, MD: Bluejacket Books, 2006.

Toll, Ian W. "Rear Seat Gunners at Midway." *Naval History Magazine*. (May 2013.) Accessed online on 9 July 2019 at https://www.usni.org/magazines/naval-history-magazine/2013/may/rear-seat-gunners-midway.

U.S. Department of Commerce. National Oceanic and Atmospheric Administration. National Weather Service. Weather Prediction Center. David Roth. "Texas Hurricane History." January 17, 2010. Accessed online on 30 April 2019 at https://www.wpc.ncep.noaa.gov/research/txhur.pdf.

U.S. Department of Commerce. National Oceanic and Atmospheric Administration. Office of Oceanic and Atmospheric Research. Atlantic Oceanographic and Meteorological Laboratory. Hurricane Research Division. "Seventy-fifth Anniversary of first hurricane eye penetration." July 27, 2018. Accessed online on 30 April 2019 at https://noaahrd.wordpress.com/2018/07/27/seventy-fifth-anniversary-of-first-hurricane-eye-penetration/.

U.S. Navy. Bureau of Yards and Docks. *Building the Navy's Bases in World War II. History of the Bureau of Yards and Docks and the Civil Engineer Corps 1940–1946*. Volume 1. Washington, D.C.: GPO, 1946. Accessed online on 13 August 2019 at https://www.history.navy.mil/content/history/nhhc/research/library/online-reading-room/title-list-alphabetically/b/building-the-navys-bases.html.

U.S. Navy. Bureau of Yards and Docks. *Building the Navy's Bases in World War II: History of the Bureau of Yards and Docks and the Civil Engineer Corps 1940–1946*. Volume II of II. Washington, D.C.: GPO, 1947. Accessed online on 13 August 2019 at https://www.history.navy.mil/content/history/nhhc/research/library/online-reading-room/title-list-alphabetically/b/building-the-navys-bases.html.

U.S. Navy. Commander, Naval Installations Command. Naval Base Coronado. "Naval Air Station North Island." Accessed online on 18 September 2019 at https://www.cnic.navy.mil/regions/cnrsw/installations/navbase_coronado/about/installations/nas_north_island.html.

U.S. Navy. Naval History and Heritage Command. "Admiral Arleigh A. Burke. Fifteenth Chief of Naval Operations August 17th, 1955–August 1, 1961." Accessed online on 4 February 2020 at https://www.history.navy.mil/browse-by-topic/people/chiefs-of-naval-operations/admiral-arleigh-a—burke.html.

U.S. Navy. Naval Air Station Kingsville. NAS Kingsville Public Affairs. "NAS Kingsville—Flying for the Future for 60 Years." 6 August 2002. Accessed on 8 May 2019 online at https://www.navy.mil/submit/display.asp?story_id=2988.

"Wilbert P. Popp." *Association of Naval Aviation*. Published for the association by Turner Publishing, Paducah, Kentucky, in 2003.

Winchester, Jim. ed. *American Military Aircraft: A History of Innovation*. London: Amber Books, 2005.

Zamaites, Jonathan. "Naval Air Station Glenview." 21 October 2017. Published on the Military History of the Upper Great Lakes website and accessed online on 7 December 2018 at https://ss.sites.mtu.edu/mhugl/2017/10/21/naval-air-station-glenview/.

Index

A6M5 Zeke (Zero) 42, 51, 128–9, 134, 136, 139–40, 148, 161–2, 170, 175, 179–80
Air Group 4 124, 136, 147, 149, 159
Air Group 6 167
Air Group 83 159, 162
Air Group 84 1, 3, 78, 81, 88, 90, 93–5, 99–100, 102, 105–6, 109–10, 112, 114, 116–8, 123, 133, 135–8, 140, 142, 147–9, 156–7, 160, 162–4, 168, 170–1, 174–81, 184, 186, 190, 192, 196, 201, 206
All Saints Episcopal Church 6–7, 194
Amami Gunto 154–7, 161, 165, 167, 171, 175–7, 185, 197, 200–1, 204, 207
Amami O Shima 171, 174–6, 179, 190, 192, 196
USS *Astoria* (CL-90) 124
Attu Island 53

B5N Kate 161, 171
B-29 Superfortress 125, 127, 129, 135–6, 139, 144, 148, 158
USS *Bataan* 58, 167, 169, 170, 174–8, 200–2
Beerhard, Alva 30
USS *Birmingham* 114
Blackburn, CDR Tommy 28, 79, 82–3, 86
Bob Crosby and the Bobcats 71
Brown, 1st Lt. Forrest P., Jr. 135
USS *Bunker Hill* 79, 80, 82–3, 110–2, 114–25, 158–160, 186–93, 196–8, 204, 206; air strikes on Japan 1, 3, 129, 133–42, 148–9, 152–3, 170–1; Amami Shunto 175–7; Kikai 175–7, 200–3; Kyushu–Inland Sea Air Raids 162–4; Okinawa 156–7, 167–9, 171, 174–5; Pearl Harbor 120; sinking of *Yamato* 178; struck by kamikaze 180–4; VB-17 80, 95; VF-17 79–80, 82–3

Burdge, Rose 6
Burdge, Sam 6
Burke, COM Arleigh 115, 122–3, 129–30, 135, 151, 180–1
Burness, ENS Jack 191
Bush, George H.W. 30

USS *Cabot* 159, 160, 162–4, 167, 169, 170, 175, 178
Calloway, Cab 27
Carmichael, CDR Joseph 117, 181
Carrier Light Air Group 29 163
Carrier Light Air Group 46 124, 136, 142, 149
Carrier Light Air Group 47 167, 176–7, 200
USS *Casco* 53
CASU-5 64
CASU-6 65–6, 69, 76
Chicago, IL 22, 25–7, 30, 34
Civilian Pilot Training Program (CPTP) 11–3, 29
Cleaves, CAPT Willis E. 53
Coconougher, LT(jg) Ralph K. 95, 108, 134, 177, 192, 200–2
Cola, Steward's Mate 1st Class Norman 119, 183
Conrad, Richard 1
Coral Sea 15
USS *Cowpens* 81, 124, 133, 136–7, 139, 140, 142, 147, 149, 156, 159

D3A Val 179
Deckard, Martha 189
DeGaspar, Ed 16, 24, 30, 35
Delaney, LT Robert E. 117, 129, 188
Dewey, Thomas 98, 100
Dickerson, James R. 51–2, 57
Dickerson, Joan 24
Dickerson, Kathryn (Nist) 2, 5–6, 24, 35, 45, 51–2, 57
Dickerson, Patricia 24
Dickerson, Walter E. 35, 52
Dickerson, Walter E., Jr. 24, 35
Diteman, LT(jg) J.E. 79, 134, 165

Dixon, LT(jg) James C. 79, 134, 179
Duckworth, LtCol. Joseph B. 37
Dyson, CDR Howell J. 117

Ellis, MAJ Henry A., Jr. 106, 139
Ellsworth, LT(jg) J.O. 79
USS *Enterprise* 54, 69, 95, 124, 161, 167, 180, 182
USS *Essex* 67, 90, 114, 116–7, 124–5, 133–4, 136–7, 140, 147, 149, 156, 159, 160, 162–4, 167, 169–71, 174–5, 178
Estelle, Margaret (née Dickerson) 185
Estelle, Margaret "Wootz" 5–6, 24, 27, 67, 92, 152
Estelle, Milton, Jr. 185
Estelle, Milton, Sr. 185

F2A Brewster Buffalo 49
F4F/FM-2 Grumman Wildcat 49, 51–2, 75, 82, 94–5, 106
F4U/FG-1 Vought Corsair 1, 23, 25, 27–8, 44, 51, 75, 78, 82–9, 92–3, 98, 102, 104, 108, 110–2, 125–6, 129, 134–5, 137–8, 140, 147–9, 153, 157, 160, 164–5, 167–70, 172, 175, 177, 184, 192, 200–2, 204
F6F/F6F-5N/F6F-5P Grumman Hellcat 1, 28, 44, 51–2, 55–6, 64, 67, 75, 80, 83, 92–6, 100–2, 107–8, 110–2, 120, 124–6, 129, 133–4, 136–7, 139–40, 142, 147, 149–51, 153, 157, 159–60, 162–5, 167–70, 172, 174–7, 200–4
Farmingdale Grammar School 7
Fast Carrier Task Force *see* Task Force 58
First (1st) Louisiana Infantry Regiment (Union) 5
Fitch, VADM Aubrey 188
Forrestal, James 192, 197
USS *Franklin* 164–5, 167

246 Index

Freeman, LT Doris 79, 108, 179, 182, 184

Galveston, TX 36–7
Gerner, LT(jg) William L. 80, 95
Gildea, LT(jg) John T. 80, 108, 148–9, 165, 182, 184
Gillen, LT Earle C. 81, 108, 168
GM-4 Betty 133–4, 161–2, 166, 170, 175, 179
Greer, CAPT Marshall R. 117–8

H5Y Cherry flying boat 170–2
Halsey, ADM William F. 105, 122–3
Hamamatsu Airfield 133–4
USS *Hancock* 167, 169, 170, 174, 176, 178
Hayes, Chester 5
Hayes, Frederick 5, 142
Hayes, Jonathan 5
Hedrick, LCDR Roger 78–81, 91, 101, 108, 121, 134, 148, 168, 178–80
Helms, LT Philip C. 75, 81, 108, 157, 170
Hickey, ENS Oscar 100
Hill, LT Raymond 78–80, 108, 165, 180
Hitoyoshi Airfield 162
Hollywood, FL 43
Honshu 132, 134, 139, 165, 172, 179
USS *Hornet* (CV-8) 31, 104, 123, 127
Howell, NJ 5–7, 98, 193, 196
Hutt, LT(jg) Wilton 80, 108, 157

Ie Shima 154–5, 168, 174–5
USS *Independence* 58, 81, 124, 167
USS *Indianapolis* 124, 159
USS *Iowa* 58, 121
Iwo Jima 123–4, 129, 141, 14–8, 151, 153–5, 157–8, 173, 197–9, 204, 206

J2M2 Jack 128–9
Japanese Home Islands 1, 123, 126–7, 129, 132, 135, 139–42. 144–5, 148, 150–2, 154, 156–7, 161, 165–6, 172, 178, 198, 206
Jefferson, ENS Curtis 149
Jones, Jennifer 68
Jones-Burdich, Lt. William 37

Kaga 69
Kanoya Naval Air Base 161, 170
Kepford, LT Ira "Ike" 80, 84, 86–7, 92, 101–2
Ki-21 Sally 161

Ki-34 Oscar 128–9, 135–6, 140, 148, 161–2
Ki-44 Tojo 44, 121, 128–9, 133–8, 140, 161, 163, 175, 179
Ki-49 Helen 134, 136, 140, 161
Ki-61 Tony 121, 138, 162–2, 179
Ki-84 Frank 128–9, 135–6, 140, 148, 161, 171, 179
Kikai 161, 168, 171, 174–7, 179, 185–6, 190, 192, 197, 200–2, 207
Kikuchi Airfield 162
King, Fleet Adm. Ernest J. 92
King, CDR Shane 117
Kiyoshi, Ens. Ogawa 180
Kure Naval Base 164–5
Kuribayashi, Gen. Tadamichi 145
Kyushu 138–9, 154–5, 161–3, 165, 170–2, 176, 200, 206–7

Lakewood, NJ 5–7, 15, 105, 194, 205, 207
Lakewood High School 7, 205
Lane, ENS Kenneth 149
Laney, LT Willis G. 95, 108, 117, 129, 148, 184, 188
USS *Langley* (CV-1) 64, 104, 114
USS *Langley* (CVL-27) 183
Larsen, LT C.T. 108, 163
Lewis, LT J.L. 108
USS *Lexington* (CV-2) 114, 124
USS *Lexington* (CV-16) 67
Lindbergh, Charles A. 68
Link, Edwin 35
Link Trainer 35–6
Littlejohn, LT Ellis 179

Maberry, LT(jg) Lewis 149
Mason, RADM Charles P. 31, 39, 48
Matthews, LT(jg) H.L. 79
Mawatori Airfield 137
McCain, VADM John S. 122
McCarthy, LCDR John R. 69–70, 75
McChesney, ENS J.A. 51, 55, 61, 76, 89
McFarlane, 1stLt. Don 133
Meek, LT(jg) William P. 79, 92
Messer, Alfred 9–10, 192
Miami, FL 43, 49–52, 68, 205
Midway 15, 31, 53
Miller, Arthur C. 68
Miller, LT(jg) Elmer "Dusty" 70, 75, 80, 93, 96, 109–10, 134, 180, 182–3, 187
Miller, Lois 93–4, 187–8, 190–1, 193
Minami Daito Shima 169, 171
Mira Loma AAF 90–1, 93
Mito Airfield 139
Mitscher, VADM Marc 105,

109–11, 122–4, 127, 129, 130–2, 135, 138–9, 141, 143, 148, 150, 158, 164, 166–7, 169, 180–2, 196
Mitsubishi 42, 127–8, 134, 136, 139, 166
Miyazaki Airfield 162
Musashi Engine Plant *see* Nakajima Tama Musashimo

N3N-3 "Yellow Peril" 22–9, 32, 40–1, 45, 55, 75
NAAF Twenty-Nine Palms 98–9
NAAS Cabanniss Field 30, 32–5, 43
NAAS Chase Field 31
NAAS Cuddihy Field 30–1, 35
NAAS Kingsville Field 31, 39–42, 46–7, 49
NAAS Redd Field 31
NAAS Waldron Field 31
Nakajima Aircraft Company 127–8, 135–7, 139–40, 143
Nakajima Koizumi Assembly Plant 135–7, 141, 149–51, 157–8
Nakajima Ota Assembly Plant 135–6, 144, 149, 157
Nakajima Tama Musashimo Engine Plant 136, 139–40, 143–4, 149, 157–8
NALF Santa Rosa 72, 76
NAS Alameda 65–7, 71–2, 76–8, 110, 112, 114, 118–9, 159, 189, 191, 206
NAS Banana River 59
NAS Corpus Christi 30–2, 34–40, 43, 45–8, 51, 60, 205
NAS Daytona Beach 52–3, 59–62
NAS Glenview 21–30, 34, 50, 61–2, 67–8, 75, 205–6
NAS Jacksonville 51–2, 61
NAS Miami 43, 48–52, 205
NAS Sanford 52
Naval Station Pearl Harbor 67, 69, 81, 104, 114, 120–2, 179, 183
Navy Yard Puget Sound 112, 117, 183
New Brunswick, NJ 8–11, 13, 39, 43, 52, 54, 83
USS *New Jersey* 58, 121, 124, 156, 162, 167
New Orleans, LA 5, 49–50
Nimitz, Fleet Adm. Chester A. 153
Nist, Ethel (Hayes) 5, 8, 26, 28, 29, 43, 99, 105, 110, 178, 185, 187–90, 192–3, 196–7, 207
Nist, Jacob 5–6
Nist, LT(jg) James A.: Army ROTC 8, 16; "Blackout" 100; USS *Bunker Hill* 1, 3, 79, 110–12, 114, 116, 118–21, 123,

Index

125, 134, 137–8, 140–2, 148–9, 157–8, 160, 169–70, 174–5, 184, 186–90, 192–3, 196–198; childhood 5–8; Civilian Pilot Training Program 11–3, 15, 29; hurricanes 37, 45–7; Iwo Jima 147–8; Kikai 127, 190, 192, 200–2, 207; Kyushu airstrikes 162–3, 170, 172, 207; Lakewood High School 7; NAAF Twenty-Nine Palms 98–99; NAAS Cabaniss Field 32–5, 40, 42; NAS Alameda 65–9, 76, 112, 206; NAS Corpus Christi 30–2, 34–40, 43, 45, 47–8, 51; NAS Daytona Beach 52–3, 58–59, 61–2; NAS Glenview 22–30, 61–3, 67–8; NAS Kingsville 39–41, 46–9; NAS Miami 48–52; NAS San Diego 64–5, 78, 92, 102, 106, 112; Okinawa 155, 157, 169, 174–5; opinion on F4U Corsair 95; opinion on F6F Hellcat 56; opinion on 1944 presidential election 98, 100; opinion on President Franklin D. Roosevelt 98, 100; opinion on SBD Dauntless 53, 57, 60; opinion on SNJ 38–40, 42–4; opinion on VADM Marc Mitscher 105; opinion on Vultee Valiant 32; USS *Ranger* 102, 110; Rutgers University 8–9, 13–16, 18, 21; USS *Takanis Bay* 99–104; Tokyo airstrikes 134, 137–8, 142, 149–50, 206–7; Truman, Harry S. 98, 179, 198; UNC Chapel Hill Pre-Flight School 16–21; VB-303 66, 69–77; VF-84 75, 78–88, 90–9, 101–2, 107–112, 116, 118–9, 134, 137, 142, 147–50, 157, 159–60, 162–3, 165, 167, 170–2, 175, 177, 179, 182, 184, 188–9, 192–3, 200–3; VSB-59 52–5, 58–62; USS *Wolverine* 17, 50, 62–4, 67, 101–2; wrestling 9–11, 16, 18–20
Nist, Johann Martin 5, 49
Nist, Magdalena 5, 49
Nist, Margaretha 5–6
Nist, Margaretha (Herbst) 5–6
Nist, Martin 5, 8, 26, 28, 43, 99, 105, 110, 178, 192–3, 196, 207
Nist, Martin Frederick 5–6
Nist, Wilhelmina 5–6
USS *North Carolina* 167

O'Hair, Lt. Ralph 37
Ohka Baka flying bomb 166, 179–80
Okinawa 117, 123, 150, 152, 154–8, 161, 165–9, 171–9, 184, 193, 197–200, 202, 206–7
OS2U Kingfisher 72, 168–9
Ottinger, CDR George 81, 93, 106, 133–4, 164, 168

USS *Pasadena* 124
Paul Kimball Hospital 6
PBY Catalina 32, 34
Perrine AAF Field 46–7
Peterson, LT(jg) Abbott 117, 129
Popp, LT(jg) Wilbert 3, 79, 83–5, 91, 119–22, 133, 140, 147–9, 160, 164, 168, 178–80, 182, 189, 190
Powell, LT(jg) Gene 70, 75, 80, 96, 108, 182–3

USS *Randolph* 120, 159, 160, 182
USS *Ranger* 81, 101–3, 106, 109, 110, 114
Reagan, Ronald 57
Rempel, LT(jg) Williard 149
Richards, Alice 61, 76–7, 89–92, 97, 99, 104, 108–10, 112–3, 123, 143, 152, 159–60, 167, 169, 178, 186–8, 190–1, 193, 204
RO-61 53
Roberts, Maj. Edwin S., Jr. 106, 133
Roberts, LT(jg) G.E. 108, 163
Roosevelt, Franklin D. 98, 100, 179, 185, 197
Rutgers University 1, 8–16, 18, 21, 39, 152, 192–3, 196, 198–9, 204

USS *Sable* 17, 50, 62
Saint Anne of the Sunset Church 77, 159
San Diego, CA 43, 61–7, 77, 81, 83, 88, 90–2, 98–9, 100–7, 109, 112, 189, 192, 206
San Francisco, CA 61, 65–6, 68, 70, 76–7, 89–91, 96–7, 99, 108–110, 112, 118–20, 123, 159–60, 185–7, 193
San Marcos AAF Field 46–7
USS *Saratoga* 104, 114, 120, 124, 148
Sargent, LT(jg) John J. 80, 108, 134, 157, 165, 175, 182, 200, 202
Satchel, Richard "Satch" 16, 18–9, 21
SB1C Helldiver 49–50, 66, 81, 88, 93, 125, 136–8, 140, 149–51, 156, 162–4, 168, 170–1, 180, 184, 192
SBD Dauntless 34, 44, 53–5, 57, 59–60, 66–73, 75, 80, 87, 98, 126, 177, 202, 204

Seigler, LT M.B. 108
Seitz, CAPT George A. 118, 181–2, 188–90
Seizo, SubLt. (junior grade) Yasunori 180
Sherman, RADM Frederick C. 124, 133, 140–1, 148, 151, 173
Shmomiro Airfield 139
Smiley, Jim 16, 104
Smith, Lt. Gen. Holland M. 153
Smith, LT(jg) John M. 79, 179, 184
Smith, June 39, 43, 51–2, 56, 59–60, 63, 69, 89, 92, 97
Snider, Capt. William N. 133, 163, 184
SNJ/Texan 35, 37–40, 42–4, 46–7, 49, 51, 53, 56, 62–4, 67–8, 71–2, 75, 85, 94–5, 101–2, 108
SNV-1 Vultee Valiant 32–4, 36–8, 75
The Song of Bernadette 68
South, ENS Robert M. 99
USS *South Dakota* 124, 159, 160, 167
The Spirit of St. Louis 64
Spruance, ADM Raymond 105, 122–5, 142, 150, 166–7, 173
Squankum, NJ 1, 10, 54
Stallknecht, Aviation Radioman 2nd Class 54–5, 57–60
Stokey, Sarah 5
Swett, Capt. James 106, 180, 184

Tachikawa Aircraft Company 136, 139, 141
USS *Takanis Bay* 99–102, 119
Task Force 58 (Fast Carrier Task Force) 1, 105, 110, 121–5, 129, 131–2, 138–9, 141–2, 145, 148, 150–4, 156–61, 165–7, 170–3, 178, 180, 182, 186, 200
Task Group 58.3 123–5, 133, 136, 140–1, 147–50, 156–61, 163–71, 174–5, 178–9, 200
Tatayama Airfield 133
TBF/TBM Avenger 67, 81, 88, 93, 124–5, 136–8, 140, 146–7, 149, 151, 157, 162–4, 168, 170–1, 176, 180, 184
Tenryu Airfield 133–4
Tokuno Shima 161, 171, 175
Tokyo 1, 72, 121, 127–33, 136–7, 139–143, 148–51, 153, 158, 190, 196–8, 206–7
Tomitaka Airfield 162

Ugaki, ADM Matome 139, 142, 161, 166
Ulithi Atoll 121–3, 150, 154, 157–60, 167, 171–2, 183

Index

UNC Chapel Hill Pre-Flight School 16–22, 24, 34–5, 104, 111, 205
U.S. Naval Academy 31, 53, 59, 81, 104, 118, 122, 124

Vaughn, LT(jg) R.J. 108, 157, 200
VB-4 124
VB-6 167
VB-83 159
VB-84 75, 81, 88, 93, 95, 100–1, 106, 118, 137–8, 149, 156, 163–4, 170, 181
VB-301 74–5
VB-302 74–5, 69
VB-303 68–76, 81–2, 78, 87
VBF-6 167
VBF-83 159
VF-4 124, 139, 163
VF-6 167
VF-29 159, 162–4, 175
VF-46 139
VF-83 159
VF-84 1, 189, 192–3; air strikes on Japan 134, 137, 142, 164–5; Amami Shunto 177; USS *Bunker Hill* 118, 134; Iwo Jima 147–50; kamikaze attack 11 May 1945 179–82; Kikai 177, 200–3; Okinawa 157, 160, 167–8, 172, 175–6; organization 75, 78–83; USS *Ranger* 102–4; re-organization 105–8; sinking of *Yamato* 178–9, 184; USS *Takanis Bay* 99–102; training in California 83–8, 90–6, 98–9, 104, 109–11
VMF-124 124, 134
VMR-213 124
VMF-221 106, 109, 119, 133, 149–50, 162–3, 179–80, 184
VMF-451 106, 109, 119, 135, 138–9, 164, 170, 175, 179, 184
VSB-59 52–3, 58–9, 60–2, 64, 66, 76
VT-4 124
VT-6 167
VT-29 159, 162–4, 175
VT-47 167, 200
VT-83 159
VT-84 81, 88, 93, 100, 106, 109, 119, 137–8, 149, 164, 170, 180–1, 184

Wallet, LT(jg) Leroy 80, 119, 179, 189
USS *Washington* 167
USS *Wilkes-Barre* 124
USS *Wolverine* 17, 50, 62–4, 67, 101–2

Yahagi 178
Yamakawa Airfield 170, 172
Yamato 165, 178–9, 184
USS *Yorktown* (CV-5) 15, 70, 114
USS *Yorktown* (CV-10) 80, 161

www.ingramcontent.com/pod-product-compliance
Lightning Source LLC
Chambersburg PA
CBHW060339010526
44117CB00017B/2889